COMPUTERS AND BUSINESS INFORMATION PROCESSING

William S. Davis
Miami University
Oxford, Ohio

ADDISON-WESLEY PUBLISHING COMPANY
Reading, Massachusetts · Menlo Park, California
London · Amsterdam · Don Mills, Ontario · Sydney

Library of Congress Cataloging in Publication Data

Davis, William S   1943–
    Computers and business information processing.

    Includes index.
    1. Business—Data processing—Study and teaching.
2. Electronic data processing—Study and teaching.
I. Title. II. Series.
HF5548.2.D375   658'.054'07   80-10946
ISBN 0-201-03161-2

Substantial portions of this text were originally published in *Business Data Processing* by William S. Davis, copyright © 1978 by Addison-Wesley Publishing Company, Inc.

ISBN 0-201-03161-2
ABCDEFGHIJ-DO-89876543210

To my Dad

PREFACE

The very first commercial computer, the UNIVAC I, was delivered in 1952. It contained miles of wire and thousands of electronic tubes, and it filled a good-sized room. It consumed vast amounts of electricity. But the machine could add about one thousand numbers in a single second! The age of the computer was upon us.

Today, electronic circuits equivalent to those miles of wires and thousands of tubes can be placed on a single chip about as big as a fingernail. A complete, comparable computer system fits in a cabinet about the size of a portable television set and weighs less than fifty pounds. Such small systems can execute as many as one *million* instructions per second, a significant improvement over the UNIVAC I. In the face of three decades of inflation, how much might you expect to pay for this "new, improved" computer? Two million dollars? More? Wrong. A computer, better than the UNIVAC I in virtually every way, can be purchased for less than $1000. If the automobile industry had followed the same price/performance curve, a Rolls Royce would cost about $250 and would get 200 miles per gallon! In town!

We are in the midst of a revolution. During the industrial revolution, machines were developed to augment muscle power. Today, the computer is being used to augment the power of the mind. The results could well change our present society as much as the industrial revolution changed the agrarian society it overthrew.

Illiteracy is a major handicap; the person who cannot read cannot function in our present society. In the coming decades, *computer illiteracy* will be every bit as much a handicap. Everyone, from the computer professional to the common citizen, will be affected. Ready or not, the revolution is coming.

Nowhere has the impact of the computer been greater than in the field of business. Already, most of our major business concerns simply could not function without their computers; they would literally drown in a sea of paperwork. The future promises even greater impact. Automation is changing the way our industrial organizations manufacture their products. Electronic information systems are changing the way these products are distributed. The firm that cannot adjust will not survive. The individual who cannot adjust will not "make it" in the business world of the very near future.

This is not to suggest that everyone must become a computer expert. You don't have to be an author to use a library. You don't have to be an expert to use a computer. The key is understanding, basically, what a computer is and what a computer can (and cannot) do. In other words, the key is "computer literacy."

Thus we come to the purpose of this book: To teach you something about the computer. Our assumption is that you are a business student or a business professional; thus computer concepts are presented from a business perspective. When you finish this course, you should have a solid understanding of common computer terminology. More importantly, you should have a sense of how all the pieces of a computer system fit together. Technology will change. However, this sense of a complete "system" will give you a framework against which to measure new technology.

The book is divided into five parts. The computer is an information processing machine; its most basic function is to accept data and process it into information. Information, as you will learn, is valuable; thus the computer is valuable. Part I, Chapters 1 through 4, concentrates on the basic ideas of data, information, and the information processing cycle. The intent is to establish *why* computers are used.

In Part II, Chapters 5 through 10, the components of a typical computer system are examined in detail. In Chapter 10, these components are pulled together to form a computer system. Three different types of computer systems—large mainframes, minicomputers, and microcomputers—are examined.

Part III, Chapters 11 through 14, concentrates on the development of a single computer application. First, a system must be designed. Within the context of this system, a program can be planned and written. The future business-oriented computer professional will find that his or her job fits into this system development cycle. The future manager must understand this cycle if he or she is to be an intelligent computer user.

The most common business computer application is file processing; thus Part IV, Chapters 15 through 19, presents file processing in some detail. Sequential files, direct access files, and modern data base systems are covered. In support of this material, you will find two brief case studies of typical file processing applications.

Modern computer systems often seem more complex than they really are. In Part V, Chapters 20 through 23, we examine such topics as multiprogramming, operating systems, teleprocessing, distributed information systems, and management information systems, carefully linking these modern concepts to the more basic ideas presented earlier. The last chapter, Chapter 23, examines both the opportunities and some problems arising from the computer revolution.

The computer is here to stay; it *will* impact your life. You have two choices. You can take the time to learn about these machines and thus participate intelligently in shaping that impact. On the other hand, you can entrust the critical decisions that will be made in the coming decades to a handful of "experts." The latter choice is dangerous. Technology can be controlled only by a population of educated individuals.

This book (and this course) will give you a good start. If you are training to become a computer professional, you will take additional computer-related courses. Other majors will encounter the computer throughout their academic and employment careers. Just remember, the computer will impact *you*. Only by gaining an understanding of these machines can you ensure that the impact will be a positive one.

Oxford, Ohio   W.S.D.
September 1980

CONTENTS

IV FILE PROCESSING

V MODERN COMPUTER-BASED INFORMATION SYSTEMS

DETAILED CONTENTS

▌▌ THE COMPUTER: AN INFORMATION PROCESSING MACHINE

III SYSTEMS DEVELOPMENT AND IMPLEMENTATION

IV FILE PROCESSING

V MODERN COMPUTER-BASED INFORMATION SYSTEMS

THE VALUE
OF INFORMATION

1

THE COMPUTER IMPACT

A FEW DAYS IN THE LIFE OF BOB SMITH

Bob Smith is a typical guy. He's married, has two children, and lives in a small house in a suburban development outside a large city. He has a pretty good job—not the most exciting work in the world, but he likes it and the pay is not bad.

It's Friday afternoon—payday. Along with thousands of his co-workers Bob eagerly awaits his weekly wages, neither knowing nor caring that his work record for the prior week was analyzed, his earnings calculated, and his check printed by a computer.

At 4:15 P.M. the end-of-shift buzzer sounds, and the nightly race to the parking lot begins. On the way out, Bob must stop to punch his time card. He inserts a card containing his name and employee number into the proper slot of a small blue machine, waits a fraction of a second, retrieves the card, places it in a rack, and rushes to his car. By punching his time card, Bob really sent the following message to a computer: "Bob Smith left at exactly 4:16 today." This little piece of data will be used in preparing the following week's pay.

Bob is the third member of his four-person car pool to reach the parking lot. Only two months ago, he didn't even know two of his three fellow riders. In response to a tight energy situation, the company's computer was programmed to suggest possible car pools by matching home addresses and work schedules.

The car starts easily, due in part to the highly efficient air/fuel ratio maintained by the tiny microcomputer behind the control panel. As he pulls into the exit lane, another car suddenly darts in front of him. Fortunately, the same microcomputer also controls the braking system and, in spite of Bob's rather "less than perfect" braking technique, a skid (and a likely minor accident) is avoided.

The trip through the city is paced by computer-controlled traffic signals. A short stretch of turnpike costs forty-five cents; the card Bob receives on entering and returns on leaving the toll road will eventually be processed by the state's computer.

As he reaches normal cruising speed, Bob presses a button on the automobile's control panel. Almost instantly, the car's current gas mileage is displayed, replacing the current time on the digital clock: 23.5 miles per gallon. The microcomputer had quickly sensed gas consumption and distance driven and used this data to compute the mileage. "Not bad," thought Bob.

Friday means a stop at the bank. As Bob waits in line, he can't help but notice the strangely shaped black numbers at the bottom of his paycheck and on the deposit slip from his checking account. The numbers are printed with a special magnetic ink and allow the bank's computer to read the documents.

Finally, it's Bob's turn. He inserts his plastic bank card into the slot in the 24-hour automated teller and types in his personal code number; in response, the heavy metal cover rises, exposing a set of push buttons. He pushes the one marked "Checking Account Deposit," and drops his paycheck through a slot; he then pushes two other buttons indicating his desire to withdraw fifty dollars in cash, and the machine dispenses the money. This 24-hour teller is a small special-purpose computer. As he leaves the bank, Bob enjoys a momentary thought about the pleasant conversations he used to have with the tellers. But the lines are shorter today and, after all, you can't fight progress.

Bob's credit card covers the cost of a full tank of gas. He leaves behind a copy of the sales slip which will eventually be read by the oil company's computer as it compiles future bills. The next stop is home, where Bob is enthusiastically greeted by his wife, Nancy, whom he met through a computer dating service.

Awaiting him is a stack of bills delivered with the aid of computer-read zip codes. Bills for electricity, gas, the mortgage, insurance, department store purchases, a magazine subscription, and the family doctor are neatly piled on his desk, every bill prepared and addressed by a computer. Bob writes a check (a message to the bank's computer) to cover each bill, and stuffs both the check and the bill into the proper preaddressed return envelope. "Next month," he thinks, "I'm going to sign up for the new bill-paying service being offered by the bank and let them simply transfer money from my account to cover some of the bills; why should I take the time to write all these checks?" The new service is part of the bank's Electronic Funds Transfer system to be implemented, as you may have guessed, through the bank's computer.

Friday is grocery night for the Smiths. As they move through the aisles, their selections are aided by computer-generated unit price information. At the checkout counter, a clerk simply moves packages over a small electronic reader, making sure that the preprinted product code is in the proper position. The product code identifies the brand and size of the package; once read, this information is sent along to the store's computer, where the current price of the item is found and added to the bill. After all the Smiths' purchases have been scanned, the clerk pushes a button and a detailed list is printed. Bob presents his bank card; the clerk inserts it into a card reader similar to that used on the 24-hour bank teller and, in a fraction of a second, funds have been transferred from Bob's checking account to the supermarket.

For the past few weeks, Nancy has been on a health-food campaign, serving her family a series of well-planned, balanced, nutritious, tasty, and reasonably priced meals. The menus were printed in the local newspaper. They had been planned by a computer.

Following dinner, the Smith family piles into their car and drives to the hospital to see Grandma Smith. Several weeks ago, she had been a very sick woman; the fact that her doctor was having a difficult time diagnosing her illness merely added to the family's concern. Finally, the results from a series of computer-controlled blood tests allowed the doctor to identify a rare form of anemia, and to prescribe medication. During her two nights in intensive care, the Smiths were very thankful for the special patient-monitoring mini-computer that maintained a second-by-second surveillance over her vital

signs. The prognosis tonight is highly positive; Grandma will be home in less than a week.

The Smiths' favorite television program won't be on tonight; it was cancelled because its rating, calculated by a computer, was too low. Fortunately, a baseball game is being televised. The antics of some cartoon characters on the million-dollar, computer-controlled scoreboard are of particular interest to the children.

The ball game is interrupted several times to report on the progress of our latest space flight. Such space probes would, of course, be impossible without the aid of computers.

Tiring of the ball game, Bob retires to his den where he engages his personal home computer in a quick game of chess. He returns to the family room just in time for the news.

A major topic of discussion on the late news is a charge made by a group of politicians that computers may have influenced the results of a recent statewide election. It seems that several hours before the polls closed, a computer predicted the outcome based on an analysis of sample "key" precincts. Perhaps a number of potential voters, having heard or read about this prediction, decided to stay home, feeling that their vote wouldn't mean anything anyway.

A special feature on the sports report is a discussion of how the computer is used to rate college football players who are eligible for the professional draft. The final news item is a reading of a computer-generated weather report indicating that there is a "thirty-percent chance of precipitation" for Saturday.

For the past few years, Bob has been attending evening and weekend classes at a local university in hopes of eventually earning a degree. Saturday morning is registration time for the next semester so, after breakfast and a quick scan of the morning newspaper (the type was set by computer, by the way), he heads for the city again. The registration process consists of filling out a number of computer-readable forms, because class registration and billing are computerized at this university.

Later that afternoon, Bob's golf game shows marked improvement as he shoots a very strong eighty-five. Perhaps a new set of computer-designed golf clubs had something to do with it. Some of the luster is lost, however, when Nancy cards an eighty-two using his old, cut-down set.

On the way home from the golf course, Bob and Nancy decide to stop and do some shopping at their favorite department store. Selecting a number of items from stock, they approach a checkout clerk, presenting Nancy's credit card in payment. As a normal part of processing the credit sale, the clerk inserts the card into a small machine; within a second or two, a green light winks on, indicating that the credit sale is approved. Actually, the little machine sent Nancy's credit card number to a central computer that checked a list of stolen credit cards and made sure that Nancy had consistently paid her bills before granting its approval.

Saturday's supper, again planned by computer, is eaten a bit earlier than usual; Bob and Nancy plan an evening at the racetrack. There, their attention is centered on a large electronic tote board, where the rapidly changing odds on each race are flashed. The track's computer recalculates these odds every ninety seconds, basing its computations on the actual amount of money wagered on each horse. Right after the fifth race, it begins to rain (the weather bureau's computer had estimated a thirty-percent chance).

On the way home, Bob is stopped by a state police officer for exceeding the speed limit. The officer radios the numbers of Bob's driver's license and automobile registration back to headquarters, where a quick check of the police department's computer files shows that the car has not been listed as stolen and that Bob's record shows no recent traffic convictions. This information is radioed back to the officer who simply warns Bob not to exceed the speed limit again.

As the officer leaves and Bob and Nancy resume their trip home, we too will leave this brief narrative of a day or two in the lives of a typical American couple living in the last quarter of the twentieth century.

THE COMPUTER IMPACT

Not too many years ago, Bob and Nancy Smith might have been characters from science fiction. As recently as the late 1950s, the computer was almost unknown outside a few large universities and research centers. Yet today, a few short years later, the impact of the computer on the everyday life of a typical citizen of the United States is staggering, rivaling that of television and the automobile.

The computer is with us literally from birth until death. In the hospital, the fact of a new birth is reported to a number of hospital and government computers. Several tests are performed, some with the assistance of a computer, to ascertain and ensure the health of the newborn. Nurses are reminded of the proper medication and diet for both baby and mother by the hospital's computer. Upon their departure, the proud parents are presented with a bill prepared by computer. At life's opposite pole, the fact and cause of an individual's death are reported to a number of hospital, government, and scientific computers, perhaps providing an important clue in the fight against cancer or heart disease.

Education takes up a significant part of our early years. Information processing machines—another, perhaps more accurate name for computers—are becoming an increasingly important factor in our educational system. Most large universities, many smaller colleges, and quite a few high schools use the computer to schedule classes, print grade reports, and maintain scholastic records. A number of examinations (the Scholastic Aptitude Test, College Entrance Examination, and many IQ tests, to name a few) are graded by computer. In some schools, a few courses are actually taught by computers.

After our formal education is completed, we enter the work force, and what could be more important to us than our paycheck? Most are prepared by computer. In addition to preparing pay checks, business people handle billing, maintain accounting and tax records, make credit decisions, and keep track of merchandise by computer. Manufacturers often assign the computer the job of scheduling and controlling production and, in some cases, have a computer guide a specific machine through the process of cutting or shaping a piece of metal or plastic without human intervention.

In the financial arena, the stock market has been computerized to a high degree, and almost every banking transaction (checks, deposits, savings account deposits and withdrawals, bond purchases) involves the bank's computer.

The police and other law enforcement agencies use the computer to keep track of stolen automobiles, analyze evidence, and identify fingerprints. Several law officers' lives have been saved when a request for information on a car they had just stopped was answered with a computer-generated report, returned in a few seconds, indicating that the occupants of the car in question had previously been reported as armed and dangerous. In some communities, the computer, using statistical techniques, identifies high-crime areas, in effect, predicting the most likely locations for a crime. Lawyers also use the computer to help research court cases.

The government is probably the biggest user of computers in this country. Income tax returns are checked and tax records maintained by computer. Social Security, the highway trust fund, welfare, Medicare, student loans, government payrolls, automobile registrations—the list of government operations that depend on the computer, at least for record keeping, is practically endless. Even our national defense system, from the early-warning system to the delivery of a missile, could not operate without the computer.

Not even sports are immune. Several National Football League teams have banded together to take advantage of computerized scouting reports and draft choice ratings. Some teams even use the computer to analyze an opponent's past games and predict the most likely play in certain situations. Television coverage of the recent Olympic Games highlighted some extremely accurate computer-controlled timing devices. The computer is actually becoming an active participant in a number of newer "sports," with computer chess and other, similar games gaining in popularity.

The entire space program and much current scientific research in such fields as atomic physics, cellular biology, and astronomy would not be possible without the computer. Engineers design bridges, chemists identify compounds, and geographers draw maps with the aid of these modern marvels.

The computer, directly or indirectly, affects almost every phase of our modern way of life; except for a few hermits, it is difficult to find an individual who has never heard the word "computer" or handled (but not bent, folded, spindled, or mutilated, of course!) a data processing card. The computer has a profound impact on all of us.

Today, computers seem to be almost everywhere; their impact rivals that of the automobile and television. It seems hard to believe that the computer was not even invented until the mid-1940s and, as recently as the late 1950s, was virtually unknown outside a few large university, research, corporate, and military centers. The computer is younger than your parents! (Maybe even younger than you!)

The first commercial computer, the UNIVAC I, was sold in 1952 for a few million dollars. Today, it is possible to purchase a personal computer system at the local shopping center for under a thousand dollars. And the new, inexpensive system is better in virtually every way. That is progress! Imagine similar progress in the automotive industry. A new, full-sized car might cost a few hundred dollars and need a tank of gas every month or so.

COMPUTERS IN BUSINESS

In no segment of our society has the impact of the computer been more strongly felt than in the field of business. You might be a manager. You might be a computer professional. You might be an employee performing virtually any job in the organization. It doesn't matter—the computer *will* have a profound impact on what you do and how you do it.

Let's assume that you are a typical business student. You selected business as a major because of a desire to prepare yourself for a management position following graduation. You have your degree, and you have just been hired as a management trainee by a large corporation. It's your first day on the job. What can you expect?

It is likely that your very first contact with your new employer will be in the personnel office. Here, you will almost certainly be asked to fill out a number of forms. What is the purpose of these forms? Basically, the objective is to collect key personal information (name, address, marital status, etc.) so that you can be entered in the firm's computerized personnel data base. You have been working less than an hour, and already you are dealing with a computer!

The afternoon of your first day is spent in a meeting. You hear about the history, traditions, products, and image of the firm you have just joined. Several corporate officials are introduced and welcome you "on board." More importantly, the manager of personnel explains to you and several other management trainees your assignment for the next 18 months. You are to be exposed to all segments of the business—if you are to be managers, you must have a broad understanding of everything the organization does. You will spend your first three months working in sales. Then you will shift to the accounting department for another three-month tour of duty. Subsequent three-month assignments will be spent with production, engineering, marketing, and financial planning, after which you will receive your first managerial job.

The balance of your first week is spent attending a number of seminars designed to introduce you to the company's organization and policies. Finally, the meetings over, you prepare for your first "real" day of work with the sales department.

Sales

You discover that selling is hard work—you may have to visit a dozen or more potential customers before making a single sale. As each sale is closed, you must fill out an order form. You are surprised to learn the primary purpose of the order form, beyond the obvious recording of the customer's needs, is to provide input data for the computer.

Each completed order form is given to the order entry department where it is entered, in coded form, into the computer. The computer performs a credit check on the customer. It also prepares a customer invoice, and calculates and authorizes the salesperson's commission. If the order is not on the computer, it literally does not exist.

You are training to be a manager; thus much of your time is spent with the office manager rather than with the sales people. You read the monthly computer-generated reports listing sales activity by customer. The reports are designed in such a way that they suggest a number of pertinent questions such as, Why has this once-good customer stopped buying our products? You learn to pass such questions to the salespeople. You also discover that computer-generated account ledgers make it very easy to identify the best customers.

The budget consumes a major part of the office manager's time. Monthly reports compare actual office expenses to budgeted expenses; and variation must be carefully explained. Once again, the computer is the source of these reports.

Perhaps even more important than the budget report is the monthly quota report. The sales office was given a target at the beginning of the year—the staff is expected to sell at least a certain amount of product. The manager knows that failure to meet the quota will be viewed with disfavor by higher management and could even lead to dismissal.

The individual salespeople have quotas too. One of the more uncomfortable moments of your first assignments occurs when the office manager finds it necessary to fire a salesperson for falling too far behind quota. The computer, of course, generates the quota performance reports.

Accounting

The first three months pass quickly, and you move on to a new assignment with the accounting department. Here, your first task is to work with the people who are responsible for the system that accepts and processes sales orders. You also have a chance to see how the budget and quota reports that so greatly influenced your earlier job are prepared.

The accounting department, however, is not concerned merely with sales. In the accounts receivable system, for example, each sale is recorded as an expected payment, and bills are produced and mailed—the salespeople almost never deal directly with billing. Another important part of the accounts receivable system is credit authorization and control. Each customer is given a credit limit; sales beyond this credit limit are simply refused. Virtually all of the accounts receivable system is implemented on the computer.

In addition to mailing bills, the accounting department must receive payments as well. This is handled by a different system and different people; almost never does the same person mail a bill and receive the payment—it is just not good business practice. The computer is used to check and record each and every payment.

Another key accounting system is accounts payable. It is through this system that all bills owed by the company are verified and paid. The computer is used to track all payments; in fact, these payments form an important part of the "actual" expense in the budget versus actual reports.

Perhaps the most significant cost encountered by the company is labor. Paychecks for both the hourly and salaried employees are prepared by computer. Before your tour in the accounting department, you may have felt that payroll ends with the distribution of paychecks, but you soon discover that it doesn't. Payroll is an expense, and this cost must be factored into the budget versus actual reports. It really is amazing how all the pieces begin to fit together.

Production

Soon your accounting assignment is over, and the production department is next. It is here that the products sold by the sales staff and tracked by accounting are actually made.

On your first day you meet several people from timekeeping. Earlier, you tended to view the numbers that represented the hours worked by labor as simply numbers—so many hours for employee X, and so many hours for department Y, for example. Suddenly you discover that there is a great deal more to it. Some hours are direct; in other words, spent doing work on a product. Others are indirect—time spent managing others, for example. Vacation time is treated one way; sick time is treated another; still a third special classification is time spent on jury duty or authorized civic projects. Each hour must be categorized and charged against the correct budget. All this time-juggling is handled by the computer; the timekeeper's job is to make certain that the input data is accurate.

Labor data is used for another purpose as well. Our production employees are paid on an incentive basis—the more they make, the more they earn. Actual production figures are collected by the production control department. Actual hours worked comes from timekeeping. Each job has a standard: so many pieces per hour. Dividing the actual production by the actual hours worked yields a similar statistic. If actual production is greater than the standard, the employee gets a bonus. The computer, of course, is used to make all these computations.

Perhaps the second biggest cost of production (after labor) is inventory. Raw materials must be kept in stock so that they are available when needed.

As production is finished, products enter finished-goods inventory until they are shipped. While a product is being produced, it spends some time just sitting (in various states of completion) on the shop floor; all the materials currently being worked on make up the work-in-process inventory.

Exactly how much of a given raw material do we have in stock? Where is a given customer order? A very good customer needs some supplies "right now." If we have it in finished goods inventory, we can ship it immediately. Do we? You quickly learn that these are important questions. Looking at row after row of materials in the various warehouses and on the manufacturing floor, how can you possibly answer them?

It's easy—you ask the computer. Each time a raw material enters or leaves inventory, each time a job is released to the manufacturing floor, each time a job moves from one work station to another, each time a product enters finished goods inventory, each time a product is shipped, the fact is reported to the computer. As a result the computer knows where everything is. There is simply no way that inventory can be effectively controlled without the aid of these machines.

One of your weekly tasks is to make a production schedule for the next week. How many workers will be needed? Are there any machines that can be scheduled for maintenance? Are adequate raw materials available? Once again, the computer is your tool. Sales orders, summarized by the computer, tell you what must be made; once again the pieces of the company begin to come together. Given a list of products to be made, the computer can easily figure out raw material requirements. Labor is a bit more difficult to predict, but, factoring in such things as known vacation plans, typical rates of personal illness, and other problems, you can at least anticipate such needs as overtime or an expanded second shift.

While you are not directly involved, you can't help but notice the work of the people in the quality control department. Their job is to inspect the product at various stages in the production process. If they discover defects, they have the authority to order changes in the production line and can literally shut the line down. Much of their work involves the computer. Statistical techniques (often implemented through the computer) are used to suggest exactly what production units should be tested. Many tests use the computer to either collect or analyze data (or both).

One of the more interesting innovations is the use of computers to directly control portions of the manufacturing process. A particular welding operation, for example, has been a headache for years. The weld must be performed right after rustproofing, in a hot, dirty, and thoroughly uncomfortable room, and people just don't want to work at this job. Several months ago, a robot was purchased. Working under computer control, the machine performs admirably. Perhaps more importantly, a very serious potential health hazard has been avoided.

Engineering

Engineering is the next stop in your management training program. Engineering budgets, payrolls, and other accounting functions are, of course, computerized; these are present in every corner of the organization. The computer, however, has other, far more important uses in engineering.

There are, you discover, many different kinds of engineering. Some engineers are concerned with product development; this group is sometimes called research and development or R&D. The R&D people are particularly interested in using small computers as components in the products built by our firm. Large computer systems are used to model possible products before they are actually created. In one fascinating demonstration, you watch an engineer draw an electronic diagram on a computer terminal screen and then instruct the machine to analyze the completed circuit.

Other engineers are concerned with facilities planning. The R&D people have designed a new product. How are we going to build it? Plants and production machinery must be designed. Once again, the computer is a very valuable aid to the planning process.

It's one thing to plan a new production facility, and quite another to actually implement it. How long will it take? What are the critical steps? How can we measure our progress? Often the computer is used at this level, too. Basically, a schedule is used to set the standard, and as work is actually completed, it is measured against this standard. The computer is needed simply because so many different things happen at the same time.

Other engineers are concerned with the human element in the production process. How can people be made more efficient? Once again the computer is used, this time to analyze human performance. Often a simple change in the way a job is done can significantly improve production.

Marketing

It seems hard to believe that an entire year has gone by as you move to your fifth assignment, the marketing department. As a student, you tended to think of marketing as a place where mildly neurotic people sit around and dream up clever advertising slogans—it isn't. In fact, your first job is rather unglamorous. The government has just released a new set of projections and economic indicators, and your job is to feed them into the computer. Your firm, you are told, has a very sophisticated economic model on the computer. The model allows marketing to make educated guesses about the probable impact of economic conditions on the sales potential of the firm's products but, if these projections are to be accurate, the very latest economic data must be available to the program.

The model involves the use of simulation techniques; your supervisor likens it to a gigantic Monopoly® board. Essentially, it allows the marketing department (and management) to ask "what if?" questions. What if we were to withhold this new product for three months? What if we were to change the name of that product? The intent of the model is to accept such questions and generate a most likely result. The company that can't project the consequences of its decisions is simply lost in today's marketplace.

Another key function of the marketing department is market research. Will customers buy a new brand of peanut butter? The only way to find out is to test market it. The results of test marketing in a selected economic area can, by using the computer and several statistical techniques, be extended to cover a larger area, yielding a good indication of the market potential of the new product. Surveys are another valuable tool of marketing; almost invariably, computer analysis of the results of a survey is necessary.

Financial Planning

Marketing was fascinating, but once again it's time to move on. Your next (and final) stop is the financial planning group. You started with sales, the "front line." Accounting and production were also concerned with the present. Engineering and marketing, on the other hand, were concerned with tomorrow. In your new assignment, you concentrate on next year or five years from now. Step by step your viewpoint changed from the short term to the long term. That was, after all, one of the major purposes of the training program.

The company president has just set the official goals for next year: Both revenues and profits will increase by ten percent. This target becomes the basis for a complete financial plan.

You know how much product the firm sold last year—revenue is simply the sum of all sales. The profit is also known. Both can be increased by 10 percent; it's a simple mathematical operation. Profit is defined as the difference between revenue and cost; thus a simple subtraction tells us how much we can spend to generate the revenue needed to meet the president's targets. The new revenue figure defines how much sales must sell which, in turn, defines how much production must make; this statistic becomes the basis for determining quotas. The new expense figure tells us how much we can spend on labor, inventory, equipment, and the like, and becomes the basis for determining budgets.

So far, the computations have been easy. Now, the complexity begins to creep in. It's one thing to argue that the entire company must sell $250,000,000 worth of products, but defining now much of that total should be the responsibility of a single salesperson in New York is quite a different problem. How much did the New York office sell last year? How much did the salesperson in question sell? What has happened to population of potential customers in New York—can we realistically expect a 10 percent increase in sales? Is there another section of the country where we want to improve our performance? These are but a few of the questions that must be considered in setting sales quotas. Some of the questions are judgmental. Others merely require the manipulation of vast amounts of data. Because of its ability to answer this latter kind of question, the computer is the financial planner's most valuable tool.

Similar arguments could be cited for planning production quotas or budgets. Projections based on historical data can be generated by the computer. Changes in direction involve human, managerial decisions. The process of developing a complete financial plan is almost symbiotic, with the computer augmenting human logic by providing, quickly and accurately, digests of vast amounts of data, and the people augmenting the computer's "brute force" data manipulations with flashes of insight and intuition. The result is far better than either the computer or the people could accomplish alone. For the very first time you begin to sense the potential of human/machine cooperation. It is downright exciting!

Management

Finally, you receive your first managerial assignment. It's a small department, but you do have your own budget to administer, your own functions to perform, your own people and equipment to manage, and your own headaches. Your training has proven invaluable.

What does the computer do for you now? It prepared your budget. It processes your actual expenses and compares them to your budget, alerting your manager when your costs begin to go out of line. It pays your employees and tracks your inventory. It even helps your secretary prepare reports and letters—the word processing system. It really is impossible for a modern business person to avoid the computer. It is equally difficult to imagine why anyone would want to. As a manager, you know that the computer is a very valuable tool.

COMPUTER PHOBIA

But (with a few exceptions) you aren't a manager yet. You are a student, just starting your education. You probably know very little about the computer. In fact, you may be just a little bit afraid of it. You've read or heard about the science fiction stories in which a computer takes over the world. Maybe you've seen *2001: A Space Odyssey;* the villain was a computer named HAL. Numerous stories echo this theme: the computer has become the Frankenstein's monster of our modern folklore.

We hear about people being replaced by a computer. Computer-controlled supermarket checkout and computer-controlled bank teller terminals may be convenient, but they eliminate two traditional entry-level job opportunities. Students are closed out of critical courses by "the computer." Errors in billing and poor service in general are blamed on "computer errors." All too often, we simply accept such things—if the computer is responsible, what are we "mere" human beings supposed to do about it?

Television is relatively new, but it was preceded by radio, the movies, and the theater. Very few of us, to be sure, really understand the details of broadcasting, but we can accept television.

Automobiles have been around for a hundred years or so. Before the automobile, we had horse-drawn carriages. We all feel reasonably comfortable with a car. We understand them, at least well enough to know how to drive them. Very few of us are capable of taking a car apart and putting it back together, but we have all come to accept the automobile.

Computers are different. Have you ever seen one? Don't count the little game-playing machines sold in a department store. Have you ever seen a *real* computer? Probably not. Real computers (the big machines) tend to be housed in special, climate-controlled rooms not accessible to "ordinary mortals." How many programmers or analysts do you know? Have you ever heard a non-computer person complain about the strange work habits, unusual personal characteristics, or special privileges of a computer person? Computer people seem to speak their own language. They seem different. Many see the special room, special treatment, and special language as characteristics of a new sort of priesthood, with the computer as the new object of worship.

Why? Perhaps it is because of the kind of work computers do. They perform clerical and bookkeeping functions—jobs that we have always associated with intelligence, with thinking. Other machines augment muscle power. The computer seems to emulate the mind. We know that it is our mind, our ability to think and reason, that sets us apart from the other animals. The mere thought that a machine might be able to do the one thing that we regard as uniquely human is troubling. Is it any wonder that so many people fear these new machines?

IGNORANCE IS NOT BLISS; IT'S IGNORANCE

The computer is here to stay. There is simply no way that you can avoid contact with these machines. They *will* have an impact on your life. The fact that you are reading this book indicates that you have an interest in business, in the computer, or both. If so, the computer will have a *significant* impact on your life. Even if we could figure out a way to get rid of all our computers, we wouldn't want to—computers have become such an ingrained part of our society that we literally could not function without them.

Illiteracy is a major handicap in our present society. In the very near future, computer illiteracy will be almost as much of a handicap. And there is no reason for it. The computer is basically a very simple machine. With a reasonable amount of effort you *can* learn how a computer works and what it can (and cannot) do. People fear computers because they don't understand them. They don't understand them because they haven't taken the time to learn. When it comes to the computer, ignorance is not bliss. It's ignorance.

Does this imply that only computer experts will "make it" in business in the future? No. Not at all. You don't have to be a great writer to use a library. You don't have to be a computer expert to use the computer. The key is to understand the computer's potential—its strengths and limitations. The computer is a tool. If you try to avoid it, the tool is useless. But if you learn how to use it, the computer may well be the most powerful and useful tool we have ever developed.

Thus we come to the purpose of this book: To introduce the computer and information processing concepts to beginners, to the uninitiated, in a readable and, hopefully, entertaining manner. As a beginner, you do not yet know the technical terms and jargon of the computer professional, and thus such terms will not be used without careful explanation. By the time you are finished you should know what the computer does, how it does it, and (perhaps most importantly) why the computer is used to perform a given task.

We begin in Part I with a discussion of the value of information, concentrating on what computers do and why they are used. In Part II, we turn our attention to the computer itself, studying exactly how these machines work. Part III is concerned with the system development process—we will follow a computer application from an initial idea to its actual implementation on a machine. Part IV covers file processing, perhaps the most important of all business uses of the computer. We end, in Part V, with a discussion of modern computer-based information systems.

SUMMARY

The chapter began with a brief discussion of the impact of the computer on our society. We then turned our attention to the subject of computers in business, following a newly hired management trainee through an 18-month training program, and highlighting the impact of the computer at each stage. There is literally no function in a modern business organization that is not directly, or indirectly, influenced by the computer; if you plan a business career, you *will* be required to work with these machines. The modern manager often finds that the computer is his or her most powerful and helpful tool.

In spite of the computer's tremendous impact on society in general and on business in particular, a surprising number of people really don't understand these machines. Many actually fear them. The computer, however, is here to stay; ignoring them won't make them go away. People who know nothing about the computer will be at a decided disadvantage in the years to come. When it comes to computers, ignorance is not bliss; it's ignorance.

KEYWORDS

At the end of each chapter, you will find a list of the keywords introduced in that chapter. You should know the meaning of each keyword; if not, you have missed something and should review. Chapter 1 was purely introductory, and thus no keywords are listed at this time. Look for the keywords list at the end of subsequent chapters, however.

EXERCISES

1. See if you can find any evidence of the computer in your daily life. Keep track of the number of times that you come across a punched card, a check, or a piece of mail addressed by a computer (if the name is printed in capital letters, it's pretty safe to assume that it has been addressed by a computer), or are required to fill out an application form or an order form.

2. Look through this evening's newspaper and see how many articles and features you can find that involve the computer in some way. Check such items as stock market prices or baseball records, which are frequently computer-prepared. Check the "help-wanted" section for such positions as computer operator, programmer, systems analyst, analyst, keypunch operator, or any position beginning with the words "data processing."

3. Read a science fiction story that in some way involves a computer and make a note of your reaction to the machine. Reexamine your reaction after you have finished this book.

4. Visit a local bank and find out what happens to your check after you cash it.

5. Unless your school is very small, you probably have a computerized registration system. Find out how it works.

6. In many large shopping centers, particularly near a city, you will find a "computer store." Visit such a store and ask the manager to show you some of the things a personal computer system can do.

7. Find out where your campus computer center is, and visit it; many campus centers will schedule tours for students. Make a note of what you see; in particular, make a list of all the equipment. Also, compile a list of all the words your guide uses that you don't quite understand. By the end of the academic term, you should know what all the words mean, what each piece of equipment is, and what each piece of equipment does.

2

DATA, INFORMATION, AND INFORMATION PROCESSING

OVERVIEW

The first chapter was concerned with just how widespread is the use of computers in our modern society. In this chapter, we'll begin to explain what computers are used for by defining and explaining a number of key terms such as data, information, data processing, and information processing. These terms will be explained by describing the data and information needs of a typical business concern.

INFORMATION

When we think of modern American business and industry, we tend to think of the corporate giants—firms such as General Motors, Ford, Chrysler, IBM, and General Electric. These companies, however, were not always big; many began as single-owner proprietorships. One person invented a new product or a new service, or thought of a better way of performing some task, and decided to go into business. In the beginning, these firms tended to be literally "one-man bands," with the owner designing, manufacturing, selling, servicing, and planning a product, and performing the necessary record-keeping functions in his or her spare time.

Eventually, if the product or service was a good one, the demand became too great for one individual to handle, and a partner or some hired help entered the scene. Soon a few salespeople, an accountant or two, and a handful of workers to help build the product were added. The proprietor, however, still exercised complete control over the business.

In a modern, large, multinational corporation, such personal control becomes impossible. How can the president of General Motors *possibly* be familiar with the details of the manufacturing, design, and marketing of all GM cars? Because of its size, the modern corporation has become very tightly organized, with lines of command and control that rival those of the military. The president sits at the top of this typical organizational pyramid (Fig. 2.1),

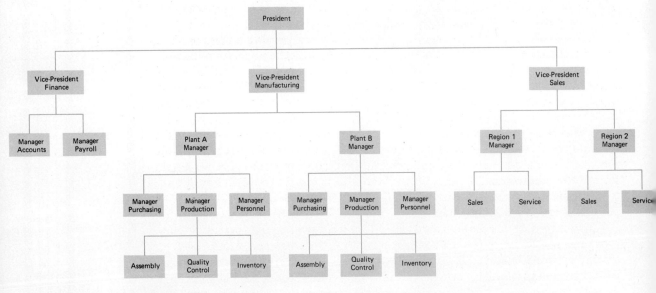

Figure 2.1
A typical corporate organization chart.

with a vice-president in charge of each of the major functions. The vice-presidents, in turn, have a number of middle-level managers reporting to them. Eventually, we reach the level of the "front-line" manager who is responsible for the people who actually perform the manual tasks. The sheer size and complexity of a modern corporation makes such organization essential.

The big problem faced by management is one of coordinating these groups. What happens, for example, if the sales department suddenly recognizes a decline in the demand for lime-green refrigerators, but manufacturing continues to build lime-green refrigerators? Without tight management control, this situation can happen (as it did with the hula hoop and oversized automobiles). Back in the days of the single proprietorship, the fact that one individual was personally responsible for all phases of the operation made such an event unlikely, but no one individual can exert such total control today. How can the president and the other officers of a large corporation control such complex operations?

Through **information.** What exactly is meant by the term information?

Perhaps the best way to illustrate the concept of information is through an example. Let's assume that the vice-president in charge of sales is to approach the president with a request that the company begin offering lime-green refrigerators for sale. It's probably reasonable for the president to assume that the vice-president has looked into the sales potential very carefully and firmly believes that "if lime-green refrigerators were available, our salespeople could sell them." To the president, the knowledge that "lime-green refrigerators will sell" becomes a single fact; i.e., a single piece of **data.**

Is this enough? Can the president, on the basis of this single piece of data, commit the company to the building and distribution of lime-green refrigerators? Probably not. Can they be built? The president might ask manufacturing or engineering for an opinion. Let's assume that the answer is "yes, they can be built." The president now knows that the sales force can sell them *and* that the company can build them. Is this enough? Again, probably not. Can they be built at a reasonable price? Once more, the president might ask engineering for an opinion. Engineering, we'll assume, estimates that "we can build them for $1.00 more per unit than the standard white unit." Now the president knows that the company can sell them and build them, and that it will cost $1.00 more per unit to build a lime-green refrigerator. Now, perhaps, the president can make a decision.

Examine this process carefully, because it illustrates an important concept. The president began with a number of individual pieces of *data,* each of which, by itself, was not enough to support a decision. It was only when the president had combined a number of different pieces of data that he or she had enough to support a decision. By combining data in a meaningful way, the president has created *information* (Fig. 2.2). Information has meaning. Data

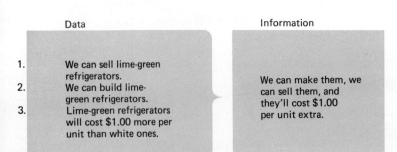

Data

1. We can sell lime-green refrigerators.
2. We can build lime-green refrigerators.
3. Lime-green refrigerators will cost $1.00 more per unit than white ones.

Information

We can make them, we can sell them, and they'll cost $1.00 per unit extra.

Figure 2.2
Data is combined to form information.

are merely individual facts that must be combined or "processed" in some way in order to give them meaning.

Let's assume that on the basis of the information available on the sales and manufacturing potential for lime-green refrigerators, the president decides to offer this product for sale. Data has been combined to form information, this information has supported a decision, and the resulting decision has led to action: start producing the refrigerators. What if some of the data had been incorrect? What if there really were no demand for lime-green refrigerators? What if a sudden increase in the cost of lime-green paint pushed the extra cost up to $25.00 per unit? The organization must have a mechanism for correcting wrong decisions.

This mechanism is usually implemented through such tools as budgets, quotas, and targets. Each salesperson might be assigned a quota of 250 lime-green refrigerators, to cite one example. If salesperson A reports only 200 sales, we have a fact. If salesperson B reports 300 sales, the average of 250 units each seems to indicate that sales are right "on target"—we now have information. If, however, salesperson B also reports 200 lime-green refrigerators sold, the average of only 200 units, when compared to the quota or target of 250 per salesperson, seems to indicate that sales are not going as well as expected—information of another sort. Management can now make another decision, to cut production or stock the product in hopes that sales will pick up, resulting in another action.

Thus we can see that the information flow through an organization is cyclic in nature (Fig. 2.3). Data is combined to form information. Information supports decision making. A decision (hopefully) leads to action. The results of an action can be measured; these measurements produce additional data that can be combined to form additional information, which, in turn, can be used to support the decisions that "fine tune" the process.

A modern large organization consists of a number of separate functional groups whose activities must be coordinated. Information is the key to this coordination. Each of the functional groups produces information that is used to communicate with the other groups.

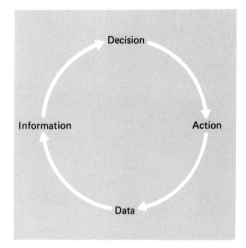

Figure 2.3
The information feedback cycle.

THE INFORMATION NEEDS OF A TYPICAL BUSINESS CONCERN

Now that we've basically defined what data and information are, let's take a look at the information needs of a typical corporation. We'll start at the very top of the organization and consider how the president, with the help of the vice presidents and others, comes up with a general strategy or plan for the entire organization. We'll then follow this strategy down to the bottom levels of the organization, showing how, through the use of such things as budgets and quotas, the total strategy is implemented, progress measured, and actual operations adjusted to meet changing circumstances.

Strategic Planning

At the very beginning of the information cycle of an organization is *strategic planning*. Normally, this is the responsibility of the president and his or her staff. During strategic planning, the goals and objectives of the organization are set.

Long-range strategic planning is concerned with determining what the organization is to be doing several years in the future. Imagine that you are involved in manufacturing automobiles. What type of car is the American public going to be demanding five years from now? Is the expected shortage of oil going to finally force a switch to smaller cars? Is it reasonable to expect the development of some totally new power system to replace the internal combustion engine within the next five years? Given that it takes three or four years to plan and build a new manufacturing plant, should we begin work on a new facility to make our current line of cars? These are examples of the kinds of questions that are dealt with in long-range planning.

Where does the information to support long-range planning come from? Many sources, really (see Fig. 2.4). The government prepares long-range economic surveys; similar materials describing the most likely pattern of international economics are also available. Private financial institutions prepare and sell long-range and short-range economic forecasts. Newspapers, magazines, and technical literature provide other sources of information, as do the publications of universities and other private research groups. Within the organization, market surveys can be conducted by a marketing group, and new products and inventions might arise in a research and development group. Finally, we have the factor of management intuition, a fancy word for informed guessing.

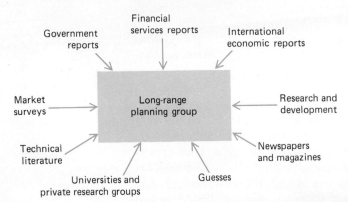

Figure 2.4
Sources of information for long-range planning.

All of these sources of information are really guesses, made (hopefully) by informed people, about what the future will hold. Long-range planning is far from perfectly accurate. Even so, the organization that has some idea of its future direction is in much better shape than the firm that just reacts, on a day-to-day basis, to what is happening "right now."

Short-Range Planning

Long-range planning sets the major goals of the organization. *Short-range planning* is concerned with what the organization is going to do in the current year.

As with long-range planning, there is a certain amount of guesswork involved in looking even one year into the future. Who, for example, could possibly predict an oil embargo, or a winter like the one we experienced in 1977? Barring such totally unpredictable happenings, however, we can do a pretty good job of guessing what the next twelve months might bring.

Within the organization, we know a great deal about what we'll be able to do over the next year. We know how many salespeople and sales outlets we have. We know how much this sales staff has been able to sell in the past, and that gives us a pretty good indication of how much they'll be able to sell this year. Our manufacturing facilities are equally well known; we have just so much manufacturing capacity and just so many workers and, based on past production, we have a pretty good idea of what they can do. We also certainly know whether any new manufacturing facilities are planned to become operational this year—the legacy of a prior year's long-range planning.

The objective of short-range planning is to set goals, budgets, and quotas for the coming year. Basically, this process starts with a reasonable estimate of how much marketing or sales thinks we can sell and how much manufacturing thinks we can produce. Assuming the numbers are different (and they usually are), a series of meetings, presentations, and strategy sessions are required to bring them together. Finally, targets that everyone can "live with" are agreed to or, if it is impossible to achieve agreement, targets are *dictated* by the president, and the goal of the organization for the next year is set.

Now comes the problem of implementing this objective. It's one thing for the president to say that "Our objective for the current year is to sell 3.5 million dollars' worth of our products." It's quite a different thing to translate this goal into the number of automobiles (or bookshelves or "gidgits") manufacturing must make or sales must sell. In most organizations, these very specific "front line" targets are set through the development of budgets and quotas.

One final comment on strategic planning, both long- and short-range, before we move into budgets and quotas. Why is planning necessary? What if sales went out and sold five million dollars' worth of product but manufacturing was able to make only three million dollars' worth? We'd have a lot of unhappy customers. What if manufacturing can make 100,000 automobiles, but sales is able to sell only 50,000 of them? Where would we park all the extra cars? The real purpose of planning is to balance and coordinate all the functions in the organization. If we force everyone to shoot for the same goal, extreme conditions such as the ones described above are unlikely to occur. Planning isn't perfect, but it is better than no planning.

Budgets and Quotas

Given a plan, the vice-presidents can now begin the task of implementing it. The vice-president in charge of sales knows that revenue totaling 3.5 million dollars, for example, is to be produced. If the Region 1 sales office accounted for 10 percent of total sales last year, the vice-president might assign the Region 1 sales manager a **quota** of $350,000, allocating the remainder of the total target to the other regions based on their past performance. Factors other than past performance, such as expected population growth in a region or the retirement of a super salesperson, might also be taken into account in setting regional quotas. A quota represents, in this case, the dollar sales that each of the regions is expected to contribute to the organization.

The regional sales manager, in turn, allocates his or her quota among the salespeople (Fig. 2.5). Salesperson A might, for example, be assigned a sales quota of $120,000 for the next year. Meanwhile, all the regional managers have been allocating their quotas to all their salespeople; if you were to add together the individual quotas of each of the salespeople, you'd come up with the total corporate objective (3.5 million, in our example).

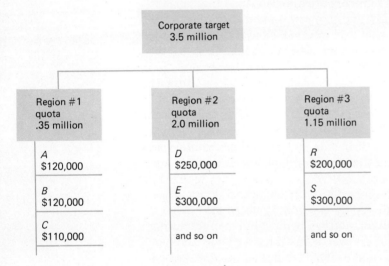

Figure 2.5
Setting individual sales quotas.

Manufacturing goes through much the same cycle. The target is divided among the various production plants. The plant managers, working from a reasonable guess of the actual mix of products that are needed to produce the planned total revenue, set quotas for each of the manufacturing departments.

Budgets are a means of controlling costs. It's not quite enough to simply say that we plan to sell 3.5 million dollars' worth of product; any business concern must also earn a profit if it is to stay in business. Let's assume that our firm is shooting for a 20 percent profit before taxes. Of the 3.5 million we hope to sell, $700,000 should be profit. That means that we can spend what's left, 2.8 million dollars, to produce and sell our product.

The available dollars are divided among the various functions of the organization, probably using the actual expenses of the past year as a guide.

The result is that each group has a budget, representing the total amount of money they are expected to spend during the current year. Now, both the expected production and the expected cost are known; each part of the organization has a budget and a quota. If everyone does exactly as planned, the organization will have no problems.

Measuring Progress

Not everyone does exactly as planned. Unforeseen problems crop up. Fuel becomes unavailable. People resign. Consumer tastes change. If the organization is to be successful, it must have a mechanism for measuring how well reality is conforming to plan. Budgets and quotas provide an excellent mechanism for making these measurements.

Usually, budgets and quotas are broken down into monthly, weekly, and even daily objectives. By comparing what actually happens to what the budget or quota says is expected to happen, we can get a pretty good idea how close to target we are. Consider a simple example. We have two salespeople, both of whom are expected to sell $2000 worth of merchandise each week. If at the end of week #1, salesperson A has sold $3000 worth but salesperson B has sold only $1500 worth, we know that A is ahead of target, B is behind target, and our store, having sold a total of $4500, is ahead of target. Expand this basic idea of comparing actual results with planned targets to each of the hundreds of salespeople in a medium-sized corporation, and you'll have a pretty good idea of how quotas can be used to measure progress. Budgets can be used in much the same way, comparing actual costs to expected costs.

Controlling Day-by-day Operations

Where do we get the data on what is really happening? If we plan to compare what is really happening to what is supposed to happen, we have to know what is really happening. Generally speaking, this data is a by-product of the firm's normal day-by-day paperwork. Let's examine the paperwork flow through a typical organization, starting with a sale to a customer and ending with delivery to that customer.

The process begins with the salesperson who, having received a firm order from a customer, fills out an order form (Fig. 2.6). The order form is then sent into an order-entry group that checks it for accuracy, checks the price quoted the customer, and schedules the product into manufacturing. Some firms, rather than manufacturing each item to a specific customer order, maintain products in inventory; if this is the case, order entry might have the product shipped directly to the customer from the warehouse, scheduling a replacement through manufacturing. The order form becomes a piece of data showing

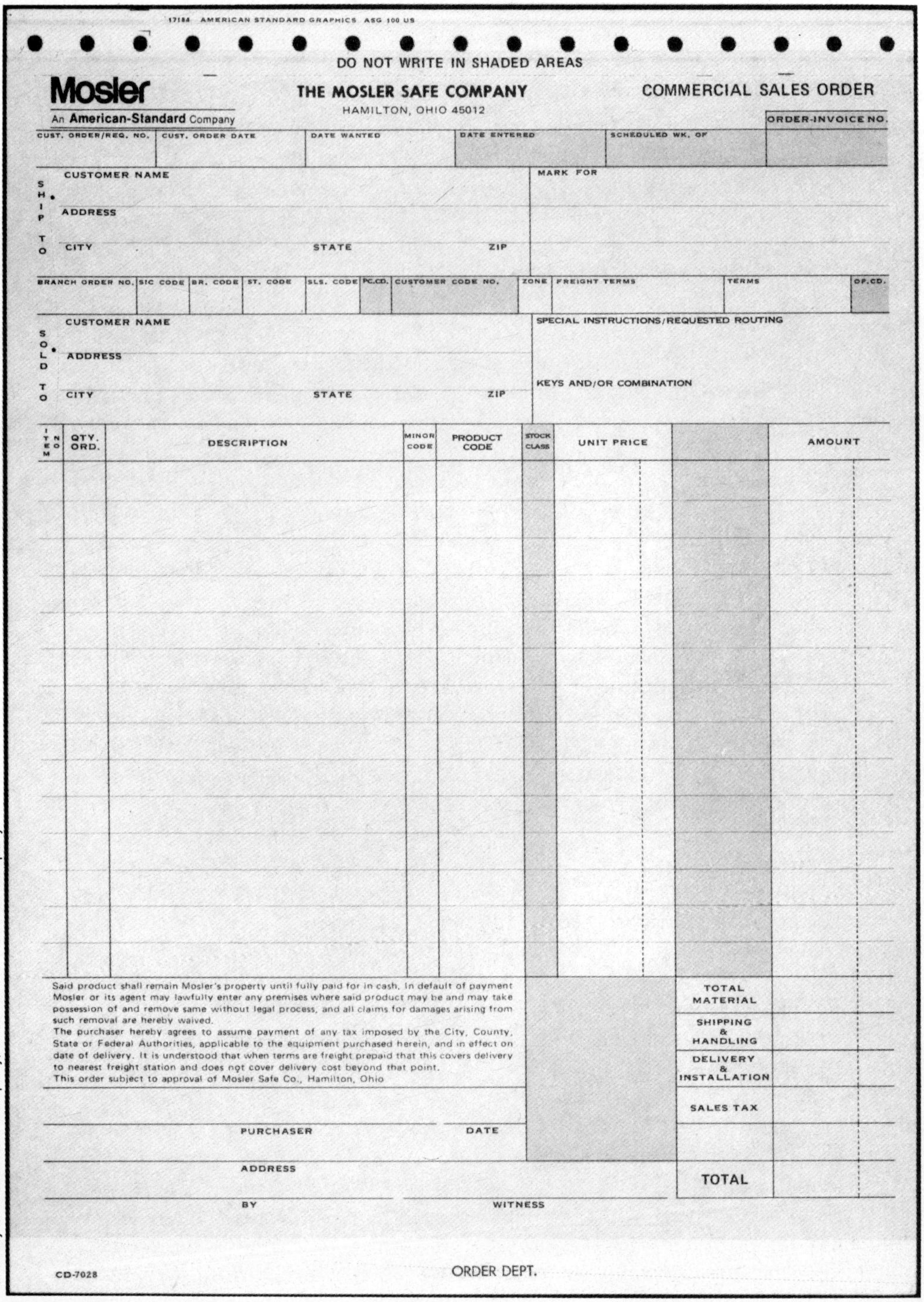

17184 AMERICAN STANDARD GRAPHICS ASG 100 US

DO NOT WRITE IN SHADED AREAS

Mosler
An **American-Standard** Company

THE MOSLER SAFE COMPANY
HAMILTON, OHIO 45012

COMMERCIAL SALES ORDER

CUST. ORDER/REQ. NO.	CUST. ORDER DATE	DATE WANTED	DATE ENTERED	SCHEDULED WK. OF	ORDER-INVOICE NO.

SHIP TO
CUSTOMER NAME
ADDRESS
CITY STATE ZIP

MARK FOR

BRANCH ORDER NO.	SIC CODE	BR. CODE	ST. CODE	SLS. CODE	PC.CD.	CUSTOMER CODE NO.	ZONE	FREIGHT TERMS	TERMS	OF.CD.

SOLD TO
CUSTOMER NAME
ADDRESS
CITY STATE ZIP

SPECIAL INSTRUCTIONS/REQUESTED ROUTING

KEYS AND/OR COMBINATION

ITEM NO	QTY. ORD.	DESCRIPTION	MINOR CODE	PRODUCT CODE	STOCK CLASS	UNIT PRICE		AMOUNT

Said product shall remain Mosler's property until fully paid for in cash. In default of payment Mosler or its agent may lawfully enter any premises where said product may be and may take possession of and remove same without legal process, and all claims for damages arising from such removal are hereby waived.
The purchaser hereby agrees to assume payment of any tax imposed by the City, County, State or Federal Authorities, applicable to the equipment purchased herein, and in effect on date of delivery. It is understood that when terms are freight prepaid that this covers delivery to nearest freight station and does not cover delivery cost beyond that point.
This order subject to approval of Mosler Safe Co., Hamilton, Ohio

PURCHASER DATE

ADDRESS

BY WITNESS

TOTAL MATERIAL	
SHIPPING & HANDLING	
DELIVERY & INSTALLATION	
SALES TAX	
TOTAL	

CD-7028

ORDER DEPT.

Courtesy of Mosler Safe Company, an American Standard Company.

Figure 2.6
A typical order form.

what this particular salesperson is doing; adding this sale to other sales provides the real data to compare against planned sales.

In most companies, several copies of the sales order are prepared. Assuming that this is a manufacturing firm, one copy would probably be sent to manufacturing, where it becomes the basic input document for creating a number of pieces of manufacturing data. Two common manufacturing documents are a bill-of-material and a router. A bill-of-material shows all the raw materials that must be assembled in building the product. A router shows all the manufacturing steps that the product must go through. Along with these two documents, many firms prepare a shop order, identifying the product to be manufactured. At the end of the manufacturing process, this shop order becomes the document that is used to measure what manufacturing is really doing.

What if all the raw materials needed to make the product are not available? Often, a part of the procedure for releasing a job to manufacturing requires a clerk to check for the availability of raw materials. If sufficient raw materials are not present, the purchasing department is called in to order more. Purchasing involves still more paperwork, as materials are ordered, delivered, and placed in inventory.

When the job has passed through manufacturing, it's time to ship it. Great care must be taken to make sure that the right product is shipped to the right customer—still more paperwork. Shipping often involves the use of independent truckers, the railroads, or some other mode of transportation, and transportation must be carefully coordinated. Every step in this process is carefully documented in writing in all but the smallest (or most irresponsible) companies.

The customer must be billed, a function performed by an accounts receivable or billing department. Raw material suppliers, shippers, and other suppliers must be paid by the accounts payable department. Payments from customers must be received; this function is often performed by still another department. The employees must be paid, often through a payroll department. In every case, the paperwork that was prepared at the time an expense was encountered is the document that supports the sending of a bill or the paying of a bill. Actual payments and receipts provide the real data that can be compared to plan.

COMMUNICATION LINES

All this is easier said than done. The organization chart of Fig. 2.1 represents a formal view of the lines of responsibility in the organization; on a day-to-day basis, Fig. 2.7 is probably a more accurate portrayal of what really happens. Each of the functional groups of the organization has a job to do. Each group must do its job if the organization is to succeed. In order to do its job, however,

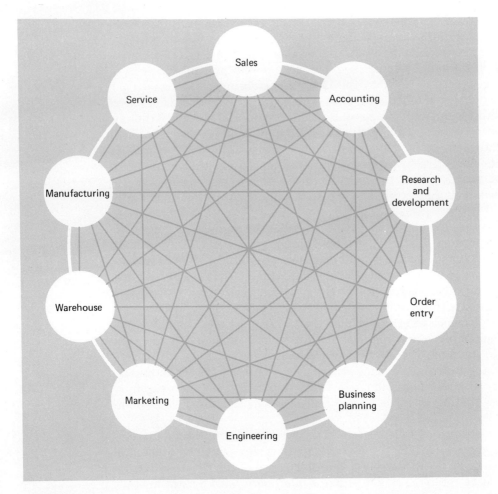

Figure 2.7
The lines of communication within an organization.

each group must communicate with every other group; often informally by telephone, but more frequently through the exchange of paperwork.

It's one thing to say that manufacturing needs the information provided by sales or that sales needs the information provided by manufacturing. It's quite another thing to actually provide that information. How, for example, can sales data be made available to other functions in the organization? The sales department writes an order form for each order. Is it reasonable to expect manufacturing to work with thousands and thousands of individual orders? Of course not. Manufacturing personnel are not interested in the details of the individual orders; what they need is summarized information—in other words,

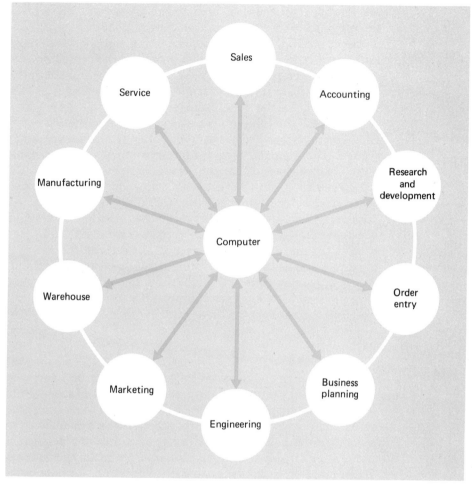

Figure 2.8
The computer as an information warehouse.

how many units of product A must be produced in a given month? Someone or some group must "process" the sales data, combining and summarizing the data on individual orders to produce information that is useful to manufacturing. To achieve this objective, many firms have an order-entry department or a similar group. The function of such a department is purely clerical; they process the paperwork. Similar groups exist throughout the organization, translating the data produced by one group into the information needed by another.

As a company continues to grow, even this arrangement becomes unwieldy. A greater volume of sales produces a greater volume of paperwork;

eventually, even the best manual paperwork system is overwhelmed. Enter the computer. A computer is very good at addition, subtraction, multiplication, division, sorting, counting, accumulating—in short, all those functions that are normally handled by clerical people. If the computer is placed in a (logically) central position (Fig. 2.8), each of the major functions in the organization can communicate its own detailed data into the computer. The computer can then summarize the data, feeding it back to the individual functions as required. Thus, the computer acts as a sort of information warehouse accepting data from various locations, processing it, storing it, and releasing it on request. The computer is an **information processing** machine. By using computers, many clerical functions can be automated.

Does this mean that all the clerical jobs in the country are about to be taken over by the computer? No. Definitely not! The fact that a task can be automated does not necessarily mean that it will be automated. Computers are expensive, and businesses do not purchase expensive equipment just to replace people. The decision to "go computer" depends on the size of the data processing job. A smaller firm might well decide that manual data processing is best. A firm of intermediate size might use a combination of manual and automatic data processing. A big firm will probably use a computer. In Chapter 3, we'll examine the reasons for these differences.

INFORMATION PROCESSING

Information processing or **data processing** (the terms are synonymous) involves taking the raw data produced as part of the regular business cycle (order forms, shop orders, shipping orders, and so on) and processing this data into a more meaningful form. By processing, we mean such things as sorting, summarizing, calculating, printing, selecting out desired bits of data, and performing any other operations that might make the data easier to interpret. By so processing the data, we get information. Perhaps a few examples of a number of typical applications will help to clarify what we mean by data or information processing.

Let's start with one of the more familiar tasks, *payroll*. Payroll processing starts with the individual employee's time card, a record of the actual hours worked for the pay period. These cards are collected and, normally, sorted into employee-number sequence to make it easier to update the books showing year-to-date earnings. A number of calculations are required to find gross pay, deductions, and take-home pay. A check is prepared, and a record of the payment is kept by the company. Often, these records of payment are the basis for a report sent to each department manager showing actual labor expenditures, to be compared with planned or budgeted labor costs.

Billing is another information processing operation. First, bills are collected and sorted by customer number; in this way, all the bills for a given customer are grouped together. Now, the total bill can be computed and prepared. *Accounts payable* is a similar application, except that what we collect are bills we owe other firms. *Accounts receivable* is concerned with actually receiving payment from customers; in this application, customer payments are collected and kept track of. Obviously, there must be a close relationship between billing and accounts receivable; why aren't these two applications combined? By keeping the billing and receipt-of-payments functions separate, we reduce the likelihood that a dishonest employee can cheat the company without getting caught.

Every business organization is required to maintain a set of books called a *ledger* reflecting actual expenditures and incomes. Keeping this ledger up to date is another information processing task.

Most firms maintain an *inventory;* often three separate inventories—raw materials, work-in-progress, and finished goods—are kept. Products are added to inventory and removed from inventory every day. Keeping track of the amount and cost of each product in inventory is yet another example.

Other information processing operations involve preparing reports comparing actual to budgeted expenses, or actual results to a quota. Typical examples include *sales analysis,* where actual orders are compared to quota for each salesperson, for each sales district, and for the company as a whole; and *production control,* where actual production is compared to quota and actual production costs are compared to budget for each department, for each plant, and for the company as a whole. These reports serve as a sort of early warning system when actual results begin to deviate significantly from plan.

Other common information processing applications will be mentioned throughout this book.

SUMMARY

This chapter started with a discussion of the difference between data and information. Data are individual facts; information is the meaning that human beings assign to facts. Data is often combined or processed in some way so as to convert it to information. The information cycle—data/information/decision/action—was then introduced.

Next, we moved into a discussion of the information needs of a typical business concern, starting with long-range strategy, moving to short-range planning, then through budgets and quotas, and finally down to the control of day-to-day activities. A quota represents a planned or expected contribution to the organization, while a budget represents a planned expense.

Controlling day-to-day activities involves a great deal of paperwork. This paperwork must be communicated among the various groups in the organization. The act of accepting data and processing it into a form suitable for the use of some other function in the organization is known as information processing. The computer is an information processing machine.

The chapter ended with a brief discussion of a number of typical information processing applications, including payroll, billing, accounts payable, accounts receivable, ledger, sales analysis, and production control.

KEYWORDS

budget	data processing	information processing
data	information	quota

EXERCISES

1. What is data?
2. What is information?
3. Explain what is meant by the information feedback cycle of Fig. 2.3.
4. What is long-range strategic planning? Who does it? Why is it important?
5. What is short-range planning? Why is it important?
6. What is a quota?
7. What is a budget?
8. Why is it important to measure how well the organization is actually doing as compared with the plan? How can budgets and quotas be used in measuring this progress?
9. What is information processing?
10. A computer is said to be an information processing machine. What does this mean?

3

INFORMATION PROCESSING TECHNIQUES

OVERVIEW

In this chapter we'll examine the basic information processing cycle, covering the steps involved in a number of typical, information processing applications. It is possible to solve most information processing problems by either manual, partially automated, or fully automated (computer) means; economic considerations will be shown to be among the more significant factors in selecting the technique to be used in solving a particular problem.

THE INFORMATION PROCESSING CYCLE

Our concern in Chapter 2 was with the data processing and information needs of the entire organization. In this chapter, our attention shifts to a specific area of application that we'll be looking at in some detail. The application chosen for our analysis is payroll.

Everyone who works expects to be paid, and we all have a pretty good idea of how our pay is calculated. First, we know our hourly rate. Second, we know how many hours we've worked. Multiplying these two numbers gives us our gross pay, but, as we all know, this is not our take-home pay. The government takes a portion to cover income taxes, the amount varying with the income level. Another portion goes to the Social Security Administration to help pay the costs of our Social Security system. Other payroll deductions might cover union dues, credit-union loan repayments, savings, bond purchases, state taxes, local taxes, and a myriad of other things. Subtracting all these deductions from our gross pay yields our actual take-home, or net, pay.

This is a pure **information processing** application. What are the major steps involved in processing a payroll?

The operation starts, in many organizations, with a time card. Each employee is expected to punch his or her time card at the start of work in the morning, and before leaving at night. Any other deviations from a normal work schedule are also recorded on the time card; some firms, for example, require their employees to "clock-off" and "clock back on" for lunch. At the end of the pay period, this time card contains a complete record of the employee's actual time spent on the job. The time card is a **source document,** containing the original raw data needed by the payroll system. This phase of the data processing cycle is known as the **data collection** phase.

Once the data has been collected, it must be **recorded** in some way. Perhaps the time cards are simply stored for future reference. Perhaps the data on the time cards is recorded in accounting books. On a computer-based system, the data on the time cards might be converted to a pattern of holes in the cards so that it can be read by machines. This is basically a bookkeeping function, but it's an important one. Since this source data is used to generate people's paychecks, the recording of this data helps to guarantee the fair settlement of any future disagreements that might arise.

Once the data has been collected and recorded, we can begin to **manipulate** or **process** it. It's during this stage that the actual calculations are performed, multiplying hours worked by an hourly pay rate, computing Social Security tax, figuring out income tax, and so on. Most of you have probably noticed the year-to-date earnings and deductions that are normally attached to a paycheck (Fig. 3.1). Employees are required by law to maintain this information, primarily for income-tax purposes. An important step in the processing part of the cycle is adding earnings and deductions for the current pay period to the year-to-date figures.

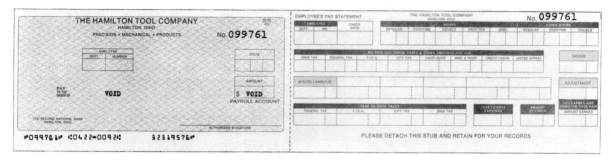

Figure 3.1
A paycheck with a year-to-date stub. (Sample courtesy of The Hamilton Tool Company.)

Once the data has been processed and the results obtained, the results must be **recorded.** Information (note that we're calling it information now; the data has been processed) on the amount of money to be paid employees will certainly be entered into the accounting books of the organization. A new set of information on the year-to-date earnings of each employee must also be compiled in preparation for the next pay period.

The final step in this cycle is **output.** Checks must be printed, typed or written, and distributed to each employee. This cycle started with the employee and ends with the employee.

INFORMATION PROCESSING TECHNIQUES

All these steps are essential, but there are many different ways of actually doing each step. The collection of source data, for example, might involve something as simple as a department manager taking notes on who arrives late or who leaves early. In other organizations, each employee is expected to maintain personal work records in pencil or pen on a slip of paper or a 3 × 5 card. More common is the time-clock approach, with employees punching on and off by using a time card. Some larger corporations have elaborate computer-controlled data entry terminals through which employees report their time directly to a computer.

The recording of source data can also be done in numerous ways. Picture an ancient clerk copying time data into a ledger book with a quill pen, and you have a good impression of a pure manual system. From this, we can move up to the use of punched cards or magnetic computer tapes.

Processing can be done by hand, using nothing more than a paper and a pencil. Calculators can help, giving a primarily manual but partially automated system. Punched card data processing, popular a few decades ago, involved even less manual labor. Finally, we come to the computer, where data can be processed into information almost totally without human intervention.

Both recording and outputting the data can be done by a variety of techniques, ranging from the fully manual to the fully automated.

Manual data processing, semi-automated data processing, and **computer data processing** are all in common use today. Which approach is best? The answer depends on a number of factors, but, primarily, the answer is an economic one. The best data processing technique for a given task is the one that allows the task to be completed at the *lowest possible cost.* Perhaps the best way to illustrate this idea is through an example. Let's take a look at how three business concerns—a small gas station, a medium-sized newspaper, and a large manufacturing operation—might handle their payroll processing problem.

Before we begin, however, it might be useful to comment briefly on our terminology. The act of converting data into information has traditionally been called *data* processing. *Data* processing tends to emphasize the raw material, while *information* processing tends to emphasize the result, the real objective of the process. The two terms are considered synonyms, but information processing is currently more favored. Our practice will be to use data processing when describing established, long-standing processes, and information processing when referring to current techniques.

Payroll Processing in a Small Business

For quite a few years, Tony has operated a service station at the corner of Fifth and Main. He has a good reputation for high-quality work and claims numerous regular customers. Tony employs seven people: two mechanics and five part-time attendants. Let's watch him as he prepares his weekly payroll.

On Monday morning, Tony posts a work schedule for the week in the station. Throughout the week, changes are simply noted on the schedule— Tom's Wednesday morning history test might prompt him to switch nights with Judy. Early Saturday evening, after closing the station for the weekend, Tony removes the schedule and takes it home. This record of the number of hours worked by each employee is essential data; we can call it Tony's basic *input* document.

Saturday evening is payroll time. Tony always starts with Lou, his number-one mechanic and second in command. The schedule shows that Lou worked from 8:00 A.M. until 5:00 P.M. (nine hours) Monday through Friday and from 9:00 A.M. until 1:00 P.M. on Saturday. Although it isn't actually on the schedule, Tony knows that Lou took an hour for lunch on each nine-hour day. Working on a sheet of scratch paper, Tony quickly computes Lou's total hours for the week: 44. Lou is paid $4.75 per hour. A simple multiplication (44 × $4.75) gives Lou's gross pay for the week; it's $209.00.

Next, Tony computes the income-tax deduction. The government publishes a set of income-tax withholding rates every year; this set of tables is circulated in a booklet called "Circular E." In this booklet are the tables Tony must use in preparing payroll. (A copy of the appropriate tables has been reproduced as Fig. 3.2). Lou has a wife and one child living at home; thus Tony must subtract $57.69 ($19.23 times 3 dependents) from Lou's gross pay before entering the table—this subtraction leaves $151.31 of taxable wages. Tony now enters the tax table. Since Lou's taxable wage lies between $127 and $210, the amount of tax to be withheld is $12.15 plus 18% of all earnings over $127. Tony computes the "excess" portion of earnings ($151.31 minus $127 equals $24.31), finds 18% of this amount (18% of $24.31 is $4.38), adds this amount to the base tax ($4.38 plus $12.15 equals $16.53), and ends up with the amount of federal income tax that must be withheld from Lou's pay.

WEEKLY PAYROLL PERIOD

(a) Single person—including head of household			(b) Married person		
If the amount of wages is:	The amount of income tax to be withheld shall be:		If the amount of wages is:	The amount of income tax to be withheld shall be:	
Not over $27 0			Not over $46 0		
Over—	but not over—	of excess over—	Over—	but not over—	of excess over—
$27	–$63 . . . . . 15%	–$27	$46	–$127 . . . . 15%	–$46
$63	–$131 . . . . $5.40 plus 18%	–$63	$127	–$210 . . . . $12.15 plus 18%	–$127
$131	–$196 . . . . $17.64 plus 21%	–$131	$210	–$288 . . . . $27.09 plus 21%	–$210
$196	–$273 . . . . $31.29 plus 26%	–$196	$288	–$369 . . . . $43.47 plus 24%	–$288
$273	–$331 . . . . $51.31 plus 30%	–$273	$369	–$454 . . . . $62.91 plus 28%	–$369
$331	–$433 . . . . $68.71 plus 34%	–$331	$454	–$556 . . . . $86.71 plus 32%	–$454
$433	. . . . $103.39 plus 39%	–$433	$556	. . . . $119.35 plus 37%	–$556

Figure 3.2

A federal income tax table: weekly payroll period. Multiply the number of dependents claimed by the employee by $19.23. Subtract the product from gross pay to get the employee's taxable wage. (*Source: Circular E, Employer's Tax Guide,* Department of the Treasury, Internal Revenue Service Publication 15. Revised November 1978, pp. 15–16.)

Next the social security tax must be computed. The current social security tax rate is 6.65% of gross pay. Since Lou's gross pay is $209.00, the deduction for social security tax is $13.90 (6.65% of $209).

Net, or take-home, pay is found by subtracting all deductions from gross pay. In Lou's case, Tony subtracts the $16.53 for income tax and the $13.90 for social security tax from Lou's gross pay of $209.00, leaving a net pay of $178.57. A check for this amount is made out to Lou.

Tony is now ready to tackle Ralph's pay. First, the total number of hours that he worked is determined—the source is the work schedule. Hours worked is then multiplied by the hourly pay rate, giving gross pay (with only seven employees, Tony knows everyone's pay rate). The gross pay figure allows income tax to be computed through the tax table. The social security deduction is 6.65% of gross pay. Net pay is found by subtracting these two deductions from gross pay, and a check is written.

He now moves on to the part-time workers, repeating what should, by now, have become an obvious pattern:

1. Find total hours worked from the schedule.
2. Multiply hours worked by the employee's hourly pay rate to get gross pay.
3. Find income tax from the tax table.
4. Multiply gross pay by 0.0665 to get the social security tax.
5. Subtract income tax and social security tax from gross pay to find net pay.
6. Write a paycheck.

Note that the same sequence of computational steps is repeated for each employee.

Every computation is checked and double-checked for accuracy, but mistakes still happen occasionally. The arithmetic is not difficult; multiplication and subtraction, even with decimal numbers and percentages, are elementary-school skills. But Tony hates this job; it's just too repetitive, too boring, and too exacting.

Tony spends roughly an hour a week on his payroll. Why not do the work on a computer? Although the cost of computers has been dropping steadily (and dramatically) in recent years, a computer is still a pretty expensive machine. Small microcomputer systems are available for $1000 or less, but Tony simply does not have the expertise or training to use such a machine. Tony has seen advertisements for small business computer systems designed specifically for people with no training or background, but these systems start at about $12,000, and that's just too much. Even though he loathes this part of his job, Tony is not willing to spend thousands of dollars just to save a few hours of his time each week. The service station is just too small for a computer. Maybe next year.

Payroll Processing in a Larger Firm

The *Evening News* employs approximately 700 people, some as reporters and others as proofreaders or typesetters. Still other individuals are involved in running the presses, selling ads, or delivering the newspapers. Although the company would certainly not be considered huge (or even big), no single individual would be capable of personally exercising total control over all these functions, making subdivision necessary.

Payday is once a week, on Friday. Since the company is a bit larger than Tony's service station, some of the informality disappears from the payroll process. Rather than simply relying on handwritten attendance records, employees record their comings and goings by punching a time clock. Since it is not reasonable to expect any one individual to keep everyone's pay rate in mind, personnel records are maintained. But the computations performed and tables used by the *News* are identical to those used by Tony; if they tried to do the job any differently, the *News* would be in violation of federal law. An individual's pay is still computed by the following six steps:

1. Find total hours worked (from the time card).
2. Multiply hours worked by the employee's hourly pay rate (from personnel records) to get gross pay.
3. Find income tax from the tax tables.
4. Multiply gross pay by 0.0665 to get the social security tax.
5. Subtract income tax and social security tax from gross pay to find net pay. (With a larger firm such as the *Evening News,* other deductions are likely, but we'll ignore them.)
6. Write a paycheck.

This procedure must be repeated once for each employee. Tony went through it seven times, needing about an hour to complete the work. The *News* must repeat the cycle seven hundred times; one hundred hours would seem a reasonable estimate of the time required to complete the job. If we assume that the company is on a standard forty-hour work week, that amounts to the services of $2\frac{1}{2}$ people. Adding various employee benefits to the basic pay of these employees means that it would probably cost the *News* at least $1000 per month for each employee; given $2\frac{1}{2}$ people, that's a total of $2500 just to produce the payroll.

What would it cost to do the job on a computer? A small microcomputer probably couldn't handle this job, so the equipment selling for under $1000 can be discounted, but the job could certainly be done by a small business minicomputer system selling for about $20,000. Spreading that cost over two years (a common amortization period for such equipment), and factoring in the cost of a service contract will generate a monthly equipment cost of about $1000. A computer can be purchased for about $1000 per month. It looks like a good deal.

But it's a bit more complex than that. In order to use a computer, even a small one, an operator is needed. A computer operator is a highly skilled individual who expects to be paid more than the average employee. Let's assume a total labor cost of $1500 per month, including benefits. The operator and the computer will cost the *News* $2500 per month; they can save the *News* $2500 per month. Should the *News* shift payroll computations to the computer? The answer is not clear; perhaps other applications of the machine will produce other savings and "tip the balance" in the computer's favor.

Payroll Processing in a Large Corporation

Tinhorn Steel is one of the largest corporations in the country; the local plant alone employs nearly seven thousand people. Laws regarding income tax and social security tax do not change as a firm grows larger; thus Tinhorn faces the same tax-withholding requirements as Tony's service station and the *Evening News*, and an individual employee's pay is computed by the same procedure used in the two smaller firms. Yet Tinhorn Steel uses a computer.

Tony repeated this set of calculations seven times a week, spending about an hour on the job. The *News* repeated the same computations 700 times, needing about 100 hours, or the services of 2½ people, to do the job. Tinhorn Steel, with 7000 employees in the local plant, must repeat the cycle 7000 times, spending about 1000 hours per week on payroll! Again, if we assume a forty-hour work week, that amounts to 25 full-time employees doing nothing but multiplying hours worked by hourly pay rate and so on. At $1000 per employee, that's $25,000 per month just to *produce* the paychecks for the other 6975 employees.

As we stated earlier, a computer can be purchased for roughly $1000 per month. With the services of an operator, a programmer, and a manager included, the total cost of computerized payroll won't exceed $6000 or $7000 per month. That's considerably less than $25,000. Tinhorn uses a computer because the computer is cheaper. It's that simple. Whenever

1. a task can be completely defined by a series of repetitious, computational or logical steps, and

2. the task must be repeated many times,

the computer may provide a solution. Both characteristics—well-defined steps repeated many times—are present in the vast majority of commercial computer applications.

THE BREAKEVEN POINT

Why should the number of repetitions make such a big difference? If a computer can be purchased for $20,000, the cost remains the same whether the machine is used to compute one, two, seven hundred, or several thousand pay checks. The computer is a **fixed-cost** item. Human labor, on the other hand, is a **variable-cost** item. If the cost of producing one paycheck by hand is one dollar, the cost of producing two is two dollars, five hundred cost $500, and ten thousand, at $1 each, $10,000.

Take a look at Fig. 3.3. Along the horizontal or *x*-axis, we have the number of repetitions; along the vertical or *y*-axis, we have the total cost. The horizontal line marked "computer cost" shows that the cost of doing a job such as payroll does not change as the number of repetitions changes; it costs the same

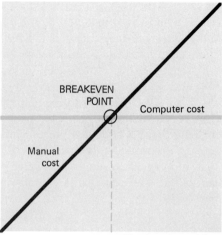

BREAKEVEN
POINT

Computer cost

Manual
cost

Figure 3.3
The breakeven point.

Number of repetitions

to compute one paycheck as it does to compute 10,000. (This is not entirely true; more checks means more paper and more ink and more paper handling, but the variable part of the computer cost is very small.) The slanted line marked "manual cost," starting at zero and going up and to the right, shows how the cost of processing checks by hand increases with each check. Eventually, as the number of repetitions increases, the "manual" line crosses the "computer" line. To the left of this point, the cost of doing the job by hand is less than the cost of using the computer; to the right of this point, the cost of using the computer is less than the cost of doing the job by hand. This point is called the **breakeven point.** The breakeven point defines a critical number of repetitions. If a company has fewer employees and, hence, fewer paychecks than this crucial number, the job will probably be done by hand. If employment exceeds this number, the computer will probably be used.

Actually, this idea is not so unusual if you think about it. Why, for example, do we use a shovel to dig a few postholes but switch to a steamshovel to dig a basement for a new house? Given enough people and enough shovels, a basement could be dug by hand, but with such a large task, the use of the machine saves money (and time). Why does a teacher grade classroom examinations by hand while lengthy exams such as the Scholastic Aptitude Test (SAT) are graded by machine? Again, it's a question of cost. Why do we type letters but print newspapers and books? Try to picture two million copies of the latest paperback bestseller being produced by monks with quill pens; even at the ridiculously low wage of one dollar per hour, the cost of a book produced in this manner would be beyond all but the most wealthy.

The breakeven concept is an important one. Manual labor is a variable cost; machine labor is a fixed cost. As the number of repetitions or copies increases, the cost of manual labor creeps closer and closer to the breakeven point; when the breakeven point is crossed, the machine will be used. This is the underlying motivation behind *all* forms of "automation"; if the machine is cheaper to use than human labor, the machine will be used. There is nothing sinister about it. Automation is not designed to put people out of work; automation is intended to save money.

How does a semi-automated approach to information processing fit in with this breakeven concept? The use of a calculator saves computation time, making the labor cost per paycheck lower than in a purely manual system, but calculators represent an initial expense that must be recovered. In Fig. 3.4, the cost picture of a semi-automated solution is shown graphically. The first horizontal line represents the cost of the equipment. If a $500 calculator is purchased to compute payroll, it doesn't matter whether 1, 2, or 2000 checks are computed; the cost of the calculator is still $500. On top of this initial cost is the labor cost needed to process each employee's payroll. This is a variable cost, which depends on the number of checks processed; this cost is shown by the line slanting upward and to the right (Fig. 3.4).

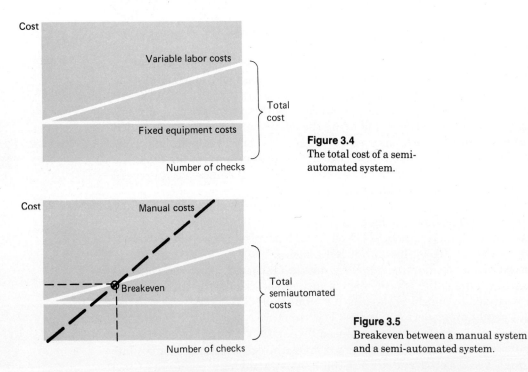

Figure 3.4
The total cost of a semi-automated system.

Figure 3.5
Breakeven between a manual system and a semi-automated system.

In Fig. 3.5, we've put the manual and semi-automated systems together on the same graph. The manual system consists of purely variable costs; we might imagine a cost of $1.00 per check just to give us a feel for what is going on. The labor cost of the semi-automated approach will be lower (let's assume a cost of 50¢ per check), but the initial cost of the equipment must also be taken into account. In effect, what we are saying is that the first check in our example costs $500.50 in the semi-automated system, but each additional check costs only 50¢. For just a few checks, the purely manual system is the least expensive; this is represented by the area to the left of the breakeven point in Fig. 3.5. To the right of this point, the labor savings gained from the equipment have paid for the equipment, and the semi-automated system becomes least expensive.

Now, let's put all three systems—manual, semi-automated, and computer—together on the same chart (Fig. 3.6). To produce just a few paychecks, the manual system is the best solution (area "A" on Fig. 3.6). To produce an intermediate number of checks, the semi-automated solution is best (area "B"). Finally, when the number of checks to be produced is high enough to cover the initial cost of the computer, the fully automated approach becomes the best solution (area "C").

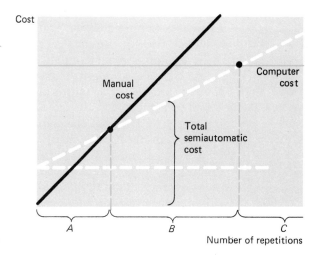

Figure 3.6
Breakeven—all three systems.

What is the best approach? The answer depends on the characteristics of the particular application being considered.

OTHER SIMILAR APPLICATIONS

Let's assume that we're selling cars and specializing in a single model. The cars on our lot make up our inventory. Each time we sell a car, we subtract one from inventory; each time a new shipment arrives from our supplier, we add the incoming cars to our inventory. The current number of cars in inventory is an important statistic; we use this number to determine whether or not to order additional cars. The computations are very easy—simple addition and subtraction.

At a more realistic automobile dealership with dozens of different models, the problem is a bit more complex, but manual records are still adequate. What happens, however, in a big department store, or a supermarket, or an industrial warehouse, where thousands of different products must be controlled and tracked? Paper-and-pencil inventory systems do not have a chance in such complex environments. The calculations are no more difficult; it's just that there are so many more of them to perform. Computers are frequently used to keep track of inventory.

Billing is another good example of a common computer application. A small company might write its bills by hand, but how can a large bank-credit-card system possibly process millions of individual purchases each month by hand? Instead, individual sales and credit slips are read into the computer and sorted and grouped by account number, and the resulting bills are compiled and printed by computer.

Banks face similar problems. To update checking account balances, all checks must be subtracted from the old balance and all deposits must be added. Again, it's simple addition and subtraction. If only a few dozen accounts are involved, this job presents no problem. But what if the bank has 100,000 or more accounts? Would you enjoy doing nothing but adding deposits and subtracting checks for eight hours a day, day in and day out? Adding interest to savings accounts is a similar problem. The computations are easy—all you do is find an account's minimum balance for the period and multiply by a constant interest rate. But, ten thousand times?

A small library can easily track its circulation by handwritten documents on 3 × 5 card files. But what about the big metropolitan library or the large university library? A small school can easily compute every student's grade point average manually, but if Ohio State or Stanford University were to try this approach, first-term averages *might* be ready by the end of the second term.

A surprising percentage of modern computer applications are really nothing more than this—very simple computations repeated many, many times. These applications represent nothing more nor less than the automation of tedious clerical functions.

SUMMARY

This chapter started with a discussion of the basic information processing cycle: data collection, recording, data manipulation, the recording of results, and output. We then contrasted manual, semi-automated, and computer data processing techniques by examining how payroll might be processed in a small, medium-sized, and large business organization. By introducing the idea of a breakeven point, we were able to show that the selection of an information processing technique for a particular application is really based on simple economics, with the lowest-cost alternative being chosen. The chapter closed with a discussion of other similar applications.

KEYWORDS

breakeven point	fixed cost	recording
computer data processing	information processing	semi-automated data processing
data collection	manual data processing	source document
data manipulation		variable cost
data processing	output	

EXERCISES

1. Discuss the information processing cycle.
2. What is a source document?
3. What happens during the data collection phase of the information processing cycle?
4. Why is it important that source data be recorded in some way?
5. What happens during the data manipulation or processing phase of the information processing cycle?
6. Why is it important that the results of data manipulation be recorded?
7. What is output?
8. Contrast pure manual, semi-automated, and computer data processing.
9. What is the difference between a fixed and a variable cost?
10. Explain the concept of a breakeven point.

4

INFORMATION PROCESSING: AN EXAMPLE

OVERVIEW

In this chapter, we'll be examining how a small firm might keep track of its inventory, processing data into information by manual means. The company is an automobile dealership that offers three models for sale: a subcompact, an intermediate, and a full-sized automobile. The problem is one of getting an accurate picture of inventory status for reordering purposes. Each of the major steps in the information processing cycle will be described; we'll be looking at exactly how this firm collects, stores, and processes the data needed to track inventory.

OUR FIRM

The company to be analyzed in this chapter is a local automobile dealership selling an average of forty to fifty new cars per week. As automobile dealerships go, that's a pretty good size, but compared to the firms in the *Fortune 500,* this is a very small organization.

The automobiles sold are manufactured by the North American Automobile Corporation. Three models are offered for sale: the subcompact Hummingbird, the intermediate Mallard, and the full-sized Pelican. The organization employs ten full-time sales people and a reasonable number of service and support personnel.

THE PROBLEM

Each week, the owner of this dealership places orders for new stock. To help make an accurate decision, the owner must know exactly what is on the lot at the time the order is placed. Basically, the boss is looking for the following information:

1. How many cars of each model type did we have at the beginning of the week?
2. How many cars of each model type were delivered by the manufacturer during the week?
3. How many cars of each model type were sold during the week?
4. How many cars of each model type are currently in stock?

THE BASIC SOLUTION

This is really a fairly simple data processing application. Let's assume that, at some point in time (probably on the day the dealership opened for business), someone counted the cars on the lot and filled out a 3 × 5 card on each. This deck of cards represents a **master file,** containing one **record** for each car on the lot (Fig. 4.1).

The problem is one of simply keeping this file up to date. Each time a new automobile is delivered to the lot, a clerk fills out a new 3 × 5 card containing information on this new car and adds it to the master file. Each time one of the salespeople sells one of the automobiles, the associated 3 × 5 card is pulled from the file. At the end of the week, assuming that the job has been done correctly, the summary information required by the owner can be obtained by simply counting the cards of each type.

Source Data Collection

How does the clerk in charge of the master file know when new automobiles arrive or when a car is sold? The obvious answer is by looking out the window

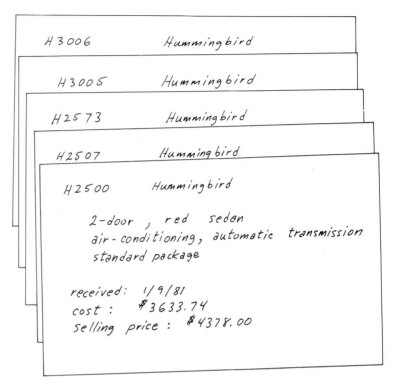

H 3006   Hummingbird

H 3005   Hummingbird

H 2573   Hummingbird

H 2507   Humming bird

H 2500   Hummingbird

2-door , red sedan
air - conditioning, automatic transmission
standard package

received: 1/9/81
cost : $3633.74
selling price : $4378.00

Figure 4.1
A portion of the inventory
master file.

and watching the delivery trucks arrive, or by talking to the salespeople. The obvious answer leaves a great deal to be desired. What if this clerk just happens to be on a break when the truck arrives? What if one of the salespeople were to lie in an attempt to increase his or her commission for the week? Informal communication just will not do; formal communication is essential.

When a car is sold, the salesperson is required to fill out a sales order (Fig. 4.2), giving one copy to the customer, one to the inventory clerk, one to the owner, and keeping one for himself. To the clerk, that copy of the sales order is formal notification that an automobile has been sold. There is no possibility of misunderstanding or misinterpretation; there either is or is not a sales order.

When automobiles are delivered to the dealership, the truck driver gives an official of the firm a delivery order (Fig. 4.3), which is checked for accuracy before any cars are unloaded. This delivery order lists each automobile on the truck. The inventory clerk is given a copy of this list, thus receiving formal notification of the arrival of new merchandise.

The clerk now has two stacks of papers to work with: one stack identifies each car sold; the second identifies each new automobile arriving at the dealership. These documents are the clerk's **source documents.**

W. C. DAVIS
NORTH AMERICAN AUTO
CINCINNATI, OHIO

BUYER'S NAME _GEORGE SMITH_ DATE _DEC. 3_ 19 _80_

ADDRESS _452 S. MAIN_ RES PHONE _____ BUS PHONE _____

I (we) hereby order from you, subject to all terms, conditions and agreements contained herein, and the ADDITIONAL CONDITIONS printed on the reverse side hereof, the following ☒ NEW ☐ USED VEHICLE

YEAR	MAKE	MODEL OR SERIES	BODY TYPE	COLOR	TRIM
1981	HUMMINGBIRD	2-dr	SEDAN	RED	STD.

MVI OR SERIAL NO.	STOCK NO. 42573	TO BE DELIVERED ON OR ABOUT _DEC. 6_ 19 _80_

CASH PRICE OF VEHICLE		3999	95
ADD: AIR CONDITIONING		349	50

FINANCING TO BE ARRANGED BY CUSTOMER

	TOTAL	4349	45
	TAX	195	73

DOCUMENTARY CHARGE AND FEES: LICENSE _20.00_ LIC. TRANSFER _2.50_ TITLE _2.50_ REGISTRATION _5.00_ | 30 | 00

(1) TOTAL CASH PRICE DELIVERED $ 4575 18

DESCRIPTION OF TRADE-IN

YEAR	MAKE	MODEL	TYPE	COLOR

MVI/SERIAL NO. _____ STOCK NO. _____

TITLE NO. _____ LICENSE NO. _____

DOWN PAYMENT
CASH DEPOSIT ON ORDER $ _500.00_ CASH ON DELIVERY $ _4,075.18_
TRADE IN ALLOWANCE AS APPRAISED _NONE_
LESS BALANCE OWING TO:

TYPE OF INSURANCE	AMOUNT	TERM	COST
FIRE AND THEFT			
COLLISION	DED.		
PUBLIC LIABILITY			
PROPERTY DAMAGE			

CREDIT LIFE INSURANCE — BUYER IS NOT REQUIRED TO OBTAIN CREDIT LIFE INSURANCE COVERAGE

THE UNDERSIGNED HEREBY AFFIRM(S) THAT THE CHARGE FOR CREDIT LIFE INSURANCE HAS BEEN DISCLOSED IN WRITING PRIOR TO EXECUTION BY THE UNDERSIGNED. BUYER SPECIFICALLY AFFIRM(S) THAT HE DESIRES TO OBTAIN INSURANCE FOR WHICH CHARGES ARE MADE.

BUYER X _____ CO-BUYER X _____

WARNING THE INSURANCE AFFORDED HERE DOES NOT COVER LIABILITY FOR INJURY TO PERSONS OR DAMAGE TO PROPERTY OF OTHERS UNLESS SO INDICATED HEREON. BUYER MAY CHOOSE THE PERSON THROUGH WHICH INSURANCE IS TO BE OBTAINED

(2) TOTAL DOWN PAYMENT	
(3) UNPAID BALANCE OF CASH PRICE (1-2)	
(4) OTHER CHARGES	NA
(5) AMOUNT FINANCED (3 + 4)	
(6) **FINANCE CHARGE**	
(7) TOTAL OF PAYMENTS (5 + 6)	
DEFERRED PAYMENT PRICE (1 + 4 + 6)	

ANNUAL PERCENTAGE RATE %

Finance charges begin to accrue on _____. The Total of Payments shall be repaid to _____ in _____ consecutive equal monthly instalments of $ _____ each on the _____ day of each month commencing _____ 19 ____ plus one final instalment of $ _____ due _____ 19 ____. If final monthly instalment is more than twice amount of an otherwise regularly scheduled equal payment, balloon payment in amount of $ _____ is due _____, 19 ____. Balloon payment shall be paid when due and may not be refinanced. If any instalment is in default more than 10 days, default charges shall be payable in the amount of _____ % of the delinquent instalment or $ _____ whichever is less. Seller shall have a security interest in the property until the Total of Payments is paid in full. If this contract is prepaid, a refund credit computed in accordance with the Rule of 78s will be made to Buyer. In computing such refund credit, an acquisition charge in the amount of $ _____ will be made.

SALESMAN _T.C. Jones_

ACCEPTED BY _W C Davis_
THIS ORDER IS NOT VALID UNLESS SIGNED AS ACCEPTED BY DEALER OR HIS AUTHORIZED REPRESENTATIVE

BUYER SIGNS X _George Smith_

CO-BUYER SIGNS X _____

ADDRESS _425 S Main_

CITY-STATE, ZIP _____

NOTICE TO THE BUYER. Do not sign this order before you read it or if it contains any blank spaces. You are entitled to an exact copy of the order you sign. BUYER ACKNOWLEDGES he has read and received a completed copy of this order comprising the entire agreement affecting this purchase, and that this order is subject to Buyer's satisfactory credit rating. BUYER CERTIFIES he is of legal age to execute binding contracts in this State, and no credit has been extended except as appears above.

FORM SA-690 (10-73)   THE REYNOLDS & REYNOLDS CO., CELINA, O., DALLAS, LOS ANGELES   LITHO IN U S A

56

◀ **Figure 4.2**
A customer sales order
begins the process.

AAAA AUTO CARRIERS, INC.				BILL NO. **BI 12293**	
SHIPPER: *NORTH AMERICAN MOTORS, INC.*	DRIVER: *ROBERT ADAMS*		FCC NO. *001*	DATE BILLED	DATE SHIPPED *12/1/80*
DESTINATION *W.C. DAVIS NORTH AMERICAN AUTO*	REMARKS				

STOCK NUMBER	MODEL	SERIAL NO.	MILES	INSPECTOR'S COMMENTS:
H4350	*H-52G*	*H 210661*	*345*	
H 4351	*H-52R*	*H 210763*		
H 4352	*H-54Y*	*H 210765*		

	RECEIVED COMPLETE AND IN GOOD CONDITION	DATE TIME

Figure 4.3
A typical delivery order.

Recording the Data

The next step in the information processing cycle is one of **recording** the data.
In our example, the master file of all cars in stock is maintained on a deck of
3×5 cards. Thus, the clerk begins the task of transferring data for each new
arrival to a 3×5 card (Fig. 4.4). Since we already have a record in the master
file for each of the cars we sold, there is no need to record the data from the
sales orders again; handling the deletions from inventory can wait until the
data manipulation stage.

Manipulating the Data

Now that we have collected the source data and performed any necessary data
recording, we're ready to begin processing or manipulating the data. The first
step is one of **updating the master file,** i.e., *adding* the cards for the new
arrivals and *pulling* the cards for the cars that have been sold.

This sounds like a very simple task, but think about it for a minute. Let's
say that a bright red Hummingbird with stock number H4573 has just been
sold. How would you go about finding the card representing this particular car
in the master file? A dealership of this size might well have 400 to 500

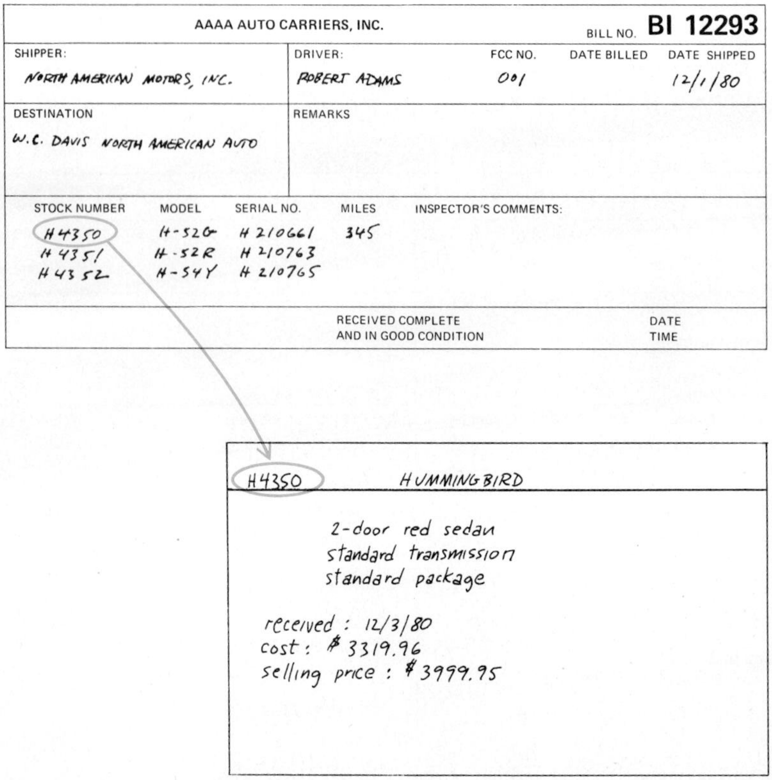

AAAA AUTO CARRIERS, INC.				BILL NO. **BI 12293**	
SHIPPER: *NORTH AMERICAN MOTORS, INC.*	DRIVER: *ROBERT ADAMS*	FCC NO. *001*	DATE BILLED	DATE SHIPPED *12/1/80*	
DESTINATION *W.C. DAVIS NORTH AMERICAN AUTO*	REMARKS				

STOCK NUMBER	MODEL	SERIAL NO.	MILES	INSPECTOR'S COMMENTS:
H4350	*H-52G*	*H 210661*	*345*	
H 4351	*H-52R*	*H 210763*		
H 4352	*H-54Y*	*H 210765*		

RECEIVED COMPLETE AND IN GOOD CONDITION   DATE   TIME

H4350   *HUMMINGBIRD*

2-door red sedan
standard transmission
standard package

received : 12/3/80
cost : $3319.96
selling price : $3999.95

Figure 4.4
Data for each new arrival is
transferred to a 3 × 5 card.

automobiles in stock. If you started at the front of the deck of cards and searched through in sequence, you'd eventually find the right card, assuming, of course, that the card is in the deck. What if you went all the way through the deck and failed to find the card that matched the automobile the salesperson claimed to have sold? Did the salesperson make a mistake, or did you just miss the card the first time through?

Such a haphazard search technique will never do; it's almost easier to simply go outside and count the cars every week. What is needed is a system of some type. How would you handle this problem?

When you are playing cards, don't you make an effort to arrange the cards in your hand in a sequence so as to make it easier for you to evaluate your hand? If you collect baseball cards, or comic books, or stamps, or coins, or dolls, don't you arrange your collection into some logical sequence for classification purposes? Why? Because when a collection of things is arranged in a predictable way, it's much easier to keep track of the individual pieces in that collection. A **file** is a collection of records. If the records can be arranged in a predictable order, it's much easier to keep track of that file.

In this example, there is an obvious order for arranging the cards in the master file. Each car has a stock number. Every Hummingbird is identified by the letter "H" followed by a four digit number. Mallards are assigned the letter "M" and four digits; Pelicans get a "P" and the four digit number. Each 3 × 5 card contains a stock number, along with other pertinent data. The cards in the master file are arranged in sequence by the stock number. Knowing the sequence, the task of finding the card identifying an automobile that has just been sold is an easy one—just look where the master file record is supposed to be.

Sorting

Now that we know the order of the master file records, let's consider a few alternatives for updating the master file. We could simply start through the file with our sales orders, pulling the deleted cards as they come. It might be easier, however, to **sort** our sales orders and new arrival cards first. If we do sort, we can perform the master file update very efficiently, by simply going through it once. With the master file and all our **transactions** in the same sequence, the sales order on top of the pile will have to be for a car whose record comes before the one identifying the second sales order. To put it another way, if both the master file and the sales orders are in the same sequence, once we find the master file entry associated with the first sales order, we know that the master file card for the second sales order will be closer to the back of the master file deck.

Sorting does something else for us, too; it allows us to group similar records. Consider the data in Fig. 4.5. Look what happens when we sort the data. Since every Hummingbird has a stock number that begins with the letter "H", and since "H" always comes before "M" in the alphabet, the act of sorting guarantees that the stock number for every Hummingbird will come before the stock number for the first Mallard. The same argument can be used with Mallards and Pelicans. Sorting is one of the most valuable of information processing operations.

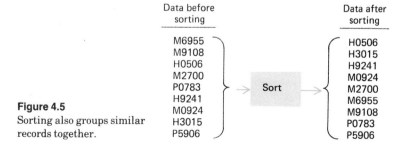

Figure 4.5
Sorting also groups similar
records together.

Data before sorting		Data after sorting
M6955		H0506
M9108		H3015
H0506		H9241
M2700	Sort	M0924
P0783		M2700
H9241		M6955
M0924		M9108
H3015		P0783
P5906		P5906

Processing the Data

Once we have the sales orders sorted into stock number sequence, we can go through the master file and pull the cards representing the automobiles that have been sold. What if there is no master file entry to match a sales order? Someone has made an error. Perhaps the salesperson made a mistake in filling out the sales order. Perhaps the master file is wrong. Once the error has been discovered, it can be corrected. The process of identifying and isolating specific records is called **selection.**

Having pulled all the cards associated with "sold" cars, we now have a new deck to work with. Since the master file is in sequence, we can, assuming that we pull the "sold" cards in sequence, take advantage of the grouping effect of sorting and determine the number of Hummingbirds, Mallards, and Pelicans actually sold this week by simply counting how many cards of each type we have pulled. Counting is a form of **calculating;** since the resulting information—three numbers—boils down quite a bit of detail to a very simple form, we're also **summarizing** our data.

Before adding the "new arrival" 3 × 5 cards to the master file deck, it might be wise to first sort and count them, too. Having done this, we know how many Hummingbirds, Mallards, and Pelicans arrived this week, another piece of the information requested by the dealer.

Knowing what the inventory level was at the beginning of the week, we are now in a position to compute the current level. By simply adding arrivals to the start-of-week inventory of each model, and subtracting sales, we get the end-of-week inventory level. Where did the start-of-week number come from? This question is best answered by asking another question. If you had 500 cars when you closed the showroom at 9:00 P.M. on Saturday, how many cars would you expect to have when you reopened on Monday morning? Barring theft or a natural disaster, you'd expect to have 500 cars. In other words, the balance at the end of last week is the same as the balance at the beginning of this week (Fig. 4.6), and the balance at the end of this week will be the same as the balance at the beginning of next week.

Last week's ending balance is the same as this week's beginning balance. We know how many of each model were sold during the current week because we counted the cards representing the "sold" cars. We also know how many of each model arrived at our dealership during the current week because we counted the "new arrival" cards. By adding arrivals and subtracting sales from the old balance, we arrive at our current inventory balance for each model of automobile. We have successfully calculated all the information requested by the owner of the dealership.

In a real automobile dealership, we'd probably be interested in calculating and summarizing more information. Any owner would certainly want information on how long automobiles are staying on the lot. Inventory-carrying costs,

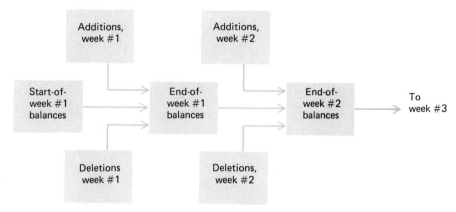

Figure 4.6
The end-of-week balance for one week becomes the start-of-week balance for the following week.

which include such expenses as maintenance, cleaning, insurance, the loss of interest on the money invested in the car, and many others, are expensive. If the owner is able to identify automobiles that are just sitting and not moving, special sales can be planned, future models with similar options or color schemes can be avoided, or the cars can be sold at wholesale. Where would such information come from? The inventory clerk could simply go through the master file deck and pull the cards (selection) for all automobiles that have been on the lot for more than a critical period of time, preparing a summary report of this information.

Information relating to the cost of each of the cars in inventory is also crucial. Management is not just interested in how many Hummingbirds we have; management wants to know how much money we have invested in these cars. If, for example, we were to receive ten very expensive Hummingbirds, loaded with options, during the week when we sold fifteen inexpensive, stripped Hummingbirds, a comparison of the counts could indicate that our inventory has decreased, while a comparison of costs could well indicate that, since the total of the ten expensive cars is greater than the total cost of the fifteen inexpensive cars, our inventory cost has really increased.

We'd also probably want to use the information generated by this system to pay our salespeople and measure their performance. Most automobile salespeople are paid, at least in part, on a commission basis, getting a percentage of the profit earned on each car they sell. The sales order is the formal document that proves that a sale has been made. Since the owner is undoubtedly interested in knowing how the salespeople are doing, a summary report listing what each salesperson did during the current week will certainly be desired. Such a report can be generated by simply sorting sales orders (or the cards removed from the master file in response to a sales order) into salesperson sequence, and then listing and accumulating sales for each employee.

Rather than complicate this example more than is necessary, we won't include these additional information requirements. You should, however, be aware that such information is an essential part of any information processing system.

Let's now take the final data manipulation step in this example and add the "new arrival" cards to our master file. Having done this, we have

1. an updated master file reflecting new arrivals and sales for the current week;

2. the old inventory balance for each model type (from last week's inventory update);

3. new arrivals by model type;

4. sales by model type; and

5. the new, end-of-week inventory balance for each model type.

The steps we took to reach this point are summarized in Fig. 4.7. We are now ready to store our results and report the output to the owner.

One final comment before we move on. The master file represents the automobiles in stock; how can we be sure that this file is accurate? The usual practice is to take an occasional *physical inventory,* during which the cars are actually counted and the counts compared with the master file. Such physical counts are scheduled at regular intervals, at least once a year. In an automobile dealership, the physical inventory will probably be run much more frequently, because the number of automobiles in stock is relatively small and the cost of each item in stock is relatively high. In a department store that stocks thousands of different, low-cost items, an annual physical inventory is the rule.

Storing the Results

Merely computing the new level of inventory isn't enough; the results must also be **stored** for future reference. The inventory clerk maintains a number of ledgers for this purpose. In this manual system, the task of storing the results for future reference consists of copying the results into a ledger.

Why is it important that results be stored? Basically, for purposes of financial control of the organization. Good accounting practice insists that careful records of all financial transactions be maintained. Such information is essential if the firm is to prove its actual level of expenses at income tax time. Such information is also essential if the organization is to be able to prove its stability when requesting a bank loan or other financial support. A business that maintains sloppy or inaccurate records is generally regarded by the financial community as suspect, and a prime candidate for bankruptcy. An organization's books represent the outside world's view of the organization.

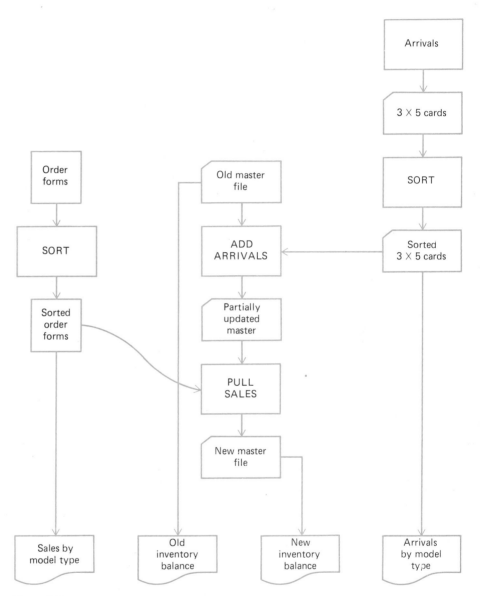

Figure 4.7
A summary of the inventory analysis information processing application.

Producing the Output

The short-term objective of this information processing exercise was to produce information for the owner to use in ordering new cars. Thus the final step is one of producing an **output** report. This report can be prepared by simply copying the information onto a sheet of paper. The resulting output can be used by the owner as an aid to decision making.

If we had computed additional information from our data, additional reports could have been prepared. We might, for example, want a report that summarizes sales by salesperson. Another report might summarize sales by model, with additional breakdowns based on such factors as color or options. Still another report might list and summarize the current inventory by time on the lot, with cars we've had over 3 months being selected out and summarized by model type. The key to generating all this information is the master file and the individual transactions.

MANAGEMENT DECISION MAKING

How would the owner use this information as an aid to decision making? Let's say that the numbers show that we sold many more Hummingbirds than were shipped to us, thus lowering our stock of the subcompact model. This might convince the owner that more Hummingbirds should be ordered this week. What if the inventory report shows that very few Hummingbirds were sold? Perhaps future orders should concentrate on the other models.

Note, however, that the information on the output report does not make the decision for the owner. The information is only an aid to decision making. Factors such as expected changes in customer demand or an expected increase in fuel prices, which might increase sales of the subcompact model, cannot be generated by data processing. Using the results of data processing as a guide allows management to make a more informed decision, but the existence of good, accurate information does not relieve management of its decision-making responsibility.

SUMMARY

This chapter was really a case study of manual information processing in a small business concern. The company, an automobile dealership, needed information on inventory levels for decision-making purposes. We followed the process of generating this information from the initial source documents (sales orders and shipping receipts), through the recording of this data, and into the data manipulation stage where, through such operations as sorting, selection, calculating, and summarizing, the required information was produced and the master file was updated. We then considered the recording of this information and the preparation of a report for management. The chapter ended with a brief discussion of how management might use this information as an aid to decision making.

KEYWORDS

calculating	**record**	**storing**
data collection	**recording**	**summarizing**
file	**selection**	**transaction**
master file	**sort**	**output**
master file update	**source document**	

EXERCISES

As our exercises for this chapter, let's consider how a small bank might handle its information processing.

The firm: A small bank handling roughly 1000 checking accounts.

The problem: To produce an updated listing of the amount of money in each checking account. This involves subtracting all checks from and adding all deposits to the old balance.

The basic solution: Each account has a unique account number. Consider checks to be much like deletions from inventory and deposits to be much like additions to inventory. Your own checking account will also provide some guidelines in answering the questions below.

1. What is the master file in this problem?

2. What are the source documents for updating this master file?

3. In what sequence would you expect to find the master file? Why?

4. Based on your own knowledge of banks, who do you suppose would be responsible for collecting the source data? In what order would you, as an information processing clerk, expect to find the source data?

5. Would you want to sort transactions before beginning the master file update? Why or why not?

6. Briefly describe the calculations needed to update the master file.

7. What would it mean if you received a check drawn against an account for which there was no master file entry? How would you select out such checks?

8. What would it mean if you received a deposit for an account for which there was no master file entry?

9. Design a reasonable format for the output from this data processing operation. Use, as a guide, the information you expect to receive concerning your checking account. Explain how each item in the output information can be produced by the system.

10. Compare this operation to the way in which you maintain your own personal checking account.

THE COMPUTER: AN INFORMATION PROCESSING MACHINE

5

WHERE DID THEY COME FROM?

OVERVIEW

In this chapter, we'll trace the history of information processing from early counting devices to modern computers. People have been processing data into information since the Stone Age, and probably before. As society became more and more complex, the need for information became greater and greater, and thus tools were invented to make information processing more efficient. As you read about the discoveries and inventions that have led to the modern computer, don't lose sight of the fact that each step in the development of these machines was prompted by a real and definable need. The key is the information, and the computer (and other information processing equipment) is merely a means to this end.

THE BEGINNINGS

Early man was primarily a hunter and a gatherer. Gradually, civilization began to develop. With civilization came individuals who specialized in a particular trade such as making arrows or dispensing medicines. Primitive barter economies began to emerge. Along with these changes came a need to keep records; the arrow maker expected payment for arrows, for example, and had to know how many animals (or whatever) each member of the tribe owed him.

The earliest record-keeping techniques were as primitive as a barter economy, consisting of such things as knots in a rope, piles of pebbles, or notches cut into a stick. Primitive though they were, they represented the beginnings of data processing.

The Abacus and Other Early Aids to Computation

The first real aid to computation, the *abacus* (Fig. 5.1), was developed in China, as early as 2600 B.C., by some accounts, and moved to Greece and Egypt by about 1000 B.C. This simple counting device is still in common use in many parts of the world. Why did the abacus become so common? With the development of economies based on the exchange of money, the need for keeping accurate records became much more crucial. Some aid to computation beyond simply counting on one's fingers or tying knots in a rope was essential. The abacus filled a need.

ABACUS
c. l200   ("Suan-pan")   China

Calculator of antiquity which historians trace
vaguely to Egypt, India and Mesopotamia

Figure 5.1
Highlights in the story of the computer. From the abacus to the electronic computer, every improvement in calculating devices has come in answer to the need for faster and more efficient means of counting, releasing people from needless figuring and leaving them free to create. (Reprinted by permission of the Fine Arts Department of the International Business Machines Corporation.)

in 1647, consisted of a series of gear-driven counters similar in design to a modern automobile odometer, and it actually worked. It was, however, not a financial success; apparently, the people of the mid-1600s were just not ready for the automation of clerical functions.

In 1666, Sir Thomas Morland used a series of disks to replace Napier's bones and developed an operational multiplier. Pascal's device was improved upon by Gottfried Wilhelm Leibniz who, in 1673, exhibited a machine capable of performing multiplication by repeated addition (Fig. 5.1). These early calculators were the ancestors of our modern pocket calculators and also contributed to the ultimate development of modern computers. All were economic failures, however, their impact blunted by insufficient need and inadequate technology.

Joseph Marie Jacquard

Weaving is a very repetitive activity. As a hobby, some people find weaving to be enjoyable and relaxing; as a full-time job, many people would find it dull.

In 1801, Joseph Marie Jacquard developed an automatic weaving loom that created perfect copies of a rug, under the control of a series of punched cards. Jacquard's loom was declared public property in France in 1804; looms based on his design are still in use today.

Why are we discussing weaving in a book about data processing? The punched cards used in Jacquard's loom were the direct ancestors of modern punched cards.

George Boole

The basic rules of logic used on a modern computer were developed by George Boole who, in 1854, published his principles of Boolean logic. This system of logic is based on manipulating true and false conditions; as we'll see in Chapter 8, a system of logic that manipulates two conditions is a perfect match for a computer.

Charles Babbage

One of the more interesting of the computer pioneers was Charles Babbage. Like many of his predecessors, Babbage dreamed of a machine to compute and print mathematical tables and, in 1823, started work on just such a machine, his *difference engine* (Fig. 5.2). With some support from the British government, Babbage began to design his difference engine, actually beginning construction in 1830. During the planning stages, however, he expanded his view of the problem and envisioned another machine, an *analytical engine,* which would be capable of solving more general problems. By 1834, Babbage had abandoned plans for his difference engine and began devoting his full energy to the analytical engine.

Photograph courtesy of IBM Corporation.

Figure 5.2
Babbage's difference engine.

Babbage's analytical engine was a most interesting device. It was composed of four basic units (Fig. 5.3): a *store* for holding data and intermediate results, a *mill* for performing arithmetic computations, a system of gears and levers for *transferring* data between the store and the mill, and a separate device for getting data *into* the analytical engine and for getting answers back *out*. These basic units may not mean much to you right now, but when you get to Chapter 6, you'll be surprised to see how closely Babbage's design parallels that of a modern computer. Charles Babbage, in the mid-1800s, had envisioned a modern, general-purpose computer!

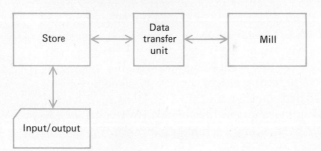

Figure 5.3
A rough schematic of Babbage's
analytical engine.

Borrowing from the ideas of Jacquard, Babbage planned to use punched cards to provide input data and control for his analytical engine. The device was completely mechanical, consisting of a complex arrangement of gears and levers, and, as a result, was quite slow when compared with a modern computer, but, functionally, all the components were there.

Why, then, did we not have working computers by 1850? Basically, for two reasons. First, the technology of Babbage's time was not capable of producing gears and levers to the precision necessary to build something as complex as an analytical engine. A second and perhaps even more important reason is that there was no real demand for such a machine in the mid-1800s. The calculators available at that time were good enough to handle most of the common data processing problems faced by people of the day. Babbage was ahead of his time.

The analytical engine was never actually constructed. The ideas of Charles Babbage were largely forgotten until after a computer incorporating many of his concepts had been built. Babbage, though a brilliant man, contributed little or nothing to the advancement of computers.

MODERN CALCULATORS

In discussing Babbage, we mentioned that calculators available in the mid-1800s were adequate for most of the data processing needs of the time. Although the technology of the nineteenth century was not able to support something as complex as an analytical engine, improvements had been made, and devices far superior to the calculators of Pascal and Leibniz were available (though hardly common). One of the more important calculator developments of this century was the Comptometer, which was invented by Dorr E. Felt in 1885. By the end of the nineteenth century, sophisticated, fairly modern calculators were being produced. These machines were mechanical; the electronic marvels available today represent a relatively recent innovation.

PUNCHED CARD DATA PROCESSING

The United States Constitution requires that a census be taken every ten years for the purpose of determining how districts will be drawn for electing members to the House of Representatives. At first, with a relative handful of people to count, the task of taking a census was fairly simple. As the population grew, however, the job of counting heads became a major data processing problem. The 1880 census, a count of roughly 50 million people, took seven and one-half years to complete. Based on expected population growth, it was entirely possible that the 1890 census would not be completed until 1902, two years after the 1900 census was to start. Without help, the logistics of simply counting all the people living in our country would make it impossible to meet the census requirements as specified in the Constitution.

Herman Hollerith was an employee of the Census Bureau during much of the time the 1880 census was being compiled. He left the Census Bureau to teach at M.I.T. for a while, and later took a job with the U.S. Patent Office in 1884. Perhaps the time spent with the Patent Office awakened the inventor's instinct in him.

The Census Bureau, recognizing the potential problem they faced with the 1890 census, created a committee to consider a better way of tabulating the data. Three systems were tested, one of which was Hollerith's. Herman Hollerith's system won, completing the tabulating of the Census Bureau's test data in two-thirds the time of his closest competitor. Hollerith was not an employee of the Census Bureau at the time; he was an independent inventor who was simply awarded the contract for the 1890 census.

The inspiration for Hollerith's new system (Fig. 5.4) was Jacquard, the French inventor who, some years before, had automated a weaving machine by punching control information into cards. If a pattern of holes in a card could be made to represent weaving instructions, why couldn't similar holes be made to stand for numbers? As the data for the 1890 census began to come in, Hollerith had it punched into cards.

To read and tabulate this data, he borrowed ideas from the rapidly developing field of electricity. Cards do not conduct electricity, since paper is a very good insulator. If a card is placed on a metal surface and a series of metal pins is brought into contact with the card, the paper material effectively separates the pins from the metal surface, cutting off the flow of electricity. Except, of course, where there is a hole. Here, the pin goes through the hole and contacts the metal, allowing a current to flow. Hollerith's device simply counted the number of times that current actually flowed through a given wire as the cards were fed one at a time by hand. Each wire corresponded to one possible hole position on the card; each hole position represented one value of one census statistic; thus, the counts gave the results of the census. The 1890 census was completed within two years.

Why was Hollerith successful when such men as Pascal, Leibniz, and Babbage had failed? Were his ideas any better? Not really, but by 1890, electronics and manufacturing technology had advanced to the point where Hollerith's ideas could be implemented.

Hollerith's association with the Census Bureau ended in 1896 when he decided to start the Tabulating Machine Company, to market his inventions. Through a series of mergers, Hollerith's company became the Computing-Tabulating-Recording Company. In 1924, under the leadership of a new president named Thomas J. Watson, C-T-R was renamed the International Business Machines Corporation.

Hollerith's successor at the Census Bureau was named James Powers. Although an employee of this government organization, Powers was sharp enough to keep for himself the rights to all patents he might be granted while

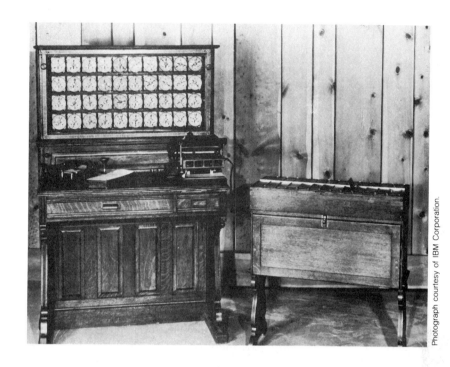

Figure 5.4
Hollerith's card tabulating
machine.

Figure 5.5
Card tabulating equipment.

Photograph courtesy of IBM Corporation.

Photograph courtesy of IBM Corporation.

working on improving Hollerith's system—and improve it he did. Powers left the Census Bureau in 1911 to found his own company, the Powers Accounting Company. Through a series of mergers, his company became a part of Remington Rand which, in turn, became a part of Sperry Rand, one of IBM's major competitors in the computer marketplace.

By the late 1920s, card-tabulating equipment had become quite common throughout the United States (Fig. 5.5). In 1935, IBM was successful in obtaining the largest (to that day) card-tabulating equipment contract when the social security system came into being. Significant improvements had, of course, been made, but the equipment was based essentially on Hollerith's original idea.

The MARK I

Punched card equipment is quite flexible, but punched card equipment doesn't quite measure up to a computer. Additional refinements were needed before the kind of machine envisioned by Charles Babbage could be realized.

In 1939, Howard Aiken of Harvard University began working on a machine to solve polynomials. IBM provided financial and engineering support and, in 1944, the MARK I (Fig. 5.6), the world's first operational electromechanical computer, was unveiled. The modern age of the computer had begun.

Figure 5.6
The MARK I.

A TOUR OF A COMPUTER CENTER

1

1. At first glance, a large computer center seems a most confusing place. What is in all those large cabinets? Where should we start?

2. Perhaps the best place to start is with the computer itself. Here, the red cabinet at the left contains the central processing unit, while the other cabinets house the computer's main memory and other key components.

2

3. Inside the central processing unit are the electronic circuits that perform arithmetic and logical functions and control the operation of the other components.

3

4. The central processing unit is itself under the control of a human being, the computer operator.

5. A computer is basically an information processing machine. Its task is to accept input data, process this data, and produce output information. Perhaps the best known of the input devices is the card reader.

4

6. The best-known computer output device is probably the printer.

5

6

7. Input and output devices are linked to the computer by a channel. Controlling input and output is a complex activity; thus the channel is itself a small, special-purpose computer. Knowing this, we are not surprised to discover that a channel looks, on the surface, much like a central processing unit.

9. Volumes of magnetic tape are accessed by the computer through tape drives.

8. Modern computer systems are used to store massive amounts of data. Here, we see a magnetic tape library. Each reel of tape (about the size of a one-inch thick, long-playing record album) could easily hold over one thousand characters of information on each of 20,000 students.

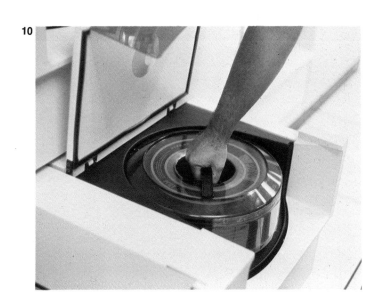

10. Perhaps the most commonly used information storage medium is magnetic disk.

11. In a typical large computer center, we will find numerous disk drives.

12. The computer is linked to the outside world through data communication equipment, such as these modems.

13. Using regular telephone lines, a student or other computer user can dial a computer center and gain access to the computer. Perhaps you have remote terminals like this at your school.

14. Even card readers and printers can be linked to a computer via communication lines.

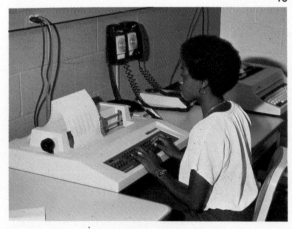

The first twelve photographs in this brief "tour" were taken in the South Road Computation Center at International Business Machines Corporation's Poughkeepsie, New York, facility. We gratefully acknowledge the help and cooperation of Mr. Earl W. Inman, Jr., and IBM. The last two pictures were taken at Miami University's Oxford, Ohio, campus by the Audio-Visual Department. Note that the terminals pictured above do not normally communicate with the IBM Poughkeepsie center, but with similar hardware located at Miami.

The MARK I, also known as the Automatic Sequence Controlled Calculator, was a massive device, stretching over 51 feet in length and standing over 8 feet high. It contained over 500 miles of wiring. Keep this size in mind as we move on to more modern computers.

ELECTRONIC COMPUTERS

In 1939, Dr. John Vincent Atanasoff, a faculty member at Iowa State College, constructed a machine to solve linear algebraic equations. In building this machine, Atanasoff used vacuum tubes and manipulated digital numbers; his device has come to be regarded as the first true electronic digital computer.

One of those who visited Professor Atanasoff at Iowa State was a professor from the University of Pennsylvania named John W. Mauchly who, along with a colleague named J. Presper Eckert, was about to undertake a project much more significant than Atanasoff's limited "breadboard" model of a computer. Whether or not Mauchly was influenced by Atanasoff's device is hard to say, but the machine developed by Mauchly and Eckert was to have a much broader impact.

By far the most significant event of the 1940s was the Second World War. War tends to accelerate invention. Accurate military ballistics tables were needed, and a contract was granted to Mauchly and Eckert at the University of

Figure 5.7
The ENIAC.

Photograph courtesy of The Moore School of Electrical Engineering. University of Pennsylvania.

Pennsylvania, to construct a computer. The result—ready in 1945, two months after the surrender of Japan—was christened the ENIAC (Electronic Numerical Integrator and Calculator). The ENIAC was the first electronic computer (Fig. 5.7).

After the ENIAC was completed, Mauchly and Eckert continued their work, developing an improved model, the EDVAC, in 1946. An important addition was the stored program concept suggested by John von Neumann, a member of the team working on this project and an outstanding mathematician in his own right.

Actually, the EDVAC was not the first stored program computer to go into operation. This honor belongs to a machine named the EDSAC (Electronic Delayed Storage Automatic Computer) which was built at Cambridge University in England in 1949. The EDVAC, though started first (in 1946), wasn't completed until 1952. The two leaders of the EDVAC project had other things on their minds.

The First Generation: The 1950s

Mauchly and Eckert left the university, founded a corporation to manufacture computers, and, in 1951, sold a computer named UNIVAC I to the Census Bureau (the machine was retired in 1963, and now rests in the Smithsonian Institute). The age of the computer was well under way.

The 1950s marked the computer's first generation. The precise dates of this generation are difficult to pinpoint exactly—the beginning is set somewhere between 1950 and 1954, and the end generally falls somewhere around 1958 or 1959. What really distinguishes the first generation from subsequent generations is technology. The key electronic component of a first-generation computer was the electronic tube. By today's standards, these machines were quite slow, being capable of executing approximately 1000 instructions per second. They were also rather small, holding perhaps 10,000 to 20,000 characters of data in their main memories. The electronic technology, speed, and size of a machine identify it as first generation; the dates are of secondary importance.

By 1956, IBM had taken a marketing lead that it has yet to relinquish, selling the IBM 650 and 700 lines of machines. Other key competitors included Monroe, NCR, Burroughs, RCA, Underwood, and, of course, UNIVAC.

Note that we have stopped talking about individual inventors and have begun to discuss corporations instead. A modern computer is a very complex machine, well beyond the capabilities of the single individual. (Even "build-it-yourself" kits include pre-wired electronic modules.) The resources and skills of a team of people are needed, and a modern corporation is uniquely qualified to coordinate such team efforts.

This is not, however, to suggest that individual human beings did not have a significant impact on the development of the computer and information processing. Consider, for example, Grace Hopper. Previously a colleague of Howard Aiken at Harvard, she worked as the head of programming for UNIVAC throughout much of the first generation. She believed very strongly in the concept of compiler languages, a concept to be covered in depth in Chapter 9 (and in subsequent chapters). Her early, pioneering work resulted in significant breakthroughs that were eventually incorporated into a new language called COBOL, perhaps the most commonly used of all the modern programming languages.

The Second Generation: 1960 through 1965

The field of electronics was not idle during the 1950s. Perhaps the most important discovery was the transistor, a device that won the 1956 Nobel Prize for three American scientists. By 1957, Burroughs had developed a fully transistorized computer for the Air Force. The higher speed and greater reliability of transistors marked the end of the electronic tube-based first-generation computers, and ushered in the second generation.

By 1960, first-generation computers were virtually obsolete. Transistors are smaller, faster, and more reliable than electronic tubes. As a result, a second-generation computer using transistors rather than electronic tubes was physically smaller, much faster (1,000,000 as opposed to 1000 instructions per second), and much more reliable than its first-generation counterpart. Such computers as the Honeywell 800, Burroughs B5500, IBM 1400, IBM 7090, Control Data Corporation 1604, and UNIVAC 1107 had become big sellers, with the improved reliability derived from solid-state electronics making such machines attractive to the business market.

Beyond the field of electronics, the second generation saw a tremendous improvement in techniques for using computers, with such concepts as operating systems, time-sharing, and user-oriented languages coming into common use. Right now, these terms probably don't mean much to you, but by the time you finish the book, they will.

You may have noticed that we haven't even *mentioned* any individuals in our brief discussion of the computer's second generation. The size, complexity, and cost of these machines made them corporate rather than individual devices.

The big news of the second generation was a phenomenal growth in computer use. As recently as 1950, the number of computers available in the world could be counted on a single individual's fingers; by 1965, the value of installed computers had risen to an estimated three to four *billion* dollars.

The Third Generation: 1965 to the Present

The field of electronics was not dormant during the period of the second generation—major advances were made in the areas of printed and integrated circuits. As a result of these advances (Fig. 5.8), electronic devices became even more compact, faster, more reliable, and less expensive. IBM's System/360 and (currently) System/370 computers, the dominant machines of the period, use these modern integrated circuits, as do the most current products of Control Data Corporation, Burroughs, Sperry Rand (UNIVAC), Honeywell, NCR, and others. By the mid-1970s, the value of installed computers had risen above 24 billion dollars.

Photograph courtesy of IBM Corporation.

Figure 5.8
First-generation tubes, second-generation transistorized circuitry, and modern, third-generation solid logic or integrated circuit modules.

The Microcomputer Revolution

The integrated circuit has today given way to an even better technology, *large scale integration* (LSI), with circuit components packed at greater and greater densities. In fact, we have reached the point where it is possible to place all the electronics for one or more of the computer's main components on a single LSI chip no bigger than the nail on your little finger. One chip might hold a processor (Fig. 5.9); another, memory; a third, the circuits needed to attach input and output devices. Linked together, these components form a complete *microcomputer*.

First developed in the early 1970s, the growth in the use of these devices has been nothing short of phenomenal. The reason is cost. It is possible today to

Photograph courtesy of Texas Instruments Inc.

Figure 5.9
A microprocessor.

purchase, for less than $1000, a complete computer system more powerful than the UNIVAC I. The UNIVAC I sold for over one million dollars!

Microcomputers and microprocessors (a microprocessor is the part of a microcomputer that actually computes) are used for such mundane tasks as keeping time, helping students do their homework, controlling the air/fuel mixture on some automobiles, helping to simplify the typing of a term paper, and many others. Small, personal computers are rapidly becoming the latest household appliance, with a cost comparable to the traditional washing machine, dishwasher, or refrigerator. The use of these machines can only increase. Among the firms marketing micros are Intel, Motorola, Rockwell, National Semiconductor, and Fairchild.

Minicomputers, as the name implies, are neither as big as a regular computer nor as small as a microcomputer; they are intermediate in both cost and power. Among the best known of the minicomputer vendors are Digital Equipment Corporation and Hewlett-Packard.

CURRENT TRENDS AND FUTURE PROJECTIONS

Look back at the time scale we've been using in describing the history of data processing. In the beginning, we were talking about centuries; in the middle period, techniques were developed over decades; since 1950, everything has happened in a matter of years. The first generation began around 1950; by 1960, first-generation computers had become obsolete, supplanted by the transistorized machines of the second generation; by 1965, integrated circuits spawned a third generation, which, in turn, was pushed aside by improved equipment in the early 1970s. The growth has been almost exponential (Fig. 5.10). At the same time, computers have gotten better and better. In Fig. 5.11 we see a number of trends projected on a single graph. Over the past several years, the speed and reliability of electrical devices such as the computer have risen tremendously, while the size and, more important, the cost of these devices have tended to drop just as dramatically. Consider the modern pocket calculator, which illustrates all these trends.

Computer
knowledge

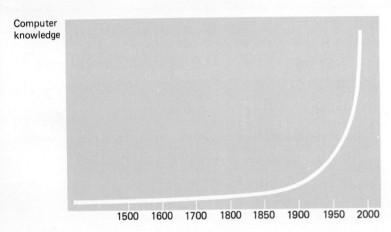

1500 1600 1700 1800 1850 1900 1950 2000

Figure 5.10
The growth of the computer.

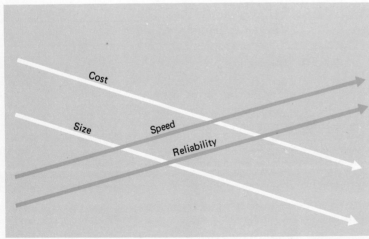

Time ⟶

Figure 5.11
Current trends.

And what of the future? Look for a continuation of the trend toward physically smaller but more and more powerful computers. Already, computers small enough to fit in a briefcase but more powerful than UNIVAC I are being offered for sale. The trend toward lower cost will also continue. Look for a proliferation of small computers (as opposed to calculators) in the not too far distant future, with very powerful devices falling into the price range of a typical household appliance. A knowledge of the computer is in fact essential to the modern educated man or woman.

SUMMARY

In this chapter, we reviewed the history of the development of modern information processing. The keywords list provides an excellent review of key topics; thus, we won't mention each contributor here in the summary.

KEYWORDS

abacus	EDVAC	Mauchly, John W.
Aiken, Howard	ENIAC	microcomputer
analytical engine	first generation	minicomputer
Arabic numerals	Hollerith, Herman	Napier, John
Atanasoff, John Vincent	Hopper, Grace	Pascal, Blaise
Babbage, Charles	Jacquard, Joseph Marie	Powers, James
Boole, George	Leibniz, Gottfried Wilhelm	second generation
difference engine		third generation
Eckert, J. Presper	MARK I	UNIVAC I

EXERCISES

1. How did Pascal and Leibniz contribute to the development of modern data processing?

2. Why are the contributions of Jacquard considered important? He was, after all, involved in weaving, and not data processing.

3. How, if at all, did Charles Babbage contribute to the development of modern computers?

4. Hollerith developed the first real data processing equipment. What was it about the problem he faced that made some form of automated data processing so desirable?

5. Why do you suppose that the requirements of World War II tended to accelerate the development of the computer? The technology to manufacture something like the ENIAC was available ten or twenty years before the machine was built.

6. What are the major characteristics of a first generation computer?

7. What are the major characteristics of a second generation computer?

8. What are the characteristics that identify a computer as being a third generation machine?

9. Modern computers seem to be becoming smaller, more reliable, faster, and less expensive, all at the same time. Why do you suppose that these trends are important?

10. Name at least three companies currently involved in manufacturing and selling computers.

REFERENCES

Four very interesting books on the subject of computer history are

1. Harmon, Margaret (1975). *Stretching Man's Mind: A History of Data Processing*. New York: Mason/Charter.

2. Goldstine, Herman (1972). *The Computer from Pascal to von Neumann*. Princeton, New Jersey: Princeton University Press.

3. Rodgers, William (1974). *Think: A Biography of the Watsons and IBM*. New York: New American Library.

4. Rosenberg, Jerry (1969). *The Computer Prophets*. New York: Macmillan.

6

THE COMPUTER: AN OVERVIEW

OVERVIEW

Part II of this text is concerned with the computer. In Chapters 7 through 10, we will investigate in some detail each of the primary components of a computer system, one at a time. This chapter is intended to provide the reader with a broad overview of the computer, showing each of the primary components in the context of a complete system. The importance of the stored program concept is a key idea. A computer's speed and accuracy will be shown to be its primary skills. The chapter ends with a few comments on computer economics and the growing trend toward the use of microcomputers and minicomputers.

COMPUTER INFORMATION PROCESSING

In Chapter 3, we considered the economics of information processing, using the concept of a breakeven point to explain how a business might choose between manual, semi-automated, or fully automated approaches. Manual data processing is done completely by manual means, with people actually recording data and making calculations (perhaps with the aid of a desk calculator). Punched card data processing is a semi-automated approach, with many of the data manipulation and computation functions being done by machines. It still involves a significant amount of manual effort, as data must be keypunched and decks of cards must be fed again and again through sorters, collators, and accounting machines.

Computer information processing, once the data has been converted into machine-readable form, is almost completely automatic, with the computer being capable of sorting, selecting, summarizing, calculating, and performing any of the other common functions without human intervention. What is it that makes a computer such a unique machine?

WHAT IS A COMPUTER?

A computer is a machine that is capable of manipulating or processing data under its own control, without the need for human intervention. It is this property that makes a computer different from a calculator. Both computers and modern calculators can perform addition, subtraction, multiplication, and division, as well as many other logical functions, at high speed and with great accuracy, but on the calculator, a human being must push a button for each logical function the calculator is to perform. A computer has the added capability of storing a series of instructions that, in effect, tell it what buttons to push and in what order to push them. This **stored program concept** is what makes a computer unique.

When most of us think of a computer, we tend to think of **hardware** such as that pictured in Fig. 6.1. The word hardware is used to refer to all the physical components of a computer system, the cabinets, electronics, and mechanical devices that can be seen and touched. The most important of these hardware components is the computer itself, a device that, in the photograph of Fig. 6.1, is housed in the large, upright cabinet with the white door near the center of the picture.

A computer is subdivided into three main components (Fig. 6.2): a **central processing unit** (better known as the CPU), a number of **registers,** and **a memory** or **storage** unit. The CPU is the place where the computer performs its arithmetic and logical functions and where the operation of all the hardware components is controlled. Memory is where data and instructions are stored. The registers provide a mechanism for transferring data and instructions between the CPU and main memory. On most modern computers, the

Photograph courtesy of Hewlett-Packard Corporation.

Figure 6.1
The hardware of a typical
small computer system.

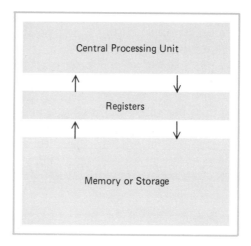

Figure 6.2
The component parts of a
computer.

registers are physically part of the CPU; the data transfer task is a description of their logical function.

Some manufacturers use the term "central processing unit" to refer to the entire computer, including the processor, the memory, and the registers. Most, however, restrict the term to those components that actually process the data. Another word which is often used to describe a computer is **mainframe,** particularly when referring to a large machine.

A computer communicates with the outside world through its **input** and **output devices** (Fig. 6.3); in Fig. 6.1, you can see two cathode-ray tube terminals (much like a television set with a keyboard), which allow data to be entered into this computer, and, to the left of the computer near the back of the picture, a printer, which allows the results of a data processing operation to be displayed.

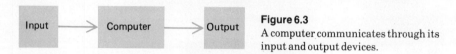

Figure 6.3
A computer communicates through its input and output devices.

Just to the left of the computer is another upright cabinet with a window through which, if you look closely, you can see two tape reels. This is a tape drive. To the right of the mainframe are two shorter cabinets; although you can't see what's inside them, they contain magnetic disks. Both are examples of **secondary storage** devices. By using disk or tape, a computer can read the data from punched cards or some other basic input medium, copy the data onto tape or disk, and retrieve it when necessary from one of these devices.

The major component of a computer that you *can't* see in Fig. 6.1 is the **program.** A program resides in the computer's main memory along with the data to be processed (Fig. 6.4). The program consists of a series of instructions designed to guide the computer, step by step, through some process. In our inventory example, the program might tell the computer to read all the additions-to-inventory cards (arrivals), sort them into sequence by stock number, read all the deletions (sales) cards, sort them into sequence by stock number, and then use these two files to update the master file, producing the desired reports in the process, all without human intervention. In effect, the use of a computer and a program frees the human operator from all but inputting the data once and collecting and distributing the results. The computer truly supports almost completely automated information processing.

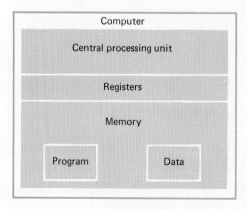

Figure 6.4
A program is stored in main memory.

A computer program, of course, must be written by a human being; a computer is just a machine and can do nothing that human beings don't tell it to do. Programs are written by **programmers.** Developing a program is time consuming and very expensive; this is one reason why the initial cost of computers is so high. The job need only be done once, however; a program, once written, can be used over and over again.

The combination of modern electronic devices and a stored program to provide control makes the computer an extremely flexible, almost general-purpose machine. One minute, a computer can be working on payroll; the next minute, acting under control of a different program, the computer can be working out the solution to a set of scientific equations. The flexibility of a modern computer is a direct result of the use of stored programs to control the machine; we'll be considering such programs in Chapter 9, and again in Chapters 12 through 14.

Programming is difficult and costly. Why do we take the time to write programs? Basically because we can't use the computer if we don't. Why do we want to use the computer? Usually, at least in most business applications, the computer is used because it can do the job at a lower cost than other alternatives. What are the characteristics of a computer that give it this level of efficiency? Essentially, there are two: computers are very fast and computers are very accurate.

A COMPUTER'S SPEED

A computer is an electronic device. One of its capabilities is addition. A computer adds by simply allowing electrical current to pass through a series of circuits, in something like the time it takes a light bulb to begin to glow once the switch has been turned on. Instantaneous? Not quite, but the time is certainly well below human comprehension.

One second is an extremely long period of time to a computer. Even on a small, "slow" computer, the execution of an instruction takes less than one **millisecond,** which is one thousandth (1/1000) of a second. That's 1000 instructions per second. Even a millisecond is a long period of time to a large, modern computer; many machines are capable of executing an instruction in one **microsecond**—one millionth (1/1,000,000) of a second—or less. New models are beginning to push into the **nanosecond** range (see Fig. 6.5). A nanosecond is one thousandth of one millionth, or one billionth, of a second (1/1,000,000,000); in one nanosecond, light travels one foot! [The next step is the **picosecond,** one millionth of one millionth of a second (1/1,000,000,000,000)!]

These speeds are inconceivable to the human mind. Let's use an analogy in order to put computer speeds into perspective. To travel from New York City to Los Angeles is a trip of roughly 3000 miles. How long would it take a human being to walk it? Assuming we can find someone who would like to try, a good

In the computer, the basic operations can be done within the order of a

NANOSECOND

One thousandth of a millionth of a second.

Within the half second it takes this spilled coffee to reach the floor, a fairly large computer could—

(given the information)
(in magnetic form)

Debit 2000 checks to 300 different bank accounts,

and *examine the electro- cardiograms of 100 patients and alert a physician to possible trouble,*

and *score 150,000 answers on 3000 examinations and evaluate the effectiveness of the questions,*

and *figure the payroll for a company with a thousand employees.*

and a few other chores.

Photograph courtesy of IBM Corporation.

Figure 6.5
The speed of modern computers is pushing into the nanosecond range.

steady walking pace would be about three miles per hour, meaning that some 1000 hours would be consumed in actually walking. Since people must take time to eat and sleep, let's assume that our walker averages ten hours a day of actual forward motion. A total of 100 days or 2400 hours would be needed to make the entire trip.

Jet airplanes have made the trip in three hours. Comparing the jet plane to the man, we find that

$$2400/3 = 800,$$

meaning that a jet plane is 800 times as fast as a human being.

A computer, even an obsolete millisecond computer, can easily handle all the computations for a 7000-employee payroll in about ten minutes, a job that would probably require a staff of at least twenty-five full-time people if done manually. Assuming a standard forty-hour work week, twenty-five workers represent (25 times 40) 1000 hours per week; multiplying by the 60 minutes in each hour yields 60,000 minutes. The computer needed only ten! Using the same kind of ratio as above,

$$60,000/100 = 6000,$$

we find that a computer is 6000 times as fast as human beings. The jet would have to make a New York to Los Angeles trip in twenty-four minutes in order to enjoy the same speed advantage over a walking human that a computer enjoys over a computing human.

Actually, the computer's speed advantage is even greater than the above analogy indicates. The slowest part of almost any computer system is the card reader. The estimate of ten minutes for a 7000-employee payroll was based on a 700-card-per-minute card reader setting the pace, and not on actual computer speeds. If we were to concentrate on the computer itself, the jet plane would have to make a 3000-mile trip in but a fraction of a minute in order to enjoy a similar speed advantage. *Computers are fast!*

A COMPUTER'S ACCURACY

A wall switch can be used to turn on a light bulb. When the switch is moved to the "on" position, electricity flows through a wire and the bulb lights. Move the switch to the "off" position, and the light goes out. A repeat of this little experiment will cause electricity to flow through the *same* wire and light the *same* bulb, and our experience tells us that no matter how often the experiment is repeated, we can expect the same result. Eventually, of course, the bulb burns out or the switch begins to wear and the experiment "fails," but, for the most part, the electrical circuit designed to control the light bulb is very "accurate."

The computer performs arithmetic and other functions through the use of electricity. Passing the same type of electrical current through the same wires will produce the same result time and time again. Thus, a computer is "accurate." Of course, the electronic circuits of a computer are much more complex than the electronic circuits that control a light bulb, but once the circuit has been designed, built, and fully tested, it is every bit as predictable. The computer almost never makes a mistake. Electrical failures do, of course, occur on occasion, but due to the advanced electronics used in modern computers, such failures are quite rare.

Imagine again a 7000-employee payroll being prepared manually. Imagine yourself working eight hours a day, five days a week, fifty weeks a year, doing nothing but multiplying hours worked by hourly pay rate to get gross pay. Do you think that you might possibly make an occasional mistake? Unlike a human being, a computer does not suffer from boredom or fatigue. A computer has no emotions. *Computers are accurate.*

COMPUTER COSTS

Computers are very fast, very accurate, and very flexible machines, but they are also very expensive, with some large-scale systems renting for as much as $100,000 per month and more. On some highly repetitive or very complex jobs, the speed, accuracy, and flexibility of the computer allow the machine to do the job at a lower cost than manual or semi-automated methods; computers are essentially used for economic reasons.

The cost of computers is, however, dropping. Consider the pocket calculator. Just a few short years ago, big bulky desk calculators were considered to be the ultimate, and the average student carried a slide rule as an aid to computation. Today, a decent calculator can be purchased for ten dollars or so, and really good calculators are priced below $100. Nobody uses a slide rule anymore.

Computers are made from the same kind of electronics as pocket calculators. The price of calculators dropped largely because the cost of electronic components dropped, and computer costs are dropping for the same reason. Big computers are still expensive, but the real news is in the area of **minicomputers** and **microcomputers.** A minicomputer is just a small computer. A microcomputer is a tiny computer, often designed to perform a single function; the electronic device inside a digital watch is a good example of a microcomputer.

Figure 6.6 shows a small, personal computer system. It fits easily on a desk, and weighs perhaps fifty pounds. The basic input and output device is a terminal—essentially, a television set with a keyboard. Secondary storage can be obtained by using magnetic tape cassettes. It is possible to purchase such a

Figure 6.6
A small, personal computer system.

system for less than $1000. And the cost is actually dropping; by the mid-1980s, you should be able to buy a very powerful personal computer system for a few hundred dollars!

What impact do declining computer costs have on the breakeven point? Consider the example of Fig. 6.7. Initially, the breakeven point was at "A." As the cost of the computer declines, the horizontal line drops, shifting the breakeven point to "B." As a result, a computer can be economically justified at a much lower level of activity than before. Small business firms are beginning to turn to the computer as a solution to their information processing problems; experts predict that soon, even the little "mom and pop" grocery store down the street will have a computer for billing, tracking inventory, processing payroll, keeping accounting records, figuring income tax, and other common information processing functions.

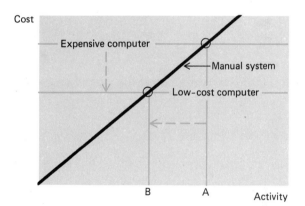

Figure 6.7
The impact of declining computer costs
on the breakeven point.

In addition to declining costs, the purchaser of a modern minicomputer is finding a product that is easier to use than its predecessors. Perhaps you've seen a television commercial showing a totally untrained computer operator inserting a diskette looking much like a long-playing record album into a minicomputer and starting payroll processing or some other information processing activity. Figure 6.8 is an example. With computers becoming easier and easier to use and lower and lower in cost, the computer is certain to assume an even greater role in the future.

The balance of Part II is concerned with the computer. In the next four chapters, we will evaluate, one at a time, the components of a typical computer system.

As you read this material, don't lose sight of the fact that the real purpose of the computer is to process data. The computer does not exist as an end in itself. Computers are used because the information they generate is valuable and because they can generate this information at a lower cost than any other alternative.

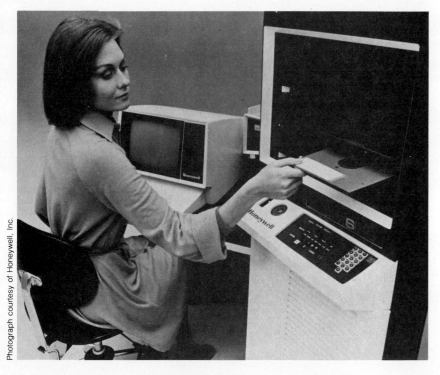

Photograph courtesy of Honeywell, Inc.

Figure 6.8
An operator inserting a program
diskette into a minicomputer.

SUMMARY

In this chapter, we introduced the major components of a computer system:
the central processing unit, registers, memory, input and output devices,
and secondary storage. The importance of a stored program was also
covered. Current trends in computer speeds and computer costs were then
discussed. This chapter serves as a sort of overview of Part II.

KEYWORDS

central processing unit (CPU)	microsecond	program
hardware	millisecond	programmer
input device	minicomputer	register
mainframe	nanosecond	secondary storage
memory	output device	storage
microcomputer	picosecond	stored program concept

EXERCISES

1. Briefly explain the function of each of the following computer components:
   a) central processing unit   b) memory or storage
   c) registers   d) input and output devices

2. Explain, again briefly, the idea of a stored program.

3. Why does a stored program concept allow a computer to become something close to a general-purpose machine?

4. What is hardware?

5. What is a program?

6. Explain the difference between the terms millisecond, microsecond, nano-second, and picosecond.

7. What is a minicomputer?

8. What is a microcomputer?

9. As the cost of computers continues to decline, what happens to the breakeven point on a graph comparing manual to computer information processing? Explain, in your own words, the significance of this shifting of the breakeven point.

7

INPUT AND OUTPUT

OVERVIEW

In this chapter, we'll be discussing a number of actual input and output devices including: card readers, printers, optical devices, magnetic devices, terminals, and a number of other types of equipment. In addition, we'll introduce the concepts of buffering and control units.

THE PUNCHED CARD

The most widely known of all computer input or output documents is the **punched card;** it's hard to imagine anyone in our present society who has never seen one. This familiarity makes the card an excellent choice for introducing basic input and output concepts.

Let's begin by analyzing the card itself. A punched card (Fig. 7.1) is divided into eighty columns each of which is subdivided into twelve rows. The columns are numbered from 1 through 80 (predictably); you can find the column numbers between the 0's and the 1's in Fig. 7.1. The rows run down the card: 12, 11, and 0 through 9. Originally, the card was intended to be used for numerical data only (Hollerith's census application); thus, early cards had only ten punch positions per column, 0 through 9. These are known as the numeric positions. Later, when the need for alphabetic data arose, the zone positions, rows 12 and 11, were added.

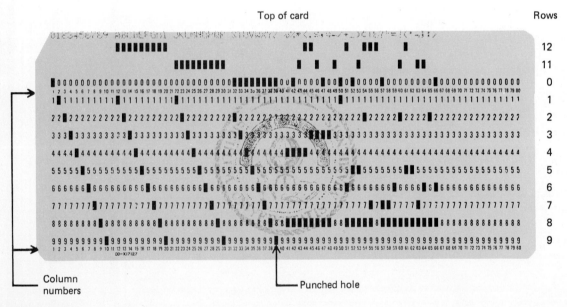

Figure 7.1
A punched card.

Each column of a card holds one **character**—a letter, a digit, or a special symbol such as a punctuation mark. The position of holes punched in the column determines the character. In Fig. 7.1, column 1 contains only a single hole in the 0 row; thus the column contains the digit zero. Column 2 contains a single punched hole in the 1 row; hence, it contains the digit one. Letters are represented by two punches, a zone and a numeric, in the same column; column 12, for example, contains punches in rows 12 and 1, which, taken together (Fig. 7.1), designate the letter A. The various special symbols are similarly represented by combinations of hole patterns; a close examination of Fig. 7.1 will reveal several examples.

Note very carefully how an individual character is represented on a punched card. Each column consists of 12 rows—12 possible punch positions. Each of these possible punch positions either does contain or does not contain a hole—there can be no ambiguity. The character is represented by this pattern of hole/no hole, in much the same way that the Morse code represents characters as a pattern of dots and dashes. The computer, you must remember, is an electronic device. It is relatively easy to design an electronic device to recognize things as being either "on" or "off," and the pattern of holes in a card row creates a rather obvious "on or off" situation.

Reading the Data

Paper (a punched card is made from a particular type of paper) is a good electrical insulator; in other words, paper will *not* conduct an electrical current. This simple fact provides the basis for a technique for reading these documents. Let's say that we were simply to lay a card on a metal surface and touch each of the 960 possible punch positions (80 columns times 12 rows per column equals 960 different possible punch positions) one at a time with an electronic probe (see Fig. 7.2). If there were no hole in a given punch position, the card would serve to separate the probe from the metal surface, thus preventing the flow of electricity. If, however, there were a hole, the probe would drop through the hole and contact the surface, thus allowing a current to flow through the wire. The presence or absence of electrical current in the wire has exactly the same meaning as the presence or absence of a hole in the card; we have succeeded in converting a pattern of holes into a pattern of electricity, thus "reading" the data.

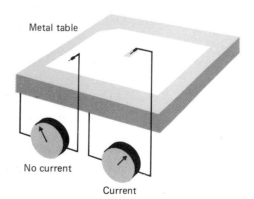

Metal table

No current

Current

Figure 7.2
An experiment to show how a
punched card is read.

Of course, the technique of reading one punch position at a time with a manual probe is much too inefficient for practical use. We must also be concerned with feeding the cards into the read mechanism; manual feeding might have been acceptable in Hollerith's day, but it isn't now. One of the most common feed-and-read mechanisms in use today consists of a metal cylinder and a set of metal "fingers" (Fig. 7.3). Using this device cards are moved from the input hopper one at a time and wrapped around the metal cylinder. The metal fingers, one for each of the twelve rows (or one for each of the 80 columns on some machines), are allowed to simply drag over the card; if there is a hole, the finger drops through and contacts the cylinder, thus allowing a current to flow. Since the cylinder rotates at a fixed speed, the time to go from column 1 to column 2 to column 3 and so on is constant, allowing the machine to distinguish between individual columns. Card readers of this type are capable of reading as many as 600 cards per minute.

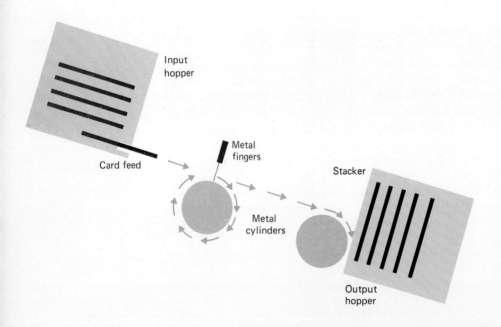

Figure 7.3
A typical card-reading mechanism.

Another important property of a card is its opacity; in other words, light won't go through it. Except, of course, where a hole has been punched. This property is the basis for another general type of card reader, one based on a photoelectric circuit. A photoelectric cell emits electricity when struck by light. Imagine a bank of twelve of these cells (Fig. 7.4), one for each possible punch position in a column. We'll shine a light on this bank of cells and then move a card between the light source and the photocells, one row at a time. The card would tend to block the light, so no current would flow. Except, again, where a hole had been punched in the card. At these spots, light would stream through to the photoelectric cells causing an electrical current to be generated. Once again, a current would be present in some wires and not in others; the card, having been converted to an electrical pattern, is read.

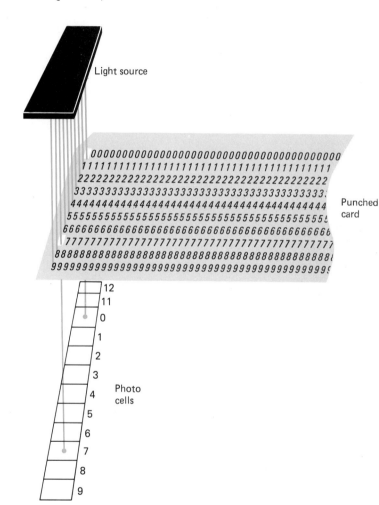

Figure 7.4
Photoelectric card reading.

The photoelectric process involves less physical contact than do the mechanical contact approaches to card reading; thus, card readers utilizing the photo-cell approach are capable of a bit more speed—1000 cards per minute is not an uncommon rate. Figure 7.5 shows an example of a typical **card reader.**

Figure 7.5
A typical card reader—this
one is a card reader/punch.

Preparation

So far we've been discussing how to read a pattern of holes in a punched card.
But how are the holes made in the card in the first place?

The most common mechanism for punching data into cards is the
keypunch (Fig. 7.6). A keypunch, as the name implies, is a keyboard device,
looking much like a typewriter. Instead of using paper, however, the keypunch
is equipped with a card-feed mechanism that moves one card at a time into the
punching position; as a key is depressed, the hole pattern associated with that
key is punched into the card. Most keypunches have a printer that prints the
content of each column at the top of the card, thus facilitating visual checking.

The most common type of keypunch punches a single column of data as the
key is depressed. Other keypunches, called **buffered keypunches,** allow the
operator to type an entire card of data, visually check that data, depress a
button, and then (and only then) actually punch the data into the card. The big
advantage of a buffered keypunch is in data accuracy; if an error is made when

Photograph courtesy of IBM Corporation.

Figure 7.6
A keypunch.

initially entering the data, the operator has the ability to spot and correct the error before actually punching the card.

Closely associated with keypunching is the process of verification. A **verifier** looks very much like a keypunch. Once data has been keypunched, it is moved to the verifier where a different operator re-keys it; the verifier marks any cards on which the two operators disagree, allowing these cards to be isolated and corrected.

A common computer output device is a card punch. Perhaps the best way to understand how a card punch is used is through an example—let's use payroll again. Each employee in a plant requires a weekly time card containing, among other things, the individual's name, social security or employee number, department number, and actual time worked. Except for the actual time worked, all of this information is known at the beginning of the week, before the card is prepared. Rather than repeat the slow, expensive, manual keypunching operation on this known data every week, a deck of partially prepunched cards (containing name, social security number, and department number) can be prepared by the computer through a card punch at a rate of 300 to 500 cards per minute with almost perfect accuracy, leaving only the actual hours worked to be filled in by the keypunch operators. Punched-card output can be used in a number of similar applications.

Another technique for preparing punched cards is the **port-o-punch** system shown in Fig. 7.7. In this system punch positions are prescored and the holes are later created by manually pushing out the hole with a stylus. This type of card is often used in vote tabulation. A ballot is inserted into a small plastic case, and the voter uses a stylus to punch the card in positions that correspond to his or her choices for the various offices; these individually prepared cards can then be read into a computer for tabulation. Other types of portable, one-card-at-a-time devices are also available.

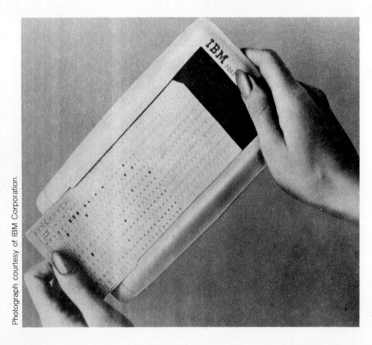

Photograph courtesy of IBM Corporation.

Figure 7.7
A port-o-punch card.

The 96-Column Card

Although the 80-column card is considered an industry standard, there are other types of cards. One of the most important alternatives is the 96-column card used in small computers (Fig. 7.8). On this card, data is punched in three sections—columns 1 through 32 are on the top, columns 33 through 64 are in the middle, and columns 65 through 96 are on the bottom. Rather than the usual twelve rows per column, the 96-column card has only six—from bottom to top, they are 1, 2, 4, 8, A, and B, respectively. The first four are numeric punches; the last two are zone punches. The number 1 is just a 1 punch; the

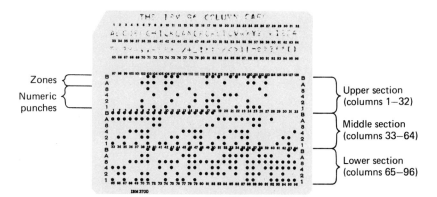

Figure 7.8
The 96-column card. (*Note:* The alphabet begins in column 33.)

number 2 is a 2 punch; the digit 3 is a 1 *and* a 2 punch; the digit 7 is 1, 2, and 4 punches in the same column (just add the punches together). Letters of the alphabet consist of a zone punch plus a combination of numeric punches. Actually, the coding scheme is quite similar to the standard 80-column code.

The 96-column card is smaller and it contains more data. Why hasn't it totally replaced the 80-column card? Basically because so many companies have such a large investment in programs and equipment that are based on the 80-column card.

Paper Tape

A close cousin of the punched card is **punched paper tape** (Fig. 7.9). As with cards, characters can be represented on paper tape as a pattern of punched holes. The most popular format divides the tape into eight channels that run parallel with the tape. Each character consists of a pattern of holes and no-holes cutting across the tape.

During the computer's first and second generations, punched paper tape was one of the most commonly used of all input and output media. With the development of more modern and more convenient devices, its use has declined, but paper tape is still used when low cost is a primary consideration.

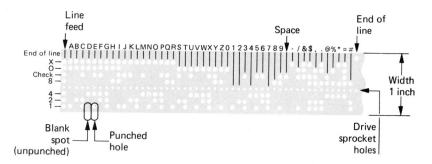

Figure 7.9
An 8-channel punched paper tape.

CHARACTERS, FIELDS, RECORDS, AND FILES

In our discussion of the punched card, we concentrated on how individual *characters* can be punched and read. Actually, we are interested in more than the individual characters. Imagine an input card on which columns 6 through 20 contain an individual's name, columns 21 and 22 his or her initials, 31 through 33 the hours worked, and 41 through 44 this same person's pay rate. Each of these groupings of characters has a meaning of its own. Such character groupings are called **fields.** A field is simply a group of characters having a logical meaning.

We would need *all* the data on a single card in order to compute one person's pay. *The collection of data fields needed to support one cycle of a program is called a* **record.** When using punched cards, one card typically contains one record; this is why punched card equipment is sometimes called unit record equipment. A program normally reads one record of data, processes this record, and produces a record of output; the program then moves on to the next record, repeating the cycle.

In any firm that uses the computer to produce its payroll, there will almost certainly be a large number of employees, each of whom has a time card. Each time card is one record, providing the data needed to compute that individual's pay. The collection of all the time cards is called the timecard file. A **file** *is a collection of all the records of a given type.* A program processes a file by reading the records in that file one at a time until the entire file has been processed.

We should note at this point that many computer applications call for the input and output of multiple files in a single program; we'll discuss such applications in later chapters.

PRINTERS

Character Printers

The simplest computer output device is basically an electric typewriter. A mechanical typewriter (Fig. 7.10a) works through a series of levers. When a key is depressed, a lever causes a type hammer to move forward and smash into a ribbon and the paper, leaving behind the impression of a character. On an electric typewriter (Fig. 7.10b), the connecting levers are replaced by an electrical switch; as the key is depressed, the switch is closed, causing a type hammer to smash into a ribbon and the paper. Since the typewriter is just a machine, it doesn't care where the electrical impulse comes from; thus, by sending the proper electrical signals to the typewriter, a computer can close the proper switches and cause a message to be printed. This is essentially how the computer prepares printed output. An electric typewriter, modified, of course, for use with a computer, can also be used as an input device; each typed character can be converted to an electrical pattern and sent to the computer.

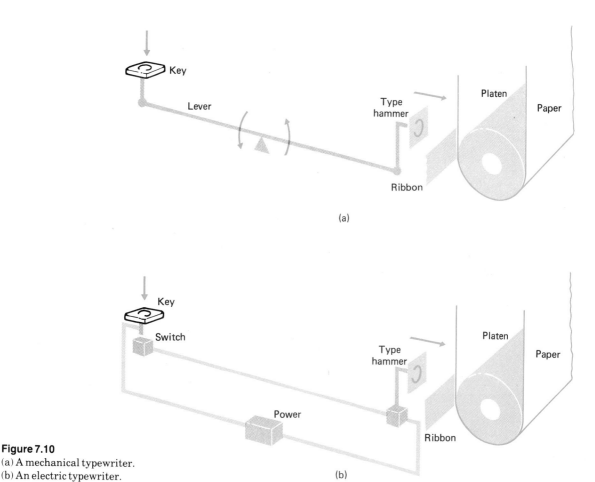

Figure 7.10
(a) A mechanical typewriter.
(b) An electric typewriter.

There are several different types of **printers** in common use. **Impact printers** that use a type hammer, ribbon, and paper are probably the most common; they are relatively inexpensive and are capable of printing at speeds in the neighborhood of 20 to 30 characters per second. **Matrix printers** are beginning to grow in popularity. On a matrix printer, the letters and numbers on the type slugs are replaced by a matrix of wires; by controlling which wires are allowed to strike the ribbon and the paper, a dot pattern forming the desired letter or number is left behind.

Non-impact printers are also available. As the name implies, a non-impact printer forms letters without actually striking the paper. Many approaches to non-impact printing are commercially available; most rely on specially treated paper. One technique called radiation printing selectively burns the paper, leaving characters (or diagrams) behind. Another approach utilizes a jet of ink that "spits" a pattern of dots to form characters. Heat-sensitive paper is used in a number of thermal techniques, where the equivalent of type is heated as the paper passes by, leaving behind an impression of a character. Non-impact printing is (or can be) a bit faster than impact printing, and it's certainly far less noisy. The disadvantages of non-impact printing are two: the specially treated paper is expensive, and it's next to impossible to make more than one copy at a time.

Line Printers

Computer reports can be extremely lengthy. To insist that such reports be printed at 20 or 30 characters per second is unreasonable—assume a 132-character line, 50-lines per page, and a 200-page report, and compute the print time at 25 characters per second. At that rate, it would take over 14 hours to produce! To support the printing of large reports, **line printers** (Fig. 7.11) are used. A typewriter prints one character at a time; a line printer prints one line at a time.

It's not quite correct to say that a line printer prints a full line at a time. One common approach to line printing (probably the easiest to visualize) consists of a rotating cylinder holding on its surface a complete set of the

Figure 7.11
A line printer.

numbers, letters, and symbols (the character set) available to this printer (Fig. 7.12); there is one set of characters for each possible print position. In front of the cylinder is a set of type hammers—again, one for each print position. The cylinder is constantly rotating and as the desired character moves over the paper, the hammer is fired and the character is printed. It's possible that one, a dozen, or even one hundred characters might actually be printed at the same time. The real speed advantage of a line printer, however, results from the fact that it is not necessary to move a type element or a carriage in order to space the characters. Other common approaches put the character set on a series of moving rods or on a moving chain; the result is the same, with the character being printed as it moves into the proper position. Try to picture a typewriter with one type ball for each and every print position, and you'll have a good mental image of how a line printer works.

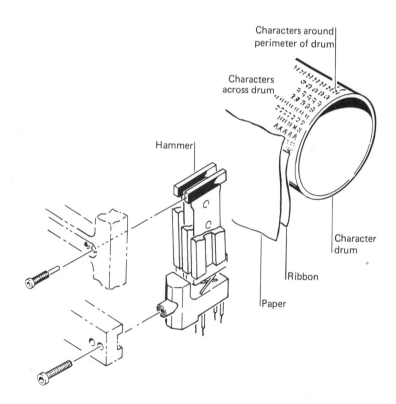

Figure 7.12
A print mechanism for a line printer. (Illustration courtesy of Dataproducts Corporation, Woodland Hills, California.)

Line-printer speeds range (in popular models) from a few hundred lines per minute into the 1000 to 1500 line-per-minute range. Non-impact line printers are also available, enjoying the same advantages and disadvantages as their typewriter counterparts.

Page Printers and Computer Output Microfilm

On very high volume printing jobs, even the 1500 line per minute speeds of a good line printer can seem unreasonably slow. **Page printers** were designed with just such jobs in mind. With a line printer, a complete line is set up in the computer's memory and then sent to the printer. With a page printer, a complete *page,* consisting of 50 to 60 lines, is set up in memory before being sent to the printer. Typically, the actual printing of a page at a time is achieved by a photographic technique similar to that used in common office copiers.

Another popular solution to the high-volume, printed output problem is **computer output microfilm,** or COM (Fig. 7.13). As the name implies, a computer output microfilm device writes characters on microfilm rather than on paper. (Ask your librarian to show you what microfilm looks like.) Often, a controlled laser beam is used to form the characters.

Photograph courtesy of Eastman Kodak Company.

Figure 7.13
A microimage processor for producing computer output microfilm.

In addition to high speed, microfilm output enjoys at least one major advantage over traditional printed output: reduced bulk. Compare, for example, the physical size of the Sunday *New York Times* with a microfilmed copy of the same newspaper. Less bulk means easier storage and easier retrieval of the printed matter. Unfortunately, there are disadvantages too. The equipment is expensive. The microimage cannot be read directly; it must be first displayed on a screen or copied to paper before it can be used by a human being. In spite of these problems, the use of computer output microfilm continues to grow.

CHARACTERS, FIELDS, RECORDS, AND FILES REVISITED

A printed report (Fig. 7.14) can, if properly prepared, be very easy to read. The column headers at the top of each page clearly identify the meaning of each field, and the individual fields are evenly spaced across the page to give an

INVENTORY MASTER LIST

PART NUMBER	DESCRIPTION	STOCK ON HAND	REORDER POINT	REORDER QUANTITY	REORDER PENDING
0001	EMERY PAPER, SHEET	1530	78	1500	
0002	COMPACTOR	278	10	300	
0007	BALL POINT PEN	1888	51	2000	
0013	ADDING MACHINE RIBBON	78	21	100	
0017	FLAG POLE	85	43	100	
0020	PAINT BRUSH	503	28	550	
0025	V-BELT	1643	85	2000	
0032	BEVERAGE COOLER	697	20	700	
0037	3/4 ELBOW	258	95	325	
0040	COPIER	772	39	825	
0043	ACETATE SOLVENT - PINT	271	22	300	
0052	ALCOHOL, QUART BOTTLE	492	32	500	
0058	THUMB TACKS - BOX	616	87	615	
0063	EXPOSURE METER	292	61	340	
0071	METAL FOIL - ROLL	414	36	500	
0074	RANGE HOOD	195	34	250	
0080	AWNING	338	20	400	
0085	GARDEN TRACTOR	151	33	175	
0091	SEARCHLIGHT	840	79	800	
0095	AIR FILTER	836	45	1000	
0099	TRIPOD	595	55	600	
0107	HEAT LAMP	619	32	700	
0108	BOOK REST	949	70	1000	
0109	AIR BRUSH	42	65	200	X
0115	HOT WATER HEATER	78	11	100	
0124	DOCK COVER	922	133	850	
0127	VINAL - YARDS	554	93	900	
0128	SEWER TAPPER	919	70	1000	
0136	NYLON SILK SCREEN	84	25	250	
0143	HINGE	233	110	200	
0148	ADHESIVE TAPE, ROLL	1157	704	700	
0153	CHICKEN WIRE - FEET	616	98	600	
0159	PRESSURE COOKER	830	79	800	
0166	BARBED WIRE, FEE	774	96	2000	
0170	OPTICAL FILTER	647	45	1400	
0172	RIVETS - POUNDS	825	29	1000	
0178	AIR COMPRESSOR	22	85	500	X
0184	HEATING PAD	60	83	1300	X
0189	KITCHEN EXHAUST FAN	169	62	400	
0194	TWO-WAY RADIO	277	20	350	
0202	ACETYLENE TOURCH	2	10	75	X
0207	BOOKSTAND	1911	71	2000	
0208	AIR GUAGE - HOSE TYPE	1359	77	2000	
0212	FM RADIO	410	61	500	
0230	AM RADIO	34	45	750	X
0231	FAN COIL ENCLOSURE	478	53	500	
0234	FLOWER POT	1379	403	1000	
0239	ALUMINUM PIPE, FEET	1884	297	1600	
0243	AEROSOL CONTAINER	1732	376	2000	
0247	ELECTRIC SAW	840	310	600	

Figure 7.14
An example of a printed report.

attractive appearance. How is this result achieved? How can the printer be made to space and to print column headers?

The answer to both questions is the same: The computer, under control of a program, tells it to. The programmer first lays out a column header and codes the instructions necessary to instruct the computer to set up this header in memory. Once the header is set up, it is sent to the printer. A similar method is used for spacing: The programmer determines the proper number of blanks, instructs the computer to set up a line of output containing these blanks, and the resulting line is sent to the printer.

Let's put it another way. The printer prints individual *characters* without regard for their logical relationship; the grouping of characters into fields is a logical function that is performed within the computer (and, of course, within the mind of the person reading the report). The same principle holds true on a card reader that simply sends one independent character at a time into the computer; the task of grouping these characters into fields is a logical function belonging to the computer itself.

OPTICAL MEDIA

A punched card can be read simply because the pattern of holes can easily be converted to a pattern of electrical pulses. It isn't the card or the holes that is really important; the critical thing is the pattern of electrical pulses. Any physical medium that can be converted to a similar pattern of electricity can be used to input data to a computer.

To read a card, we take advantage of certain physical properties of that card. The card is opaque, so we can use light and photoelectric cells to read it. The card is a nonconductor of electricity, so we can use direct contact through the holes to read it.

A number of commonly used data entry media rely on a different physical property—the reflectivity of light from a white or lightly colored surface. Consider, for example, the sheets on which students record their answers to a standardized test. You probably recall the instructions: Use a number 2 pencil to blacken the space between the two parallel lines, and so on. Such tests are designed to be scored by computer, but how are the answers read? Very simply, light is shined on a selected region of the surface. If a great deal of light is reflected back, the spot must be white; i.e., there is no black mark. If very little light is reflected, the spot must be black—there is a mark. Photoelectric cells can be used to measure the intensity of the reflected light. Low intensity means a black mark; high intensity means no black mark. Again, the data is converted into a pattern of electronic pulses.

The general name for this technique is **mark sense.** A simple black mark on a sheet of paper or a card, in a very precise location, of course, is all that is needed to record data. Mark sense forms have been used for grading tests,

Figure 7.15
A Universal Product Code (UPC)
is printed on most products
offered for sale in the modern
supermarket.

registering students for classes, recording personal health histories, correcting
the amount due on a utility bill, and hundreds of other applications.

Many of you have probably noticed the black and white bar code that
appears on most packaged products available for sale today (Fig. 7.15). It's
called the **Universal Product Code** or UPC, and it relys on the same optical
technique as does mark sense. The bar code is scanned by a light source; the
black bars reflect little light, while the spaces between the bars reflect considerably more. Combinations of two bars are used to represent individual
characters, with the relative thickness of the two bars allowing for differentia-
tion between characters.

Perhaps the best-known application of the Universal Product Code is
found in the supermarket. Many experts believe that, in the store of tomorrow,
the checkout clerk will no longer ring each item individually on a cash
register. Instead, the clerk will simply locate the UPC, pass the product over a
scanner, and let the computer keep track of the amount of the order. Later in
the text, we'll look at the computer controlled supermarket in more detail.

The supermarket is not the only place where bar codes and **bar code
scanners** (Fig. 7.16) can be used effectively. Recording inventory, keeping
track of samples in a chemical testing laboratory, and controlling circulation

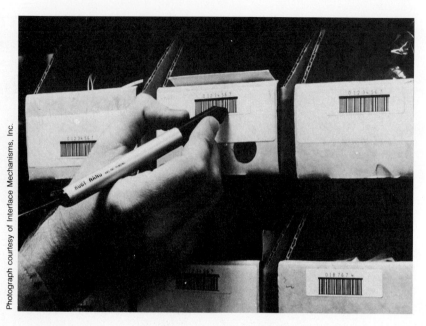

Figure 7.16
A bar-code scanner
or "light pen."

in a library are but a few examples of the rapidly growing use of this optical technique.

Another, related technique is called **optical character recognition** or **OCR.** Under OCR, typed and even carefully handwritten characters are read directly by machine. One method of reading OCR characters breaks a possible print position into a matrix of dots and measures the reflectance of each dot; the pattern of high and low reflectance defines the character. Although substantially more expensive than either mark sense or bar-code scanning, OCR is significantly more flexible, and is also enjoying growing popularity.

MAGNETIC MEDIA

One of the first of the commonly used alternatives to punched cards was **MICR,** or magnetic ink character recognition, developed by the banking industry to ease the flow of checks. The oddly shaped black numbers on the bottom of every bank check are printed in a special machine-readable magnetic ink. The first of these three fields identifies the bank; the second field (Fig. 7.17) identifies the individual account number; and the third field, added after the check has been cashed, shows the amount of the check. Once these three fields have been read, the bank has all the information it needs to update an individual's checking account. A MICR reader, similar in appearance to a card reader, converts the magnetic intensity of a MICR character into an electrical pulse (or pulses), thus reading it.

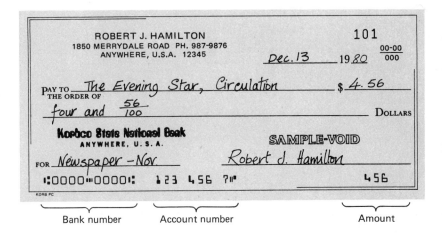

Figure 7.17
MICR fields on a check.

Bank number   Account number   Amount

As the number of checks in circulation continues to grow, many experts believe that the banking industry may soon find itself swamped in a sea of individual, MICR-encoded pieces of paper. The solution may well be a new approach to banking known as *electronic funds transfer* or EFT. Under an electronic funds transfer system, rather than writing a check to pay a utility bill, for example, the customer would simply present an identification card and authorize the bank to transfer funds from his or her account directly to the electric company's. Eventually, perhaps, most bills will be paid this way.

The key to such a system will almost certainly be an identification or account card similar to a modern credit card. Look on the back of almost any bank credit card such as a VISA® or Master Card® (Fig. 7.18). Most already contain a narrow strip of magnetic tape. On this strip it is possible to record such data as an account number, a credit limit, the current balance of an account, certain security characters, and a number of other fields. Individual characters are stored as a pattern of magnetic spots; at any given spot there either is or is not a properly aligned magnetic field, thus allowing the magnetic strip to be read in a manner analogous to a punched card or punched paper tape.

Magnetic strip

Figure 7.18
A magnetic strip card.

Photograph courtesy of Honeywell, Inc.

Figure 7.19
Operators preparing computer input
data on a key-to-tape system.

Banking is not the only industry using such magnetically encoded "credit" cards. Employee identification, health plan identification, and student identification are but a few of the applications of this technology.

Perhaps the major competition for the punched card today is provided by a number of **key-to-tape** and **key-to-disk** systems (Fig. 7.19). Essentially, these devices work much like a keypunch, with an operator entering one character at a time via a keyboard. The data, rather than going directly onto a card, is displayed on a small cathode-ray tube (like a television set). Once an entire record has been entered, the operator visually checks the data for accuracy before depressing a button that causes the data to be recorded (so far, it's pretty much like a buffered keypunch). Rather than punching a card, however, the key-to-tape or key-to-disk devices record the data on magnetic tape or magnetic disk. The use of tape and/or disk allows data to be read into the computer at rates much higher than are possible with punched cards.

TERMINALS

In our discussion of typewriters earlier in this chapter, we mentioned the possibility of using such devices to input data to a computer. When a typewriter device is used in this way, it is called a **terminal** (Fig. 7.20). Often, terminals are used for both input and output.

Figure 7.20
A terminal.

    In Chapter 6, we discussed the speed of computers, using such terms as microsecond and nanosecond to describe computer capabilities. Compare your own typing speed to a machine capable of adding over one million numbers in one second. Unless you are very unusual, the comparison favors the computer.

    It is unrealistic to expect an expensive computer to wait while we type our one or two characters per second. Instead, as we type, our characters are stored in a **buffer,** which is part of the terminal (Fig. 7.21). As we complete the line, our final act is to hit the RETURN key, moving the carriage back to the left margin. At this signal, the complete line (or record) of data can be transferred into the computer at something closer to computer speeds.

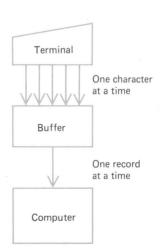

Terminal

One character
at a time

Buffer

One record
at a time

Computer

Figure 7.21
The concept of buffering.

The concept of buffering is an important one. A buffer is nothing more than temporary memory or storage. Its function is to allow the speed of input or output devices to more closely match the speed of the computer. Although the need is not as obvious, buffering takes place on card readers and printers, too; a rate of 600 cards per minute may seem very fast, but, to a computer, it's really quite slow. Rather than force the computer to wait for the card reader to read each column one at a time, the contents of the individual columns are placed in a buffer, with the actual transfer of data taking place after the complete record has been read. On a line printer, a complete record is moved from the computer to a buffer, and the individual characters are fed to the printer one at a time. If you think about it, it's possible to print position 100 before printing position 10 on a line printer; without buffering, would this be possible?

Typewriters are not the only variety of terminal in common use. **Cathode-ray-tube** terminals, essentially television sets with a keyboard and the ability to display characters (Fig. 7.22), are becoming increasingly popular. Often called CRTs or *tubes,* these terminals allow for the rapid display of a limited amount of information.

One growing application of CRTs is in data entry; essentially, a CRT terminal can be used to replace a keypunch. When keypunching, the keypunch operator transfers data from a **source document,** such as a time sheet or an engineering drawing, to a punched card; eventually, the card is read into a

Figure 7.22
A cathode-ray-tube (CRT) terminal.

computer. Using a CRT, the terminal operator can enter the data through the keyboard and *directly* into the computer. To simplify the task of the terminal operator, a pattern identifying the data that must be entered can be displayed on the screen; note, in Fig. 7.22, the words NAME, STREET, CITY, STATE, and ZIP. Using this approach, all the operator need do is fill in the blanks.

The use of a CRT rather than a keypunch for preparing computer input data tends to produce more accurate data. Why? Basically, for two reasons. First, since a CRT terminal is normally attached to a computer, the computer can be used to check on the accuracy of the data, making such comments as "There is no such customer number," or "Four hours is a bit low for a typical work week; are you sure the decimal point is in the right place?" Little things such as misplaced decimal points and inverted digits (1324 rather than 1234) are common human errors; the computer is very good at catching such errors.

The second reason for the improved accuracy of CRT-based data entry has to do with the ability to capture data closer to its source. For example, imagine that you are a salesperson and that you have just written an order. The chances are that your order will go directly to an order-entry clerk or a secretary who types the order and checks it for accuracy. Next, the typed order is sent to keypunch, where it is copied to a punched card and, eventually, submitted to the computer. What exactly is done in the keypunch operation? The data is copied from one document to another. Period! It's just copied. And copying is a source of error. (Try typing the material on this page, and then have someone count your errors.)

Why not allow the order-entry clerk or secretary who typed the order in the first place to enter the data directly into the computer? Using a CRT terminal, this person could produce computer input data with roughly the same effort needed to type the document in the first place. Thus the keypunch step could be completely bypassed, eliminating both a cost and a significant source of error. In some firms, the salesperson is responsible for entering order information via a CRT, thus eliminating the need for an order-entry specialist.

Besides eliminating copy errors, placing data entry responsibility close to the source of the data has another important impact on data accuracy. What would happen, for example, if a timekeeper dropped a decimal point and submitted a total of 400 (rather than 40.0) hours worked for an individual employee during a given week? The keypunch operator would probably punch 400, but a professional timekeeper entering the data through a CRT would immediately recognize the absurdity of a 400-hour work week and correct the data on the spot. The individual whose actions produce the data should know what the data should be, an advantage that a professional keypunch operator would almost certainly not enjoy.

In addition to being accurate, CRT data entry tends to be a bit faster than keypunching, simply because the data is entered directly into the computer and does not have to go through another device (a card reader) before becoming available to the computer. Combining the quicker data accessibility with improved accuracy makes CRT data entry quite attractive; more and more organizations are using this approach.

Management is also beginning to make heavy use of CRT terminals. Information is essential to good management, and the computer is a virtual treasure trove of information. In many modern offices, the manager has at his or her disposal an on-line CRT connected directly to the computer. By asking simple questions such as "What's the current stock on hand for part number 228654?" the manager can selectively query the computer's data base. This approach is rapidly developing into a very important management tool; it's the key to a management information system, a topic we'll be discussing in more detail later.

We've considered some of the advantages of CRTs, but there are also disadvantages. Several years ago, the argument was that CRT terminals were more expensive than typewriter terminals. This is no longer true; advances in electronics have brought the cost of a CRT terminal into a very competitive range.

Another common argument holds that whenever CRT terminals are used, special equipment and special programs must be available to support them. (We'll consider this equipment and software in more detail in a later chapter.) But these special support modules must be present for any terminal, not just a CRT.

Actually, the biggest argument against the use of CRTs is the fact that they produce only an image on a screen rather than a hard copy on paper. The user of a CRT is glued to the terminal, while the user of a typewriter terminal can tear off information and carry it to "where the action is." A "hard copy" terminal leaves a complete audit trace of all the day's activities; it is very difficult to accurately trace what has happened on a CRT. What's better, a CRT or a hard copy terminal? It depends on the application.

Buffering is essential on a CRT terminal. The image on a cathode-ray tube screen is not permanent and must be constantly refreshed by retransmitting the image. One alternative would be to have the computer simply retransmit the data several times a second, but a computer has better things to do with its time. A more reasonable approach is to send the data to a buffer, allowing electronic circuits within the terminal to refresh the image from the buffer as required.

Special-purpose Terminals

Other terminals are designed to perform special functions. Consider, for example, **data entry terminals** such as the one shown in Fig. 7.23. These terminals typically consist of a card reader, a badge reader, and a simple keyboard. A worker might, upon entering a manufacturing plant in the morning, insert his

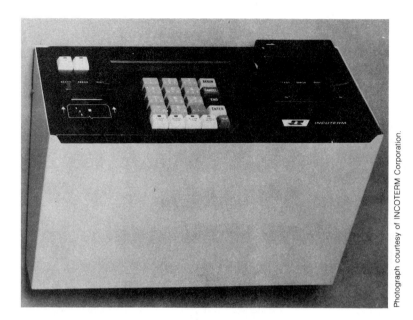

Photograph courtesy of INCOTERM Corporation.

Figure 7.23
A simple data entry terminal.

or her badge into the terminal, thus reporting the time of arrival to the computer. Upon completing a unit of work, this same individual might insert this badge (for personal identification) and a card identifying the work just completed into the machine, using the keyboard to report such variable data as quantity. This approach, often called **source data automation,** eliminates the need for keypunching the data at a later time.

The idea of capturing data at the source is also quite prevalent in retailing, with cash registers either being directly connected to a computer or producing machine-readable register tapes. Even more common are the little terminals that allow a salesclerk to enter an account number and the amount of a purchase into a credit verification system. You've probably seen these at the local department store.

In some supermarkets, a scanning device, a special type of terminal, can read the bar codes printed on most packages, allowing the store's computer to locate the current price and update the store's inventory. Even banks, with various automatic-teller devices, are using special-function terminals.

A special-purpose terminal is designed for convenience. Such a terminal may not be very flexible, limited as it is to one or two very specific applications, but the applications that it does support are greatly simplified. Figure 7.24, for example, shows a small, hand-held data entry terminal designed to allow a limited amount of numeric data to be collected and entered into a computer. The unit, looking much like a pocket calculator, can be equipped with such extras as internal memory, the electronics needed to communicate over regu-

Photograph courtesy of Norand Corporation.

Figure 7.24
A portable, hand-held data
entry terminal.

lar telephone lines, and a bar code scanner similar to the ones described earlier. These little data entry terminals fit in a vest pocket and are as easy to use as a calculator.

COMPUTER GRAPHICS

Anyone who has watched television (and who hasn't?) knows that it is possible to display much more than simple letters and digits on a TV screen. A CRT terminal is much like a television set; it too can display noncharacter data. Figure 7.25 shows a CRT screen displaying a grid pattern. In this example, the task of a data entry clerk is going to be greatly simplified as he or she enters data by simply filling in the blanks, with the grid providing an excellent visual guide. CRT screens are commonly used to display charts, graphs, bar charts, engineering drawings, and even schematics of three-dimensional objects such as an automobile. The objective of a computer is to convert data into information. Such visualizations carry a great deal of information content, so why not have the computer produce graphical output?

One of the first of the computer graphics devices was the **plotter** (Fig. 7.26). A plotter, as the name implies, draws or plots graphical output from a computer. Typically, the plotter defines a reference point on a set of X-Y coordinate

Photograph courtesy of Hewlett-Packard, Inc.

Figure 7.25
A CRT displaying graphic
data.

Photograph courtesy of California Computer Products, Inc. (CalComp).

Figure 7.26
A plotter.

axes and then simply moves a pen from point to point, making the drawing.
Graphs, engineering drawings, even works of art have been produced by
plotters.

A plotter is exclusively an output device. A CRT screen can be used for
both input and output. There are light-sensitive, and even touch-sensitive,
screens that allow a user to enter graphical material directly into the computer.

A **digitizer** (Fig. 7.27) is the exact opposite of a plotter. A plotter draws by
moving a mechanism from point to point, dragging a pen along with it; in
effect, it acts like a child playing "connect the dots," except that the dots don't
actually appear on the paper. With a digitizer, the user starts with a finished

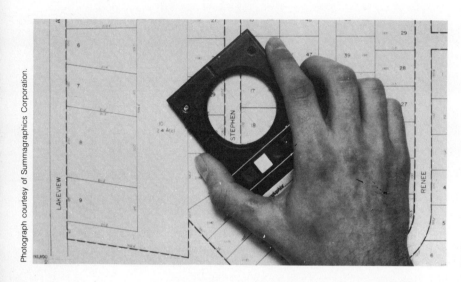

Figure 7.27
A digitizer.

drawing and, by moving the device from point to point, enters the points into the computer. Once the points have been entered, the drawing can later be reproduced by a computer-controlled plotter.

VOICE RESPONSE AND VOICE RECOGNITION

Perhaps the ultimate in computer input and output is to have the machine actually speak to us. Nothing could be more natural. Most of us, however, tend to visualize a "talking computer" as a prop in *Star Trek* or *2001, A Space Odyssey*. Not any more. Voice response and voice recognition are already with us!

Consider, for example, a popular child's toy designed to teach spelling. The little, microcomputer-controlled unit first speaks a word. The child responds by typing the word through a keyboard, and the computer tells the child if the spelling is correct. You probably didn't even know that little toy was really a very sophisticated computer, equipped with a state-of-the-art **voice response** unit.

Banks are also using voice response. In many cities, a customer can call the bank, enter an account number through the buttons on a touch tone telephone, and receive, verbally, his or her current account balance. Other banking functions can also be handled in this way. New uses for voice response are being discovered almost daily.

It's one thing to have a computer respond verbally, and quite another to have the machine recognize sounds. Voice response merely involves having the computer select the proper sounds or phrases from its memory bank and then feed the associated electronic signals to a speaker. **Voice recognition,** on the other hand, implies being able to distinguish specific words as spoken in various contents by different human beings. Have you ever had trouble under-standing someone speaking your own language in a slightly unfamiliar di-alect? Imagine the problems faced by the designer of a computer voice recogni-tion unit.

Most existing voice recognition systems are designed to allow a single individual to "teach" the computer the meaning of a limited vocabulary of perhaps 100–200 words or phrases. Once this teaching has been completed, the computer is able to understand these specific phrases as spoken by this indi-vidual.

Imagine a quality control inspector carefully checking the dimensions and other properties of a complex electronic circuit under a microscope. The inspec-tion requires deep concentration and close attention to detail. Both hands are actively involved. As measurements are made, they must be recorded, but the very act of recording using traditional paper-and-pencil methods tends to disturb the essential concentration. Voice recognition is perfect for such ap-plications. As measurements are made, the inspector simply speaks into a microphone, and the data is entered into the computer. As a result, the inspector can concentrate on the primary activity, inspection, rather than on the secondary activity of data collection; thus, he or she becomes more efficient.

Numerous other examples could be cited—the pathologist conducting an autopsy, an inventory clerk accepting several shipments in a short period of time, a salesperson placing a customer order via telephone. In some cases, full attention must be paid to the primary task, and data collection tends to detract from performance. In others, both hands are fully involved in the work, and paper-and-pencil methods are impossible. In others, the delays inherent in transmitting written documents are unacceptable.

Of course, a regular tape recording can always be made, with the results later being transcribed for computer data entry. But transcribing is extra, nonproductive work. Why not capture the data in computer-acceptable form the first time? That is exactly what computer voice recognition does.

Today, computer voice recognition is economically feasible for a number of very specific applications such as the ones described above. It is not yet a general purpose technique, and it will be some time before it is competitive with punched cards, optical techniques, and magnetic media. Still, it is hard to imagine a more natural, easier-to-use approach to data entry. Improvements will be made. The potential for voice recognition is enormous.

CONTROL UNITS

Throughout this chapter, we've been discussing the need for buffering. In many cases, the physical buffer is not located in the input or output device itself, but resides in an intermediate device called a **control unit** (Fig. 7.28). The control unit sits between the **I/O** (for input/output) **device** and the com-puter acting, with its buffering capability, as an intermediary.

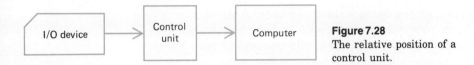

Figure 7.28
The relative position of a
control unit.

Control units perform another, less obvious function as well. Consider the many different I/O devices we've discussed in this chapter. The 80-column card uses a code derived from the twelve possible punch positions in each column. The 96-column card uses a six-hole code. Paper tape uses a code based on eight different hole positions. A printer expects an electrical impulse which can be converted to a switch position, so that the proper hammer can be fired. A MICR device reads magnetic intensity. An OCR or mark sense device reads the degree of reflected light. Imagine the complexity of a computer capable of dealing with all of these different forms of electronic codes!

In order to save expense and to simplify the design of the computer, the task of converting all these codes is housed in a control unit. The control unit for the card reader (Fig. 7.29) accepts punched card code and converts it to a standard computer code (for the computer being used). The printer's control unit (Fig. 7.29) accepts this standard computer code and converts it electronically into the pulses that fire the proper print hammers. Similarly, with each input or output device, the intermediate control unit always works with the standard computer code on the computer's side and whatever code is called for on the device side. Thus, no matter what the electronic characteristics of the device might be, the computer always "sees" the same code (we'll introduce some common codes in the next chapter). This control unit function is called **standard interface.**

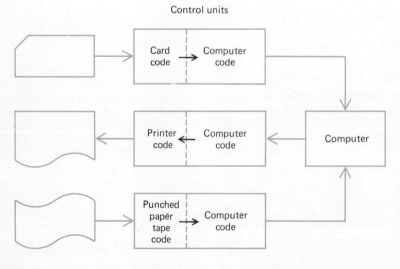

Figure 7.29
The standard interface
function.

If you were to walk into a modern computer center and ask to see the various control units, you probably wouldn't be able to find them; almost all are physically contained within the box that houses the input or output device itself. But the control unit is still there, performing an essential function.

SUMMARY

In this chapter, we've introduced a number of basic input and output devices including card readers, printers, card punches, optical and magnetic devices, graphical devices, voice response, and terminals. Key concepts included the use of codes to stand for characters, buffering, and the standard interface function of control units.

KEYWORDS

bar-code scanner	keypunch	plotter
buffer	key-to-disk	port-o-punch
buffered keypunch	key-to-tape	printer
card reader	line printer	punched card
cathode-ray tube terminal (CRT)	magnetic strip card	record
character	mark sense	source data automation
computer output microfilm (COM)	matrix printer	source document
	MICR (Magnetic ink character recognition)	standard interface
control unit		terminal
data entry terminal	nonimpact printer	Universal Product Code (UPC)
digitizer	OCR (Optical character recognition)	verifier
field		voice recognition
file	page printer	voice response
impact printer	paper tape	
I/O device		

EXERCISES

1. Keypunch your name and address into a data processing card.
2. What is a field?
3. What is a record?
4. What is a file?
5. Explain buffering.

6. What are the functions of a control unit? What does standard interface mean?

7. Explain how a line printer differs from a character printer.

8. What advantages do key-to-disk and key-to-tape systems enjoy over standard punched cards?

9. Data on cards and other unit record media is stored as a series of independent, coded characters. Why is this desirable?

10. Explain how a card reader works.

11. A major topic in this chapter is the use of CRT terminals for data entry. What are the advantages of this approach over keypunching?

12. Discuss the advantages and disadvantages of computer output microfilm.

13. Explain the physical property that allows data to be read optically.

14. Why is graphical output sometimes desirable?

8

THE COMPUTER

OVERVIEW

In this chapter, we'll consider the basic components of an actual computer: memory, the central processing unit, and the registers. In order to gain an understanding of how these internal components work, it is first necessary to have an idea of the language used inside a computer; thus the chapter begins with a discussion of the binary number system.

THE BINARY NUMBER SYSTEM

Modern digital computers are designed to work with **binary** data; thus a basic appreciation of the binary number system is essential if you are to gain a real understanding of how a computer works. It is *not* essential that you become extremely proficient in handling binary numbers. You do *not* have to begin thinking in binary, and personal difficulties in converting from decimal to binary and back again will *not* doom you to certain failure in any computer-related course. Even the professional programmer finds proficiency in handling pure binary numbers to be, at best, of marginal importance. Should you decide to major in a computer-related field, you will eventually encounter a real need for working with binary data. At this point, however, what is really important is that you realize that it's not only possible to store and manipulate binary data, but that this approach makes a great deal of sense on a computer. The purpose of this section is to give you an appreciation for the value of using binary and to create in your mind a willingness to accept the use of binary data on a computer as being reasonable, quite possible, and very sensible.

Since the decimal numbering system is more familiar to most of us, let's start our discussion of binary numbers by taking a close look at a few decimal numbers. Consider the two numbers 3 and 30. Both contain a common digit, a three, but we all know that we are looking at two different numbers. What's the difference between the three in the number 3 and the three in the number 30? The answer is its position: The first three is in the units position, and the second three is in the tens position. Closer analysis reveals that the number thirty (30) is really another way of saying "three tens and no ones."

To put it another way, *any* decimal number consists of a series of digits—0, 1, 2, 3, 4, 5, 6, 7, 8, 9—written in precise, relative positions. The number twenty-three is written as 23, while a different combination of the same two digits, 32, represents a completely different number.

Take a look at the number 3580; what is really represented by this combination of digits is

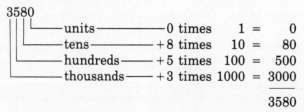

In other words, to find the value of *any* number, multiply each digit by its positional (or place) value, and add these products. This is known as the **digit-times-place-value rule.**

Take a closer look at the sequence of place values. In the example shown above, we started with 1, then went to 10, then 100, then 1000. What would you expect the next higher place value to be? It would, of course, be 10,000. Just add one more zero. What does this really mean? We started with 1. To move up to the tens position, we multiplied this starting value by 10 (our **base**—this is a base-ten numbering system). The hundreds position, stated another way, is 10×10. The thousands position is $10 \times 10 \times 10$. Next comes the ten-thousands position: $10 \times 10 \times 10 \times 10$. Do you perceive a pattern? Each time we move up one position, we multiply by one more ten.

Eventually, we reach a point where it becomes a bit tedious to write down all those tens. You probably know that 10×10 can be written as 10^2 and that $10 \times 10 \times 10$ can be written as 10^3; the exponent or "power" of ten indicates the number of times that the number is to be multiplied by itself. This saves writing a lot of zeros when a number becomes very large. Numbers expressed in this way are written in scientific notation.

In Fig. 8.1, we have written a series of place or positional values along a horizontal line, showing these same values, in scientific notation, below the line. Starting at the right, we find that the number 1 can be written as 10^0; in fact, by mathematical definition, *any* number (except zero) raised to the zero power is equal to 1. Given this starting point, the place values for the decimal numbering system can be written as 10, the base, raised to a series of sequential integer powers—0, 1, 2, 3, 4, 5, 6, 7, ...

100,000	10,000	1000	100	10	1
$10 \times 10 \times 10 \times 10$	$10 \times 10 \times 10$	10×10	10	1
10^5	10^4	10^3	10^2	10^1	10^0

Figure 8.1
Decimal place values.

Let's summarize a few of the key ideas brought out in our discussion of decimal numbers. First is the idea of place or positional value represented by the base ten (10) raised to a series of sequential integer powers. The use of the digit zero (0) to represent "no value" in a given position is the second key concept. Third, a total of ten digits—0, 1, 2, 3, 4, 5, 6, 7, 8, 9—are needed to write decimal numbers. Finally, only values less than the base (in this case, ten) can be written in a single position; numbers exceeding nine must be written in at least two positions.

There is nothing to restrict the application of these rules to a base-ten numbering system. If the positional values are represented as powers of two instead of ten, we have the framework of the base-two or binary numbering system (Fig. 8.2). As in the decimal numbering system, the digit zero (0) is needed to represent "no value" in a given position. In addition to zero, the binary numbering system needs only one other digit, a one (1), in order to form numbers. Why only these two digits? Only values less than the base can

32	16	8	4	2	1
$2 \times 2 \times 2 \times 2 \times 2$	$2 \times 2 \times 2 \times 2$	$2 \times 2 \times 2$	2×2	2	1
2^5	2^4	2^3	2^2	2^1	2^0

Figure 8.2
Binary place values.

be represented in a single position. Since the base of the binary system is two (2), only numbers less than two can be so represented—0 and 1.

Once again, as in the decimal numbering system, the digit-times-place-value rule still works; it's just that the place values are different, representing powers of *two* rather than powers of ten. Consider, for example, the binary number 1101. Using the digit-times-place-value rule and remembering that we have a binary number, we can perform the following analysis:

$$
\begin{array}{l}
1101 \\
\quad 2^0 \text{ or units} \longrightarrow 1 \text{ times } 1 = 1 \\
\quad 2^1 \text{ or twos} \longrightarrow +0 \text{ times } 2 = 0 \\
\quad 2^2 \text{ or fours} \longrightarrow +1 \text{ times } 4 = 4 \\
\quad 2^3 \text{ or eights} \longrightarrow +1 \text{ times } 8 = 8 \\
\hline
\qquad\qquad\qquad\qquad\qquad\qquad\quad 13
\end{array}
$$

giving us the decimal equivalent of the binary number 1101.

Any whole number can be written in binary. How do we tell the difference between a binary 11 (which is equal to three in decimal) and a decimal eleven? Normally, the binary number is enclosed within a set of parentheses, and a subscript is used to indicate the base—for example, $(1101)_2$. This is merely a convenient way of differentiating between numbers with different bases.

We use the base-ten system because we are used to it; since our childhood, the numbers 1, 2, 3, 4, 5, 6, 7, 8, 9, and 10 have been drilled into us. There is, however, nothing inherently "better" about base-ten numbers; in fact, if humans were to have six fingers on each hand, we might well be using a base-twelve number system in our everyday activities. Since we all know base-ten, base-ten is convenient for us. That's why we use it.

For a computer, an electronic device, binary numbers are much more convenient to use than are base-ten numbers. Since data representation requires only the two digits, 0 and 1, the computer, using binary numbers, can work with the simple on/off logic of electrical circuits. Binary is truly an electronic numbering system.

Throughout the remainder of this text, we'll be talking about the manipulation of binary data by the computer. When we refer to binary data, we are simply talking about a string of 0's and 1's. Occasionally, we'll concentrate our attention on one or two of these binary digits, using the term **bit,** which is an acronym for *binary* dig*it*.

CODES

We have seen that numbers can be represented in binary form. Patterns of 0's and 1's can, however, be used to represent more than numerical data. In Morse code, for example, letters are represented by a pattern of dots and dashes; for instance, (. . . – – – . . .) is the international distress signal SOS. If we were to substitute a 1 for each dot and a 0 for each dash, we would have a binary code capable of communicating letters as well as digits. Braille is another example of a code that, at its core, is binary; there either *is* or *is not* a raised dot.

A game that you may have played as a child involves the coding of secret messages. A very common code in such games simply converts each letter to a number, with 1 meaning A, 2 meaning B, and so on. Using such a code,

8–5–12–16

can be interpreted to mean "H–E–L–P." Why are the dashes used? Is 851216 really "HELP," or is it "HEABAF"? The dashes are used to separate letters and allow the reader to make sense of the code.

Suppose we were to take a different approach and decide that each and every letter will be represented by exactly two digits—A is 01, B is 02, J is 10, K is 11, and so on. Now our message can be written as

08051216

without any dashes. Since each and every letter is represented by exactly two digits, all we need do is break the message into two-digit groups. We have a fixed-length **code.**

Suppose we were to do the same thing with the binary number system. Starting with only the numbers 0 through 9, we might write the binary equivalent of each digit and use the resulting four-bit number as a code (Fig. 8.3). Using this code, the number 12 could be *represented* as 00010010. Note that we are *not* talking about the binary number system right now; we are talking about a code. If we were to take the string of digits $(00010010)_2$ and treat it as a binary *number,* we would have

1 times 2^1, plus 1 times 2^4 or (2 plus 16),

which is *not* 12. Coded numbers and real numbers are not the same, simply because the code ignores positional value.

Decimal	Code	Decimal	Code
0	0000	5	0101
1	0001	6	0110
2	0010	7	0111
3	0011	8	1000
4	0100	9	1001

Figure 8.3
A binary code for decimal digits.

A	11 0001	S	01 0010
B	11 0010	T	01 0011
C	11 0011	U	01 0100
D	11 0100	V	01 0101
E	11 0101	W	01 0110
F	11 0110	X	01 0111
G	11 0111	Y	01 1000
H	11 1000	Z	01 1001
I	11 1001		
		0	00 1010
J	10 0001	1	00 0001
K	10 0010	2	00 0010
L	10 0011	3	00 0011
M	10 0100	4	00 0100
N	10 0101	5	00 0101
O	10 0110	6	00 0110
P	10 0111	7	00 0111
Q	10 1000	8	00 1000
R	10 1001	9	00 1001

Figure 8.4
The six-bit BCD code. Other unlisted codes are used for special symbols.

Many computer applications require *alphabetic* as well as *numeric* data; thus, something more than this simple numeric code is needed. One solution to this problem is the six-bit **BCD code** (Binary Coded Decimal) shown in Fig. 8.4. Using this code, individual characters are represented by a series of six bits: two zone bits and four numeric bits. The letters A through I are all assigned zone bits 11. Since A is the first letter in this group, its numeric part is 0001; B, being the second letter in the group, has the numeric part 0010; C is 0011, and so on. In other words, a zone-bit configuration of 11 is attached to a numeric part that indicates the relative position of the letter within the group. A second group of letters, J through R, is assigned zone bits 10; once again, the numeric bits show the relative position of each letter within the group. The letters S through Z are formed by attaching numeric bits 0010 through 1001, respectively (that's 2 through 9) to zone bits 01 (there are only eight letters in this group, which explains the unusual start). Numbers all have zone bits 00 followed, essentially, by the number itself expressed in binary. The digit zero deviates somewhat to allow for the existence of a blank character. It's actually a fairly simple code. All things considered, it makes a great deal more sense than the code Mr. Morse developed for the telegraph.

In Chapter 7, we talked a bit about control units. Do you remember the standard interface function? The control unit, on input, accepts whatever code is used by the I/O device and converts it to computer code (Fig. 8.5). On output, the control unit accepts computer code, transforming it to whatever the output device requires in the way of a code. BCD is sometimes used as an internal computer code. The I/O devices treat each character as a separate entity, passing their own codes along to a control unit where the data is converted to BCD and stored (or copied) into the computer's memory as separate and independent characters. The job of putting the individual characters together to

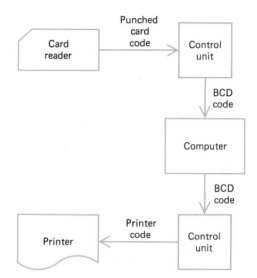

Figure 8.5
The function of a control unit.

form fields is a logical function performed by the computer under the control of a program.

One point should be restated at this time. Coded data and numeric data are not the same. The two decimal digits 12 obviously form the number twelve which, in pure binary form, is $(1100)_2$. Using the BCD code, the digit 1 is 000001, and the digit 2 is 000010; putting them together yields

$$000001000010 \qquad or$$

$$\underline{\qquad}\ 1 \text{ times } 2^1 = 2$$
$$\underline{\qquad}\ + 1 \text{ times } 2^6 = 64$$
$$\overline{66}$$

which is *not* 12. A card reader passes individual digits to a computer in BCD form. If, however, the two digits in question really do mean twelve, we *must* have a mechanism for converting from *coded* form to *numeric* form. Fortunately, most computers possess special instructions to perform this conversion.

The code allows individual characters of data to be transferred between the computer and its input and output devices. The code also allows these individual characters to be stored in the computer's memory. The computer, under program control, groups these characters into logical fields and performs any data format conversions needed to produce meaningful data. Any code will do, so long as it is known and consistently applied. Two codes enjoying great popularity on modern computers are IBM's **EBCDIC** (Extended Binary Coded Decimal Interchange Code, pronounced "ebb-see-dic") and the **ASCII-8** code of the American Standards Institute (Fig. 8.6). Both are eight-bit codes. If you glance back at the punched-card codes of Chapter 7, you should recognize the hole/no-hole pattern as still another binary code.

Character	EBCDIC	ASCII-8
A	1100 0001	1010 0001
B	1100 0010	1010 0010
C	1100 0011	1010 0011
D	1100 0100	1010 0100
E	1100 0101	1010 0101
F	1100 0110	1010 0110
G	1100 0111	1010 0111
H	1100 1000	1010 1000
I	1100 1001	1010 1001
J	1101 0001	1010 1010
K	1101 0010	1010 1011
L	1101 0011	1010 1100
M	1101 0100	1010 1101
N	1101 0101	1010 1110
O	1101 0110	1010 1111
P	1101 0111	1011 0000
Q	1101 1000	1011 0001
R	1101 1001	1011 0010
S	1110 0010	1011 0011
T	1110 0011	1011 0100
U	1110 0100	1011 0101
V	1110 0101	1011 0110
W	1110 0110	1011 0111
X	1110 0111	1011 1000
Y	1110 1000	1011 1001
Z	1110 1001	1011 1010
0	1111 0000	0101 0000
1	1111 0001	0101 0001
2	1111 0010	0101 0010
3	1111 0011	0101 0011
4	1111 0100	0101 0100
5	1111 0101	0101 0101
6	1111 0110	0101 0110
7	1111 0111	0101 0111
8	1111 1000	0101 1000
9	1111 1001	0101 1001

Figure 8.6
The EBCDIC and ASCII-8 codes. Once again, unlisted bit combinations are used to represent punctuation marks and other special symbols; these symbols are not shown since the pattern of the code is not as obvious. A full listing of these codes can be found in almost any reference manual.

PHYSICAL MEMORY DEVICES

As we can see from the preceding discussion, the ability to manipulate just two characters—a 0 and a 1—limited though it may seem, gives us all kinds of capabilities. We can treat a given combination of 1's and 0's as a pure binary number, giving us the ability to manipulate numbers. Alternatively, we can treat the string of bits as coded data and subdivide it into code groups, giving us the ability to handle alphabetic messages. (Incidentally, computer codes are almost universally fixed-length codes because it is easier to design electronic equipment around a fixed-length format than around a variable-length format.) Anything that can be done with numbers and letters can be done with bits.

How do we go about storing these bits? Almost any device that is capable of holding two states—a light (on/off), a wire (current flowing/no current flowing), an electronic tube (current/no current), a transistor (current/no current), a switch (open/closed)—can be used to store bits. Some devices are better than others, but all could work.

Early computers used electromagnetic relays similar to those shown in Fig. 8.7. An open switch stored a 0-bit; a closed switch stored a 1-bit. To read the contents of memory, all the computer had to do was to pass a current across the wires. If the current flowed, the switch must have been closed, indicating a 1-bit; if no current flowed, the switch must have been open, indicating a 0-bit. However, electromagnetic relays proved to be too bulky, too slow, and too costly, and they have disappeared from the market as memory devices. The big breakthrough leading to their demise was the development of **magnetic core memories**.

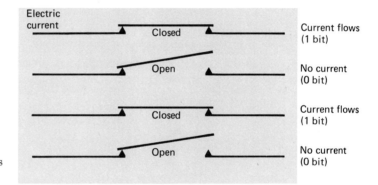

Figure 8.7
Electromagnetic relays as storage devices.

Magnetic core memory takes advantage of the directional properties of a magnet and of the relationship between electricity and magnetism. It is made from tiny donut-shaped rings (cores) of magnetic material (Fig. 8.8). We've all played with bar magnets as children, and most of us know about the north and south poles of a magnet—magnets possess directional properties. But how do we tell the north from the south pole on a ring magnet? Actually, what gives a magnet its directional properties is the alignment of the electronic forces within the material. If enough individual molecules are lined up in the right direction, we have a magnet; that direction determines which is the north and which is the south pole. On a ring magnet, this alignment results in clockwise or counterclockwise magnetization (Fig. 8.9), giving us the necessary two states. We'll arbitrarily use the clockwise state (although the other choice would be just as good) to indicate a 1-bit and the counterclockwise state to indicate a 0-bit and design a computer memory around this assumption.

Core memory is fairly fast, with "slow" core being capable of transferring close to two million characters per second, and "fast" core nearly four million

Figure 8.8
A close-up of magnetic core memory.
Each tiny donut-shaped core is
about the size of the head of a pin.

Clockwise   Counterclockwise

Figure 8.9
The two states of a magnetic core.

characters per second. The cost of core is approximately one-half cent per bit, and, until recently, that price was hard to beat. However, newer solid-state technologies have begun to produce memory devices that are cost-competitive with core, while offering substantially better performance at transfer rates of over eight million characters per second.

Most computer manufacturers are shifting from core to solid-state memories on their latest computers. The primary reason for this is cost. Today, core and solid-state memories are cost-competitive, with core perhaps enjoying a slight edge. But core manufacture is a predominantly manual process, while solid-state devices are made by largely automated processes. The trend in manual labor costs is up; the cost of automated production tends to remain, at worst, constant.

Figures 8.8 and 8.10 show, respectively, core memory and a type of solid-state memory, MOSFET (for Metal Oxide Semiconductor Field Effect Transistor). Solid-state memory is compact, highly reliable, and very fast. Costs are actually dropping on these newer memory technologies.

Core is an example of **random access memory.** The programmer can usually address, access, and change any memory location in core. Solid-state memory having the same characteristics is often called **RAM,** which is short for random access memory.

In some cases, it is not a good idea to allow the programmer to access and (perhaps) change the content of certain memory locations. Consider, for example, the memory holding the program that controls access to a 24-hour bank teller terminal. A skilled but dishonest programmer might be tempted to change the program so that it instructs the machine to dispense all the cash he (or she) wants. Clearly, this is a risk that the bank cannot afford to take. Before solid-state memory became available, the problem might have been solved by designing a hardware circuit to replace the program, a very expen-

Photograph courtesy of IBM Corporation.

Figure 8.10
Solid-state memory chips. These MOSFET (for Metal Oxide Semiconductor Field Effect Transistor) chips each hold 24,576 bits of storage capacity; they are used in the IBM 5100 computer. Yes, that is a teaspoon of sugar.

sive solution. Today, the program is simply stored in a special type of solid-state memory called **read-only memory** (or **ROM**); the name is quite descriptive.

Computer people often refer to a machine's **main memory** as core. In the past, it really was core, and the name made sense. Today, however, most new computers no longer use core, although the term continues to be used to describe the main memory. Over the years, this usage has created a new meaning for the word core: main memory. It will probably continue to be used in this context, in spite of the swing to semiconductor memories.

ADDRESSING MEMORY

Individual bits might be stored on cores or on solid-state devices but, at any rate, we store bits. As we saw earlier in the chapter, bits can be grouped together to form coded characters or binary numbers. Every digital computer has the ability to group bits.

Since IBM is the largest supplier of computers in the world, the reader is more apt to have access to an IBM computer than to the product of any other manufacturer; thus, we will use the IBM System/370 series of computers as an example of how bits are grouped and **addressed.**

The basic unit of memory on an IBM System/360 or System/370 computer is a set of eight bits called a **byte** (Fig. 8.11). Two codes, EBCDIC and ASCII-8, use eight bits to identify a single character. IBM uses the EBCDIC code, storing one EBCDIC character in each byte.

A very simple addressing scheme is used to allow the programmer to indicate a specific byte location in a program. The bytes are numbered sequentially. The first byte in memory is byte number 0 (Fig. 8.11), the second is number 1, the third is number 2, and so on, until all bytes in a given memory have been numbered (the largest possible address in an IBM System/360 or System/370 computer is 16,777,215).

Not all data in the computer is character data; at times, numeric data is needed. If the computer were limited to groupings of eight bits, the largest

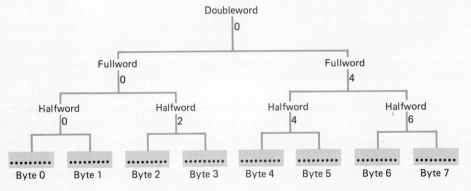

Figure 8.11
Addressing main memory on an IBM System/370.

number that could be stored would be $(11111111)_2$, which is 255. That is not even big enough to compute take-home pay. Additional data groupings are needed. Thus, most computers have the ability to handle a **word** of data.

On an IBM machine, groups of 16 bits or two bytes are wired together to form halfwords (see Fig. 8.11), and groups of 32 bits or four bytes (or two halfwords) are wired together to form (as you may have guessed) fullwords. A halfword, assuming that the first bit is used as a sign, can hold a maximum value of $(0111111111111111)_2$, which is 32,767. A fullword of 32 bits can hold numbers in excess of two billion!

THE CENTRAL PROCESSING UNIT

If a computer could be said to have a brain, the **central processing unit** would be that brain. It's in the central processing unit (or CPU) that the computer carries out its arithmetic and logical functions and where the operation of the entire computer system is controlled.

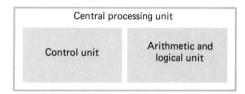

Figure 8.12
The central processing unit.

The CPU is divided into two parts (Fig. 8.12): the **control unit** and the **arithmetic and logical unit.** The function of the control unit is to get a single instruction and to decode it. Once the control unit has figured out what is to be done, control is turned over to the arithmetic and logical unit, which does it. The first step in this cycle is called instruction time, or **I-time.** The second step, involving the arithmetic and logical unit, is called execution time, or **E-time.** Completion of both parts represents one **machine cycle** (Fig. 8.13). That's how a computer works: The control unit figures out what is to be done and turns control over to the arithmetic and logical unit, which performs the task and turns control back to the control unit, which decodes the next instruction and returns control to the arithmetic and logical unit, and on and on in a cyclic pattern.

What exactly do we mean by an **instruction?** Perhaps the best way to visualize the meaning of an instruction is to look at a familiar, close relative of the computer—the pocket calculator. Let's assume that we have a number in the calculator's memory and wish to add another value to it. Depending on the type of calculator we are using, either we enter the number and push the ADD (or +) button, or we push the ADD (or +) button and enter the number; the result in both cases is the same, a very rapid computation of the correct sum. The typing or keying of the number is an input operation. Pressing the ADD

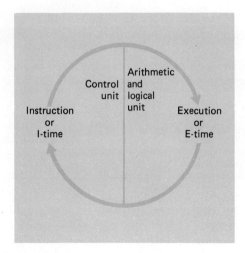

Figure 8.13
A machine cycle.

(or +) button causes the two numbers in question to be allowed to pass through the addition circuitry. The display of the answer is an output operation. In effect, each function button on the calculator represents one instruction in the calculator's instruction set.

THE STORED-PROGRAM CONCEPT

On the calculator, each action (each instruction) involves two distinct steps on the part of the person using the machine. First is a "decision" phase ("What should I do next?") analogous to the function of the control unit of the central processing unit. Second is an "action" phase (push the proper button) analogous to the function of the arithmetic and logical unit.

A computer does *not* work by pushing buttons. The approach described in the preceding paragraph is fine for computing your own grade point average or your own take-home pay, but picture the problems involved in pushing the right buttons in the right sequence 20,000 times to compute everyone's grade point average or everyone's take-home pay. Impossible!

Imagine a mechanical device capable of pushing the right buttons in the right sequence. To help visualize this device, think of a player piano with a paper or rubber roll controlling the striking of the keys. Given such a device, the problem of multiple repetitions would disappear. To do a given computation 20,000 times, we would merely turn the machine on and let it run 20,000 times. The right buttons would be depressed in the right sequence with mechanical precision.

The computer works in much the same way. Rather than using buttons, a computer uses *instructions*. The format of an instruction (Fig. 8.14) is pretty

Figure 8.14
An instruction.

Operation code or op code	Operands

simple, consisting of an operation or **op code** telling the machine *what* to do (add, subtract, multiply, divide, compare, copy) and a series of **operands** providing the machine with such information as

1. where in memory data can be found,
2. where in memory an answer is to be placed,
3. the length of an element of data.

A **program** is simply a series of these instructions stored in main memory. The control unit of the CPU goes into memory, *fetches* one of these instructions, and decodes it. The op code of the instruction tells the machine what to do (this is equivalent to telling it which button to push) and the operands tell the machine what elements of data to do it to. After decoding the instruction, the control unit passes control to the arithmetic and logical unit, which executes the instruction. Then it's back to the control unit, which fetches the next instruction and repeats the cycle.

What makes this approach particularly effective is the fact that the program is stored in the computer's main memory in electronic form. Once an instruction is in the computer, it is nothing more than a string of binary digits. This means that no mechanical motion is involved in executing an instruction. Why is the lack of mechanical motion important? Mechanical motion is very slow when compared with the very rapid speed of electricity moving through a wire; also mechanical components tend to wear out.

Thus we have a **stored program,** so called simply because it is stored in main memory. The program controls the CPU by guiding it through the right instructions in the right sequence. One program might guide the CPU through the computation and printing of payroll checks. Another might cause the machine to compute an arithmetic average, while still another program might read a magnetic tape and print a list of address labels. Since the program exists only as a pattern of binary 1's and 0's in main memory, it is easy to change. By reading a new program (from cards, tape, or a direct access device) into main memory, a computer that had been processing payroll is transformed into an inventory machine or an accounting machine. By simply changing the program, the same set of hardware can be used for any number of different applications; this *general-purpose* nature of the computer is one of its more powerful features.

The ability to work under control of a stored program is what distinguishes a computer from a calculator. (Some of our newer calculators are actually programmable, making the dividing line a bit fuzzy.) We'll cover programming in more detail in later chapters.

THE COMPUTER'S INSTRUCTION SET

A computer adds by allowing two binary numbers to pass through a set of electrical circuits. It multiplies by allowing two binary numbers to pass through another set of electronic circuits. It copies by using still another set of circuits. In fact, each instruction valid on a given computer has its own set of circuitry. The collection of all these electronic components is known as the computer's **instruction set.**

On early computers, these instructions were handwired. They were very expensive, and modifications were made only after careful study. On a modern computer, the circuits are equally complex, but modern production methods have reduced the cost and improved reliability tremendously.

On a modern computer, a set of instruction circuits might be placed on individual circuit cards or boards. These electronic components are then slipped into a cabinet (Fig. 8.15) to form the computer. This approach makes

Figure 8.15
The modular design of a modern computer. This photograph of a Honeywell Level 6 minicomputer shows a CPU, main memory, and control for a number of peripheral devices and communication lines implemented on a series of circuit boards.

the selection of an instruction set a bit more flexible. A business data processing installation might, for example, decide *not* to purchase the floating-point instruction set, having no need for it; the mainframe supplier can easily comply with the customer's wishes by simply pulling or not installing the card containing the floating-point instruction set.

REGISTERS

How does data or an instruction get from main memory to the CPU? On many computers, the answer is "through the registers." A **register** acts as a path or conduit, connecting the two major components of the computer.

Once again, it seems that the best way to explain the functions of a register is by referring to the familiar pocket calculator. We've already seen that the electronic circuits of a calculator are analogous to a CPU. Since most calculators have very limited memory, let's say that our main memory is a sheet of scratch paper. If we wish to add two numbers, it is first necessary to transfer them from the scratch pad (our main memory for this analogy) into the calculator; we do this by keying in the numbers to be added, digit by digit. In effect, we have transferred the data from main memory into a register.

Most computers are designed in a similar manner. Data is first stored in main memory. If two numbers are to be added, one (or both) must first be copied into a register before the ADD instruction can be executed.

Following execution of an ADD on a calculator, the answer is usually displayed (the display is nothing more than a visual copy of what is in the register) so that the operator can copy it to the scratch paper (main memory). Following the execution of an ADD instruction on a computer, the answer is usually dropped into a register, allowing a subsequent instruction to copy it into main memory.

Logically, the registers serve to connect main memory and the CPU. Physically, the registers are actually part of the CPU on most modern computers. Some machines use general-purpose registers, which are available for both addressing and arithmetic. On other computers, the addressing and arithmetic functions are separated. In some cases, the programmer may have access to two special registers called the ACCUMULATOR and the COUNTER, the functions of which should be apparent if you've ever tried to compute a simple average. Many machines have special registers for handling floating-point arithmetic.

The size of a register and the number of registers on a machine varies from manufacturer to manufacturer. Most often, the word size used on a given computer matches the register size; common word sizes include 8, 16, 24, and 32 bits.

Although the size, number, and type of registers can vary, their function remains constant; they are used to transfer information between the CPU and main memory.

A COMPUTER: THE WHOLE PACKAGE

We have finally reached the point where we can put all the components of a computer together. At the top of Fig. 8.16, we see the central processing unit, better known as the CPU, where all the logical and control functions of the computer are carried out. The CPU is subdivided into two parts: the control unit and the arithmetic and logical unit. The control unit is responsible for figuring out exactly what the computer is to do next; the arithmetic and logical unit is responsible for doing it.

At the bottom of the figure is the computer's main memory, consisting of a series of magnetic or electronic devices, each capable of existing in either of two states (0 or 1). These individual bits are grouped together to form bytes, characters, words (depending on the computer manufacturer), or, in general, memory locations. On almost all computers, these memory locations are addressed by assigning them consecutive numbers beginning with 0; we can find the address of a given memory location by simply counting how many memory locations it is away from the first one.

Between the CPU and main memory are a number of registers that serve as pathways or conduits connecting these two components. Registers are actually located in the CPU; Fig. 8.16 illustrates their *logical* position.

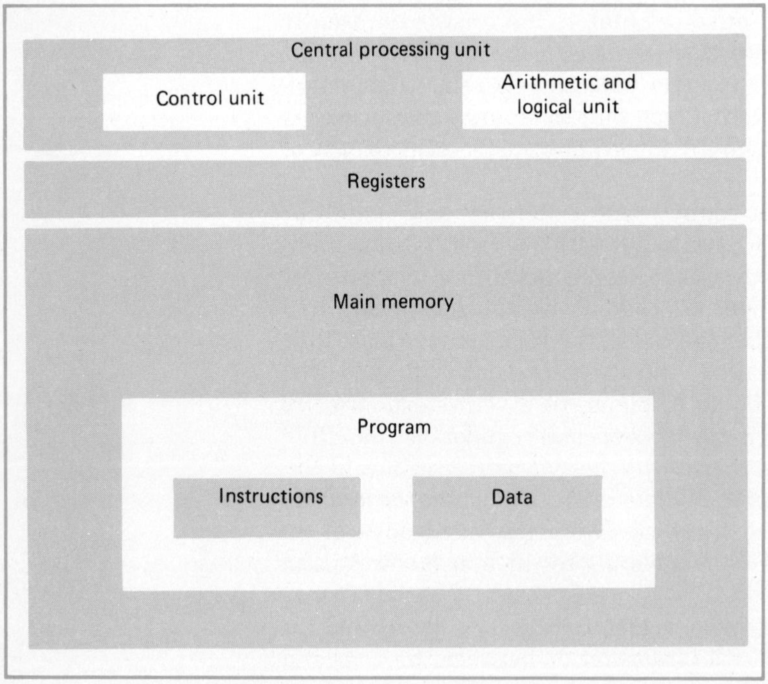

Figure 8.16
The entire computer.

According to many sources, the term *central processing unit* should be applied to the entire computer; in other words, everything shown in Fig. 8.16. If this definition were applied, the CPU would actually include main memory and the registers. However, the standard definition clearly limits the term central processing unit to "the interpretation and execution of instructions," which is the meaning assigned to the term in this text. Although the broader definition of the CPU is technically not correct, you'll still find many people using it.

Another term used to describe a computer is **mainframe.** To many, a computer's mainframe is simply the CPU. Others include the registers and main memory in the definition. Still others argue that the mainframe consists of every component actually included in the same physical "box" as the CPU; this latter definition seems to be the one that is currently popular. Thus, we speak of a computer's mainframe, which houses a CPU, main memory, registers, and perhaps other electronic components as well.

SUMMARY

In this chapter, we introduced the basic concepts of computer memory or storage devices. The chapter began with a discussion of the binary number system, the language of the computer. Key concepts included digit and positional value, the zero (0) digit, and the computer's need for only two digits—0 and 1.

Following the introduction to binary numbers, several binary codes were introduced, including BCD, EBCDIC, and ASCII-8. Finally, we entered a discussion of physical storage media. Until recently, core was *the* primary memory device. Lately, computer technology has been shifting to solid-state memories.

Memory is grouped and addressed within a computer. IBM groups every eight bits together to form a byte; the individual bytes are consecutively numbered from zero up to the limit of a given installation's available memory, thus providing an addressing scheme. Bytes are grouped to form halfwords, which are subsequently grouped to form fullwords; fullwords are themselves grouped into doublewords. Other manufacturers use different schemes for grouping and addressing memory; many use the word as the basic addressable unit. Word sizes may vary, too.

Following the discussion of memory, we turned our attention to the central processing unit or CPU, describing the two main components of the CPU: the control unit and the arithmetic and logical unit. I-time or instruction time and E-time or execution time, the two components of a machine cycle, were defined and illustrated, along with the idea of a stored program. After putting registers in their context, we then presented all the components of a computer as a single package.

KEYWORDS

address

arithmetic and
logical unit

ASCII-8

base

binary

binary coded
decimal (BCD)

bit

byte

central processing
unit (CPU)

code

control unit
portion of CPU

core memory

decimal

digit

digit-times-place-
value rule

EBCDIC

execution time
(E-time)

instruction

instruction set

instruction time
(I-time)

machine cycle

mainframe

main memory

memory

operand

operation (op) code

positional value

program

random access
memory (RAM)

read-only memory
(ROM)

register

storage

stored program

word

EXERCISES

1. Why is binary so well suited to the computer?
2. What is meant by place or positional value?
3. Explain the "digit-times-place-value rule."
4. Explain the difference between numeric and coded data.
5. How is main memory addressed?
6. Integrated circuits and semiconductor memories are beginning to replace core in many modern computers. Why?
7. What is RAM? What is ROM?
8. Explain what is meant by a computer's machine cycle.
9. What are the functions performed by the control unit portion of the central processing unit?
10. What is the difference between the control unit portion of the CPU and the control unit that is found between the computer and an I/O device?
11. What is meant by a stored program?
12. Explain how the idea of a stored program allows a computer to be a general-purpose machine.
13. What is meant by a computer's instruction set?
14. What is the function of a computer's registers?

9
SOFTWARE

OVERVIEW

To this point, we've covered the major hardware components of a computer system in some detail. Software (the actual programs) is different. It's not a physical thing (like hardware) that can be seen or felt; to a certain extent, it's much like a thought. We'll begin this chapter by considering the idea of program logic. The intent of this section is to clearly illustrate that programs must be carefully planned by human beings before being implemented on a computer. Planning is a thought process and not a mechanical or electronic process; don't lose sight of this basic idea. As part of our discussion of the program planning process, we'll consider a very popular aid to planning—flowcharting.

After illustrating a number of basic program planning concepts, we'll move along to the topic of program implementation. Program implementation refers to the task of actually writing and testing a program. Starting with an individual instruction, we'll build from a number of basic concepts, through groups of instructions, to the idea of assembler and compiler languages, finally introducing the idea of complete program logic by showing how a program to compute an arithmetic average can be implemented in several different languages.

SOFTWARE: BASIC CONCEPTS

Software is a collective term for programs. Hardware is physical, while software is *not*. Within the computer, a program is nothing more than a pattern of 1's and 0's in memory, existing only so long as the power remains on. You can't see software, nor can you feel, smell, taste, or hear it.

The transient nature of software allows a computer system to be very flexible. At any given moment, the computer might be running a payroll program, with the collection of hardware components, working under control of a program, producing paychecks from time cards. A few minutes later, following completion of the payroll job, a new program might be placed in the computer, allowing the same collection of hardware components to compute and print end-of-term grade reports for 20,000 students. Another program change might allow a mathematician to use the same hardware to analyze a large amount of data. Still another program change might convert the same physical machine into an inventory processor. The flexibility of software allows a computer to become a true **general-purpose machine.**

What is a program? In Chapter 8, we discussed the computer's instruction set. Most computers are restricted to various forms of the following basic functions:

1. addition,
2. subtraction,
3. multiplication,
4. division,
5. copying,
6. simple yes/no logic,
7. requesting input, and
8. requesting output.

A **program** is nothing more than a series of these instructions. That statement does oversimplify the concept a bit, since the instructions must be the right instructions in the right sequence, but that is *basically* all a program is.

In Chapter 8, as you may recall, we discussed the idea of a stored program. We began by pointing out that in order to solve a problem on a pocket calculator, it is necessary to attack the problem step by step. We then imagined a machine capable of pushing the proper buttons in the correct sequence, in effect putting the calculator under automatic control.

This is essentially what a program does for a computer. The program consists of a series of instructions that tell the computer, step by step, exactly what it is to do. Each instruction tells the computer to perform one of its basic functions—addition, subtraction, multiplication, or any of the other operations listed above. The sequence of instructions determines the order in which these instructions will be performed. A correctly written program will cause the computer to convert input data to accurate output information.

THE PROGRAMMING PROCESS

Programs do not simply "spring into being." Where do they come from? Programs are written by **programmers.** Some human being must tell a computer, step by step, exactly what must be done before a computer can do anything. How does a programmer go about writing a program?

Programming is not quite a science; there is a touch of art involved. Thus it is not surprising to find that different programmers go about the task of writing a program in different ways. There are, however, a number of clearly identifiable steps that are almost always involved in the programming process and that provide a convenient framework for studying this process. In very general terms, these steps are to

1. define the problem,
2. plan a solution,
3. implement that solution, and
4. maintain the program or programs.

In this chapter, we will follow the process of developing a simple program to compute an arithmetic average, moving from problem definition, through planning, and onto the actual coding of the program in a variety of languages. Later, in Part III of the text (Chapters 11 through 14), we will consider the program development process in greater detail.

PROBLEM DEFINITION

The first of these steps, **problem definition,** asks a key question: "What is it we want to do?" It would seem as though this is an obvious starting point, but problem definition tends to be the most frequently bypassed step in the entire process. Almost every computer installation in the country produces at least one report that no one wants and no one uses, a situation that we can probably attribute to the fact that the programmer never thought to ask, "What exactly do you want me to do?"

Thus it is essential that we know what we are going to do *before* we start to do it. Common sense? Sure. But all too often common sense is ignored.

In this chapter, we'll be writing a program to compute an arithmetic average. Assuming that most students know how to compute an average, our problem is defined.

One final comment before we move on to planning. Who is responsible for defining the problem? In some organizations, it's the programmer who, hopefully, arrives at a definition by talking with those who will eventually use the information produced by the program. In other organizations, this responsibility belongs to the systems analyst, another professional. Part of the analyst's job is to clearly define (and in some cases, plan) the work to be done by the programmer.

PLANNING

Planning is a more detailed step. By this stage, the fact that a program will be created has been established, and what is needed is a detailed set of specifications to guide the programmer as he or she begins programming. It is still a good idea to know exactly where you are going before you start, thus the planning step is often subdivided into a number of separate steps, starting with a very general view of the solution to the problem and gradually adding more and more detail.

Often, the very first step in the planning process is to define any **algorithms** needed to solve the problem. An algorithm is simply a rule that leads to an unambiguous solution. We might express the rule using algebraic notation, as in

$$\text{MEAN} = \frac{\sum\limits_{i=1}^{n} X_i}{n}.$$

We might express the rule in English:

1. Add together all the values you wish to average.
2. Divide by the total number of values.

The algorithm need not be a mathematical formula; *any* unambiguous set of rules will do.

The algorithm defines what must be done. Next, we turn our attention to how we might do it. Many programmers start by asking a simple question, "How would I solve this problem by hand?" You might do the following:

1. Write all the numbers in a column.
2. Add the column of figures.
3. Count the number of figures in the column.
4. Divide the sum by the count giving the average.

Now we'll make the job a bit easier by giving you a few machines to aid in making these computations—specifically, a pocket calculator and a mechanical counter. Given this equipment, you might view the problem in a different way. First of all, a pocket calculator doesn't add a column of figures in the same way that you would. When using such a device, you enter the first number, add the second to it, add the third to the sum of the first two, and so on. A calculator adds two numbers at a time. This process is sometimes called accumulation.

The availability of a mechanical counter might change your view of the counting process too. Why go back after adding or accumulating the numbers and count them? Why not simply add 1 to the counter as each number is added to the accumulator? Your method of computing an average with electronic and mechanical aids might include the following steps:

1. Set the accumulator to 0.

2. Set the counter to 0.

3. Add a number to the accumulator.

4. Add 1 to the counter.

5. Repeat steps 3 and 4 until there is no more data.

6. Divide the value in the accumulator by the value in the counter to get the average.

What we have here is a program. It's a series of logical steps that, if followed to the letter, will always result in the computation of an arithmetic average. Although the form of the program is not quite suitable for the computer, it is, logically speaking, a program.

As we begin to analyze this program from a computer's point of view, we must keep in mind the fact that a computer is not a human being. We are capable of exercising independent judgment; a computer is not. The most obvious point of difference, at least in this problem, lies in how people and computers discover that there is no more data to be processed. Consider the fifth step in the set of directions listed above: "Repeat steps 3 and 4 until there is no more data." How do we determine that there are no more numbers? "Simple," says the human, "there aren't any more numbers!" We'd be insulted if someone were to imply that such a simple exercise in logic was beyond us.

This kind of logic *is* beyond the computer. A computer is, as you may remember, restricted to simple yes/no logic. What if a line in our column of figures were to be left blank? What if the numbers were continued on a second or third page? What if a few extra numbers were written along the margins? These situations would pose no problem for us, but such variables involve more than simple yes/no logic.

A computer gets its data from some input device—in our example, we'll use a card reader. We cannot allow the computer to assume that if there is no more data in the card reader, there is no more data to be processed. What if the operator hasn't yet loaded some of the cards? What if the card reader breaks down? What if another program is in the card reader immediately following ours? A human being would be capable of dealing with these problems, but a computer needs a very complex program to deal with every possible contingency.

All this discussion amounts to a very lengthy way of stating something very simple: A computer must be provided with an unambiguous mechanism for determining when there is no more data to be processed. With card input, this objective is usually achieved by using a special "last card." The letters "EOD" might be punched in the first three columns of this last card; the first two columns might contain the characters "/*" or "/&"; or the card might start with "$EOJ". Any combination of unique characters will do equally well. Given this end-of-data marker, the process of identifying the end of data becomes a simple yes/no decision, as follows:

1. Read a card.
2. Are the first two columns equal to /*?
3. If yes, it is the last card.
4. If no, it is not the last card.

With these ideas in mind, we move along to the next step in the program development process: detailed planning.

DETAILED PLANNING

We began the planning process by defining, in very general terms, the steps involved in computing an average. We then proceeded to define in detail the rules for implementing each of these steps. We are now about to begin the process of restating these rules in terms of the basic functions of a computer. Thus, we enter the final planning stage—detailed planning.

Incidentally, you may be wondering why "detailed planning" has been given its own topic heading. Isn't detailed planning a part of planning? Yes it is, but it's very important that you understand the value of step-by-step planning, because many realistic computer problems are much too complex to allow even the best programmer to simply jump in and begin working with the details. By giving detailed planning its own heading, we are emphasizing the importance of this step-by-step approach.

Programmers use a number of different tools to aid in this detailed planning step. One of the more commonly used tools is flowcharting.

Flowcharting

A **flowchart** is a graphical representation of a program. Program logic is defined by using a few standard symbols (see Fig. 9.1); these symbols are connected by lines to indicate the flow of logic through the program. Let's say,

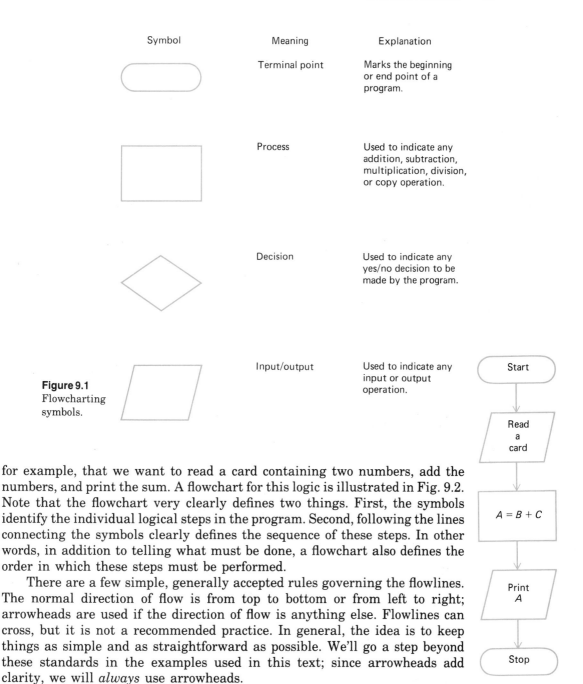

Symbol	Meaning	Explanation
	Terminal point	Marks the beginning or end point of a program.
	Process	Used to indicate any addition, subtraction, multiplication, division, or copy operation.
	Decision	Used to indicate any yes/no decision to be made by the program.
	Input/output	Used to indicate any input or output operation.

Figure 9.1
Flowcharting
symbols.

for example, that we want to read a card containing two numbers, add the numbers, and print the sum. A flowchart for this logic is illustrated in Fig. 9.2. Note that the flowchart very clearly defines two things. First, the symbols identify the individual logical steps in the program. Second, following the lines connecting the symbols clearly defines the sequence of these steps. In other words, in addition to telling what must be done, a flowchart also defines the order in which these steps must be performed.

There are a few simple, generally accepted rules governing the flowlines. The normal direction of flow is from top to bottom or from left to right; arrowheads are used if the direction of flow is anything else. Flowlines can cross, but it is not a recommended practice. In general, the idea is to keep things as simple and as straightforward as possible. We'll go a step beyond these standards in the examples used in this text; since arrowheads add clarity, we will *always* use arrowheads.

Now we're about ready to begin a flowchart of our average program. The finished product is shown in Fig. 9.3. Let's go through it step by step; the steps

Start → Read a card → $A = B + C$ → Print A → Stop

Figure 9.2
A simple flowchart.

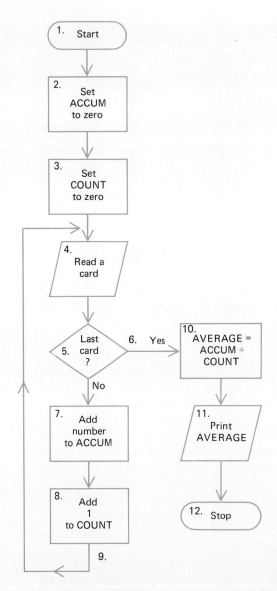

Figure 9.3
A flowchart of the "average" program.

have been numbered to aid in this process. Follow the flowchart carefully as we move through the program, and be sure that you understand exactly what happens in each and every step. The steps are as follows:

1. This is the start of the program.
2. Set ACCUMULATOR register to zero.

3. Set COUNT register to zero. Why must these two steps be completed first?

4. Read a card.

5. Test for last card. Why do we test for last card before accumulating and counting? Do we want to count this last record?

6. If it is the last card, skip to instruction 10.

7. Add the number to the ACCUMULATOR register.

8. Add 1 to the COUNT register.

9. Go back to instruction 4.

10. Divide ACCUMULATOR register by COUNT register.

11. Send a line of output to the printer.

12. Terminate the program.

Having developed a flowchart of our program, we have just about completed the planning phase. The flowchart of Fig. 9.3 very clearly shows, step by step, exactly what the computer must do in order to compute an average. Coding the program now becomes a task of simply translating this logic into the proper computer language, a problem that we will discuss next.

PROGRAM PLANNING: A SUMMARY

The main objective of program planning is to carefully define a solution to a problem down to the point where it can be implemented on a computer. Ideally, the solution should be so well defined following planning that programming becomes little more than the translation of this solution into "computerese." Planning is a step-by-step process, beginning with a very general view of the problem and gradually introducing detail until a computer solution is clearly defined.

IMPLEMENTATION AND MAINTENANCE

The four basic steps in the programming process are definition, planning, implementation, and maintenance. We have already covered the first two in some detail; we must now turn our attention to program implementation and maintenance.

By program implementation, we mean the task of actually converting a problem solution, existing perhaps in the form of a flowchart, into a computer *program.* This task involves a number of clearly identifiable steps. The first of these is **coding;** in other words, actually writing the instructions. It's a rare programmer who can write error-free code; thus a second step in this process is program **debug,** which simply means removing the errors (or *bugs*) from the program. The final step is program **testing.** In this step, the program is used to process realistic, representative data, and the results are compared with expected results. These three steps overlap a great deal, with errors frequently being detected during testing and removed (debugged) by recoding portions of the program.

Maintenance begins after the program is finished. As an example, consider payroll processing. Income tax rates change from year to year, and the new rates must be incorporated into the program; such program changes are part of maintenance. Another common maintenance problem involves the removal of bugs that, for some reason or another, had not been removed during the implementation stage. It's almost impossible to test a program for every possible contingency; even the best of plans will always miss one or two extreme or unusual conditions.

Since maintenance begins after the program has been written, it involves some special problems. The original programmer may well have forgotten the program, hence needing a refresher, or he or she may have left the organization, meaning that someone else must find and fix the bug or make the modification. If a program is to be successfully maintained, it is essential that a very clear and complete description of the logic of the program be available.

A detailed description of a program is normally prepared as part of the implementation stage in a step known as **documentation.** Program documentation consists of program listings, flowcharts, decision tables, narrative descriptions, data formats, and any other information that might help a future maintainer to understand the program. Many organizations have standard formats for program documentation. Frequently the original programmer is required to prepare an acceptable documentation package before a program is officially declared finished. Without good program documentation, maintenance becomes very difficult, if not impossible. Ideally, the programmer should be preparing documentation throughout the implementation stage, integrating this essential task into his or her daily activity.

Programming is the task of actually writing a program; it involves all four steps. A *program* is a series of instructions that tells a computer what to do. What do these instructions look like, and how do they fit together to form a program?

GETTING THE PROGRAM ON THE COMPUTER

Back in Chapter 8, we spent quite a bit of time on the binary number system, explaining that the language of the computer is binary. Main memory is designed to store binary data. The CPU is designed to manipulate bits. If a program is to be stored in main memory and acted upon by the CPU, it must be in binary form.

Clearly, if programmers were required to write all programs in pure binary, there would be very few programmers around. Instead, programs are written in languages such as BASIC, FORTRAN, COBOL, and RPG. Before a computer can actually use the instructions generated by such languages, translation into a binary form is necessary. This translation process is the subject of the next several pages.

We'll begin our discussion at the bottom, with an analysis of the contents and meaning of a single instruction. We'll then combine several of these instructions and show how the translation to binary can be achieved.

AN INSTRUCTION

In Chapter 8 we explained how the central processing unit gets an **instruction** from main memory and figures out what is to be done, turning control over to its arithmetic and logical unit for the actual execution of the instruction. Obviously, if a computer is to work in this way, each instruction must contain the information needed to tell the CPU what to do.

A typical instruction (Fig. 9.4) contains two major fields: an **operation code** (or op code) and a series of **operands.** The op code tells the machine *what* to do: add, subtract, multiply, divide, copy, compare, ... The operands tell the computer "what to do it *to.*" For example, if we, as programmers, wanted to instruct the computer to add the contents of registers 2 and 3, the parts of our instruction might be the following:

Op code   ADD REGISTERS
Operands
  First   2
  Second   3

The op code tells what is to be done (ADD REGISTERS), while the operands tell what memory locations or registers are to participate in the operation (registers 2 and 3 in this example).

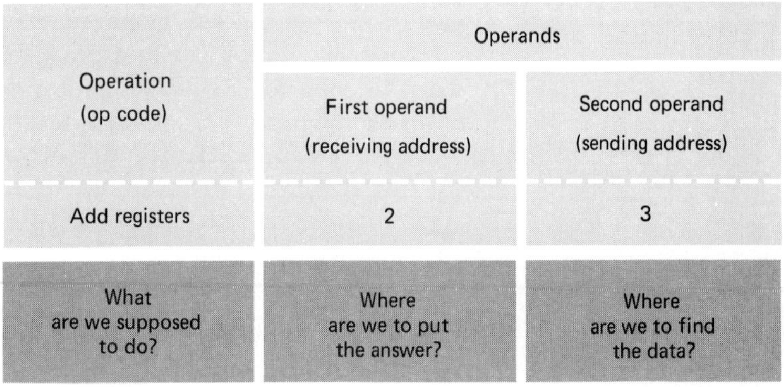

Operation (op code)	Operands	
	First operand (receiving address)	Second operand (sending address)
Add registers	2	3
What are we supposed to do?	Where are we to put the answer?	Where are we to find the data?

Figure 9.4
The parts of a typical computer instruction.

Let's look at another situation. What if our application calls for us to copy an employee's name from the image of an input card (in main memory) to the image of an output line that we are in the process of building in main memory? What is it that we want to do? Copy, or MOVE, data from one memory location to another. Let's assume that the individual's name starts at memory location 1000, and we want to make a copy of this field at memory location 2000. Our instruction might contain the following:

Op code	MOVE
Operands	
First	2000
Second	1000

Why is the target address given first? The designers of the computer used in this example decided that data would move from the second operand location to the first operand location. This decision is an arbitrary one, but if you want to use this computer, that's the way it is. Once you understand the rules, the instruction very clearly says that the data found at memory location 1000 is to be moved to memory location 2000. There is no ambiguity. What do we mean by memory location? Remember (see the discussion in Chapter 8) that every character, or byte, or word (depending on the computer) in main memory is assigned a number indicating its relative position away from the first memory location. This relative position is called an *address*. By memory location, we mean address.

A SINGLE LOGICAL OPERATION: ADDING TWO NUMBERS

Now let's see how a series of instructions can be used to perform a simple logical function such as the addition of two numbers.

Before getting into the actual instructions, it might be wise to review briefly a few hardware concepts. Data, once in the computer, is stored in main memory. Data is processed in the central processing unit. In order to add two numbers, it is first necessary to copy (or LOAD) them into registers, the conduits connecting memory and the CPU. Following addition, we will probably want to copy (or STORE) the answer from a register (where the CPU places it) into memory. Thus, a task as simple as the addition of two numbers really involves four distinct instructions (Fig. 9.5): LOAD/LOAD/ADD/STORE. Instructions, like data, are stored in main memory, which is capable of storing only patterns of 1's and 0's; thus an instruction at the machine level *must* exist in binary form.

On an IBM System/360 or System/370 computer, the op code for loading a number from memory into a register is

01011000

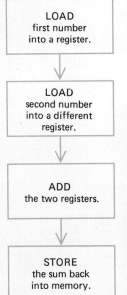

Figure 9.5
Adding two numbers on a computer.

in binary; thus, the first of these four instructions (Fig. 9.6) begins with this eight-bit operation code. The second eight bits are subdivided into two parts: The first four indicate the register that is to receive the data (register 3) and the second four bits hold an index register, a field that we are not using in this instruction. The final 16 bits hold the address of the sending field in main memory (in other words, where, in main memory, the number that is to be loaded into register 3 can be found).

The second instruction (Fig. 9.6) is another load instruction, so its op code is identical to that of the first instruction. Note, however, that the first operand indicates register 4 rather than register 3 and that the address of the second

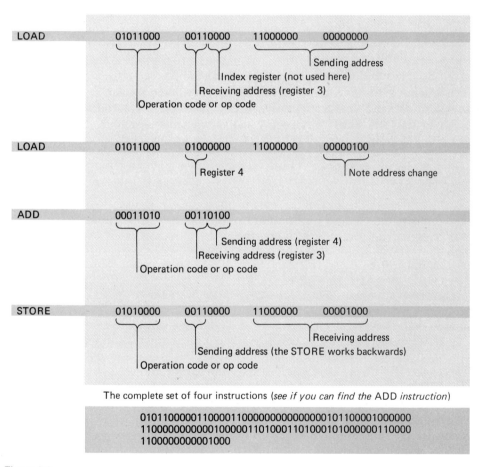

Figure 9.6
The instruction needed to
add two numbers.

operand field in memory is also different. This is a different instruction; it loads a different number into a different register.

Next is the add instruction, whose op code is

00011010

The first operand (four bits) indicates register 3; the second operand (the next four bits) indicates register 4; this instruction (see Fig. 9.6) adds registers 3 and 4, dropping the sum into register 3 (the receiving address register).

Finally, the answer is copied back into main memory. The op code for a store instruction is

01010000

in binary. The first operand identifies register 3 as the one that is to be stored; the second operand gives the address (main memory) where it is to be stored.

At the bottom of Fig. 9.6 is the string of bits representing these four instructions. In the early days of computing, programs were written at this level. Imagine how difficult it would be to find one incorrect bit in that string. And we're only looking at four instructions. A typical program might consist of thousands of such instructions! Fortunately, programmers don't have to get down to the "bit level" anymore because we have assembler and compiler programs to help simplify the task of writing a program.

AN ASSEMBLER PROGRAM

Coding at the binary level is difficult to put it mildly. Even in the early days of data processing, many programmers took shortcuts. One common approach was to write the program in a shorthand form, as follows:

```
LOAD     3,1000
LOAD     4,1004
ADD      3,4
STORE    3,1008
```

After coding the program at this level, the programmer could logically "desk-check" it before converting the **mnemonic codes** shown above to true binary. The conversion was straightforward; the programmer knew that when "LOAD" was coded, he or she really meant $(01011000)_2$ and that "3" really meant $(0011)_2$. Essentially, the programmer converted the program from his or her own mnemonic (meaning "memory aiding") language by replacing each field with its binary equivalent, perhaps using a simple conversion table to aid in this translation process.

Why not write a program to take these mnemonic codes to binary? Logically, the conversion process is fairly simple: Just match the coded operation with an entry in a table and, when an equal code is encountered, substitute. Fig-

Description	Mnemonic	Binary op code
Add memory to register	A	01011010
Add register to register	AR	00011010
Branch on condition	BC	01000111
Compare memory locations	CLC	11010101
Compare registers	CR	00011001
Divide register by memory	D	01011101
Divide register by register	DR	00011101
Load from memory into register	L	01011000
Move data (copy)	MVC	11010010
Multiply register by memory	M	01011100
Multiply register by register	MR	00011100
Store register in memory	ST	01010000
Subtract memory from register	S	01011011
Subtract register from register	SR	00011011

Figure 9.7
Some typical mnemonic operations codes
(IBM System/360 and System/370).

ure 9.7 shows a series of mnemonic operation codes that are valid on IBM's
System/360 and System/370 computers, along with their associated binary op
codes. Using the codes in this table, it is relatively easy to convert mnemonic
operation codes to their binary equivalents. Can this be done by a program? Of
course. All we're dealing with is the yes/no logic available to a computer.

To illustrate this idea, let's try converting a mnemonically coded instruction such as

AR   3,4

to a binary instruction. The op code is AR. Refer to Fig. 9.7, and start at the
top. Is AR equal to A? Obviously not. Move along to the next op code. Is AR
equal to AR? Yes! We've found the correct op code. Our table tells us to use

00011010

as the binary op code for this instruction. What about the operands? Do you
remember the computer instructions designed to convert data type? Simply
convert the "3" and the "4" to binary, and you have a complete instruction

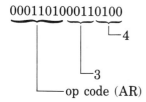

Other instructions can be converted using the same method.

The program that performs this job is called an **assembler.** An assembler
program (Fig. 9.8) reads a programmer's **source code,** written in the mnemonic language, and converts it to **object code,** which is another term for

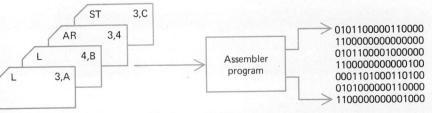

Figure 9.8
An assembler program.

machine-level binary code. A programmer writing at this level is said to be programming in an *assembler-level* language.

Note the instructions in Fig. 9.8. We load a value into register 3 by coding

L   3,A

which is much easier to understand than its binary equivalent

0101100000110000110000000000000000

The responsibility for converting assembler-level instructions into machine-level object code belongs to the assembler program. All the programmer must do is follow the rules.

We do pay a price for this benefit. We are no longer writing programs that can be directly executed on a computer. Programming is now a two-step operation: (1) load the assembler program and convert the source code to object code, and (2) load and execute the object code.

Most computer mainframe manufacturers provide an assembler program with their machine. There are no national standards on assemblers; they vary significantly from manufacturer to manufacturer. However, these languages do share one common feature: The programmer codes one mnemonic instruction for each machine-level instruction.

COMPILERS

Why must the programmer code two loads and a store just to add two numbers? Logically, all he or she wants to do is add; the loads and store are used because that's the way the machine works. Why not assume these steps? That's the basic idea behind a **compiler** (Fig. 9.9).

A scientist or engineer who wishes to add two numbers would probably express the problem as an algebraic equation:

$$C = A + B.$$

The computer may need the two loads and the store, but the programmer logically has no need for anything but the add instruction. Why not let a program take care of inserting these instructions, particularly when we know

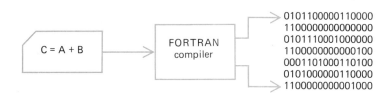

Figure 9.9
A FORTRAN compiler.

that in almost all cases, the addition of two numbers involves essentially these same four instructions?

FORTRAN, which stands for FORmula TRANslator, was developed in the mid-1950s with exactly this idea in mind. The FORTRAN programmer can express program logic by writing a series of instructions that look very much like algebraic expressions, ignoring the details of exactly how these operations will be implemented on a given computer. These source statements are fed into a FORTRAN compiler, which converts or translates the statements into acceptable machine-level object code (Fig. 9.9).

Note, by comparing Figs. 9.8 and 9.9, that the same object code is produced by both the assembler program and the FORTRAN compiler. This shouldn't surprise you. The instructions that are actually executed by the computer *must* be binary instructions. You must have valid binary instructions in the computer before it can do anything.

COBOL programs are written according to the rules imposed by a COBOL compiler; COBOL source statements pass through the COBOL compiler (Fig. 9.10) on the way to becoming machine-level instructions. RPG source statements pass through an RPG compiler; a BASIC program goes through the BASIC compiler.

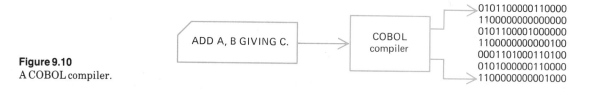

Figure 9.10
A COBOL compiler.

Other compilers, which we'll just mention at this time, include APL (A Programming Language), PL/1 (Programming Language One), ALGOL (ALGOrithmic Language), GPSS (General-Purpose System Simulator), and many, many more. If you were to define your own set of rules for producing valid machine-level code, you could design your own personal compiler. More often, however, assemblers and compilers are provided by the computer manufacturer.

Take very careful note of the fact that each of these compilers is different; a FORTRAN source program would be pure gibberish to a COBOL compiler.

Each compiler is designed to accept source statements written according to a particular set of rules and convert these statements to machine-level instructions. Imagine that the machine-level language is Latin and that each of the compiler languages is a modern language such as English, Spanish, French, German, Japanese, Russian, Chinese, or Swahili. Now imagine a number of translators whose job it is to translate from the source language into Latin. The objective of each translator is the same: Latin. Each translator is, however, different, since the source languages are different. That's the basic idea of a compiler.

THE COMPILATION PROCESS

A compiler is a program designed to translate source statements, written according to a specific set of rules, into object code. The program in its original, compiler language form is called a source program or source module. After translation, the machine-level version of the program is called an **object module.** A flowchart of this translation process is shown in Figure 9.11.

The compilation process (Fig. 9.11) is a two-step process. First the proper compiler (or assembler) program must be loaded into memory. The compiler reads the source statements and translates them into object-module form; usually, the object module is written to a high-speed storage medium such as magnetic tape or disk, although punched-card output (an *object deck*) is sometimes used. Later, this object module is itself loaded into the computer's main memory, and the **application program** begins to execute.

Incidentally, not all object modules can be directly loaded and executed. Programmers often make use of subprograms and other prewritten modules that must be added to the object code by another special program called a linkage editor. We'll discuss this program in more detail in a later chapter.

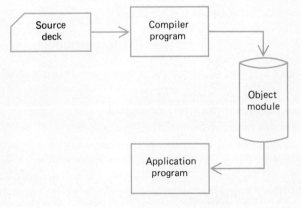

Figure 9.11
The compilation process.

CODING OUR SOLUTION

Earlier in the chapter, we planned a solution to the problem of computing an arithmetic average, developing a flowchart (Fig. 9.3). The time has come to convert that plan into a program. Without getting into excessive details, let's consider how this program might look in three of the more commonly used programming languages: BASIC, FORTRAN, and COBOL. Later, in Part III, we'll get into the detailed rules of each of these languages; for now, just read the programs.

A **BASIC** version of the average program is shown in Fig. 9.12. The first instruction, LET A = 0, initializes an accumulator called A to the value zero; the second instruction does the same for the counter. These two instructions correspond with blocks 2 and 3 of the flowchart of Fig. 9.3.

The next series of instructions is to be repeated until all input data has been accumulated and counted. Basically (no pun intended), the logic calls for us to read a record, add the value to an accumulator, add 1 to a counter, and then come back and read the next record, continuing this process until there is no more data. See if you can follow the logic in Fig. 9.12. The only trick is the last record check; we will simply enter a negative number to indicate that all records have been processed.

Move on to statement number 100 (Fig. 9.12), where the instruction says LET M = A / C. Can you see how this instruction tells the computer to compute an average? Finally, the functions of the PRINT statement and the END statement should be obvious. See if you can relate the BASIC logic to our flowchart (Fig. 9.3). A program really isn't difficult to follow if you simply take your time and read carefully.

A **FORTRAN** version of our program should be even easier to follow, if only because FORTRAN allows the programmer to more fully define variable names. Rather obviously, the first two instructions in Fig. 9.13 tell the computer to set an accumulator and a counter to zero. The next five tell the machine to read a record, accumulate, count, and then to go back and read another

```
100 LET A=0
110 LET C=0
120 INPUT X
130 IF X<0 THEN 170
140 LET A=A+X
150 LET C=C+1
160 GOTO 120
170 LET M=A/C
180 PRINT "AVERAGE = ";M
190 END
```

Figure 9.12
The "average" program in BASIC.

```
      ACCUM=0.0
      COUNT=0.0
30    READ (5,35,END=80) X
35    FORMAT (F5.2)
      ACCUM = ACCUM + X
      COUNT = COUNT + 1.0
      GO TO 30
80    AVG = ACCUM / COUNT
      WRITE (6,95) AVG
95    FORMAT (' AVERAGE = ',F6.2)
      STOP
      END
```

Figure 9.13
The "average" program in FORTRAN.

record; the "END = 80" part of the READ instruction tells the system what instruction to *branch* to after the last-record indicator has been encountered. The only potential mystery in this group of statements is the FORMAT instruction; it tells the computer that X is a 5-digit number with two digits to the right of the decimal point. The last few instructions clearly tell the machine to compute and print (or WRITE) the average and then to STOP the program.

BASIC and FORTRAN are examples of *computational* languages. They were designed primarily for the scientist or engineer who wants to use the computer to solve a problem. As a result, both tend to emphasize making the initial coding task as easy as possible. A good percentage of typical BASIC and FORTRAN programs are one-time applications, written to solve a current problem and then discarded.

The typical business application is quite different. Consider, for example, payroll. Because there are so many factors to be considered in processing payroll, such programs are usually quite large. Employees must be paid week, after week, after week; thus the payroll program is expected to have a very long life. During this long lifetime, changes (a new income tax rate, for example) will occur, and must be accommodated. Many other business applications could be cited as having the same general characteristics: large, frequently changed, and long lived. The "quick-and-dirty" code of the BASIC or FORTRAN programmer simply will not do in such an environment. What is needed is a language that clearly, explicitly, and thoroughly describes the logic of a program. In the majority of business establishments, that language is **COBOL.**

Consider the COBOL version of our average program as shown in Fig. 9.14. It begins with an IDENTIFICATION DIVISION that gives the reader some general information about the program—pure documentation. Next comes the ENVIRONMENT DIVISION; here, the environment (computer and I/O devices) under which the program is designed to run is clearly defined. The third division is the DATA DIVISION, where the precise format of the input record, output record, and any necessary work fields (such as the accumulator and the counter) are defined.

Finally, we reach the PROCEDURE DIVISION, where the actual program logic is coded; BASIC and FORTRAN started here. Read the COBOL logic. Just read it. Isn't it much easier to follow than either the BASIC or the FORTRAN program? That's the strong point of COBOL. Now consider the other side of the question: which program would you rather type, the BASIC, the FORTRAN or the COBOL version?

BASIC and FORTRAN will be covered in greater detail in Chapter 13; COBOL and another business language, RPG, will be discussed in Chapter 14. The point of this exercise was not to teach you how to write computer programs, but to give you some feel for the logic of a program.

```
IDENTIFICATION DIVISION.
   PROGRAM-ID. AVERAGE.
   AUTHOR. DAVIS.
   REMARKS. THIS PROGRAM READS A SERIES OF DATA CARDS,
            COUNTS THE CARDS, ACCUMULATES THE VALUES
            PUNCHED ONE TO EACH CARD, AND, AFTER THE
            LAST CARD HAS BEEN READ, COMPUTES THE
            AVERAGE VALUE.


ENVIRONMENT DIVISION.
   CONFIGURATION SECTION.
    SOURCE-COMPUTER. IBM-370-148.
    OBJECT-COMPUTER. IBM-370-148.
   INPUT-OUTPUT SECTION.
    FILE-CONTROL.
     SELECT CARD-FILE ASSIGN TO UT-S-SYSIN.
     SELECT PRINT-FILE ASSIGN TO UT-S-SYSOUT.


DATA DIVISION.
 FILE SECTION.
   FD   CARD-FILE        LABEL RECORD IS OMITTED.
   01  INPUT-CARD.
      02 NUMBER-IN       PICTURE 999V99.
      02 FILLER          PICTURE X(75).


   FD   PRINT-FILE       LABEL RECORD IS OMITTED.
   01  OUTPUT-LINE.
      05 FILLER          PICTURE X(14).
      05 MESSAGE-OUT     PICTURE X(10).
      05 AVERAGE         PICTURE 999.9999.
      05 FILLER          PICTURE X(100).


 WORKING-STORAGE SECTION.
   77 ACCUMULATOR        PICTURE 99999V99.
   77 COUNTER            PICTURE 999.


PROCEDURE DIVISION.
        OPEN INPUT CARD-FILE.
        OPEN OUTPUT PRINT-FILE.
        MOVE ZEROS TO ACCUMULATOR, COUNTER.


    TOP-OF-LOOP.
        READ CARD-FILE    AT END PERFORM FIND-AVERAGE.
        ADD NUMBER-IN TO ACCUMULATOR.
        ADD 1 TO COUNTER.
        GO TO TOP-OF-LOOP.


    FIND-AVERAGE.
        MOVE SPACES TO OUTPUT-LINE.
        DIVIDE ACCUMULATOR BY COUNTER GIVING AVERAGE.
        MOVE 'AVERAGE = ' TO MESSAGE-OUT.
        WRITE OUTPUT-LINE AFTER ADVANCING 3 LINES.

        CLOSE CARD-FILE.
        CLOSE PRINT-FILE.
        STOP RUN.
```

Figure 9.14
The "average" program in COBOL.

SUMMARY

This chapter began with a basic definition of software and then moved into a discussion of the programming process. The four major steps in this process are (1) problem definition, (2) planning, (3) implementation, and (4) maintenance.

Problem definition, as the term implies, involves determining exactly what must be done. It is essential that the programmer know the purpose and intent of a program before beginning to write that program.

The planning stage represents an attempt to fully define a specific solution to the point of implementation on a computer. Starting with a general view of the essential steps in the program, details are added layer by layer until a detailed plan, often in the form of a flowchart, is produced. Moving along, we covered the last two steps in the program development process: implementation and maintenance, starting at the bottom, with a single instruction. The parts of a typical instruction, operation or op codes and operands, were discussed.

Next, we moved up to a series of instructions designed to perform a single logical function—adding two numbers. The instructions were first shown at a binary, machine level and, subsequently, in assembler FOR-TRAN, and COBOL; in this way, the basic idea of compilation was introduced.

Moving up one level, we showed the logic of a typical application, computing an average, and proceeded to write this program in BASIC, FORTRAN, and COBOL. The idea of compilation, with source statements being converted to an object module, was then covered.

KEYWORDS

algorithm	FORTRAN	program
application program	general-purpose computer	program implementation
assembler language	instruction	program planning
BASIC	maintenance	program testing
COBOL	mnemonic code	programmer
coding	object module	software
compiler	operand	source code
debug	operation code	
documentation	problem definition	
flowchart		

EXERCISES

1. What is software? How does it differ from hardware?
2. What is a program?
3. What is meant by problem definition? Why is it important that this step be completed first?
4. What is the objective of the planning phase of the program development process?
5. What is a flowchart? Develop a flowchart showing all the steps involved in starting an automobile.
6. Explain the two major parts of a typical instruction: the op code and the operands.
7. Why must machine-level programs be in binary form?
8. What advantages are derived from using the mnemonic codes of an assembler language rather than coding at the machine level?
9. What is a compiler?
10. What is a source program or source module?
11. What is an object module?
12. It has been said that once a problem has been fully defined, the task of programming it becomes one of simply translating the solution into a computer programming language. Do you agree or disagree? Why?

10

THE COMPUTER SYSTEM

OVERVIEW

A primary purpose of this chapter is to tie together all the material covered in Chapters 6 through 9 and present it in the form of a complete, integrated computer system. There is one key component we have yet to cover—the channel; thus channels will be our first major topic. Finally, we will move inside a computer, discuss a few basic concepts of computer architecture, and use this discussion as a springboard for explaining the differences between microcomputers, minicomputers, and the large main-frames.

THE PARTS OF A COMPUTER SYSTEM

Throughout this section, we've been concentrating, one at a time, on the various components of a computer system. Our analysis began in Chapter 5, with a discussion of computer history. An overview of the computer's components followed. Next, we examined the devices that are used to transfer data into a computer and to transfer information out—the input and output devices. After I/O, we turned our attention to the computer itself, describing the functions and characteristics of main memory, the central processing unit, and registers. Finally, we considered the programs that control the actions of a computer.

Individually, these components are useless. It's only when they are combined to form a complete computer system that they become useful. In order for a computer to successfully convert data into information, all the components—the input device, main memory, the registers, the CPU, and the output device—must function together, in concert. The failure of any one component means the failure of the entire system.

Our objective in this chapter is to summarize Part II of the text, showing how all the parts of a computer system fit together. Before we do this, we must spend some time discussing one key component which, until now, has gone unmentioned. That component is the data **channel,** and its function is to connect input and output devices to the system.

TYING IN I/O

Back in Chapter 7, the concept of a control unit was introduced. (The control unit we are now discussing is quite different from the control unit portion of the CPU, which decodes program instructions.) The control unit, as you may remember, is responsible for converting the code used by an I/O device (the card reader's 12-bit code, for example) into the computer's internal code, a process known as **standard interface.** The control unit serves to connect an I/O device to a computer but cannot do the entire job alone.

There are a number of logical functions that must be performed during an I/O operation. Let's use a simple example, that of reading a card, to illustrate. What is really meant when a computer requests the input or transfer of "one card's worth" of information from a card reader? If we assume a standard 80-column card is used it means that 80 characters of data are to be moved, one at a time, from the card reader through a control unit, where they are converted into EBCDIC (or similar coded) form, and then into 80 consecutive memory locations in the computer's main memory. There are two very important logical functions that must be performed in support of the transfer of data. The first function is counting. How is the equipment to "know" that exactly 80 characters of data have been transferred if it doesn't count them? Counting is a logical function.

The other logical function is addressing. Following the transfer of the 40th character from the card to, let's say, memory location 1023, where does the 41st character go? Memory location 1024, obviously. How do we get from 1023 to 1024? Simple—we add 1. Addition is also a logical function.

Within a computer, logical functions are performed by the CPU. Thus on early computers, the CPU was responsible for physically controlling an I/O operation by keeping track of the number of characters transferred and the address of the "next" character in main memory. Many modern computers, particularly minicomputers and other small or mid-sized machines, still use the CPU in this way, attaching control units to a device called an **integrated adapter** (Fig. 10.1), which is physically located in the same "box" as the CPU. These integrated adapters function by "stealing" machine cycles from the CPU to support the character-counting and addressing operations.

There is nothing wrong with cycle stealing; it is a reasonable and fairly inexpensive way of controlling I/O. When the central processing unit is concentrating its energies on counting characters and updating addresses, however, it isn't performing useful work on an application program. On a smaller machine, this does not represent a great deal of waste, but as computers become bigger and faster and as more and more input and output devices are attached to the mainframe, controlling each and every I/O operation becomes a burden. The solution to the problem is the **channel** (Fig. 10.2), which is

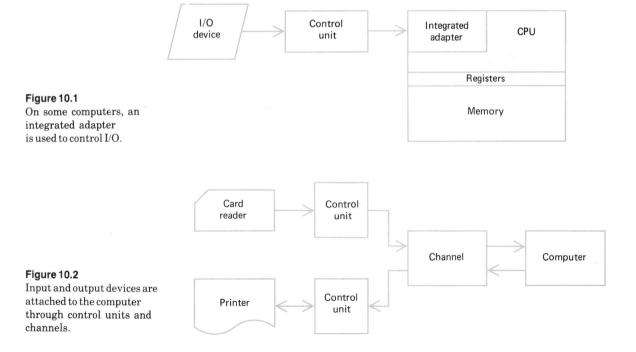

Figure 10.1
On some computers, an integrated adapter is used to control I/O.

Figure 10.2
Input and output devices are attached to the computer through control units and channels.

essentially a special-purpose minicomputer placed between one or more control units and the computer. The channel's functions are to count characters and update main memory addresses, thus taking over responsibility for controlling an I/O operation and freeing the central processing unit to perform other tasks.

Most computers support two different types of channels. The first, called a **multiplexer** (Fig. 10.3), is designed to attach low-speed I/O devices such as card readers and printers. Compare the speed of a card reader—a rate of perhaps 1000 characters per second—with the speed of a computer, which is capable of manipulating millions of characters per second. Obviously a computer can easily keep up with a number of card readers. The multiplexer allows dozens of low-speed I/O devices to be handled concurrently by overlapping, or **multiplexing,** their operation, getting one character from a card reader, sending one character to a card punch, sending one character to a printer, and then coming back to the card reader to wait for the next character to be read at the relatively low rate of 1000 characters per second.

Multiplexing implies buffering. Think about it for a minute: How can a device such as a multiplexer channel possibly handle a number of devices

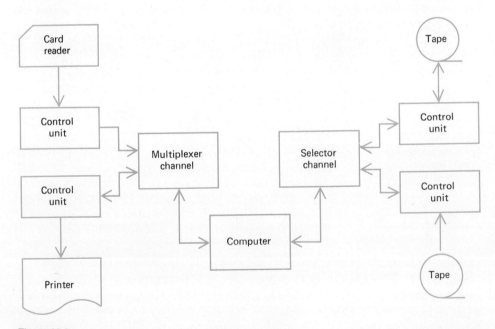

Figure 10.3
Multiplexer channels are used to connect slower I/O devices; selector channels are used for high-speed I/O.

concurrently without some means of "taking up the slack" when the inevitable conflict occurs? In our discussion of buffering (Chapter 7), we mentioned the need for a buffer to overcome the rather obvious disparity between the speed of a human typist and that of a computer, indicating that the buffer is frequently found in the control unit. Buffering at the control unit level is important to the proper functioning of a channel. What happens, for example, if a multiplexer channel is working on so many concurrent operations that it doesn't get back to a given card reader before the "next" column is read? With the use of buffering, the card reader simply drops the character into the control unit's buffer and proceeds to the next column; when the channel does get back to the card reader, it will find the data in the buffer.

In order to avoid possible conflicts in transferring data into main memory, many channels contain buffers. The steps involved in a typical I/O operation, to cite one example, begin with data moving from a card through a card reader and into a control unit's buffer, from the control unit into the multiplexer channel's buffer, and, eventually, into main memory.

High-speed input and output devices, such as magnetic tape, disk, and drum (to be covered in detail in a subsequent chapter), are normally attached to the computer through a different type of channel called a **selector** (Fig. 10.3). Unlike the multiplexer channel, a selector channel is designed to handle the transmission of data between main memory and a single I/O device at a time. Since these devices are relatively fast, the advantages of overlapping or multiplexing I/O operations are not as great. In effect, a selector channel serves as a high-speed data path connecting a single I/O device to the computer, with data being transferred in what is known as the *burst mode*. After completing an operation, the channel can then be used to connect the computer to another high-speed I/O device. A selector channel, like its multiplexer counterpart, counts characters and updates addresses, freeing the central processing unit from this responsibility.

Although the so-called high-speed devices (such as tape, drum, and disk) are very fast when compared with card readers and printers, they are still quite slow in relation to the computer's internal-processing speeds. On some extremely fast computers, special selector channels actually overlap a number of high-speed I/O operations; these channels are called **block multiplexers.**

Interrupts

The function of a channel is to free the CPU from the responsibility for actually controlling an I/O operation, thus allowing it to devote its time to other activities. If a channel is to really free the CPU, it must be capable of working independently of the CPU. Channels do work independently; in fact, during an I/O operation, the channel and the CPU each goes about its own business, giving absolutely no consideration to the actions of the other. In technical terms, we say that the two devices function *asynchronously,* with no regular time relationship.

How then can the CPU know when an I/O operation is completed? It must know, since it makes no sense to start processing data until that data is actually in the computer. In order to inform the central processing unit that an input or output operation has been completed, the channel sends an electronic signal called an **interrupt.** The word "interrupt" is very descriptive of what happens; in effect, the channel, by sending this electronic signal, tells the CPU to stop what it's doing and make a note of the fact that the I/O is done. After processing the interrupt, the computer simply continues its work as if nothing had happened.

Interrupts are used for purposes other than CPU/channel communications. Other examples include communication between two CPU's, communication between the computer operator and the CPU, and the recognition of certain types of error. Whenever we want the CPU to stop its normal activity, handle some unusual condition, and then return to normal activity, we use an interrupt.

COMPUTER SYSTEMS

We have now covered all of the major components of a **computer system** (see Fig. 10.4). Let's put the pieces together. The system begins with the computer itself, which is subdivided into three major parts: the central processing unit (CPU), registers, and memory. Within memory, we find both program instructions and data; since programs and data are stored as nothing more than a pattern of 1's and 0's on a two-state device such as core (or its equivalent), they are easily changed, allowing the machine to process a number of records and then to switch quickly to another program that can process several "different" records.

The central processing unit is subdivided into two parts: the control unit and the arithmetic and logical unit. The control unit is responsible for getting (fetching) an instruction from memory and decoding it—in other words, for figuring out what the program is to do. Control is then transferred to the arithmetic and logical unit, which executes the specified instruction. Next, it's back to the control unit, where the process is repeated. The registers serve as paths or conduits connecting main memory and the CPU.

Outside the computer, we find low-speed I/O devices such as card readers and printers attached to the computer first through a control unit (Fig. 10.4), which buffers the data and converts the code of the input or output device to the code expected by the computer (standard interface), and then through a multiplexer channel, which again buffers the data and performs the logical functions of counting characters and keeping track of main-memory addresses. A multiplexer channel can multiplex or overlap a number of I/O operations.

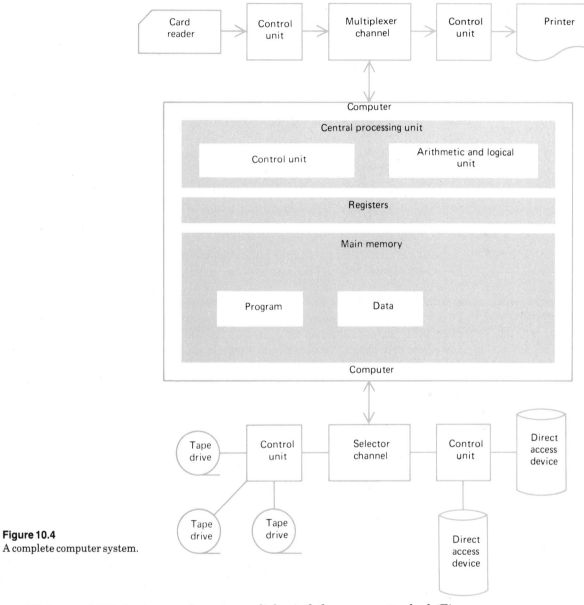

Figure 10.4
A complete computer system.

High-speed I/O devices such as tape, disk, and drum are attached (Fig. 10.4) first through a control unit and then through a selector channel. A selector channel performs the same counting and addressing functions that a multiplexer does, but it doesn't overlap I/O operations, transmitting data between main memory and one device at a time in burst mode.

All these components together compose a typical computer system. The term **system** is important, since it implies a collection of different components, all of which must work together to achieve an objective. Without input data, the computer, which is a data processing machine, would have no data to process. Without control units and channels, the input of data would be impossible. Once in the computer, data is processed through the combined efforts of memory, registers, and the control unit and arithmetic and logical unit of the central processing unit. Of course, without output, there's no point in processing data. Computers work for the benefit of people, not computers; thus, if people cannot read and analyze the computer's results, those results are meaningless.

LINKING THE COMPONENTS

Bus Lines

A computer consists of a number of components that must work together. We have seen how instructions are stored in main memory, transferred to the control unit portion of the CPU during I-time, and executed by the arithmetic and logical unit of the CPU during E-time. We have seen how data is transferred from an input device, through an I/O control unit, through a channel, and eventually into main memory. In our earlier discussions, we have concentrated on how these components are *logically* related; in other words, we have discussed what takes place without really explaining *how* things happen. Obviously, if you think about it, the fact that instructions are transferred between main memory and the CPU implies that there must be some physical connection between these two components. Likewise, a physical connection is needed to support the transfer of data between the channel and the main memory. These physical connections are normally achieved by using special electric cables or links called **bus lines.**

Consider, for example, the relationship between the control unit portion of the CPU and other internal components. One bus line (Fig. 10.5) will be used to connect the control unit with main memory. During I-time, a command will be sent over this bus line requesting the transfer of a single instruction. The instruction will, consequently, be transferred over the bus line and into the CPU, where it can be decoded. A signal over the bus line from the control unit to the arithmetic and logical unit (Fig. 10.5) is used to start the execution of the instruction.

An instruction manipulates data. The data is most likely found in main memory and must be transferred to the CPU for processing. A command from the arithmetic and logical unit to main memory via the bus line (Fig. 10.6) causes the desired data to be placed on the line and transferred. Perhaps, this bus line terminates in a register; thus the data is now accessible to the CPU.

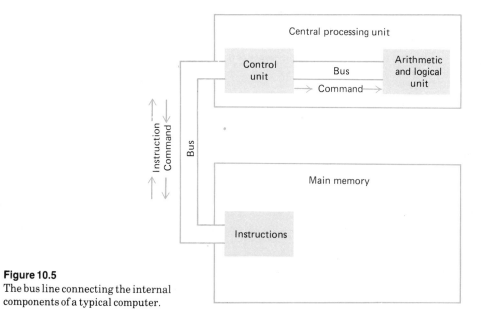

Figure 10.5
The bus line connecting the internal components of a typical computer.

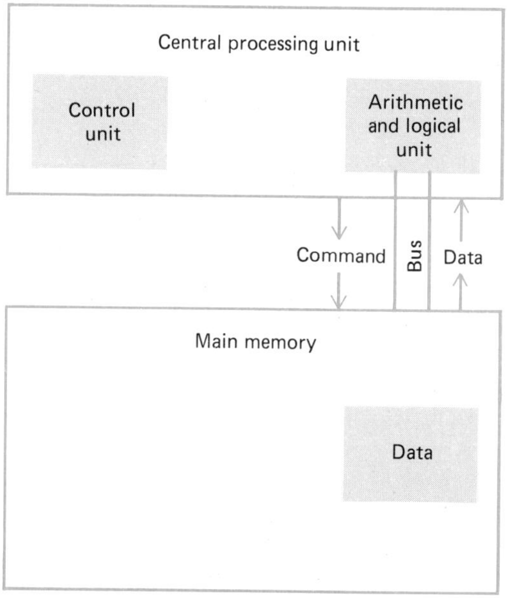

Figure 10.6
The arithmetic and logical unit and main memory are also linked by a bus line.

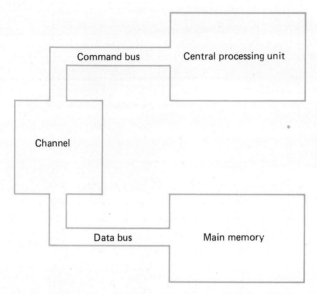

Figure 10.7
A typical computer/channel linkage.

The CPU, main memory, and a channel are linked in a similar manner. One bus might connect the channel and the CPU (Fig. 10.7), while a different line connects the channel and main memory. An I/O operation begins when the CPU (control unit portion) sends a command to the channel over the first bus line. Data is transferred from the device, through a control unit (I/O), through the channel, and into main memory via the second bus line. The CPU is notified on completion of the operation by an interrupt signal sent over the first bus line.

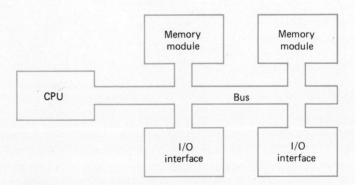

Figure 10.8
Single-bus architecture. (*Note:* An "I/O interface" might work as a channel or an integrated adapter, depending on the computer.)

Not all computers are designed the same way. Some use multiple bus lines, with a command bus transmitting commands such as "start I/O" or "fetch memory contents," an address bus transmitting addresses, an instruction bus sending instructions between main memory and the CPU, and a data bus for data transfers. Other machines are designed around a single "uni-" bus (Fig. 10.8), with all components communicating their commands, addresses, instructions, and data over a single line. Which architecture is best? That depends on the application.

Word Size

In Chapter 8, the idea of a computer **word** was introduced. We started with bits and grouped them to form bytes. A byte was too small for all but the most trivial arithmetic, so we considered a larger (usually) grouping of bits and called it a word. In one example, on the IBM System/370 series of computers, 32 bits (or four bytes) formed a word.

Actually, a word is more than just a grouping of bits in main memory. Often, all the internal components of a computer are designed around a word size. On a 32-bit word computer, for example, data is transferred from main memory to the CPU over a 32-bit bus line, placed in a 32-bit register, and manipulated by an arithmetic and logical unit designed to work best with 32-bit numbers. On a 16-bit word computer, data is transferred over a 16-bit bus line, dropped into a 16-bit register, and manipulated by a 16-bit capacity arithmetic and logical unit.

Why are these numbers so important? Consider bus lines first. Imagine that a great deal of traffic must cross a river. What would be faster, a single lane bridge or a 4-lane bridge? Obviously, we can move more traffic over a multilane bridge in a given amount of time simply because the cars can pass in parallel, rather than in single file. What would be faster, a 4-lane bridge or an 8-lane bridge? Clearly, the wider the bridge, the more cars can cross in parallel, and thus the more cars can cross in a given period of time.

A bus line is used to transfer bits between the various components of a computer. The wider the bus line, the more bits we can transfer in parallel. The more bits we can transfer in parallel, the faster we can transfer those bits. A 32-bit word computer will typically have a bus line that is 32 bits wide. A 16-bit computer will typically have a 16-bit bus. The 32-bit machine will be faster.

Consider also the amount of data transferred over the bus line. A 32-bit number is clearly bigger than a 16-bit number. Imagine that the number represents an address. The big machine might be able to manipulate addresses as big as 32 bits (about 2 billion in decimal terms), while a 16-bit machine will be limited to a 16-bit address (about 32,000). Memory locations on a computer are addressed by simply counting them—0, 1, 2, ... With 16 bits, we can't count beyond about 32,000, and thus we cannot have more than 32,000 main memory locations. On a 32-bit machine, we could have as many as 2 *billion* memory locations. In general, the bigger the word size, the more memory we can address, and thus the more memory we can have on the computer.

Now, consider the registers and the arithmetic and logical unit. A 32-bit word computer will have 32-bit registers and will be designed to manipulate 32-bit numbers. A 16-bit computer will have 16-bit registers and will be designed to manipulate 16-bit numbers. The more digits we have to work with, the greater the accuracy we can achieve. (Contrast, for example, the level of accuracy a student can obtain from a slide rule, 3-digits, and a pocket calculator, often eight or more digits.) A big computer will tend to be more accurate.

It is possible, of course, to add two 32-bit numbers on a 16-bit computer. The secret is to break the big numbers into two 16-bit pieces, add them separately, and then put the partial answers together. That involves at least two distinct operations, however. A bigger machine can do the same job in a single operation. Thus, the bigger word-size machine will tend to be faster.

In summary, virtually all the internal components of a computer are designed around a common word size. A larger word size means that the computer is likely to be faster, more accurate, and able to access more main memory than a computer with a smaller word size.

MICROS, MINIS, AND MAINFRAMES

Let's return to a potentially confusing subject, the difference between a microcomputer, a minicomputer, and a large computer (often called a **mainframe**). We can now define these terms with a bit more precision than "small," "medium," and "large."

A microcomputer is a small computer, typically having a word size of eight bits. There are 4-bit, 12-bit, 16-bit, and even 24-bit micros, but the most common varieties are 8-bit machines. The small word size limits the amount of main memory that can be attached to a micro; thus micros are usually small in memory capacity. The small word size limits the speed and accuracy of these machines. For many applications, however, they are ideal. To continue an earlier analogy, you wouldn't consider building a 4-lane bridge in a lightly travelled rural area.

There is another term that you might find confusing—**microprocessor.** A microprocessor is simply a small CPU, usually small enough to fit on a single integrated circuit chip. A microprocessor is the central processing unit of a microcomputer.

A minicomputer is an intermediate machine, typically having a word size of 16 bits. There are 8-, 12-, 24-, and even 32-bit minis, but the 16-bit mini is probably the most common. A 16-bit machine will have more memory, be faster, and be more accurate than an 8-bit machine.

A mainframe is a larger computer; a typical word size might be 32 bits, although other word sizes are common too. A 32-bit machine will be bigger, faster, and more accurate than a micro or a mini.

Word size, of course, does not tell the whole story. Cost is an important consideration, with micros usually costing in the neighborhood of $1000, minis costing around $10,000 or so, and mainframes costing $100,000 and more. Unfortunately, there is a great deal of overlap; it is possible to find a $20,000, 16-bit word "micro" to contrast with a $15,000, 12-bit "mini". The terms micro, mini, and mainframe are not absolutes; they are simply guidelines.

Before moving on, it might be wise to briefly consider a very serious problem in the information processing field: the precise meanings of our terms. Often, like a creature from *Alice in Wonderland,* an information processing expert will use technical terms to mean exactly what he or she wants them to mean, "no more and no less." Mainframe is such a term. According to the official definition, "mainframe" and "CPU" are synonyms. Nobody uses the word mainframe that way. To some, a mainframe is a box containing a CPU, main memory, registers, and perhaps other components as well—in short, the mainframe is the physical unit containing the CPU. To others, the mainframe is the computer system without its peripheral input, output, and secondary storage devices. To others, the term mainframe is restricted to large computers, and this latter use is probably the most common one today. Computer people do not play with words for the express purpose of confusing non-computer people. It just seems that way.

SUMMARY

The intent of this chapter was to tie together all the material covered in Part II of this text. We began by discussing the one component not yet covered: the channel. Integrated adapters, which function by stealing an occasional CPU cycle, were covered first; we then moved up to multiplexer channels, selector channels, and block multiplexer channels. A channel and the CPU function asynchronously; the channel notifies the CPU of the successful or unsuccessful completion of an I/O operation through an interrupt.

Having added channels to the input and output devices, control units, CPU, main memory, registers, programs, and data introduced in prior chapters, we had covered all the crucial components of a modern computer system. We thus turned our attention to the idea of a computer system, tying all these components together.

Physically, the components of a computer system are linked by bus lines. Bus lines are used to carry control signals, data, addresses, and instructions. Typically, all the internal components of a computer—the bus lines, registers, and the instruction set of the arithmetic and logical unit—are designed to manipulate a single word at a time. A bigger word size generally means that a computer is faster, more accurate, and able to address more main memory than a machine with a smaller word size. Word size is a convenient way to distinguish among microcomputers, minicomputers, and mainframes.

KEYWORDS

block multiplexer	interrupt	selector channel
bus line	mainframe	standard interface
channel	microprocessor	system
integrated adapter	multiplexer channel	word

EXERCISES

1. Explain (once again) the difference between the control unit that is used in controlling I/O and the control unit portion of the CPU.
2. What is an integrated adapter? Where are they used? What functions do they perform?
3. What is cycle stealing?
4. What is a channel? What functions are performed by a channel?
5. What is a multiplexer channel?
6. What is a selector channel? What is meant by burst mode?
7. What is a block multiplexer channel?
8. What is an interrupt? How are interrupts used in CPU/channel communications? Why are interrupts necessary?
9. Explain what is meant by the word "system" when we talk about a computer system.
10. Explain the function of each of the components described in Fig. 10.4.
11. What is a bus line? What is transmitted over a bus line?
12. Why is a computer's word size so important?
13. How does word size impact a computer's speed? It's accuracy? The amount of main memory it can have?
14. Distinguish among a microcomputer, a minicomputer, and a mainframe.
15. What is a microprocessor?

SYSTEMS
DEVELOPMENT
AND
IMPLEMENTATION

11

THE SYSTEM DESIGN PROCESS

OVERVIEW

In Part II, we considered the components of a computer system, both hardware and software. Here in Part III, we return to the subject of software, studying the task of developing a computer program in considerably more detail. It is not enough that a program be written. The important thing is that it be the right program solving the right problem. That is the subject of Chapters 11 through 14.

Chapter 11 is concerned with the system design process. System design involves identifying the "right" problem and defining (but not writing) the "right" program to solve that problem. We begin by considering the job of the systems analyst. We then turn to an example of a typical system design process, starting with a problem definition from management, working through an initial feasibility study, a broad analysis step, system design, and detailed planning, and culminating in a set of specifications for the programmer. Then, it's on to Chapter 12, where we will consider the first steps in the program development process.

THE RIGHT PROGRAM FOR THE RIGHT PROBLEM

In Chapter 9, we discussed software. Software is a general term for programs. We know that a program is a series of instructions that guides a computer through some process. We know that just "any old series of instructions" will not do; if a computer is to solve a specific problem, it must be given the right instructions arranged in the right sequence. For our purposes in Chapter 9, that was enough.

The time has come to be a bit more specific. Where does the program come from? That "series of instructions" represents a step-by-step solution to a problem; it is really a form of logic. Logic implies intelligence. Machines, even sophisticated machines like computers, are not intelligent. People are intelligent. A computer program is written by a human being, a programmer. The job of the programmer is to carefully and meticulously solve a problem, define the solution as a set of precise logical steps, and then translate the logic into a form that the computer can understand. Without this human-generated program, a computer is useless.

Programs *are* written by programmers, but there is much more to it. Programmers are well paid; their time is quite expensive. As a result, a program can be quite expensive. No business concern can afford to waste money on unnecessary expenditures. Thus, management's real concern is not merely that a program be written, but that the *right* program be written to solve the *right* problem.

How might this objective be achieved? Perhaps the best way to answer this question is by example. Let's consider how a specific program, a payroll program, might come to be written. Before we begin, however, it might be wise to introduce another computer professional who, in many business organizations, is deeply involved in system design—the **systems analyst**.

THE SYSTEMS ANALYST

In a real business environment, it is a very rare program that stands by itself. Consider, for example, a very simple payroll. A program might be written to multiply hours worked by an hourly pay rate and then print the resulting gross pay. Where did the hours worked and hourly pay rate come from? Obviously, someone had to collect these data elements, probably following carefully established procedures to ensure their accuracy. How are the results to be distributed? Other human beings following other carefully defined procedures will almost certainly be involved. The objective is not simply to write a program to compute payroll. The objective is to compute, print, and distribute correct paychecks. This broader objective involves numerous human beings, a number of procedures, several pieces of equipment (including the computer), and the payroll program. All components must work together, in harmony, if the objective is to be achieved. Whenever a number of components, human, machine, and procedural, must work together to achieve an objective, we have a **system.** The program exists in the context of the system.

Every system consists of a number of interrelated components. In order for the system to function properly, these components must work in harmony. Consider, for example, a football team. What good is a truly outstanding quarterback who throws so hard that none of the "just-average" receivers on the team can catch his passes? Of what use is the best defensive line in the league if the weaknesses of the secondary give opponents an opportunity to pass over the strength? Coordination and balance are crucial.

A few simple examples might help to illustrate this point. What happens if manufacturing breaks all efficiency and production records during a time when sales are down? The company must keep the completed but unsold products in storage, and storage is expensive. What happens if the sales department breaks all sales records during a strike when delivery is not possible? The cost to the company arising from customer annoyance could be quite high.

Interrelationships are important and must be taken into account when plans and decisions are made. This requires a broad point of view, a total-system point of view.

Such a broad viewpoint is characteristic of management. It is management that is charged with the control and coordination functions—with the interrelationships. Designing a large computer-based system requires a similar, broad point of view; it is the kind of work that a manager or administrator might be expected to do.

On the other hand, designing a computer system requires a knowledge of computer technology. What kind of computer should be used? What language? What data management techniques? How do all these pieces fit together? While most people can grasp the basics of computer technology, the computer system designer must possess a level of expertise that is not generally available. Very few managers can claim such in-depth expertise.

Designing a computer-based system is a rather demanding task, calling for management's broad viewpoint *and* a high level of technical expertise. The programmer tends to be too technical. The manager tends to be not technical enough. Increasingly, in between these two functions is a new professional, the **systems analyst.**

What exactly is a systems analyst? The analyst is a professional problem solver, combining management's broad point of view with solid technical expertise. Basically, the analyst begins with a problem. After careful study, the problem is fully defined, and several alternative solutions are suggested. A more-detailed analysis, if justified, then begins; the objective is not merely to produce *a* solution to the problem, but to produce the *best* solution. Finally, following management approval, a detailed plan for implementing the solution is developed.

Generally, that is what a systems analyst does. Note that the best solution need *not* involve the computer; a good analyst will consider manual, mathematical, semi-automated, and other noncomputer solutions before making recommendations. Usually, however, the systems analyst is assigned to work on problems that do call for computer solutions—most business organizations view the analyst as a computer professional.

Frequently, particularly in smaller organizations, the analyst and the programmer are one and the same. If the budget for information processing is limited, it may simply be impossible to hire independent analysts and programmers. Other firms with plenty of money simply do not believe in separating these two functions. The important thing to remember, however, is that the job of systems analysis must be done if the right program is to be written to solve the right problem.

THE PAYROLL SYSTEM AT THINK, INC.

Let us now turn our attention to our example. For the past several years, the payroll for our company, Think, Inc., has been prepared by a local bank. A few months ago we bought our own computer. We've been using it as an aid to market analysis—more specifically, as a tool for compiling and analyzing the results of the various market surveys we conduct. We have programmers. We have analysts. A natural question has arisen in the minds of our management: Why not use our own computer to process our payroll? We know how much the bank charges us. We might be able to save some money. Thus our systems analysis team is asked to investigate the possibility of moving payroll onto our own computer.

Where should we start? It is tempting to immediately begin considering the details of implementation on a computer. The technical questions are most interesting and most challenging. Do we need any new hardware? If so, what kind? Should we consider a different commercial computing service? What about software? Should the program be written in FORTRAN or COBOL? Should we buy an already-written payroll program? How should our data files be set up?

Such questions, at least at this early stage, tend to miss the point. Management has not asked us to implement a payroll system on our own computer. Rather, they have asked us to *investigate* the *possibility* of implementing a payroll system on our computer. That's a very different problem. It implies a very important question. Are the benefits we might expect from implementing payroll on our own computer greater than the cost of developing the system? In other words, is the job worth doing at all?

It is easy to fall into the trap of considering the technical details prematurely. In almost any large organization, you will find expensive, computer-generated reports that are simply filed in the waste basket on the day they are received. Clearly, no one thought to ask if the job of generating these reports was worth doing. If they had, we wouldn't find so many worthless reports lying around. How can the analyst avoid falling prey to this trap?

TOP-DOWN SYSTEM DESIGN

One way is to use a **top-down approach** to systems analysis and design. We start with a broad view of the problem and attempt to define what must be done; the details of how the solution is to be implemented are left until later. By concentrating on the problem first and leaving the technical details until last, those technical details are planned in the context of a broad, general solution.

There are a number of steps in the top-down system design process. We begin with **problem definition.** In this phase, the analyst tries to determine exactly what the problem is. Commonly used tools include personal interviews with affected people, a study of the existing system, and, perhaps, intuition and common sense. Often the problem-definition stage ends with a report to management identifying the problem, estimating the potential benefits to be gained from solving the problem, pointing out the risks, and asking for a decision on the advisability of continuing.

The next stage is **analysis,** during which the analyst attempts to define, broadly, a number of possible solutions to the problem. Rough estimates of cost and benefit are developed. Again, management is consulted, and the best of the alternative solutions is selected.

As we enter the **system design** phase, we know, generally, what the finished system is going to look like. We can now begin the process of defining how the system is to be implemented—outlining, at a block level, the major components, and showing how these components will fit together. Reasonable cost estimates and expected completion dates might be established. Once again, management approval may be required before moving on.

Next comes **detailed planning.** The format of each file is defined. Specifications for each of the programs are developed. The objective is to prepare a complete system plan with enough detail so that the programmers can take over.

During the **implementation** stage, the programmers actually code, debug, and document the programs. Sometimes, the analyst is a programmer too. Increasingly, programming and systems analysis are treated as separate functions, so the analyst can spend this time preparing operating procedures, security procedures, backup procedures, and a solid test plan for the system.

The last stage is **testing.** It is important that the system be tested under realistic conditions, and it is the analyst's responsibility to develop a test plan. Ideally, the user (in our example, the payroll manager) should be deeply involved in developing and executing the test; normally, the system is not considered complete until the user formally accepts it, agreeing, in writing, that the system does what it was designed to do.

THE SYSTEM DEVELOPMENT PROCESS

We'll be following the top-down approach as we design a payroll system for Think, Inc. Our first concern, therefore, is with problem definition: What exactly is it that management wants us to do?

The problem would seem to be well defined: plan and implement a payroll system on our own computer. But there is more to it. Would moving payroll to our own machine be an improvement over the present way of doing things? Is there an even better alternative? A good analyst is expected to advise management and not just blindly follow orders.

In an attempt to answer such questions, we begin an initial **feasibility study.** We know how much the old system costs—accounting records are very precise. Can we do the job on our own computer for less? We might talk with the programming department and ask their opinion. The supplier of our computer system might have valuable insight. Friends from other local firms, perhaps people we met while attending a professional society meeting, might be willing to share their own personal experiences. Let's assume that the potential for significant cost savings is present. This is, of course, the key factor, and we will recommend that the project be continued; but other, intangible factors should also be considered. By moving payroll onto our own machine, we will gain better control over this very important business expense. We will not continue to incur increasing costs as our firm grows, and we will no longer be subject to the annual price increase that the bank has accessed for the past several years. On the negative side, we will be responsible for program maintenance, and we may have to hire another programmer at roughly $18,000 per year.

Our objective is to complete such a feasibility study quickly, ideally within a few weeks. We are not trying to solve the problem; we have not even indicated that payroll *should* be implemented on our machine. Our intent, instead, has been to fully understand the problem and to determine if it is worth our trouble to even attempt to solve it. Many ideas can, and should, die at this level.

Our findings are reported to management. They are pleased, and tell us to continue. Thus we enter the analysis stage and begin to identify exactly what must be done to compute a weekly payroll.

Analysis

Our objective in the analysis stage is to discover exactly what must be done to compute payroll. Our feasibility study has indicated that the job is worth doing; thus we can anticipate that, at some time in the future, we will have a payroll program running on our own machine. We are not, however, ready to begin writing that program.

   Our first stop is in the accounting department; more specifically, with the two people who are responsible for the payroll system. They are the experts in our existing way of doing things. While we do not want to simply take the present system and copy it (improvements are certainly possible), the existing system does provide a reasonable starting place, very clearly showing the major functions that must be performed.

   As a result of our interview with the two payroll clerks, we are able to develop the system flow diagram shown in Fig. 11.1. The system begins with the individual employees who, throughout the week, record their times of arrival and departure on timecards by "punching the time clock." Every Friday morning, just after starting time, the cards are collected by members of

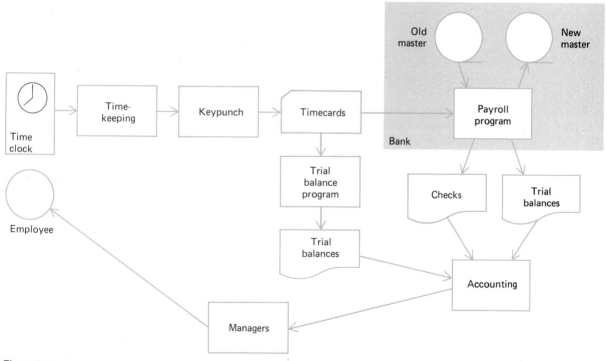

Figure 11.1
An example of a small payroll system.

the timekeeping department and checked for accuracy. Then it's on to the keypunching department, where the actual hours worked for each day are keypunched and verified. (The cards are pre-punched with such information as social security number and the employee's name.) Think, Inc.'s existing small computer system is used to prepare a trial balance that lists such information as the total number of employees to be paid and the total number of hours worked. The completed cards are then picked up and delivered to a local bank.

At the bank, the timecards are given to the computer operator. The old master file, which shows the year-to-date earnings of all Think, Inc. employees as of last Friday, is loaded onto a tape drive. Another tape to hold the new year-to-date file is loaded. Checks are fed into the printer. The timecards are then placed in the card reader, and the payroll program begins. Output includes the checks, the new master file reflecting year-to-date earnings as of today, a series of reports for Think, Inc. management, and a new deck of timecards with everything but hours worked pre-punched in preparation for next week. The completed package is handed to the courier before 2:30 that afternoon.

The checks are returned to the Think, Inc. accounting department. Here, the trial balances generated by the bank's computer are compared with those produced earlier by the internal system. Assuming things match, the checks are signed and distributed to the department managers. Eventually, just before the 4:15 quitting time, the cycle is completed as the checks are distributed to the workers.

Note all the components in this system. There is, of course, a computer—two really. Programs control the computers. Even more important, however, are the people—timekeepers, keypunch operators, couriers, computer operators, accountants, managers, and workers. And, don't forget the procedures, the schedules, the controls, the files, the forms. All these components—hardware, software, data, people, procedures—make up the system. All must work together if the system is to be effective.

Our interview with the payroll clerks is not, of course, limited to the existing system. After all, they are Think, Inc.'s payroll experts, not us. They are the ones who must tell us what must be done. Our job is to translate their requirements into a workable system. Thus, we continue to ask questions. We learn about federal, state, and local laws governing payroll. Union agreements also must be considered. Procedures for distributing the paychecks have been carefully worked out. At the end of the year, employee W-2 forms must be distributed; these are the forms that must be attached to each individual's federal income tax. Finally, the various federal, state, and local taxes must be paid on a quarterly basis.

We discover that other departments are interested in the results of the payroll operation too. The accounting system sees payroll as a large cash payment that must be entered into the books. The budgeting system needs actual labor costs by department. The hours-worked figures from the original time cards are used in the work measurement system to compare actual and expected performance.

Other interviews are conducted with production management, the people in charge of the accounting, budgeting, and work measurement systems, the programming department (again), several representatives of the bank currently doing our payroll, and numerous other people. Government regulations are read. The union contract is carefully studied. Eventually, we are able to clearly identify five major functions that must be performed (Fig. 11.2) in our payroll system.

Now we can begin, generally, to consider how each of these functions might be performed. Several alternatives are available. Data collection might be done with on-line terminals. The existing data collection and data preparation procedures might be kept as is. An honor system might be instituted. Payroll computations might be done using new programs on our existing computer. We might, instead, buy a new, small microcomputer system to be used for payroll. The existing system (the bank) is certainly an alternative. We might buy a commercially available payroll program to run on our system. Time-sharing networks represent still another alternative. Similar alternatives might be developed for each major function.

Note that these alternative solutions are identified in the context of a reasonable system plan. We already know the five functions that are to be performed. We already know the other systems that are affected by payroll,

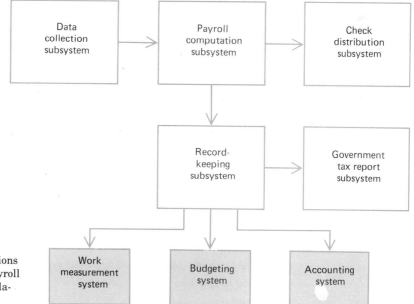

Figure 11.2
During analysis, five major functions that must be performed by the payroll system are identified. Note the relationship to other systems.

and we have made provision for them. Now, we can safely begin to consider how these functions might be implemented. Our analysis, however, is still quite general. We have not attempted to select a supplier of a commercial payroll program, nor have we started to develop the programs for an internal system. Our options are still open.

Rough cost estimates of the various alternatives are developed, and we once again approach management with a status report. Certain alternatives are ruled out by the management team. We will not, for example, continue to use the bank's payroll service, nor will we contract with a time-sharing service—the advantages of internal control and fixed costs in the face of anticipated inflation outweigh the cost of developing our own system. We will not collect data by using an "honor system"; recent labor/management problems make this approach too risky, in spite of the very attractive low cost. As we near the end of the analysis stage, management has given us very clear guidelines and has authorized us to proceed. Thus we begin the system design phase.

System Design

There are five functions that must be performed. A decision made in data collection may well influence or constrain the payroll computation subsystem; all five subsystems must blend. Where should we start? Our preliminary studies have clearly shown that the payroll computation subsystem will almost certainly be the most expensive component of the payroll system, and thus it makes sense to start here. We might, of course, change our minds as we consider the impact of early decisions on other subsystems, but, in general, it makes sense to start with the most expensive element.

At least two programs will be needed (Fig. 11.3), one to edit the input data for accuracy and the other to actually compute the payroll. A commercial payroll package written for computer systems like ours might be worthy of consideration. Even if we decide not to buy it, a study of the system parameters could identify factors we have overlooked, and the purchase or lease price will give our programming department something to shoot for.

Note that Fig. 11.3 shows the old and new master files as magnetic tape. We have not really decided to use magnetic tape, however; the circle is just a convenient symbol to represent a file of some kind. One of the weaknesses of flowcharting is the tendency of an arbitrarily selected symbol to influence future decisions. We must be careful not to let this happen.

Data collection might be the next subsystem considered in detail. Several alternatives exist, including the present timecard/keypunch system and on-line data collection. Let's assume that, after careful study, we have decided to go with on-line data collection using special-purpose terminals spread throughout the plant. Our developing system plan might now look like Fig. 11.4.

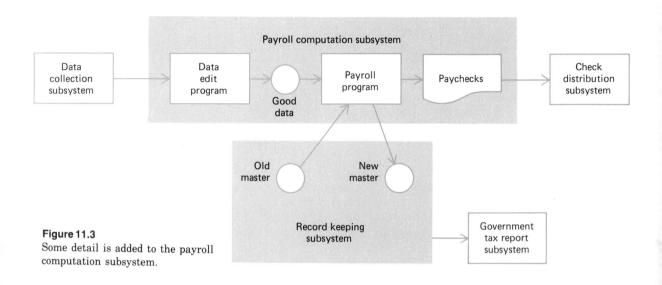

Figure 11.3
Some detail is added to the payroll
computation subsystem.

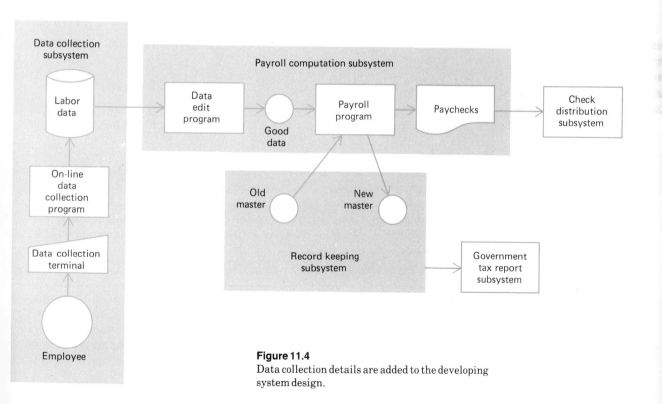

Figure 11.4
Data collection details are added to the developing
system design.

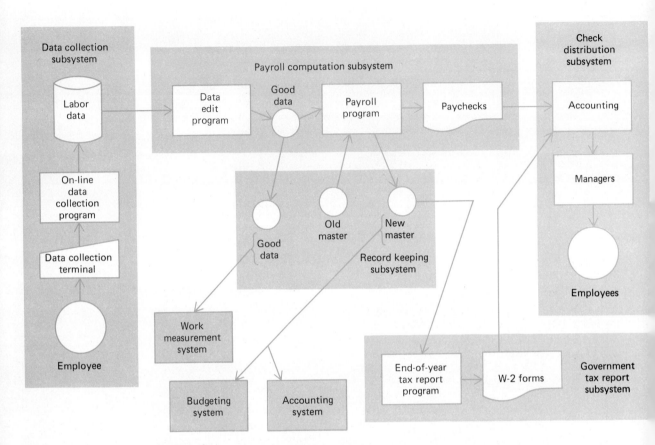

Figure 11.5
A complete plan for our new payroll system.

Each of the subsystems would be planned in turn, with careful attention being paid to the impact on planning already done. Eventually, we might develop a system like the one pictured in Fig. 11.5. User groups and programming would then be asked to comment. Eventually, management approval would be sought. We are now ready to move on to detailed planning.

Detailed Planning

The function of detailed planning is to provide the programmers with enough information to write the programs. File formats are carefully designed. Program specifications are written; in some organizations, the analyst will actually go so far as to develop flowcharts for each program. Tax tables and computational algorithms are collected and clearly identified. Given these design details, the programmers can now take over.

Implementation

Programming will be the subject of the next three chapters. It is often difficult to say exactly where programming begins and systems analysis ends; this is one reason why so many business organizations employ analyst/programmers. We will assume that our analysis team has developed the system plan of Fig. 11.5 and then defined, in general terms, the input to, output expected from, and basic functions to be performed by each of the programs, leaving to the programmer the responsibility for planning the details.

Assume, also, that the analyst and the programmer are different people; what does the analyst do while the programs are being written? Much work remains to be done. Operating procedures must be established. At what time of day must the paychecks be ready for distribution? Working backwards, how long will the payroll programs take to run? These times determine when the collection of labor data must end so that payroll computation can begin. How is the operator to identify the old and new master files? How are these files to be stored following the program run? What about file backup procedures?

Security procedures must be established too. How do we minimize the risk of fraud in the preparation of paychecks? What controls, over and above the usual accounting controls, must be instituted? Who is to be in the computer room when payroll is run? Who signs the checks, and how are we to ensure that the checks are safely delivered to this person?

Testing

A test plan is needed too. We'll assume a simple test plan in this case: for two weeks, payroll will be run both at the bank and on our computer—a **parallel run.** We will not phase over to the new system until there are no errors, or at least until all discrepancies have been explained to the satisfaction of the accounting department.

Eventually, the programs are completed, and the programming department is satisfied with the results. We can now run our test. A few minor problems are ironed out, but in general the phase-over goes smoothly—thanks, in large measure, to the intelligent planning that has gone into this system.

SUMMARY

We began with a very real management concern—that the right program be written to solve the right problem. Often, a systems analyst will be hired by management to deal with this concern. We discussed the definition of the word system, and the job of the systems analyst. We then turned our attention to an example of a typical system development process.

The analyst's first concern should be with the desirability of performing a task. To avoid becoming immersed prematurely in the technical details of system design, the analyst will often follow a top-down approach.

The steps in the top-down approach include problem definition, analysis, system design, detailed planning, implementation, and testing. We then followed a team of analysts as they developed, step by step, a new payroll system for Think, Inc. The implementation of this system will begin with Chapter 12.

KEYWORDS

analysis	parallel run	systems analyst
detailed planning	problem definition	testing
feasibility study	system	top-down approach
implementation	system design	

EXERCISES

1. Management is concerned with making sure that the right program is written to solve the right problem. Why?

2. What is a system?

3. What is a systems analyst? What does the analyst do? Why can't management do this job? Why can't a programmer do it?

4. What is the first question a good systems analyst should ask?

5. What is meant by a top-down approach to systems analysis and design? What are the steps in this process?

6. What is a feasibility study?

7. What is the analyst's objective during the analysis stage?

8. Why is an understanding of the existing system so valuable in planning a new system?

9. What happens during system design?

10. What is the objective of detailed planning?

11. What is a parallel run?

12. What does the analyst do while the programmer is writing the programs?

12

SOFTWARE DEVELOPMENT: PROBLEM DEFINITION AND PLANNING

OVERVIEW

In Chapter 11, we developed a plan for a payroll system. In this chapter, we will develop a detailed plan for one of the programs in that system, the payroll program. Initially, we'll concentrate on a simplified version of the payroll program, defining the inputs and outputs, the algorithms, and the flow of logic. Eventually, this simplified payroll program will be coded in a variety of languages in Chapters 13 and 14.

After planning a simple payroll program, we'll consider how a more realistic, highly complex program might be developed. Hierarchy charts and IPO charts will be two of the keys to this process. Throughout program planning, a top-down approach, similar in many ways to the system design process, will be followed.

The chapter ends with a discussion of language selection: what is the best language for a given application?

THE PROGRAM DEVELOPMENT PROCESS

In Chapter 9, we considered the topic of software. We discovered that a program is a series of instructions that guide the computer through some process. We then covered the programming process, showing that a programmer must

1. define the problem,
2. plan a solution,
3. implement that solution, and
4. maintain the program or programs.

Our emphasis in the earlier chapter was on the individual program. We now know that most business programs exist as components in a broader system. We have planned a payroll system. How does the system plan affect the program development process?

Essentially, it is the system plan that provides the problem definition, the first step in the program development process. If the job of systems analysis has been properly performed, we *know* the problem to be solved. In this case, we might define a payroll program that is to compute and print paychecks in the context of our system. Thus, we can move on to program planning.

PLANNING

Often the programmer will begin the planning process by carefully analyzing the problem, perhaps with the help of a systems analyst. We have already determined what must be done during the problem-definition stage; the question now is to define, in very general terms, the steps that must be taken to achieve that objective. For our payroll program, we might define the following key steps:

1. Compute gross pay.
2. Compute income tax.
3. Compute social security tax.
4. Compute any other deductions.
5. Subtract all deductions from gross pay to get net pay.
6. Print or type a paycheck.

Notice how general this first planning stage is. We haven't attempted to define *how* any of these basic steps will actually be implemented; we concentrate instead on *what* must be done.

Now we begin to add detail. How do we compute gross pay? Usually the computation is simply one of multiplying the number of hours worked by the hourly pay rate. But what about overtime? Often, the number of hours worked over 40 in a given week are paid at 1½ times the normal pay rate, but some organizations use slightly different rates. What about weekend and holiday hours? Do we calculate a double-time pay rate for those hours? It is essential that all the rules for computing gross pay be clearly defined *before* the programmer begins coding.

How are we to compute income tax? Once again, before the programmer begins to write the instructions to compute income tax, the rules must be clearly defined. In this case, the Internal Revenue Service publishes a booklet, Circular E, which very clearly defines the various income tax rates for different levels of income and different pay periods. Figure 12.1 shows a weekly tax table taken from this document.

Social security tax appears to be a much simpler computation; it is calculated as a constant percentage of gross pay. But there is a limit. Once total gross pay for the year passes a cutoff figure, social security tax is no longer withheld. This must be taken into account before writing the program.

Other deductions follow a similar pattern. How exactly is state income tax computed? What about local income tax? Are union dues to be withheld? Under what circumstances? What about "bond of the month" plans or credit union payments? All these questions must be answered before the program can be completed. What we are doing is defining the specific **algorithms** or rules for each of the primary steps in the payroll computation process.

This is not to imply that *everything* must be completely defined before the first instruction can be written. More frequently, planning and implementation overlap a bit, with the program being written in stages. We will discuss this in more detail later.

Figure 12.1

A federal income tax table: weekly payroll period. Multiply the number of dependents claimed by the employee by $19.23. Subtract the product from gross pay to get the employee's taxable wage. (*Source: Circular E, Employer's Tax Guide*, Department of the Treasury, Internal Revenue Service Publication 15. Revised November 1978, pp. 15–16.)

WEEKLY PAYROLL PERIOD

(a) Single person—including head of household

If the amount of wages is:		The amount of income tax to be withheld shall be:	
Not over $27 0			
Over—	*but not over—*		*of excess over—*
$27	−$63 . . . . . 15%		−$27
$63	−$131 . . . . $5.40 plus 18%		−$63
$131	−$196 . . . . $17.64 plus 21%		−$131
$196	−$273 . . . . $31.29 plus 26%		−$196
$273	−$331 . . . . $51.31 plus 30%		−$273
$331	−$433 . . . . $68.71 plus 34%		−$331
$433 . . . . $103.39 plus 39%			−$433

(b) Married person

If the amount of wages is:		The amount of income tax to be withheld shall be:	
Not over $46 0			
Over—	*but not over—*		*of excess over—*
$46	−$127 . . . . 15%		−$46
$127	−$210 . . . . $12.15 plus 18%		−$127
$210	−$288 . . . . $27.09 plus 21%		−$210
$288	−$369 . . . . $43.47 plus 24%		−$288
$369	−$454 . . . . $62.91 plus 28%		−$369
$454	−$556 . . . . $86.71 plus 32%		−$454
$556 . . . . $119.35 plus 37%			−$556

Let's return to the program we're actually going to be implementing—a simplified version of the payroll problem. Gross pay is simply the number of hours worked multiplied by an hourly pay rate; for our purposes, we will ignore overtime. Social security is a straight 6.65 percent of gross pay. The income tax rate structure we'll use is a simple one:

Gross less than	Tax is
$100.00	5% of gross
Infinity	10% of gross

For this example, we will ignore all other deductions. After going through the detailed planning of this program, we will, however, spend some time discussing how we might approach a more complex problem.

DETAILED PLANNING

We began the planning process by defining, in very general terms, the steps involved in computing payroll. We then proceeded to define in detail the rules (algorithms) for implementing each of these steps. We are now about to begin the process of restating these rules in terms of the basic functions of a computer. Thus, we enter the final planning stage—detailed planning.

If you look back at the steps required to compute payroll, you'll see that they could be applied to *any* technique for computing payroll, using either simple paper and pencil, a desk calculator, or a computer. Now that we've defined the detailed rules for each of those general steps, we're ready to begin defining how we might implement payroll *on a computer*. We're moving from very general planning to very detailed planning, step by step.

Programmers use a number of different tools to aid in this detailed planning step. Two of the more commonly used tools are flowcharting and decision tables.

Flowcharting

Flowcharting was introduced in Chapter 9. Using combinations of a few symbols (Fig. 12.2), connected by flowlines, a graphic representation of the logic of a program can be developed. A flowchart shows two important things: (1) the individual logical steps in a program, and (2) the sequence in which those steps must be executed. It is a very powerful planning tool.

A flowchart for our simplified payroll program is shown in Fig. 12.3. Let's go through it step by step; the steps have been numbered to aid in this process. Follow the flowchart carefully as we move through the program, and be sure

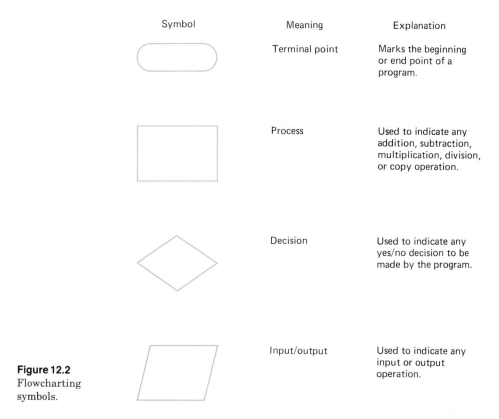

Symbol	Meaning	Explanation
	Terminal point	Marks the beginning or end point of a program.
	Process	Used to indicate any addition, subtraction, multiplication, division, or copy operation.
	Decision	Used to indicate any yes/no decision to be made by the program.
	Input/output	Used to indicate any input or output operation.

Figure 12.2
Flowcharting symbols.

that you understand exactly what happens in each and every step. The steps are as follows:

1. This is the start of the program.
2. Read a card containing an employee's name, the number of hours worked, and the hourly pay rate. Remember that the computer is an information processing machine. Its basic pattern is to read a record of data, process that data, and write a record of information.
3. Here, we have reached a decision point: Is this the last card? There are two possible answers: yes and no. A computer "knows" that a job is done only when the programmer tells it so. In this program, a special card containing no actual data will be placed at the end of the deck. When the computer reads this card, it "knows" that the job is completed.
4. This is the end of the program, reached only when the last card has been read.
5. Gross pay is computed by multiplying the number of hours worked by the hourly pay rate. Why must this *follow* the reading of an input card?

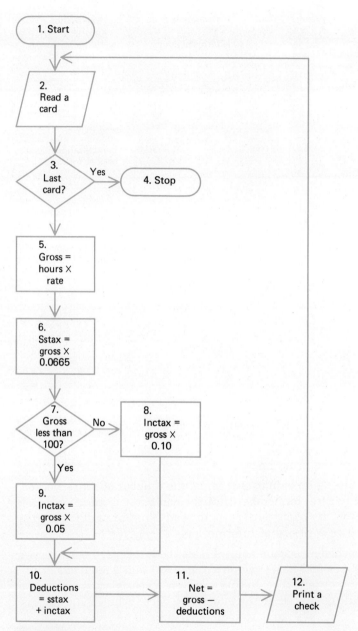

Figure 12.3
A flowchart of our payroll program.

6. Social security tax is computed by multiplying gross pay by 6.65 percent (which is, in decimal terms, 0.0665). Why must this step follow the computation of gross pay?

7. This decision is the first step in the computation of income tax. What are the possible answers to the question: "Is gross less than $100.00?"

8. If gross pay is *not* less than $100, then income tax is 10 percent (0.10) of gross pay.

9. If gross pay *is* less than $100, then income tax is 5 percent of gross pay. Why must the computation of income tax follow the computation of gross pay? Would it be possible to compute income tax before computing social security tax? Sure you could. Do you have to know the social security tax in order to compute income tax?

10. In order to get total deductions, we add income tax and social security tax.

11. Net pay is computed by subtracting total deductions from gross pay. Why couldn't we compute net pay before this point in the program?

12. Finally, we print a check.

Note the flowline that follows step 12. It goes back to the top of the program—specifically, back to step 2. Why do you suppose this is done? The answer is simple: Having read one record of data, processed this data, and written one record of output information, we are ready to repeat the process on another record of data. This is called a **loop.** The ability to loop—to go back and repeat a number of instructions—means that the programmer need only solve the problem once and simply repeat those steps for subsequent data. (Before we move on, it is important that you completely understand the flow of logic shown in the flowchart of Fig. 12.3. If you weren't sure of the answers to all of the questions asked in the step-by-step description of the flowchart, go through it again.)

The flowchart of Fig. 12.3 very clearly shows, step by step, exactly what the computer must do in order to compute payroll. Coding the program now becomes a task of simply translating this logic into the proper computer language, a problem that we will discuss in Chapters 13 and 14.

Programmers and Flowcharting

Not all programmers use flowcharts in planning their programs. Flowcharting is simply a tool that allows us to visualize the logic of a program. Flowcharting is extremely valuable to the beginning programmer, but once an individual has gained considerable experience as a programmer, it becomes just as easy (if not easier) to visualize logic in a programming language. Programming languages, as we'll see in Chapters 13 and 14, are languages having specific punctuation and grammar rules and possessing a certain style of their own.

Much as the true expert in a foreign language learns to *think* in that language, the expert programmer learns to think in COBOL, or FORTRAN, or assembler language; and once an individual has reached this point, some (but not all) stop using flowcharts as a planning tool.

Does this mean that the study of flowcharting is a waste of time? Certainly not! Designing flowcharts is an excellent way to train your mind to think in the kind of logical pattern required by a computer.

There is another use for flowcharts that even the best programmers have come to accept as essential. A flowchart is a great *documentation* tool. After a program has been written (possibly even years later), it is often necessary to go back and make corrections and changes. Given a flowchart, the programmer finds it much easier to figure out exactly what the program does. Documentation flowcharts are sometimes prepared after the program.

Decision Tables

A programmer will sometimes use a **decision table** as a supplement to a flowchart, particularly when a related set of conditions makes the logical flow of a program very complex. As an example, let us assume that the basketball coach has asked us to look through the student records and produce a list of all full-time male students who are at least 6 feet 5 inches in height and who weigh at least 180 pounds. We might want to write a program that will check the records for us, asking the following questions:

1. Is the student male?
2. Is the student taking at least 12 credit hours?
3. Is the student at least 77 inches tall?
4. Does the student weigh at least 180 pounds?

If the answer to all four questions is yes, we want to print the student's name and address; if we receive a single no, however, we will simply move on to the next student.

With four logical tests, we have a fairly complex program segment. However, by using a decision table, we can express these four tests and their necessary conditions in an easy-to-follow, standard way.

A rough outline of a decision table is shown in Fig. 12.4. The table is divided into four segments: a condition stub at the upper left, a condition entry at the upper right, an action stub at the lower left, and an action entry at the lower right. Within this framework, we'll list our questions (the conditions) in the condition-stub section (Fig. 12.5). Below the questions, we'll list our possible actions in the action-stub section. Note that each of our questions is restricted to a yes or no response.

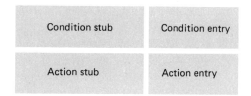

Condition stub	Condition entry
Action stub	Action entry

Figure 12.4
The framework of a decision table.

Is the student male?	Y	N		
Is the student taking at least 12 credit hours?	Y		N	
Is the student at least 77 inches tall?	Y			N
Does the student weigh at least 180 pounds?	Y			
List the student's name and address.	X			
Skip to the next student.		X	X	X	X

Figure 12.5
A decision table for the basketball problem.

Now we can begin to fill out the decision table. The first question (Fig. 12.5) has two possible answers: yes and no. These answers are listed in the condition-entry section of the table: "Y" for yes and "N" for no. If the answer to the first question happened to be yes, would we have enough information to make a decision? No; we would still have three more questions to go through. But if the answer to the first question happened to be no, we would know enough to take a specific action, ignore this student, and move on. To indicate this fact, we put an "X" in the action-entry section of the decision table directly under this "N" response (see Fig. 12.5). Continuing on a question-by-question basis, we will eventually produce the table shown in Fig. 12.5. Reading the table carefully, you will notice that the first action (list the student's name and address) is called for only when all four conditions are true. You will also notice that a single response of no to any of the four conditions is enough to support the alternate decision (skip to the next student). The decision table has allowed us to express a fairly complex series of yes/no conditions and their associated actions in a standard, easy-to-follow format.

The only part of our payroll program that might call for a decision table is the computation of income tax, although it is doubtful that a programmer would consider anything as relatively simple as a tax table to be worth the effort. A more realistic application of this tool is in the computation of state or local income taxes, where the amount collected depends on a number of complex conditions such as place of residence, place of employment, tax rate collected by the government of the place of residence, and so on.

The use of decision tables is not common, but they are, nevertheless, a useful tool. You should at least be familiar with this planning and documentation aid.

Informal Planning Aids

Not all programmers use standard flowcharts and decision tables. Many have devised their own personal techniques. However, if flowcharts and decision tables are to be used for documentation purposes rather than as a planning tool, standardization is essential.

DEFINING DATA FORMAT

The first real step in the flowchart of the payroll program (see Fig. 12.3) was to read a card. In the description of the flowchart, the fact that this card contained an employee's name, the number of hours worked, and hourly pay rate was mentioned. That's about all we, as human beings, would need to figure out the meaning of the fields on the card. However, a computer needs a bit more.

A card reader "reads" the data punched on a card one column at a time, transferring the data into the computer one character at a time. Within the computer, these individual characters must be put together to form fields. It is the responsibility of the programmer to tell the computer exactly how to do this.

Before the programmer can possibly tell the computer exactly what to do, the programmer must know. Thus another step in the planning process involves laying out, column by column, the contents of the data cards; an example of the card layout for our payroll program is shown in Fig. 12.6. Every data card must be keypunched in exactly the same way or the program will not work. The employee's name, for example, must *always* start in column 6 and must *always* consume exactly 15 columns; hence the name "ROSE" would be followed by eleven blanks, while, on another card, the name "COTTERMAN" would be followed by six blanks.

A similar argument can be stated for output. What exactly does a paycheck look like? Consider your own personal checks for a moment. Does it make any difference where you write the name of the person or organization to be paid? Does it make any difference where you write the amount of the check? The answer, of course, is yes. For a human being, a simple instruction such as "enter the amount of the check on the line under the date and toward the right" would be more than adequate. Using a computer, however, we must be a

Card columns	Field length	Content
1 – 5	5	Blanks – unused
6 – 20	15	Last name
21 – 22	2	Initials
23 – 30	8	Blank – unused
31 – 33	3	Hours worked to nearest tenth
34 – 40	7	Blank – unused
41 – 44	4	Hourly pay rate
45 – 80	36	Blank – unused

Figure 12.6
Input card format for the payroll program.

Positions	Field length	Content
1 – 10	10	Blank
11 – 12	2	Initials
13	1	Blank
14 – 28	15	Last name
29 – 38	10	Blank
39 – 46	8	Net pay
Balance of line		Blank

Figure 12.7
Output line (check) format for the payroll program.

bit more precise. An example of how a single line of output might be carefully defined for eventual computer use is shown in Fig. 12.7.

Carefully defining the format of each record input to or output from a program is an important part of the planning process.

PROGRAM PLANNING: A SUMMARY

The main objective of program planning is to carefully define a solution to a problem down to the point where it can be implemented on a computer. Ideally, the solution should be so well defined following planning that programming (the subject of Chapters 13 and 14) becomes little more than the translation of this solution into "computerese." Planning is a step-by-step process, beginning with a very general view of the problem and gradually introducing detail until a computer solution is clearly defined. An ideal plan will include a description of each input and output record, a set of well-defined algorithms for each logical step in the program, and a flowchart or other description of program flow to define the sequence in which the algorithms are executed.

TOP-DOWN DESIGN AND STRUCTURED PROGRAMMING

The sample payroll program described to this point has intentionally been kept simple. A real payroll program, however, would be much more complex. Consider, for example, one component of this program: the computation of gross pay. The simple algorithm, gross pay is the product of hours worked and an hourly pay rate, is only part of the logic; other factors must be considered. Overtime is normally paid at 1½ times the normal rate. Often a shift premium is paid to those workers assigned to the night shift. Occasionally, a bonus is paid. Often, Sunday and holiday hours are paid at double or even triple the regular rate. And we have not even considered the problems associated with salaried employees or with salespeople who are paid a commission.

Similar details could be cited for any one of the deductions. Hundreds of instructions would be needed to compute gross pay. Hundreds more would be needed for income tax; hundreds more for state tax, and so on. The resulting program would be large, well beyond the capacity of a single programmer. A traditional flowchart of this program would contain so many blocks and flowlines that it would be literally impossible to follow.

The very complexity of such a program creates a number of problems. Even the best programmers make errors and, given the vast number of instructions in the program, these bugs become very difficult to find and to remove. Changes (a new income tax rate structure, for example) must be made, and the bigger the program the more difficult such changes become.

Few competent programmers would have difficulty with the code needed to compute gross pay or the code needed to compute income tax; it is only when all of these modules are linked together that the complexity begins to appear. Why not break the program into a number of independent functions, write each functional module separately, and then put the pieces together? In other words, why not break a complex problem into a number of simple ones?

In many computer centers this is exactly what is done. Each logical function (each algorithm) is written as an independent **subroutine.** A control module, the **mainline** serves to tie together all these subroutines. The programmer can thus concentrate on one problem at a time, perhaps using flowcharts and decision tables much as we did earlier. If more than one programmer is involved, the subroutines provide an ideal framework for subdividing the work. With all the logic for implementing a single function (income tax computation, for example) housed in a single subroutine, any errors in performing this function can be isolated, thus simplifying program debug. Changes, such as a new tax rate, affect only the code in the associated module; thus maintenance is made easier.

The real problem with designing a large program as a collection of small, relatively independent subroutines is one of coordinating and organizing those subroutines. To minimize this danger, many programmers and systems analysts rely on a top-down approach to program design.

The key idea of **top-down design** is to begin looking at a problem in the broadest possible way, introducing detail gradually, layer by layer. In developing a complex payroll program, for example, we might begin by stating an objective: compute payroll. Next, we would list the steps needed to compute payroll:

1. Compute gross pay.
2. Compute federal income tax.
3. Compute state tax.
4. Compute local tax.
5. Compute social security tax.
6. Compute any other deductions.
7. Compute net pay.
8. Prepare and print a pay check.

This list is not unlike the one we compiled earlier in solving a much simpler problem. Note that we have not yet commented on *how* any one of these steps is to be implemented. At this level we are concerned with *what* must be done, and *not* how it must be done. The objective of the first steps in the top-down design process is to provide a broad overview of the entire program; the details are defined within this broad framework.

A traditional flowchart is not very effective for illustrating such a broad framework. Often, a **hierarchy chart** (Fig. 12.8) is used to visually represent the structure of the entire program. The chart resembles a business (or military) organization chart, with a president (or a general) at the top and the workers at the bottom. In business or the military, those at the top issue orders and coordinate the activities of those below them, while the actual work is done by those at the bottom. The relationship of the modules in a hierarchy chart is a direct parallel.

The modules making up the program illustrated in Fig. 12.8 would, for example, be executed in the following order:

1. *Payroll.* Execution always begins with the main control module.
2. *Get valid timecard.* "Payroll" would cause control to be transferred to this level II module.

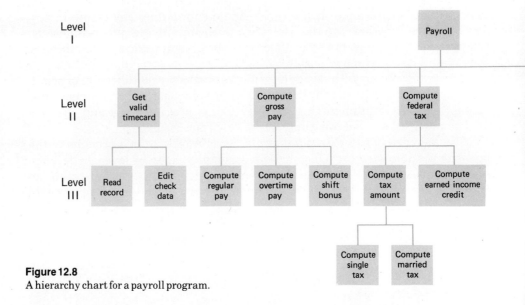

Figure 12.8
A hierarchy chart for a payroll program.

3. *Read record.* This level III module is under the control of "Get valid timecard".

4. *Get valid timecard.* After the level III module has finished, control is returned to the proper higher-level routine.

5. *Edit check data.* This is another level III module. We are still under the control of "Get valid timecard."

6. *Get valid timecard.* Again, when the level III module has finished, control is returned to the proper level II routine.

7. *Payroll.* There are no more functions under the control of "Get valid timecard"; thus, since the level II module has finished, control is returned to the next highest level, in this case to the main control module.

8. *Compute gross pay,* and so on.

The level I module, Payroll, provides overall control. Level II modules are responsible for controlling and coordinating their own lower-level modules, and so on. In this way, the pieces of a large, complex program can be linked together, from the top, down.

Although traditional flowcharts and decision tables can be used to plan and document the individual modules, many programmers and analysts prefer to use another tool, the input/processing/output (or **IPO**) chart (Fig. 12.9).

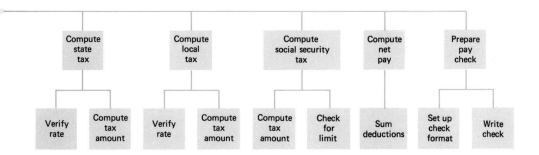

Compute state tax		Compute local tax		Compute social security tax		Compute net pay	Prepare pay check
Verify rate	Compute tax amount	Verify rate	Compute tax amount	Compute tax amount	Check for limit	Sum deductions	Set up check format / Write check

IPO CHART				
PROGRAM: PAYROLL		PROGRAMMER: W.S. DAVIS		DATE: 11/1/80
MODULE: COMPUTE GROSS PAY		LEVEL: II	ACCESSED BY: PAYROLL - LEVEL I	
INPUT	PROCESSING		OUTPUT	
1. HOURS WORKED	1. COMPUTE REGULAR PAY		1. GROSS PAY	
2. HOURLY PAY RATE	2. COMPUTE OVERTIME PAY			
3. SHIFT CODE	3. COMPUTE SHIFT PREMIUM			
	4. COMPUTE GROSS PAY			

Figure 12.9
An IPO chart for the payroll program showing
the *compute gross pay* module.

Perhaps the best way to understand an IPO chart is to look at one; we have chosen the chart for the level II module, "Compute gross pay" (see Fig. 12.8). Three fields—hours worked, the hourly pay rate, and a shift code—must be available before gross pay can be computed; these three fields are listed under the header INPUT. Regular pay, overtime pay, any shift premium, and, of course, gross pay itself must be calculated, and these steps are listed under PROCESSING. Finally, the output from this module, listed under OUTPUT, is the computed gross pay. In other words, the IPO chart lists each input field required by the module, the processing steps contained in the module, and each output field generated by the module.

Typically, an IPO chart is prepared for each module shown in the associated hierarchy chart. The hierarchy chart provides a broad overview of the program, while the IPO charts provide the supporting details. The package, often called a **HIPO** (for hierarchy and input/processing/output) diagram, is an excellent documentation and communication tool.

Note how planning proceeds from the broad and general to the specific—from the top, down. Compare the process of planning a program to the process of planning a system; you should see a direct parallel. In both cases, we started by defining *what* must be done. Only after we had gained a complete understanding of exactly what we must do did we turn our attention to how to do it. It's a bit like building a house. First we draw a blueprint. Then we build a framework. Only when this preliminary work (none of which really shows in the finished product) has been successfully completed can we even begin to put on the finishing touches. The system plan was our blueprint. The HIPO charts provide a framework for writing the program. Now we can turn our attention to the actual implementation of our program.

Imagine that we have a hierarchy chart and a set of IPO charts for the payroll program. Are we really ready to begin writing code? Probably not. The programmer may well want to do a bit more planning. The gross pay module, for example, might require flowcharting to more clearly define the sequence of logic. It is at this level that the traditional planning tools, flowcharts and decision tables, are still most valuable.

Finally, all planning done, the actual coding of the program can begin. Does the top-down approach end here? No. Many programmers subdivide their code into a series of short modules, each of which performs a single logical function. This is the essential idea behind **structured programming.** When following the structured approach, the programmer uses only a few well-defined logical structures. The result is a program that is relatively easy to read. If it's easy to read, the logical flow is easy to follow. If the logic is easy to follow, it is easier to debug, to document, and to maintain. The use of structured programming techniques is one of the strongest trends in the software industry.

THE COST OF A PROGRAM

We have spent a great deal of time discussing planning. First we planned a system. Then we planned a program to function as part of that system. Why is planning so important? Why should management care about the planning process?

Management is concerned with the planning of its information processing activities for the same reasons it is concerned with planning its inventory position, its sales, and its production activities. Information processing is essential to the well-being of the organization. Information processing is also expensive. An effective management wants to get the most value it possibly can for the money it spends. Planning simply helps to improve the efficiency of the information processing activities.

What are the costs of information processing? The most obvious cost is hardware—all that equipment. Software is expensive too; programmers and systems analysts must be paid. Historically, the big cost of information processing was hardware. Thus, computer professionals tended to concentrate on efficient use of the equipment. Today, given the sharply falling cost of computers and computer equipment and the soaring cost of human labor, software has come to be the dominant cost of information processing. Thus, the emphasis has shifted to the control of software costs.

What does a program cost? That is a very complex question. It is sometimes difficult to pinpoint the exact cost of software. We do know, however, that every program goes through the following stages:

1. Problem definition.
2. Planning.
3. Implementation, including
    a) coding,
    b) documentation,
    c) debug,
    d) testing.
4. Execution, including
    a) main memory space,
    b) CPU time.
5. Maintenance.

Each stage has a cost. Attempting to minimize only execution costs or only implementation costs is not a proper objective. The ideal is to minimize *total* program cost. When the hardware was the bulk of the information processing budget, execution costs were the proper target for concentration. Today, coding, documentation, debug, and maintenance are the big cost items. Since structured programming shows promise of helping to reduce these costs, it is easy to see why structured programming is enjoying such popularity today.

LANGUAGE SELECTION

One important factor in helping to control software costs is selecting the proper language. Consider, for example, three very popular languages: FORTRAN, COBOL, and assembler. They are quite different. Each has its own strengths and weaknesses.

FORTRAN was designed with scientific computation in mind. The typical user is a scientist, engineer, or student who has a problem to solve. Planning a solution will probably result in a series of algebraic expressions; the purpose of the program is to solve the equations. Usually, there is a very small amount of input and output data. Often, only a single number or set of numbers is expected as output. Such applications are said to be **compute bound,** because most of the computer's time is spent calculating and not doing input and output. Frequently, once the problem is solved, the program is no longer needed.

What are the primary costs of such an application? In reality, the big costs are probably concentrated in problem definition and planning, but the selection of a language will have little or no impact on these costs. Once planning is completed, coding and debugging the program take the most time. Do we have to worry about program maintenance? Not really; the program may never be reused. What about documentation? If there is no need to maintain a program, why spend a great deal of time documenting it? How about execution costs? The program will be run once or twice, using perhaps an hour of computer time. That's insignificant.

FORTRAN programs are relatively easy to write. The code generated by the FORTRAN compiler is relatively efficient on computations. As a result, the language is ideal for scientific applications.

Now consider a typical business application—payroll is a good example. The computations involved in processing a payroll are rather simple. The problem is that they must be repeated many times. Thus there is a great deal of input and output (read a timecard and print a paycheck for each employee), and relatively little computation—such programs are said to be **I/O bound.**

How many times will a payroll program be used? Once a week. For how many weeks? Ideally, forever. Business applications have long lives. Of course, there will be changes to the payroll program. Federal income tax withholding rates will change. Social Security tax rates will change. Local and state rules will change. The union contract will include new provisions each time it is renegotiated. As a result, program maintenance is very important.

Another key problem is the accuracy of the results. If a scientist gets incorrect results from a FORTRAN program, the scientist is the only one who sees the error. Corrections can be made, and the program rerun. If the business programmer makes a similar error, incorrect paychecks will be distributed. It is much more difficult to recover from an error when many different people are involved. As a result, program debug and testing become critical on a typical business application.

COBOL was designed with precisely this type of application in mind. The language is most efficient on input and output, sacrificing some computational efficiency—no problem on an I/O bound application. COBOL is self-documenting; the programmer is required to write a great deal of code that serves only to explain what is happening. That tends to increase coding costs, but it also tends to produce clearer, easier to follow code. Clearer code, in turn, tends to simplify documentation, debug, testing, and maintenance, and it is in these four categories that the major cost of a typical business program lies.

We might consider a third variety of program. This one directly controls a piece of manufacturing equipment. The program runs 365 days per year, and thousands of times per day. The real cost of this program is its execution cost. We can afford to spend a bit more time writing the program if we can make it smaller and reduce the number of instructions. Fewer instructions means that the program will run faster, needing less CPU time. A smaller program requires less main memory. Both factors tend to reduce the cost of actually running the program.

Assembler language tends to produce the most efficient programs on the computer. The assembler programmer writes one instruction for each instruction the machine executes. As a result, it takes longer to write an assembler program. But that one-to-one relationship gives the programmer precise control over what the computer does, allowing the last ounce of waste to be squeezed from the program.

The scientist would not choose assembler, because the primary concern is coding the problem, and it takes longer to code an assembler program than it does to code a FORTRAN program. The business programmer would probably not choose assembler either, because COBOL code is easier to document, debug, test, and maintain, and those are the key considerations on a typical business application. If on-the-machine efficiency is crucial, however, assembler is the best choice.

Are there any trends that might affect the future language selection decision? Yes. Hardware costs are dropping. Labor costs are increasing. As hardware costs drop, the execution costs also drop. As a result, program efficiency becomes less important. As labor costs rise, the costs of coding, documentation, debug, testing, and maintenance also rise. This tends to favor compiler languages such as FORTRAN and COBOL. While assembler language will probably never disappear, its popularity is slowly declining.

IMPLEMENTATION AND MAINTENANCE

Having covered problem definition and planning, we are now ready to move on to the next two stages in the programming process: implementation and maintenance. *Implementation* is the task of converting the solution to a problem into a form suitable for a computer's use; in other words, by implementation we mean actually writing a program. Implementation involves *coding* (the actual writing of the program), *testing* to make sure the program is correct, *debugging* (the removal of errors), and *documentation*. Program *maintenance* involves a number of activities that take place after the program is completed; this includes making any necessary changes and removing any errors not detected in the testing phase. In Chapters 13 and 14, the simple payroll program planned earlier will be coded in a variety of languages.

SUMMARY

This chapter began with a basic definition of software and then moved into a discussion of the programming process. The four major steps in this process are (1) problem definition, (2) planning, (3) implementation, and (4) maintenance.

Problem definition, as the term implies, involves determining exactly what must be done. It is essential that the programmer know the purpose and intent of a program before beginning to write that program.

The planning stage represents an attempt to fully define a specific solution to the point of implementation on a computer. Starting with a general view of the essential steps in the program, details are added layer by layer until a detailed plan, often in the form of a flowchart and/or several decision tables, is produced; we actually developed such a flowchart for a simple payroll application.

We then turned our attention to a more complex and more realistic payroll application. Following top-down design principles, we developed a hierarchy chart and explained how each of the modules shown on the chart could be defined by using IPO charts. Once planning had been completed, we turned our attention to the cost of a program, ending with a discussion of several language selection considerations.

KEYWORDS

algorithm	HIPO	structured programming
compute bound	I/O bound	
data format	IPO chart	subroutine
decision table	loop	top-down design
hierarchy chart	mainline	

EXERCISES

1. What is software? How does it differ from hardware?

2. What is a program?

3. What is meant by problem definition? Why is it important that this step be completed first?

4. What is the objective of the planning phase of the program development process?

5. What is a flowchart?

6. Why don't all professional programmers use flowcharting as a planning tool? Does the fact that many professional programmers skip flowcharting mean that flowcharting is useless? Why or why not?

7. What is a decision table?

8. Why is it necessary to fully define the format of each and every record to be input to or output by a program?

9. Discuss some of the advantages of the structured, modular approach to large-scale programming.

10. What is meant by a top-down approach to program planning and design?

11. A reasonable business objective is to keep the total cost of a program at a minimum. What does this mean?

12. How can the choice of a language impact the cost of a program?

13

PROGRAM IMPLEMENTATION: BASIC AND FORTRAN

OVERVIEW

Continuing with the discussion of the programming process we started in Chapter 12, this chapter covers the task of actually implementing or coding a program in two commonly used languages: BASIC and FORTRAN. A programming language consists of a number of very specific rules for describing the logic the computer is to follow. As we look at BASIC and FORTRAN, we'll point out some of the key rules, and, eventually, use these rules to actually code a solution to the payroll problem we flowcharted in Chapter 12 (Figure 12.3); for your convenience, a copy of this flowchart is repeated here as Fig. 13.1.

FORTRAN and BASIC were developed with the idea of scientific computation in mind. As a result, program statements in both languages tend to resemble algebraic expressions. In Chapter 14, we'll consider two languages that were developed with business data processing in mind: RPG and COBOL.

One final comment before we begin. It is impossible, in a few pages of a general, introductory-level text, to train you to be a proficient programmer. The intent of these two chapters is simply to give you a feel for a number of common languages. If you continue as a major in a computer-related discipline, you will be exposed to individual languages in much more detail.

COMPILER LANGUAGES

A computer is a binary device. It stores and manipulates data in a binary form. Main memory is designed to hold binary data; the central processing unit is designed to work on binary data. Since program instructions are to be stored in main memory and executed by the CPU, program instructions must also be in a binary form.

People do not work well with binary; it's just not natural for us. We feel comfortable with words written in our alphabet, numbers written in the base ten, and algebraic expressions. Somehow, the gap between normal human forms of communication and the binary codes required by a computer must be bridged.

Compilers are designed to bridge this gap, allowing the programmer to write a program in close-to-normal language and then translating this programmer source code into the binary-level codes required by the computer. A compiler is a special program. Its purpose is one of translation.

Many different types of compilers are available. Some allow the programmer to use program instructions that are similar to algebraic notation; others allow the use of English-like phrases and sentences. In this chapter and the next we'll be discussing four of the more common compiler languages: BASIC, FORTRAN, COBOL, and RPG. The first three, you may recall, were covered briefly in Chapter 9, where we discussed a number of essential software concepts.

BASIC

We will begin with one of the easier to use languages, BASIC. A BASIC program consists of a series of program **statements**, each one instructing the computer to take a specific action. BASIC statements are written in a form similar to algebraic notation. Rather than being forced to worry about memory locations and addresses, the programmer manipulates **variables** and **constants.**

The key statement supporting all processing steps (represented by a rectangle in a flowchart) is the LET statement. The statement

10   LET A = B

indicates, for example, that a copy of what is currently stored in the memory allocated to variable B is to be copied into the space allocated to variable A.

Variables are represented by a single letter of the alphabet or by a single letter followed by a digit; valid variables include A, A0, A1, B, C, D, D0, D8, and so on. Constants are represented as simple numbers, with or without a decimal point; the constant π is, for example, 3.1416.

Perhaps the best way to illustrate the LET statement is through an example. The formula for finding the area of a circle is

Area = $\pi \cdot$ radius^2.

A BASIC LET statement to perform this computation is

    5   LET A = 3.1416 * R ** 2

Note that on the left side of the equal sign only a single variable, A, is found. The LET statement really says, "Do whatever is indicated on the right side of the equal sign, and then copy the answer into the variable indicated on the left side of the equal sign."

To the right of the equal sign is an **expression** defining the arithmetic steps involved in computing, in this case, the area of a circle. The expression consists of variables, constants, and **operators.** Valid operations include addition (a + sign), subtraction (a − sign), multiplication (indicated by *, an asterisk), division (a slash, /) and exponentiation (a double asterisk, **). In some versions of BASIC, an arrow pointing upward (↑) is used to indicate exponentiation.

By combining these components, we get a valid LET statement. The statement

    10   LET A = 0.5 * B * H

computes the area of a triangle using the formula

Area = ½ $\cdot$ (base) $\cdot$ (height).

To compute gross pay, we might write

    10   LET G = H * R

where H represents the number of hours worked and R represents the pay rate. This statement can be interpreted as follows:

1. Multiply whatever is currently found in the variable H by whatever value is currently stored in the variable R.
2. Copy the answer into the variable G.

You will note that these two statements imply that there must be some value already stored in variables H and R *before* this statement can be executed. How do these values get there? We might write a series of BASIC statements. The statements

    10   LET H = 40

    15   LET R = 4.25

    20   LET G = H * R

would cause the computer first to copy the constant 40 into variable H and then to copy the constant 4.25 into variable R. Now, when the third instruction is executed, both variables on the right side of the equal sign have values, and the multiplication can take place. Do you remember the process of substitution in algebra? We are simply substituting an actual value for a variable before using that variable in a computation.

Rather than coding the actual value of a variable in a LET statement, we can instruct the computer to request the values through an INPUT statement. The statements

10	INPUT H,R
20	LET G = H * R

would first get values for H and R from an input device, store these values in the space allocated to the two variables, and then perform the multiplication, storing the answer in G.

The INPUT statement is coded by typing the word INPUT, followed by a list of variables separated by commas; the computer will expect a value for each and every variable in the list. The statement

5	INPUT X,Y,Z

for example, represents a request for three values from an input device.

What if the programmer wants to see the results of a computation? Output can be obtained by using a PRINT statement. The BASIC program segment

5	INPUT R
10	LET A = 3.1416 * R ** 2
15	PRINT R,A

would get a value for R from an input device, compute the area of a circle of this radius, and display the values of both the radius and the area on an output device (a printer or a terminal). The PRINT statement is coded by typing the word PRINT followed by a list of the variables to be printed, again separated by commas.

It makes little sense to write a computer program to compute the area of a single circle; pocket calculators can do this job quite easily. What if, however, we needed to compute the areas of dozens of circles? Performing the same steps over and over again would become tedious; we might consider writing a program in this case.

Recall the concept of a loop introduced earlier. By coding the solution to a problem once and then telling the computer to go back and repeat those instructions, we can have the computer go through a program any number of times. If we are to take advantage of looping in BASIC, we must have a method for identifying individual instructions and a special instruction to tell the computer to go back to the top of the program. In BASIC, individual instructions are identified by assigning a number to each statement; in fact, every instruction *must have* a valid statement number. The instruction that tells the computer to go back to the top of the program is the GO TO. The program

10	INPUT R
20	LET A = 3.1416 * R ** 2
30	PRINT R,A
40	GO TO 10

tells the computer to get a value for R from the input device, compute the area of a circle of this radius, print the radius and the area, and then go back to statement number 10 and repeat the program.

There is only one problem with this little program; how can the computer tell when we have computed the areas of all the circles in which we are interested? It can't; the computer will just keep asking for more input data. We must have a mechanism to tell the computer when we are finished. By using an IF statement, we can have the computer perform a logical test. The program

10	INPUT R
15	IF R < 0 THEN 50
20	LET A = 3.1416 * R ** 2
30	PRINT R,A
40	GO TO 10
50	END

includes an IF test after the INPUT statement. If the value for the radius provided by the programmer is less than (the < symbol) zero, the program *branches* to statement number 50, which says END. The END statement is how the programmer tells the computer to quit. If a value is less than zero, it is negative. Since a negative radius is impossible, this is a good "end-of-data" test.

The IF statement allows the programmer to compare a variable to a constant or to another variable. Possible conditions include equal to (=), less than (<), greater than (>), and any combination of two of these conditions. The general form of the instruction is

IF condition THEN statement number.

If the condition is true (if R is less than zero, in our example), then the branch to the indicated statement takes place; if the condition is not true, no branch takes place and the program continues on to the next instruction in sequence.

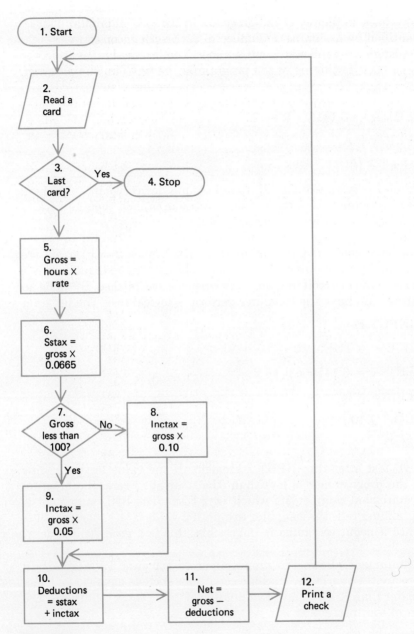

Figure 13.1
A flowchart of our payroll program.

We'll be using the IF statement for two purposes in our payroll program: first, to test for the end of data, and second, to find the proper income tax rate.

Although a standard for "minimal BASIC" was established in 1978, there really is no such thing as a true national standard for this language; many different versions exist. Some include the key logic blocks of structured programming; many do not. In describing BASIC, we have tried to include only those language features that are common to most commercially available versions—basic BASIC, so to speak. We will use this elementary version in coding a BASIC version of the payroll program (Fig. 13.2).

There are a few points in this program that have not yet been covered. There is a difference between coded and numeric data within a computer. The variables and constants described in the preceding discussion were all numeric. When the programmer wishes to store alphabetic data in coded form, a

```
100                     REM * THIS PROGRAM COMPUTES AND PRINTS   *
110                     REM * AN INDIVIDUAL'S TAKE-HOME PAY.      *
120                     REM *                                     *
130                     REM *    WRITTEN BY: W.S. DAVIS           *
140                     REM *              NOV. 1                 *
150                     REM * * * * * * * * * * * * * * * * * * * *
160                     REM
170                     REM * THE PROGRAM STARTS BY READING
180                     REM * ONE INPUT RECORD CONTAINING:
190                     REM *   N$        EMPLOYEE NAME
200                     REM *   I$        EMPLOYEE INITIALS
210                     REM *   H         HOURS WORKED
220                     REM *   R         HOURLY PAY RATE
230                     REM * IF HOURS WORKED IS NEGATIVE,
240                     REM * THIS IS THE LAST RECORD.
250 INPUT N$,I$,H,R
260 IF H<0 THEN 450
270                     REM * COMPUTE GROSS PAY (G) AND
280                     REM * SOCIAL SECURITY TAX (S).
290 LET G=H*R
300 LET S=G*.0665
310                     REM * COMPUTE INCOME TAX (I)
320 IF G<100 THEN 350
330 LET I=G*.1
340 GOTO 380
350 LET I=G*.05
360                     REM * COMPUTE NET PAY (N) AND PRINT CHECK;
370                     REM * THEN GO BACK AND READ NEXT RECORD.
380 LET D=S+I
390 LET N=G-D
400 PRINT N$;I$,"$";N
410 GOTO 250
420                     REM * * * * * * * * * * * * * * * * * * * *
430                     REM * AT END OF DATA, TERMINATE PROGRAM *
440                     REM * * * * * * * * * * * * * * * * * * * *
450 END
```

Figure 13.2
Payroll in BASIC.

variable name consisting of a letter of the alphabet followed by a dollar sign ($) is used. In the payroll program (Fig. 13.2), the programmer's name and initials are stored in variables named N$ and I$, respectively. Alphabetic constants are represented by a string of characters between a set of quotation marks; in statement 400, for example, the "," and "$" tell the computer to actually print a comma and a dollar sign.

Note also the statement numbers: They run from 100 to 450 in increments of ten. The programmer may use any numbering scheme desired, so long as the program statements are in sequential order. Leaving gaps is advantageous in that additional statements can be easily inserted into the program if necessary; statement number 115, for example, would be inserted between statements 110 and 120.

Read the program in Fig. 13.2 carefully, comparing it with the flowchart shown in Fig. 13.1. If you follow it step by step, you should have little trouble understanding the logic.

FORTRAN

The first of the compiler languages, FORTRAN was designed to support mathematical and scientific applications. Thus, it is not surprising to find that FORTRAN statements, like BASIC statements, resemble algebraic expressions.

Unlike BASIC, however, there is an accepted national standard for FORTRAN. Initially developed in 1966, the American National Standard (or ANS) version of FORTRAN has been used by most computer manufacturers and software houses as a guide in developing their own compilers. Recently, on April 3, 1978, a new standard, FORTRAN 77, became the official standard. Slowly but surely, FORTRAN compilers are being revised to conform; we'll be referencing this new standard in the discussion that follows.

Like BASIC, FORTRAN allows the programmer to write statements by using a combination of variables, constants, and operators. The operators are the same: + for addition, − for subtraction, * for multiplication, / for division, and ** for exponentiation. The variables and constants are, however, a bit different.

The most obvious difference between FORTRAN and BASIC variables lies in the number of characters that the programmer may use in a variable name. A FORTRAN variable consists of from one to six letters or digits, the first of which must be a letter. Valid FORTRAN variable names include X, X1, RADIUS, AREA, and TAX. Given these longer names, the FORTRAN programmer can more clearly indicate the actual operations to be performed; for example,

$$AREA = 3.1416 * RADIUS ** 2$$

Note that the added clarity is for the benefit of the programmer (documentation); it doesn't matter to the computer.

In BASIC, a number is a number. In FORTRAN, there are two different kinds of numbers: **integers** and **real numbers.** An integer, as the name implies, is a whole number without fractional part. A real number has a fractional part. A word of explanation: Integers are pure binary numbers; a FORTRAN real number is stored in floating-point form. The computer is a bit more efficient when using pure binary, but the mathematician or scientist has frequent need for very large and very small values; hence the floating point.

The first letter in the variable name determines the type of variable. Names beginning with I, J, K, L, M, or N identify integer variables; names beginning with any other letter are real. Constants are written as numbers, much as they are in BASIC. A real constant contains a decimal point, and any constant written without a decimal point is assumed to be an integer. In the FORTRAN statement for the area of a circle shown above, the constant 3.1416 is real, while the constant 2 is an integer.

Except for the number of characters in a variable name and the two different types of numeric data, a FORTRAN **assignment statement** looks like a BASIC LET statement without the LET. The area of a triangle might, for example, be computed by

AREA = 0.5 * BASE * HEIGHT

Gross pay might be found by coding

GROSS = HOURS * RATE

As in BASIC, every variable appearing in an assignment statement must have been assigned an actual value before the statement is executed. Thus we could code

HOURS = 40.0

RATE = 4.25

GROSS = HOURS * RATE

and use the combination of these three statements to compute gross pay for an individual who worked 40 hours and who earns $4.25 per hour.

Once again, the data can be input from an input device rather than initialized through an assignment statement. In FORTRAN, the basic input statement is the READ statement. In the BASIC language, an INPUT statement is followed by a list of variables to be read; on the input card or input line (assuming a terminal is used), the individual elements of data are separated by blanks or commas. FORTRAN 77 includes a similar, list-directed READ statement. A more general form of the READ statement, however, is

READ (n,m) list

where "n" is the number of an input device, "m" is the number of a FORMAT statement, and "list" is a list of the variables to be read. The statement

READ (5,15) X,Y,Z

gets values for variables X, Y, and Z from device number 5.

The READ statement requires further explanation. First let's consider the device number. In BASIC, the programmer is usually working through a terminal; thus it is reasonable to assume that INPUT means, "Get some data from the terminal." FORTRAN is a bit more general, being designed for use with terminals, punched cards, or any other input or output medium. Rather than have a series of different statements for each of the different possible input or output devices, FORTRAN uses the device number to designate a specific piece of I/O equipment. The actual numbers used can vary with the computer installation, but 1 or 5 are commonly used to designate a card reader, and 2 or 6 are typical printer device numbers.

The second number enclosed within the parentheses of the READ statement identifies the associated FORMAT statement. What is a FORMAT statement? It is a column-by-column description of the input or output record. For example, let's say that during the planning stage we determined that an input card to a program designed to compute the area of a triangle would contain the following data fields:

Columns	Contents
1–5	base, correct to two decimal places
6	blank
7–11	height, correct to two decimal places

A FORMAT statement to describe this card is

FORMAT (F5.2,1X,F5.2)

Within the parentheses, the card format is described column by column. The first field, F5.2, indicates that the first variable is real (the F), is five digits long (the 5), and that two digits are to be assumed to the right of the decimal point (the 2). The next field, 1X, indicates that one column on the card is to be skipped before encountering the next value, which is another five-digit real number with two digits to the right of the decimal point.

The function of the FORMAT statement is to describe, column by column or position by position, the format of an input or output record. An F-type format item, as we've seen, is used to designate a real variable. An X-type format is used to indicate blank or unused spaces. Integer values are designated by an I-type format item; for example,

FORMAT (I6)

indicates a six-digit integer value.

By combining a READ statement and a FORMAT statement, we have a very flexible set of I/O instructions. The instructions

READ (5,10) HOURS, RATE

10   FORMAT (F3.1,F4.2)

will result in values for both hours and rate being read from device number 5 (the card reader); instruction number 10 describes the precise format of the input card.

Output also uses a combination of statements—the WRITE and FORMAT statements. The WRITE statement looks very much like a READ statement:

WRITE (n,m) list

The "n," "m," and "list" have the same meaning as before.

Note the use of statement numbers in FORTRAN. A statement number need be assigned only when the programmer wishes to refer to a statement. Since FORMAT statements are always referenced by a READ or a WRITE, a FORMAT statement always has a number. The only other time that a statement number is needed is when the programmer wishes to branch to a given point in a program.

FORTRAN also has an IF statement; its general form is

IF (condition) expression

An example of the FORTRAN IF is shown in the following program:

```
1      READ (5,11) RADIUS

       IF (RADIUS .LT.0) GO TO 99

       AREA = 3.1416 * RADIUS ** 2
       WRITE (6,12) RADIUS, AREA
       GO TO 1

99     STOP
11     FORMAT (F5.2)
12     FORMAT (1X,F6.2,3X,F9.4)
       END
```

The IF statement tests the condition enclosed within the parentheses. If the condition is true (if RADIUS is less than zero, in our example), then the expression following the parentheses is executed; in this case, the computer would branch to statement number 99, and stop. If the condition is not true, the computer continues on to the next statement in sequence.

The principles of structured programming had a significant impact on the committee that developed FORTRAN 77; thus it is not surprising to find that several structured logic blocks have been added to the new standard. One of the more valuable new features is an **IF . . . THEN . . . ELSE** logic block. The basic form of this block is

IF (condition) THEN
    one or more statements
ELSE
    one or more statements
END IF

Let's briefly compare how a problem like computing the amount of income tax due would be handled both with and without this IF . . . THEN . . . ELSE structure (see Fig. 13.3). Note how much clearer the newer, FORTRAN 77 version is.

FORTRAN 77	FORTRAN 66
`IF (GROSS .LT. 100.00) THEN`	`   IF (GROSS .GE. 100.00) GO TO 25`
`   INCOME = GROSS * 0.05`	`      INCOME = GROSS * 0.05`
`ELSE`	`      GO TO 30`
`   INCOME = GROSS * 0.10`	`25    INCOME = GROSS * 0.10`
`END IF`	`30 CONTINUE`

Figure 13.3
A comparison of the IF. . .THEN. . .ELSE structure (as implemented in FORTRAN 77) with equivalent nonstructured logic.

One of FORTRAN's main advantages is the tremendous collection of scientific and mathematical subroutines that are available in support of this language. FORTRAN has been around for quite some time, and many common scientific problems have already been solved. Rather than "re-invent the wheel," the FORTRAN programmer can simply attach several subprograms to his or her own program, linking to these routines through a CALL statement.

As we have seen, larger programs are often broken into smaller modules before coding is begun. FORTRAN supports the writing of such original subroutines, and the CALL statement is used to provide a link between these secondary modules and the mainline.

The FORTRAN version of our payroll program is shown in Fig. 13.4. Comments are identified by the letter "C" in the first position of the line. Like the BASIC REM statements, these comments are not actually part of the program; they serve instead as an aid to documentation.

```
C              * * * * * * * * * * * * * * * * * * * *
C              * THIS PROGRAM COMPUTES AND PRINTS   *
C              * AN INDIVIDUAL'S TAKE-HOME PAY.     *
C              *    WRITTEN BY: W.S. DAVIS          *
C              *               NOVEMBER 1, 1980     *
C              * * * * * * * * * * * * * * * * * * * *
       CHARACTER*2 INIT
       CHARACTER*15 NAME
       REAL   NET,INCOME
C              * THE PROGRAM STARTS BY READING THE  *
C              * NAME, INITIALS, HOURS WORKED, AND  *
C              * PAY RATE. THE FORMAT STATEMENT,    *
C              * NUMBER 10, DESCRIBES THE FIRST TWO *
C              * AS ALPHABETIC FIELDS. HOURS WORK-  *
C              * ED IS A DECIMAL NUMBER WITH ONE    *
C              * DIGIT TO THE RIGHT OF THE DECIMAL  *
C              * POINT. THE PAY RATE IS A FOUR      *
C              * DIGIT NUMBER WITH TWO DIGITS TO    *
C              * THE RIGHT OF THE DECIMAL POINT.    *
C
   1   READ (5,10,END=99) NAME,INIT,HOURS,RATE
C
C              * COMPUTE GROSS PAY AND SOCIAL       *
C              * SECURITY TAX.                      *
       GROSS = HOURS * RATE
       SSTAX = GROSS * 0.0665
C              * FIND INCOME TAX RATE FROM TABLE    *
C              * AND COMPUTE INCOME TAX.            *
       IF (GROSS .LT. 100.00) THEN
           INCOME = GROSS * 0.05
       ELSE
           INCOME = GROSS * 0.10
       END IF
C              * COMPUTE TOTAL DEDUCTIONS AND NET   *
C              * PAY. PRINT A PAY CHECK; THEN GO    *
C              * BACK AND READ ANOTHER CARD.        *
       DEDUCT = INCOME + SSTAX
       NET = GROSS - DEDUCT
C
       WRITE (6,50) INIT,NAME,NET
       GO TO 1
C
C              * * * * * * * * * * * * * * * * * * * *
C              * AFTER THE LAST CARD HAS BEEN READ, *
C              * STOP THE PROGRAM.                  *
C              * * * * * * * * * * * * * * * * * * * *
   99  STOP
   10  FORMAT (5X,A15,A2,8X,F3.1,7X,F4.2)
   50  FORMAT (10X,A2,1X,A15,10X,'$',F7.2)
       END
```

Figure 13.4
Payroll in FORTRAN.

In BASIC, the use of a dollar sign as the last character in a data name was sufficient to identify it as being of character type. In FORTRAN, we must be a bit more precise. The first two statements in the program (not counting comments) indicate that INIT and NAME are character variables. Both are read in the statement numbered 1 under control of an A-type format item. The REAL statement identifies the variables NET and INCOME as being real variables; had we not so indicated, the FORTRAN compiler would have assumed that these variables were integer (they begin with one of the letters between I and N), and simply ignored the decimal point. Both net pay and income tax have fractional parts.

The READ statement (number 1) contains an extra field:

```
1       READ (5,10,END = 99) NAME,INIT,HOURS,RATE
```

It is standard procedure in many computer centers to place a special end-of-data marker at the end of a deck of data cards; this marker might take the form of a special card with a number of unusual characters (/*, or/&, or //, or EOD) punched in the first several columns. By coding END = 99, the programmer is telling the system that when this special card is encountered, the computer is to branch to instruction number 99.

Once again, read the program (Fig. 13.4) carefully, comparing it step by step to the flowchart shown in Fig. 13.1.

SUMMARY

In this chapter, we considered how a program might be coded in each of two computational languages: BASIC and FORTRAN. The payroll program (first developed in Chapter 12) was implemented in both languages; the best way to review this chapter would be to reread these two programs, Figs. 13.2 and 13.4.

KEYWORDS

BASIC

BASIC	**IF statement**	**REM statement**
constant	**INPUT statement**	**statement**
END statement	**LET statement**	**variable**
expression	**operator**	
GO TO statement	**PRINT statement**	

FORTRAN

assignment statement	**FORTRAN**	**READ statement**
CALL statement	**GO TO statement**	**real number**
comment	**IF statement**	**STOP statement**
END statement	**IF . . . THEN . . . ELSE logic**	**subroutine**
FORMAT statement	**integer**	**WRITE statement**

EXERCISES

1. Explain the difference between a variable and a constant.

2. In FORTRAN, explain the difference between real and integer numbers.

3. What is the function of the BASIC REM statement and the FORTRAN comment?

4. What is a loop? What is a branch? How does the GO TO statement (in both languages) allow the programmer to implement these two concepts?

5. What is the function of an IF statement?

6. Relate the statements that control input and output in BASIC and FORTRAN. How do the statements in these two languages differ; how are they the same?

7. Relate the FORTRAN assignment statement and the BASIC LET statement to each other. How are they similar? How are they different?

8. What is a subroutine? Why are subroutines useful?

9. What are the operators used to designate addition, subtraction, multiplication, division, and exponentiation in each of these two languages?

10. Explain the IF . . . THEN . . . ELSE logic structure.

11. Why do you suppose that a national standard version of a programming language is an important consideration? This question was not explicitly answered in the text. Think about it.

14

PROGRAM IMPLEMENTATION: RPG AND COBOL

OVERVIEW

Continuing with our discussion of common programming languages, this chapter introduces RPG and COBOL. As we did in Chapter 13, we'll point out many of the key rules for writing programs in these two languages and then use these rules to code a solution to the payroll problem; once again, for your convenience, a copy of the flowchart we developed in Chapter 11 is included here as Fig. 14.1.

Unlike BASIC and FORTRAN, RPG and COBOL were designed with business data processing in mind. Business data processing is concerned primarily with file processing activities; thus, both RPG and COBOL are more concerned with input and output than with processing. In BASIC and FORTRAN, most of the actual program code represented program logic—the actual arithmetic and control operations needed to process the data. As we move into RPG and COBOL, you will very quickly realize that a considerable part of the programmer's time is taken up with specifying input and output. You will also notice that the actual logical operations look a bit simpler in these two business data processing languages.

RPG

Report Program Generator, normally known as RPG, is a programming language designed to allow the programmer to easily format and generate standard business reports, one of the most common of all data processing activities.

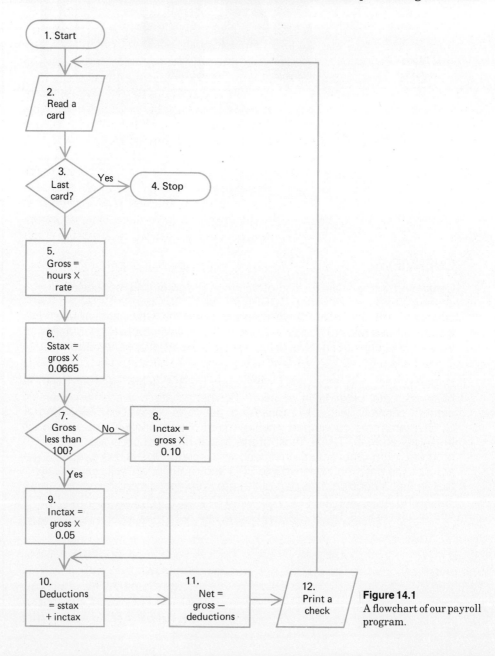

Figure 14.1
A flowchart of our payroll program.

The RPG language was developed by IBM during the 1960s. It was aimed at the small user; it was intended to allow the less sophisticated computer user to develop simple business-report programs without the need for a high-powered staff of full-time professional programmers. RPG is simple and straightforward, with program logic resembling the logic of a punched card data processing system (not surprising when you consider that many smaller users were moving up from punched card systems during the 1960s). The language has gained wide acceptance. In 1970, a new and more powerful version of RPG, known as RPG II, was announced; this version will be used throughout the discussion of the next several pages. Recently, RPG III was released.

The key to understanding RPG is the standard data processing sequence: input, processing, output. The programmer, following this same approach, first describes the input record, then the processing steps, and finally the output record. Special preprinted forms are used for describing each.

The first form (Fig. 14.2) is used to specify the physical files. A second form (Fig. 14.3) gives a column-by-column description of the contents of the input record or records. Next (Fig. 14.4) comes a form for the calculation specifications, where the sequence of additions, subtractions, comparisons, and other computer operations is specified. Finally (Fig. 14.5), we come to the output specification form, where a detailed, position-by-position description of the output record is provided.

Before going on to a detailed description of each of these forms, there are a few common fields we should discuss first. Near the top right of each form is a space to hold the page number. Each RPG form is assigned a page number; this number must be punched into the first two columns of each program statement card. Just to the right of the page number is a six-character field, identified as columns 75 through 80, intended to hold a program identification. This field is optional; if coded it will be punched into columns 75 through 80 of each RPG program card. Other boxes near the top of the form allow the programmer to identify the program and himself. The punching instructions provide a means of communication with the keypunch operator; in this example, the programmer has drawn a slash through each digit zero so as to differentiate between it and the letter O.

A number of spaces on the forms are precoded. Columns 3 and 4 of the card, for example, will hold the two high-order digits of a 3-digit line number. In column 6, the form type is precoded: H means a **control card,** F means a **file description specification** card, I identifies an **input specification** card, C designates a **calculation specification** card, and O stands for an **output specification** card.

Let's now consider each of these specification forms, one at a time, concentrating briefly on what the programmer must code in writing an RPG program. The first specification sheet (Fig. 14.2) actually designates two different cards: a control card and a series of file description cards. The function of the control card is to specify such things as the use of European notation on decimal points

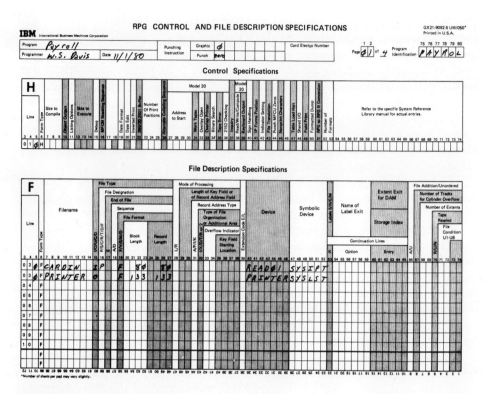

Figure 14.2
RPG control card and file
description specifications form.

and commas, the way in which signs are to be handled, special forms-handling procedures, and other control procedures. In many versions of RPG, this card is not required; in other versions, particularly older versions that are still in use in many data processing centers, it is required, even if all that is coded is a page number, a line number, and the letter H in card column 6. Incidentally, to avoid any possible misunderstanding on your part, the third digit of the line number is always coded by the programmer; the digit zero is normally used.

Following the control card (Fig. 14.2) comes a series of file description specification cards, one for each data file accessed by the program. In our example, we'll be reading cards and printing output lines; thus two file description entries are needed. The first, line 020 on Fig. 14.2, is for the input card. We've assigned the name CARDIN to this file. The I in column 15 identifies this as an input file; the P in column 16 tells the RPG compiler that this is a primary (as opposed to secondary) file. In column 19, we've indicated that the records are all of fixed length (the F). Since each record consists of exactly 80 columns, and cards are a unit record medium, the block length (to be discussed in Chapter 15) and the record length are both 80 characters. In columns 40 through 46, the device is identified: READ01 defines a particular type of card reader. The symbolic device name in columns 47 through 52, in this case SYSIPT, is required on some computers and not on others; this example just happens to be based on a computer running under a control program called the Disk Operating System (DOS), which requires the use of this field.

The output file, named PRINTER, is described in much the same way; the O in column 15 stands for output. Any other physical files needed by this program would be identified by a similar card coded on this form. There must be one file description specification for each file accessed by the program. Since the rules for specifying files can vary from installation to installation, you should check on the requirements of your own computer center before coding these cards.

Moving along to the second specification sheet, we come to the RPG input specifications (Fig. 14.3). The function of this sheet is to describe, field by field, the contents of each input record. The first card identifies a **filename.** Each

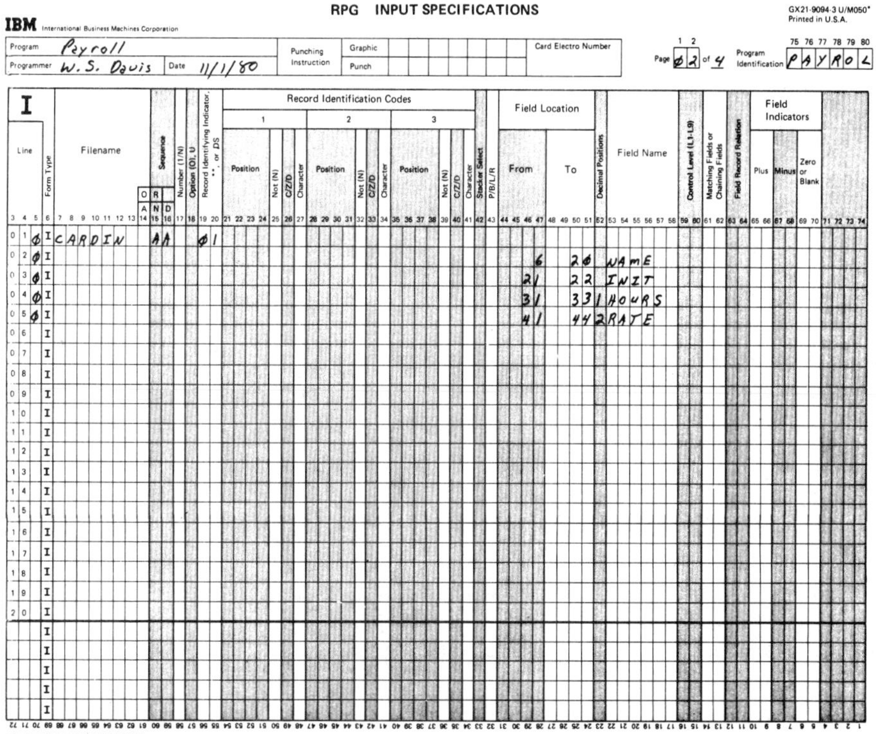
RPG INPUT SPECIFICATIONS

IBM International Business Machines Corporation

GX21-9094-3 U/M050*
Printed in U.S.A.

Program: Payroll
Programmer: W. S. Davis Date: 11/1/80
Page 02 of 4 Program Identification: PAYROL

Line	Form Type	Filename	Sequence	Number (1/N)	Option (O), U	Record Identifying Indicator	From	To	Decimal Positions	Field Name
01	I	CARDIN	AA			01				
02	I						6	26		NAME
03	I						21	22		INIT
04	I						31	33	1	HOURS
05	I						41	44	2	RATE

*Number of sheets per pad may vary slightly.

Figure 14.3
RPG input specifications form.

record description is associated with a particular file; in this case, it's CARD-IN. In columns 19 and 20, a record identifying **indicator** is punched; more about the meaning of these switches a bit later. The second card in Fig. 14.2 indicates that starting in column 6 and ending in column 20 is an input field that is to be called NAME. In subsequent lines of the form, each of the other input fields is specified, one per line. Column 52 is used to indicate the number of positions to the right of the decimal point in a numeric field.

Had there been any other input records, they would have been specified on this same form. In our example, there are none.

The key to understanding RPG program logic is the idea of setting switches or indicators. We already mentioned the fact that each input record was assigned an indicator, using 01 in our example. Each calculation specification is preceded by an indicator number. The calculation is executed only if the associated indicator is on (Fig. 14.4).

Consider, for example, the first step in the program,

01   HOURS   MULT RATE   GROSS,

which says that HOURS is to be multiplied (MULT) by RATE to get GROSS. This statement is preceded (Fig. 14.4, line 010) by the digits 01 in columns 10 and 11; these two digits identify the indicator controlling this operation. The multiply instruction is executed only if indicator 01 is on. How can this indicator be turned on? Remember the indicator associated with the input record (Fig. 14.3)? CARDIN was identified as using indicator 01; what this means is that whenever an input card is read, indicator 01 is turned on.

Perhaps the best way to understand the meaning of the indicators is by looking at the logical test incorporated in this program. Income tax, you may remember, is computed at 5% if the gross pay is less than or equal to $100.00, and at 10% if it's over $100.00. Look at the instructions in lines 030, 040, and 050 of Fig. 14.4; these lines are reproduced below for convenience:

030C	01	GROSS	COMP	100.00		101111
040C	11	GROSS	MULT	0.50	INCTAX	
050C	10	GROSS	MULT	0.10	INCTAX	

The first of these lines, line 030, asks the computer to compare (COMP) GROSS to 100.00. There are three possible outcomes: GROSS might be higher than 100.00, GROSS might be lower, or GROSS might be equal to 100.00. Depending on the result of this test, an indicator will be turned on.

The indicator to be used if the result is "high" is designated by the programmer in columns 54 and 55; the indicator to be used in the event of a low comparison is found in columns 56 and 57 (Fig. 14.4); the indicator for an

RPG   CALCULATION SPECIFICATIONS

GX21-9093-2 UM/050* Printed in U.S.A.
*No. of forms per pad may vary slightly

IBM International Business Machine Corporation

| Program | Payroll |
| Programmer | W. S. Davis | Date 11/1/80 |

Punching Instruction — Graphic / Punch

Page 03 of 4 Program Identification PAYROL

Line	Form Type	Control Level	Indicators (And / And / Not)	Factor 1	Operation	Factor 2	Result Field Name	Length	Dec Pos	Resulting Indicators	Comments
01	C		01	HOURS	MULT	RATE	GROSS	6	2		GROSS PAY
02	C		01	GROSS	MULT	0.0665	SSTAX	6	2		SOC SEC TAX
03	C		01	GROSS	COMP	100.00				10 11 11	TAX RATE TEST
04	C		11	GROSS	MULT	0.05	INCTAX	6	2		INCOME TAX 5%
05	C		10	GROSS	MULT	0.10	INCTAX	6	2		INCOME TAX 10%
06	C		01	SSTAX	ADD	INCTAX	DEDUCT	6	2		DEDUCTIONS
07	C		01	GROSS	SUB	DEDUCT	NET	6	2		NET PAY
08	C		01		SETOF					10 11	RESET FLAGS

Figure 14.4
RPG calculation specifications form.

equal comparison is in 58 and 59. If, for example, the computed GROSS pay is $150.00, indicator 10 would be turned on, and indicator 11, which is used for both low and equal, would not be.

Now, consider instructions 040 and 050. The indicator for 040 is 11; this instruction will be executed only if indicator 11 is on. Line 050 is associated with indicator 10. If GROSS had been $150.00, indicator 10 would have been turned on by the COMP instruction. Since the indicator for instruction 040 is 11, this instruction would not be executed. Since instruction 050 uses indicator 10, and since this indicator is on, income tax (INCTAX) would be computed at a 10% rate.

Finally, note the SETOF instruction (number 080). The purpose of this instruction is to "set off" indicators 10 and 11 so that, on the next program cycle, the only way either indicator could be turned on would be as a result of the COMP instruction analyzing the content of the next record.

Each logical operation is given one line on the RPG coding form. Standard operations include ADD, SUB, MULT, DIV, MOVE, and COMP, along with several others. An RPG programmer specifies the sequence in which these operations are to be performed. With each operation, a field called "factor 1," a second field called "factor 2," and a "result field" must be specified; the two factors identify the fields that are to participate in the operation, while the result field indicates where the answer is to be placed.

You may have noticed that there are no read or write instructions in this program. RPG uses a standard **fixed logic,** which is based on perhaps the most common of all business data processing applications. Consider, for example, the task of updating checking accounts. We might start by sorting all checks and deposits into account-number sequence. Subsequently, as these transactions are read in sequence, a simple check of the account number "just" read against the "prior" account number serves to clearly signal when the processing of one customer's account is finished and another customer's has begun; this is known as a **control break.** A control break is a signal to summarize activity (subtract total checks and add total deposits) or to update a master file; we'll be investigating this application in more detail in Chapter 16. The logic of this program is simple—read a record, check for control breaks, perform computations, and write a line of output. All RPG programs follow this pattern; since input and output are standard, all the programmer must code is the computational logic. There is a READ instruction available for specifying input at other than the standard points in the program, but we won't need it.

The final form to be filled out by the RPG programmer is the output specifications form (Fig. 14.5), on which the format of each output record is specified in a manner similar to the input specifications. There are a few differences. On the input specifications, both the start and ending position of each field was specified; on output, only the *ending* position is needed. In columns 45 through 70, a constant (a column header, for example) or an edit word can be coded. An edit word tells the computer how to punctuate the output field; on card 040, for example, the edit word '$ 0. ', tells the computer to print a dollar sign followed by four digits (three blanks and a zero), followed by a decimal point, followed by two more digits; the zero indicates that a digit is to be printed in this position even if no significant digits have yet been encountered.

A compiler-generated listing of the RPG program for solving our payroll problem is shown in Fig. 14.6. Follow the program step by step, comparing each logical operation with the flowchart of Fig. 14.1. Don't forget that RPG starts by defining the input and output files, specifies the input records, and only then moves on to the program logic. Remember also that normal input and output operations are not coded, being a part of RPG's fixed logic; the statement returning control to the first instruction and the last record check are other parts of this fixed logic.

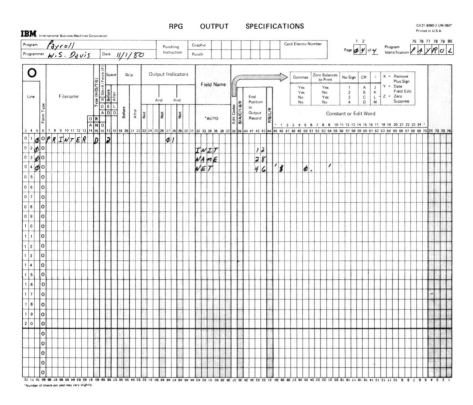

Figure 14.5
RPG output specifications form.

```
01 010 H
01 020 FCARDIN   IP  F   80   80           READ01 SYSIPT
01 030 FPRINTER  O   F  132  132           PRINTERSYSLST
02 010 ICARDIN   AA      01
02 020 I                                          6   20 NAME
02 030 I                                         21   22 INIT
02 040 I                                         31  331HOURS
02 050 I                                         41  442RATE
03 010 C         01        HOURS    MULT RATE    GROSS   62        GROSS PAY
03 020 C         01        GROSS    MULT 0.0665  SSTAX   62        SOCIAL SECURITY
03 030 C         01        GROSS    COMP 100.00            101111TAX RATE
03 040 C         11        GROSS    MULT 0.05    INCTAX  62        INCOME TAX
03 050 C         10        GROSS    MULT 0.10    INCTAX  62        INCOME TAX
03 060 C         01        SSTAX    ADD  INCTAX  DEDUCT  62        DEDUCTIONS
03 070 C         01        GROSS    SUB  DEDUCT  NET     62        NET PAY
03 080 C                            SETOF                  1011    RESET
04 010 OPRINTER D 2         01
04 020 O                             INIT     12
04 030 O                             NAME     28
04 040 O                             NET      46  '$      0.   '
```

Figure 14.6
Payroll in RPG.

COBOL

The COmmon Business Oriented Language (COBOL) was designed, as the name implies, with business data processing in mind. Business computer applications usually involve the processing of files; payroll, inventory, accounts receivable, and accounts payable are typical examples. Such applications tend to be long-lived; in other words, once a payroll program is written, it will probably be used for years. Therefore, the maintainability of these programs is of great concern. This places a premium on documentation, and COBOL is designed to be almost self-documenting.

Every COBOL program is divided into four divisions. The first of these, the IDENTIFICATION DIVISION, contains such information as the name of the program, the name of the programmer, and remarks concerning the function of the program. The primary purpose of the IDENTIFICATION DIVISION is documentation.

The second division of a COBOL program is called the ENVIRONMENT DIVISION. Here, the environment in which the program is designed to run is clearly spelled out, including such information as the make and model of the computer for which the program was written and a list of all the I/O devices used by the program. In addition to providing important documentation, the ENVIRONMENT DIVISION houses the code needed to logically link the program to its I/O devices.

Following the ENVIRONMENT DIVISION is the DATA DIVISION, where the format of each input and output record is defined. Consider, for example, the input card to the "area of a triangle" program described on page 238. In COBOL's DATA DIVISION, the format of this record might be defined as follows:

```
01    INPUT-CARD.
      05   BASE     PICTURE IS 999V99.
      05   FILLER   PICTURE IS X.
      05   HEIGHT   PICTURE IS 999V99.
      05   FILLER   PICTURE IS X(69).
```

These PICTURE clauses have been used to describe, column by column, the entire 80 columns of the card. The variable called BASE is a five-digit number with two digits to the right of the decimal point; the 9 identifies a numeric character, and V designates the implied location of the decimal point. The second item of data, called FILLER, has as its PICTURE a single X, which designates a non-numeric field. Next comes the HEIGHT, another numeric field. The final field, holding the unused remainder of the card, is also called FILLER. FILLER is a special name that can be used to identify any and all data fields not actually referenced by a program.

In the DATA DIVISION's FILE SECTION is listed the format of each input and output record. In the WORKING-STORAGE SECTION, work space to hold intermediate results, column headers, and other work areas can be defined.

All variables must be defined in the DATA DIVISION. A COBOL variable name can consist of from 1 to 31 characters; letters, digits, and the dash (—) character are valid. Why such large names? COBOL, remember, was designed with the idea of self-documentation in mind. Since the programmer has 31 characters to work with, names like SOCIAL-SECURITY-NUMBER can be used. This very clearly indicates the content of a field, and therefore aids documentation.

The final division of a COBOL program is the PROCEDURE DIVISION. It is here that the actual logic of the program is coded. The designers of COBOL wanted to create a language that is easy to read; thus a COBOL statement is much like an English-language sentence, complete with a verb and a period at the end. COBOL arithmetic is performed by statements such as the following:

ADD A,B GIVING C.

MULTIPLY HOURS-WORKED BY PAY-RATE
        GIVING GROSS-PAY.

In BASIC and FORTRAN, input and output statements are designed to read values of individual variables; in COBOL, we read and write entire records. The statement

READ CARD-FILE AT END CLOSE CARD-FILE
        CLOSE PRINT-FILE
        STOP RUN.

reads a single record of the card file; both the file and the record must be defined in the DATA DIVISION. The AT END clause attached to the READ statement is a test for the special end-of-data card. When this card is encountered, the program will, as the instructions making up the clause indicate, close the two files and stop the run.

Output is controlled through the WRITE statement, as in

WRITE PAY-CHECK AFTER ADVANCING 2 LINES.

PAY-CHECK is the name of a record defined in the DATA DIVISION. The AFTER ADVANCING clause controls printers spacing; in this case, the printer is to skip two lines and then print.

Standard COBOL contains an IF . . . THEN . . . ELSE structure. Consider, for example, the following statement:

IF GROSS-PAY IS LESS THAN 100.00
    THEN   MULTIPLY GROSS-PAY BY 0.05
               GIVING INCOME-TAX

    ELSE   MULTIPLY GROSS-PAY BY 0.10
               GIVING INCOME-TAX.

What if the condition is true (GROSS-PAY is less than 100.00)? Then IN-COME-TAX will be computed at a five-percent rate. What if the condition is not true? INCOME-TAX will be computed at a ten-percent rate. An easy way to remember how IF . . . THEN . . . ELSE logic works is to remember the following sentence:

IF condition-is-true THEN do-this
                     ELSE do-this-instead.

Business computer applications are typically large, involving many different programmers. Under such conditions, structured modular programming makes a great deal of sense. Typically, the necessary link between the program's mainline and its detailed computational routines is achieved by using the PERFORM statement. In its most basic form, the PERFORM statement causes the computer to branch to a secondary routine and then to come back to the mainline following execution of the secondary routine statements. The instruction

PERFORM INCOME-TAX-ROUTINE.

might well imply that the programmer has instructed the computer to link to an income tax computation routine, compute the tax, and return.

A COBOL version of our payroll program is shown in Fig. 14.7. There are a few points not mentioned in the above discussion. Look first at the DATA DIVISION. The line beginning "FD CARD-FILE" contains a reference to a LABEL RECORD; the clause indicates the type of label used to identify the file.

Moving along to the PROCEDURE DIVISION, a close examination should reveal two OPEN statements and two CLOSE statements. The purpose of these statements is, at the beginning of the program, to make sure that the I/O devices required are ready to be used and, at the end of the program, to return the devices to the system so they can be used by another program.

Finally, we must consider the target of a GO TO statement. In BASIC and FORTRAN, statements are assigned numbers, and a branch instruction simply refers to the number of the target statement. In COBOL, a **paragraph name** is assigned to each branch point; in Fig. 14.7, for example, we refer to the paragraph PAY-COMPUTATIONS. Strict structured programming practice often prohibits the use of any GO TO statements. Instead, the programmer writing structured COBOL would code a mainline instruction telling the program to, essentially, "PERFORM the PAY-COMPUTATIONS paragraph until there is no more data"; this is called a DO WHILE or DO UNTIL logic block. Our intent in this section is to compare several different languages, and not to introduce strict structured programming; thus we will use a single GO TO, just as we did in BASIC and FORTRAN. The reader should, however, be aware that standards may be different in a COBOL course.

```
IDENTIFICATION DIVISION.
 PROGRAM-ID. SALARY.
 AUTHOR.        DAVIS.
 REMARKS.       THIS PROGRAM COMPUTES AND PRINTS
                AN INDIVIDUAL'S TAKE-HOME PAY.


ENVIRONMENT DIVISION.
 CONFIGURATION SECTION.
  SOURCE-COMPUTER. IBM-370-168.
  OBJECT-COMPUTER. IBM-370-168.

 INPUT-OUTPUT SECTION.
  FILE-CONTROL.
   SELECT CARD-FILE  ASSIGN TO UT-S-SYSIN.
   SELECT PRINT-FILE ASSIGN TO UT-S-SYSOUT.



DATA DIVISION.
 FILE SECTION.
  FD  CARD-FILE         LABEL RECORD IS OMITTED.
   01 TIME-CARD.
    02  FILLER            PICTURE X(5).
    02  IN-EMPLOYEE-NAME  PICTURE X(15).
    02  IN-INITIALS       PICTURE X(2).
    02  FILLER            PICTURE X(8).
    02  IN-HOURS-WORKED   PICTURE 99V9.
    02  FILLER            PICTURE X(7).
    02  IN-PAY-RATE       PICTURE 99V99.
    02  FILLER            PICTURE X(36).


  FD  PRINT-FILE         LABEL RECORD IS OMITTED.
   01 PAY-CHECK.
    02  FILLER            PICTURE X(10).
    02  OUT-INITIALS      PICTURE X(2).
    02  FILLER            PICTURE X(1).
    02  OUT-EMPLOYEE-NAME PICTURE X(15).
    02  FILLER            PICTURE X(10).
    02  NET-PAY           PICTURE $$999.99.
    02  FILLER            PICTURE X(86).



 WORKING-STORAGE SECTION.
    77  SOCIAL-SECURITY-TAX PICTURE 9999V99.
    77  INCOME-TAX          PICTURE 9999V99.
    77  DEDUCTIONS          PICTURE 9999V99.
    77  GROSS-PAY           PICTURE 9999V99.



PROCEDURE DIVISION.
    OPEN INPUT  CARD-FILE.
    OPEN OUTPUT PRINT-FILE.


 PAY-COMPUTATIONS.
    READ CARD-FILE    AT END CLOSE CARD-FILE
                             CLOSE PRINT-FILE
                             STOP RUN.


    MULTIPLY IN-HOURS-WORKED BY IN-PAY-RATE GIVING GROSS-PAY.
    MULTIPLY GROSS-PAY BY 0.0665 GIVING SOCIAL-SECURITY-TAX.

    IF GROSS-PAY IS LESS THAN 100.00
       THEN MULTIPLY GROSS-PAY BY 0.05 GIVING INCOME-TAX
       ELSE MULTIPLY GROSS-PAY BY 0.10 GIVING INCOME-TAX.


    MOVE SPACES TO PAY-CHECK.
    ADD INCOME-TAX  SOCIAL-SECURITY-TAX GIVING DEDUCTIONS.
    SUBTRACT DEDUCTIONS FROM GROSS-PAY GIVING NET-PAY.

    MOVE IN-INITIALS       TO OUT-INITIALS.
    MOVE IN-EMPLOYEE-NAME TO OUT-EMPLOYEE-NAME.
    WRITE PAY-CHECK AFTER ADVANCING 2 LINES.

    GO TO PAY-COMPUTATIONS.
```

Figure 14.7
Payroll in COBOL.

255

Read the program in Fig. 14.7 carefully, comparing the PROCEDURE DIVISION step by step with the flowchart of Fig. 14.1.

COBOL has long been standardized. The most recent standard, ANS 74 COBOL, was used as a reference for the discussion above.

SUMMARY

In this chapter, we considered how a program might be implemented in each of two business data processing languages: RPG and COBOL. The payroll program of Chapter 12 was implemented in both languages; the best way to review this chapter would be to reread the two programs, Figures 14.6 and 14.7.

KEYWORDS

RPG

calculation specifications	filename	RPG
control break	fixed logic	RPG II
control card	indicator	
file description specifications	input specifications	
	output specifications	

COBOL

CLOSE	IDENTIFICATION DIVISION	paragraph name
COBOL		PERFORM
DATA DIVISION	IF . . . THEN . . . ELSE logic	PICTURE
ENVIRONMENT DIVISION	OPEN	PROCEDURE DIVISION

EXERCISES

1. Why must the RPG or COBOL programmer spend so much time specifying input and output while the BASIC or FORTRAN programmer is able to ignore most of the details of I/O?

2. What is meant by the fixed logic portion of RPG? Why is such fixed logic desirable in this language?

3. How is basic program I/O defined in RPG?

4. COBOL is said to be a self-documenting language. What does this mean and why is it valuable?

5. In Chapter 12, the need to fully specify the format of an input or output record was expressed. How is this objective achieved in COBOL? In RPG?

6. The first RPG specification sheet defined the physical files accessed by the program. Where, in a COBOL program, are the equivalent functions performed?

7. Where in COBOL do you find the equivalent of RPG's input and output specifications?

8. Where in COBOL do you find RPG's calculation specifications?

IV
FILE PROCESSING

15

SEQUENTIAL FILE PROCESSING AND MAGNETIC TAPE

OVERVIEW

Now that you have a basic idea of how a computer works, we can begin to discuss a number of more realistic examples of computer use. One of the most common applications of the computer is simply keeping records. We'll be examining this application throughout this section.

Computer record keeping often involves the processing of sequential files. Magnetic tape is a common medium for storing such files; thus we'll be covering a number of magnetic tape concepts. Finally, the idea of an access method will be introduced; look for it, because the concept is an important one.

CHARACTERS, FIELDS, RECORDS, AND FILES

The **character** is the basic building block of computer data. Letters, digits, and special symbols such as commas, periods, dollar signs, and other punctuation marks are all examples of characters.

By themselves, individual characters have little meaning; it's only when they are grouped together that they convey information. Consider the card shown in Fig. 15.1. Columns 6 through 20 contain an individual's last name. Columns 21 and 22 contain this individual's initials. Although it is not quite so obvious, the same person's hours worked and hourly pay rate are punched, respectively, in columns 31 through 33 and in columns 41 through 44. In computer terminology, a group of characters that forms a single, logical "chunk" or piece of data is called a **field.**

Fields alone are not particularly useful either. You can't do very much with SMITH. But these four fields, when combined, do serve a very useful purpose. They allow us to compute this particular individual's pay. The card contains one **record** of data; in other words, all the data needed to support one complete cycle of a program. A record is a collection of fields.

In our example, the next card would contain the name, initials, hours worked, and hourly pay rate of another person. The third card would contain the same fields for still another person. If "A. C. SMITH" works for a typical company, there are probably hundreds, perhaps even thousands, of similar records, one for each employee. Such a collection of similar records is called a **file.**

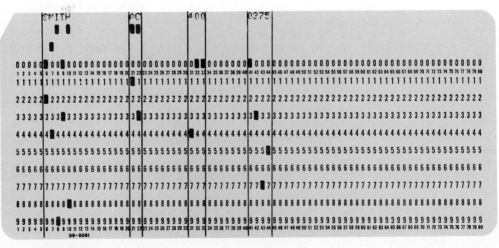

Figure 15.1
A punched card record showing a number of fields.

Files are very common, particularly in business applications. A firm's accounts receivable file is a collection of records, each identifying an amount due the firm; accounts payable is a file of bills to be paid. Payroll involves a number of files, including time cards, year-to-date earnings records, and personnel records for each employee. Banks maintain files of checking-account and savings-account balances. Most companies keep track of their inventories by keeping a record for each part number showing the amount currently in stock or on order.

The computer is often used to maintain these files; in fact, record keeping and **file processing** are probably the most common business applications of the computer. Let's take a look at a familiar file processing application: keeping track of the current balance of a number of checking accounts in a bank.

UPDATING CHECKING ACCOUNTS

Let's begin our analysis of this problem by considering how we might go about handling it manually. We have two files to work with. The first contains a list of all the active checking accounts in the bank, showing the old, or "start-of-day," balance for each. The second holds a collection of all the checks and deposits handled by the bank today. Our objective is to compute the new, or "end-of-day," balance for each account. To do this, we must use the old balance as a starting point and subtract all checks and add all deposits, account by account.

If there were only a few accounts, this would be a very simple process; we would merely read the transactions (checks and deposits) one at a time, find the old balance for the same account, and either add or subtract, depending on the type of transaction.

But what if we have thousands of accounts? Since the transactions are processed by different tellers at different times of day, they are not in any particular order. Trying to update the master file by looking up the proper account for each transaction would be a very time-consuming operation. Wouldn't it make sense to sort the transactions into account-number sequence first?

Sorting achieves two primary purposes. First, obviously, it places things in a known sequence. If both the master checking-account file and the transactions (checks and deposits) file are sorted in the same sequence by the same key (in this case, by account number) we know that we can start at the top of both files and go through them together, making the file update activity easier. There is a second advantage derived from sorting. If the transactions are sorted into account-number sequence, we know that all checks and deposits against account number 0001, for example, will come before *any* transactions for account number 0002. (In other words, the process of sorting gathers together all records having the same key.) What this means to our master-file update application is that we can process all the checks and deposits for account number 0001 before moving on to account number 0002. Looking at it from another perspective, we know that we are finished with account number 0001 as soon as we encounter the first transaction against account number 0002.

If we were to try to update the checking-account master file by hand, we might begin by sorting the transactions into account-number sequence. Once this has been done, assuming that the master file is itself sorted into account-number sequence, the problem becomes one of simply starting with an old balance, adding all deposits and subtracting all checks drawn against the same account, and writing a new balance to the new master file before moving on to the next customer's records. The logic of the "program" assumes that both the old master file and the transactions file are in sequential order. In computer terminology, we would say that these two files are organized *sequentially* and that the activity we have been performing is **sequential file processing.**

Updating Checking Accounts on the Computer Using Cards

It is not at all unusual for a bank to have over 100,000 checking accounts. Although the calculations are no different from what we've already discussed, the tremendous number of additions and subtractions needed to update a master file of 100,000 records makes this job a candidate for automation.

A computerized version of the checking-account master-file update problem is shown in Fig. 15.2. First the checks and deposit slips are sorted into

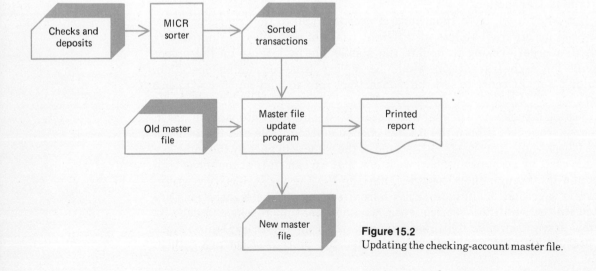

Figure 15.2
Updating the checking-account master file.

account-number sequence using a special machine called a MICR sorter (recall our earlier discussion of the magnetic characters imprinted on the bottom of a check). These sorted transactions are then read into the **master-file update** program and merged with the records from the old master-file card deck. Two output files are produced by this program: a printer listing showing the current end-of-day balance for each account, and a punched-card new master file.

Why Cards Just Won't Do for This Application

A single box that measures roughly 8 by 3½" by 15" holds 2000 cards. For a master file of 100,000 records, we would need 50 boxes. That's 50 boxes for the old master file and another 50 boxes for the new master file—one hundred boxes of cards that must be handled by the computer operator just to update the master file! The volume alone creates a serious problem.

Perhaps even more important than the physical bulk is the difficulty that an operator would face in maintaining the sequence of 50 separate boxes of cards. The master-file update program, as you may remember, assumes sequence; in fact, the program logic is written to take advantage of sequence. Try maintaining the sequence of 50 boxes of cards (not to mention the cards in each individual box) day after day after day. It's only a matter of time before an all-too-human operator makes a mistake or drops a box.

By far the most serious problem with cards (as if the previous two weren't enough) is the extreme slowness of card readers and card punches compared to the internal processing speed of a computer. With card input and output, the computer will spend most of its time waiting for I/O rather than accomplishing useful tasks.

A final problem with cards, one that is becoming more and more important these days, is the fact that cards are not reusable; there is no way to fill up the holes and use the cards again. With a continuing activity like record keeping, this tends to make punched cards a rather expensive storage medium.

The ideal medium for this application would store a great deal of data in a compact space, maintain this data in a tightly fixed sequence, support very rapid data transmission between an I/O device and the computer, and be reusable. Magnetic tape scores high on all these tests.

Magnetic Tape

Magnetic tape stores data at very high densities. A common density is 1600 characters per inch. If we assume an 80 character record (the capacity of a punched card), 20 of these records could be stored on a single inch of tape! Our 100,000-record file would require only 5000 inches of magnetic tape. A standard **reel** of tape holds 2400 feet, considerably more than is needed, and such a reel fits in a plastic case about the size of an imaginary, one-inch thick, long-playing record album. That is compact!

What about sequence? Data stored on tape is arranged in sequence along the surface of the tape. The only way to break the sequence is to physically break the tape. Magnetic tape is normally constructed of a very tough plastic called mylar, which is extremely difficult to break.

Magnetic tape is also fast—at least 100 times faster than punched cards. And magnetic tape is reusable. Anyone who has a reel-to-reel tape recorder will tell you that sound-recording tape can be reused simply by recording (or writing) new information directly over the old; magnetic computer tape is made from the same material as magnetic sound-recording tape.

Updating Checking Accounts Using Magnetic Tape

Substituting tape for the card files we used before gives us a more typical version of the checking-account update problem (Fig. 15.3). Rather than simply sorting the transactions on a mechanical sorter and then reading them directly into the master-file update program, the transactions have been read, sorted, and copied to magnetic tape. The most obvious reason for using tape to hold the sorted data is that tape can be read into the master-file update program at a higher speed than can the individual unit records of the transactions. A second advantage arises from the fact that most banks return checks to the customer; the magnetic tape allows the bank to keep a copy of the information.

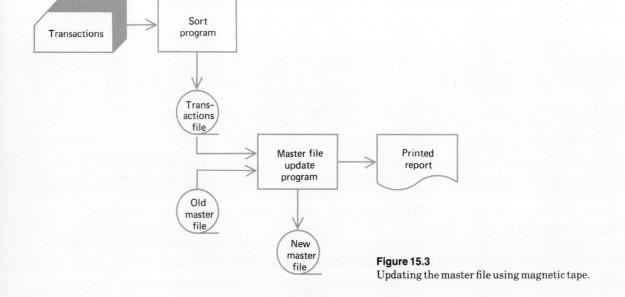

Figure 15.3
Updating the master file using magnetic tape.

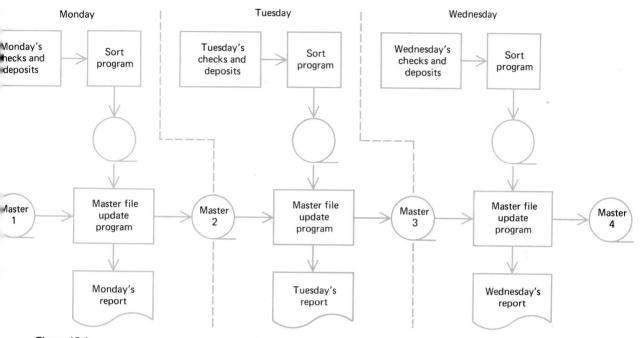

Figure 15.4
The master file is updated on a daily basis.

Another important idea is the link between successive runs of this master-file update program (Fig. 15.4). Monday's output (or "new") master file becomes Tuesday's old master file; Tuesday's output becomes Wednesday's input, and so on. In effect, the balance of a checking account at the close of "today's" business is the same as the balance at the start of "tomorrow's" business.

OTHER EXAMPLES OF RECORD-KEEPING APPLICATIONS

Look back at Fig. 15.3, and note that it does *not* refer to checks and deposits or account balances. Instead, the figure has been generalized to refer to transactions, the old master file, the new master file, and a report. The reason for making this change is simple: Record keeping is a very common computer application that is not restricted to processing checks and deposits. In fact, the sequential master-file update application is, without a doubt, the most common business application of the computer. Let's take a look at a number of other examples.

In addition to checking accounts, a bank must also maintain savings-account balances. This application involves reading deposit and withdrawal slips, sorting them into sequence, and changing the old master file to reflect these transactions, creating a new master file in the process. Computing and adding interest to savings accounts is another example of a sequential file-processing activity, involving the multiplication of a field in each old master file record by a constant, adding the computed interest to compute the new balance, writing a new master file record, and preparing a written report showing interest earned by each account holder.

Banks also make loans, and loan payments are processed in much the same way. Usually a card or other record is prepared to accompany the payment. These "transactions" are sorted into loan-number sequence and processed against the old master file of loans "outstanding," producing a new master file reflecting current payments and overdue accounts. A written report often highlights such overdues.

As those of us who pay taxes know all too well, employers are required to keep track of our earnings throughout the year. This is yet another master-file update problem, with transactions being represented by time cards that are sorted into social security number (or employee number) sequence and used to compute pay for the current period. This current income (along with current deductions) is added to the year-to-date earnings from the old year-to-date file, and a new year-to-date file is generated. The report consists of paychecks. Other reports are usually prepared for accounting and budgetary purposes.

An inventory master file might show the stock-on-hand of various products or raw materials. Transactions (additions to and deletions from inventory) are used to update this master file. Credit card companies keep track of the "balance due" on each account in a master file. Current purchases and credits are used to update this file on a regular basis.

Accounting records are updated in a similar fashion, with the start-of-period balances being updated by receipts and expenditures. Another common business application is the maintenance of an order backlog, a list of pending customer orders; new orders and shipments are the transactions that are used to update this master file.

Even in the field of education, this program is common. Unless your school is very small, your academic record is kept on computer. The old master file holds student records as of the end of the previous marking period. Current grades are sorted into student-number sequence, and the master file is updated to reflect this new data. The written report, as you've probably already guessed, is a grade report. Dozens of other examples could be cited.

CHARACTERISTICS OF THE MASTER-FILE UPDATE PROBLEM

These applications all have a number of characteristics in common. First, consider their timing. Student records are updated at the end of each grading period; interest is added to savings accounts at regular intervals; billing and the updating of accounting records usually follow a monthly cycle; inventory and order backlog are updated on a regular basis with the period determined by the firm; payroll is computed weekly, biweekly, monthly, or quarterly. All of these activities can be scheduled. In each case, transactions are collected into a batch and processed at a predetermined, scheduled time. This type of information processing is called **batch processing.**

Another characteristic of this general category of application is high **activity.** When used in this context, activity means that a significant percentage of the records in the master file are accessed each time the program is executed. It would make little sense, for example, to update the checking-account master file each time a teller cashes a check; since the master file is sequential, the computer would have to go through half the records on the file (on the average) in order to find and update the correct one. It is much less expensive to collect a batch of transactions and process them all at the same time.

If we can afford to wait long enough to collect a sufficiently large batch of transactions to create enough activity to make sequential file processing economically justifiable, then we have a candidate for this type of master-file update. But what if activity is "slow"? Or what if the data is so important that we cannot wait until an economical batch can be collected? In such cases, the file should not be organized sequentially; some examples and some alternative file organizations will be discussed in Chapters 17 through 19.

MAGNETIC TAPE

Its Physical Characteristics

We have already seen that magnetic tape is an ideal medium for sequential files. It is compact, holds data in sequence, can be read into or written from a computer at high rates of speed, and can be reused. What are the physical properties of magnetic tape that give it these advantages?

Magnetic computer tape is made from a ½-inch wide ribbon of mylar coated with a magnetic material (Fig. 15.5); it's very much like reel-to-reel sound-recording tape. If you want to play the fifth song on a reel of recording tape, it is necessary to at least move the tape holding the first four songs past the recording head; likewise, to access the 500th record on a reel of magnetic computer tape, it is first necessary to move the first 499 records past the **read/write heads.** Both types of tape store data in a fixed sequence. Another similarity involves the reusability of the tape. To reuse a reel of sound tape, simply record new information on top of the old; computer tape works in the same way. Magnetic tape is both sequential and reusable.

The speed and compactness of tape are both factors of the tape's **density.** Data is normally stored on magnetic tape at a density of 800 or 1600 characters per inch, with some modern tape units capable of recording as many as 6250

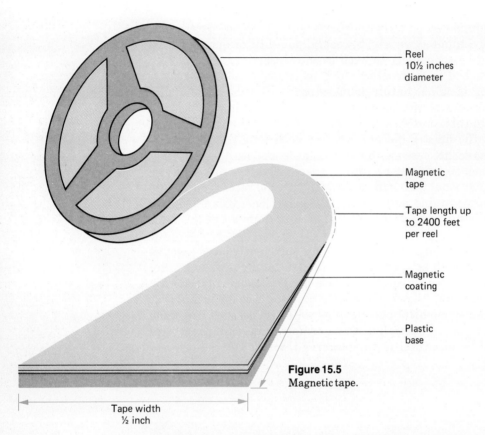

Reel
10½ inches
diameter

Magnetic
tape

Tape length up
to 2400 feet
per reel

Magnetic
coating

Plastic
base

Figure 15.5
Magnetic tape.

Tape width
½ inch

characters per inch! Even at the lower figure, a card containing 80 columns of information can be stored in only one tenth of an inch of ½-inch wide magnetic tape! A file of 100,000 records can be contained in less than 900 feet of tape, even at 800 characters per inch. A typical 10½-inch reel of tape holds about 2400 feet. That is compact!

Magnetic tape's density also leads to high data-transmission speed. A good card reader can handle roughly 600 cards per minute, a rate of ten (10) cards per second. If we were to lay these cards end to end, we would have 73.75 inches of card stock (each card is 7.375 inches long). Given that each card contains 80 characters of information, these 73-plus inches of card stock would hold a total of 800 characters of information (Fig. 15.6). Lay the same length of magnetic tape next to the cards (see Fig. 15.6 again). At 800 characters per inch, the tape would hold 59,000 characters of information, which is over 73 times as much as the cards. If the tape moves at the same physical speed as the cards, it's going to be 73 times as fast—59,000 as opposed to 800 characters per second. In fact, since the cards are separate pieces of paper while the tape is a smooth, continuous piece of plastic, the tape can move much faster. Tape can be processed at speeds of up to 800,000 characters per second!

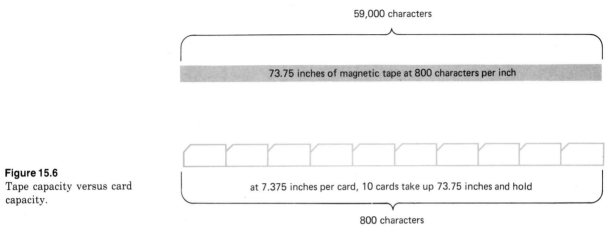

Figure 15.6
Tape capacity versus card capacity.

We've been discussing characters of data on magnetic tape for some time now and have not yet explained how these characters are actually stored. Data are stored on tape as a series of invisible magnetized spots, using the BCD, EBCDIC, or ASCII codes. Picture the upper surface of the tape divided into a gridlike pattern (Fig. 15.7). Each square on the grid represents one bit of data. If the spot is magnetized, it holds a 1-bit; if it is not magnetized, it holds a 0-bit.

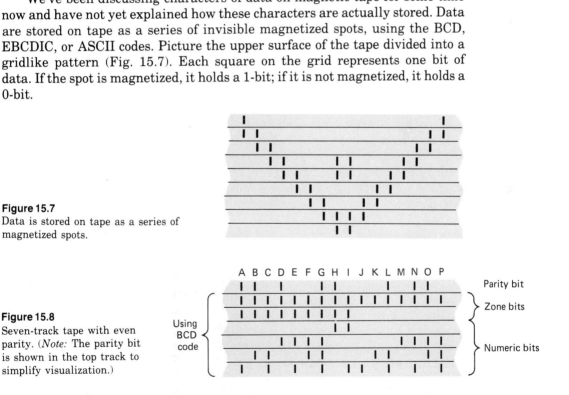

Figure 15.7
Data is stored on tape as a series of magnetized spots.

Figure 15.8
Seven-track tape with even parity. (*Note:* The parity bit is shown in the top track to simplify visualization.)

One common variety of tape is known as seven-track tape, which uses the six-bit BCD code, storing one character of data on a single cross section of tape (Fig. 15.8). Even more popular is nine-track tape, which uses one of the eight-bit codes such as EBCDIC or ASCII (Fig. 15.9).

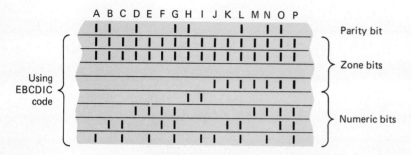

Figure 15.9
Nine-track tape with even parity.
(*Note:* The parity bit is shown in the top track to simplify visualization.)

Note that seven-track tape uses a six-bit code and nine-track tape uses an eight-bit code; what about that extra track? Data on tape is stored at such high densities and is read at such speeds that something as simple as a piece of dust in the wrong place can cause an error. This extra bit is used to help catch such errors before they enter the computer. The extra track holds a **parity bit.** Under *even* parity, an even number of 1-bits will be stored for each character. In EBCDIC, the digit 1 is represented by $(11110001)_2$; the code for the digit 1 contains exactly five 1-bits. If the parity bit were set to 1, this particular cross section of tape would contain six 1-bits, which would meet the requirements of even parity. The digit 3, $(11110011)_2$ in EBCDIC, would have a parity bit of 0. The parity bit is set when the data is written to tape. Later, assuming even parity, if a character with an odd number of 1-bits (including parity) is read, it is known to be an error. *Odd* parity is the exact opposite of even parity.

Parity checking is not restricted to magnetic tape; it is also used in main memory as part of the computer's internal error checking circuitry. Its ability to check and correct its own errors is one reason for the computer's unbelievable accuracy.

Reading the Tape

Before reading or writing tape, a reel must first be loaded onto a tape drive; this is normally the responsibility of the computer operator. The operator begins by visually checking the serial number that is normally printed on the surface of the plastic case that holds the tape, making sure that the proper tape has been selected. Each reel of tape is called a **volume;** the identifying number is called the **volume serial number.** How does the operator know the volume serial number of the correct tape? Basically, from two sources. First, a programmer is normally required to provide a **runbook** to accompany each program run on the computer system, and this runbook should contain detailed operator instructions. A second level of control is gained by having the program, just before the tape is needed, print a message on the operator's console calling for a specific tape by volume serial number.

Photograph courtesy of IBM Corporation.

Figure 15.10
A tape drive.

Having selected the correct volume of tape, the operator proceeds to mount it on a tape drive (Fig. 15.10). Some newer systems have self-threading tape drives; if this is the case, the operator simply gets things started. Other, less expensive drives require manual tape mounting. The operator first places the tape reel on the initial or "feed" sprocket. A length of roughly three feet of tape is unwound to allow for threading through the read mechanism and onto the takeup reel (Fig. 15.11). Next, the operator turns the takeup reel by hand until a clearly visible reflective strip called a **loadpoint marker** moves past the read/write heads. When this happens, the operator pushes the load and start buttons on the tape-drive control panel, telling the system that the tape is loaded and ready to be accessed. As the tape is read or written, magnetic devices in the read/write assembly (Fig. 15.12) sense (or create) the magnetized spots as the tape moves over the heads.

One final comment before we end our discussion of the responsibilities of the computer operator. The fact that tape can be reused represents a danger as well as an advantage. If data is accidentally written to a tape that already contains valuable data, the data that used to be on the tape will be destroyed. In order to minimize the risk of accidental destruction of data, a plastic ring called a **file ring** must be in place in the back of a tape volume before data can be written to that volume. Standard operating procedure often calls for the

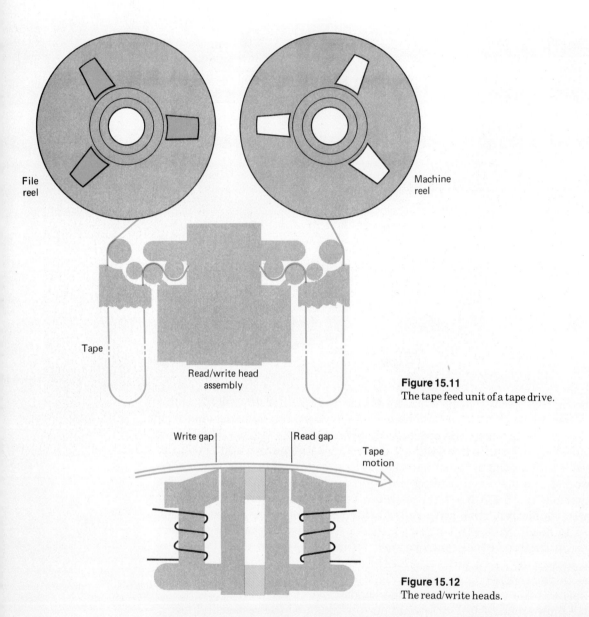

File
reel

Machine
reel

Tape

Read/write head
assembly

Figure 15.11
The tape feed unit of a tape drive.

Write gap

Read gap

Tape
motion

Figure 15.12
The read/write heads.

operator to insert a file ring in the back of a tape volume to be created, and to remove that file ring as soon as the tape is dismounted. In this way, if the tape is accidentally remounted at a later time, the absence of a file ring prohibits writing to the tape, and thus cancels the risk of data destruction. If these procedures are followed faithfully, the only way key data can be destroyed is through the conscious action of inserting a file ring.

Cassettes and Data Cartridges

A growing trend, particularly in using small computers and some terminals, is toward the use of smaller tapes such as the **data cartridge** shown in Fig. 15.13. Even standard sound-recording **cassettes** are sometimes used.

Figure 15.13
A data cartridge.

Photograph courtesy of IBM Corporation.

Fields, Records, and Files on Tape

As with cards, the basic building block of data on tape is the character. On cards, one character is stored in each column; on tape, a single character is stored across the width of the tape.

A group of characters still forms a field, but a field can be different on tape. Within the computer, a series of two, three, or four storage locations might hold a single field in numeric rather than coded form. Such data could not be sent to the printer without conversion; a printer can print only certain characters. Although it is possible to send numeric data to a card punch, the resulting punched-card codes are tricky and require special handling on subsequent input; therefore, this is not normal practice. Sending numeric data to tape, however, creates no problem. The tape drive simply transmits or accepts a stream of eight-bit plus parity-bit characters (assuming nine-track tape) and, so long as the parity bit is correct, the fact that a particular combination might not be a valid EBCDIC or ASCII character does not matter. Thus, a field on magnetic tape might hold coded, pure binary, packed-decimal, or floating-point data.

As with cards, a logically complete collection of fields forms a record on tape. The physical nature of cards normally limits us to exactly 80 characters per record. No such natural limitation exists on magnetic tape; records can be of almost any size. The records within a single file can even vary in length. A perfect example of a variable-length record is an academic history file. As a first-quarter freshman, your record holds only personal and family data, but, as you progress, courses and grades are added at the end of each marking period, making the record longer and longer.

A collection of records of similar type forms a file. A very large file might span two or more reels of tape. It is also possible, at the other extreme, to store two or more smaller files on a single reel of tape. In data processing terminology, a single reel of tape is called a **volume**. A single file spanning two or more volumes is called a *multivolume file,* while a single volume holding two or more files is called a *multifile volume.* The concept of a file has nothing to do with a physical piece of tape or a physical box of cards; a file is simply a collection of similar records. A file is a logical, not a physical, concept.

There is no visible mark on the surface of magnetic tape—people cannot read tape. How then can we be sure that the correct tape is mounted? Normally, each tape volume is assigned a serial number that is affixed to the side of the reel. If we ask the operator to mount tape #IPS001, the volume with this serial number can be found and mounted on the tape drive.

But what if there are two files on the same volume? How do we tell them apart? And how can we be sure that the operator has in fact mounted the correct volume? Mistakes do happen. The answer is really very simple. Tape files are normally preceded on the tape by a header **label** (see Fig. 15.14), which identifies the file. Before file processing begins, this label can be checked by the program.

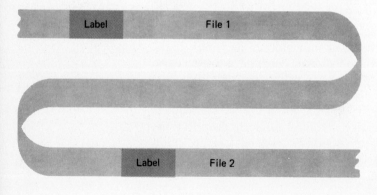

Figure 15.14
Tape files are usually labeled.

Processing Tape Records: The Interrecord Gap

A program that processes tape data is like any other program. It reads a record of data from the input file, processes the data, and writes a record to the output file before going back to the beginning and repeating the cycle. This implies that there will be some delay between reading the first record and reading the second record (or between writing subsequent records).

This delay creates a very real problem on a magnetic tape device. Tape drives are designed to read or write data at a constant speed. The fact that there is some time delay between the reading of adjacent records implies that the tape drive will stop between I/O operations, and this is in fact what it does. Imagine what would happen if records were jammed together at 800 characters per inch. After reading the first record, the drive mechanism would have to bring the tape from a constant speed to a dead stop within the 1/800 of an inch separating the last character in the first record from the first character in the last record, which would be something like an automobile running into a brick wall. The result would be destruction of the tape (and probably the tape drive). Reading the second record would be equally impossible; no physical device can go from a dead stop to full speed in "nothing flat."

The solution to this problem is to place a gap of unused tape between the records. Picture the read/write heads being located right in the middle of the gap between records 1 and 2 (Fig. 15.15). It is necessary to move the tape one-half gap in order to bring it up to speed. The record is read at a constant speed. When the end of the record is reached, the drive has one-half gap available to slow the tape to a safe stop, leaving it in position for the next read. The gap between records is called an **interrecord gap.**

How big is this gap? On nine-track tape, the usual length of the interrecord gap is six tenths (0.6) inch; on seven-track tape, the gap is even wider. Imagine an 80-character record being stored at 800 characters per inch. Given a file of such records, the tape would hold a series of 0.1-inch records separated

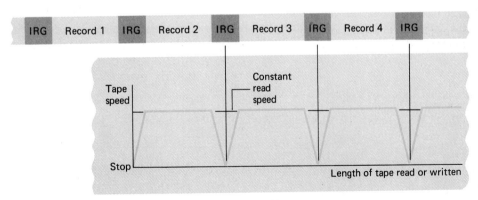

Figure 15.15
The interrecord gap.

by 0.6-inch gaps. That's like putting six blank cards for every data card in a deck! This is hardly an efficient way of utilizing the tape, but for physical reasons the gap must be there.

Blocking

One solution to making better use of the tape is to **block** the data. Rather than write a series of individual records separated by interrecord gaps, why not combine a number of records into a single block (Fig. 15.16)? If we use a **blocking factor** of 10 (that is, ten logical records per block), we could store ten 80-character records on one inch of tape, to be followed by a 0.6-inch gap, to be followed by another inch of data, and so on. Figure out the amount of tape needed to store 1000 records, each 80 characters long, assuming 800 characters per inch and a 0.6-inch gap, using no blocking. Then try using a blocking factor of 10. Do you begin to see the advantage of blocking? Now try it with a blocking factor of 20. By blocking data, we cut down on the amount of dead space.

Of course, we can't call the gap an interrecord gap; when the data is blocked, the term **interblock gap** is used. An individual block of data lying between two interblock gaps is called a **physical record,** while the individual records within this block are called **logical records.**

A record has been defined as a collection of fields needed to support a single iteration of a program. To compute pay for employee number 0001, we need a record containing data for *only* employee number 0001. On the next iteration of the program, we would need a record for employee number 0002.

A single **physical record** on tape might contain individual **logical records** for employees 0001, 0002, 0003, 0004, and 0005. What is it our program expects? A program is written to process logical records. What is going to be transferred between the tape drive and the computer? Because of the physical nature of tape, the drive will read and transfer all the data lying between two gaps. We will get (or send) a physical record.

This creates a new problem for the programmer. A request for input data might result in the transfer of 5, 10, 15, 20, or any number of logical records depending on the blocking factor used. If the program is to work properly, these logical records must be separated and handled individually. On output, if blocked data is to be sent to the tape drive, the program must collect a series of logical output records in main memory before sending the physical record to the tape drive.

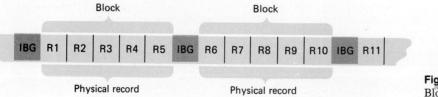

Figure 15.16
Blocking.

The process of building a physical record in main memory from a number of logical records is called **blocking.** The process of breaking a physical input record into individual logical records is called **deblocking.** The main-memory space needed to hold a block is called a **buffer.** Control units and channels contain buffers too; this one just happens to be in main memory.

SEQUENTIAL ACCESS METHODS

We began this chapter by discussing sequential file processing; lately, we have been concentrating on the characteristics of magnetic tape. Let's now pull together the application, the physical device, and the data that is accessed through this physical device.

The master-file update application involves reading a series of transactions, using these transactions to update an old master file, and creating a new master file. The individual who writes this program is not at all interested in the physical characteristics of the file. The real problem lies in making sure that the individual records are updated correctly. The fact that they are stored 10, 15, or 20 to the block is not important; it is a detail that the programmer really doesn't want to worry about. (Note that we haven't even used the terms logical and physical record; the programmer visualizes "good old-fashioned" records.)

But the data *is* stored on a *physical* file. A physical device *will* transfer *physical* records because it can do nothing else. And these records *must* be blocked and deblocked.

In most installations, the problems of blocking and deblocking are handled by an **access method.** An access method is a special **subprogram,** a collection of previously written, machine-level code that is grafted to the program. These instructions perform the functions of blocking and deblocking, allowing the programmer to "pretend" that only logical records must be handled.

A program consists of three distinct parts (Fig. 15.17). At the top is the object module produced by a compiler from the programmer's object code. In

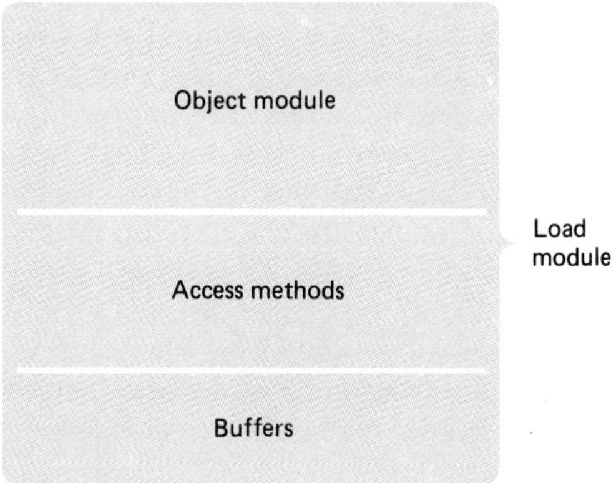

Object module

Access methods

Load
module

Buffers

Figure 15.17
A load module with access methods and buffers.

the middle is the access method—in this case, a sequential access method. At the bottom are the buffers needed to hold blocks or physical records of data. Physical records are read, under control of the access method, into a buffer. Logical records, again under control of the access method, are made available to the main program one at a time. As the main program creates output records one at a time, these logical records are transferred by the access method to a buffer for eventual transfer to an output device. Where did the access method come from? How was it "grafted" onto the main program?

THE LINKAGE EDITOR

The first step in going from programmer source code to a machine-level program is, as you may remember, compilation (Fig. 15.18). A compiler produces an object module, which by itself (except in a few special cases) is incomplete, needing access methods and buffers before processing can begin. A special program called a **linkage editor** has, as part of its function, the responsibility for adding these necessary pieces. The linkage editor produces a **load module** (see Figs. 15.17 and 15.18), which can be executed by a computer.

The process of producing and then executing a load module is a good example of **bootstrapping.** First, a compiler must be loaded into the computer so as to produce an object module. Next, another program, the linkage editor, must be loaded so it can produce a load module. Finally the load module can itself be loaded and executed. The compile, link-edit, and execute sequence is illustrated in Fig. 15.18.

Where does the linkage editor find the access methods and other subroutines that it needs to produce a load module? On a **library.** When most of us think of a library, we picture a place in which books are kept. A library, however, is much more; it is really a place in which books are carefully cataloged and stored in such a way as to make them easy to find again. A book that cannot be found is not very useful.

A program library is a place where computer programs are carefully cataloged and stored. Some libraries exist on magnetic tape; occasionally, decks of cards are used; more frequently, the library exists on a direct access device, the subject of Chapter 17. When the linkage editor program encounters a need for an access method or a subroutine, it checks the library *catalog,* finds the physical location of the needed routine, reads a copy into main memory, and adds it to the developing load module.

Sequential file processing implies the use of magnetic tape or some other bulk storage medium. Tape implies blocking. Blocking implies that such functions as blocking, deblocking, and buffering must be added to the application program. These functions are usually implemented through an access method. A compiler translates a source deck into object code. Since an access

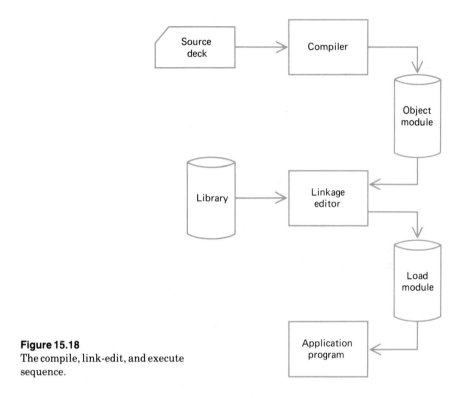

Figure 15.18
The compile, link-edit, and execute
sequence.

method is not normally part of the source deck, the compiler has nothing to translate; thus the access method is not part of the object module. It must, however, be added before the program can execute on the computer. As one of its functions, the linkage editor adds the access method and buffers to the object module in building a load module.

SECONDARY STORAGE

Magnetic tape is sometimes called **secondary storage** or **bulk memory,** a distinction that it shares with direct access devices. Like main memory, data on tape or a direct access device is stored as an electronic pattern (rather than as physical holes, as on cards). Data can be written to and retrieved from these devices quite rapidly. Any form of data valid within the computer—coded, pure binary, packed-decimal, or floating-point—can be stored without modification on tape or a direct access device; in effect, data or programs can be moved back and forth between tape or direct access devices and main memory with a minimum of difficulty; thus, the term **secondary storage.**

Why not put all data in main memory? Main memory is too expensive. Why not put it all on a secondary storage device? Even though these devices are fast, they are many times slower than main memory.

SUMMARY

We began this chapter with a discussion of characters, fields, records, and files, reviewing Chapter 7. We then moved into the master-file update application, using checking-account maintenance as an example. Key characteristics of this application include the sorting of a number of transactions into sequence, followed by the merging of this transaction file with an old master file to produce a new master file and, usually, a report.

We demonstrated that cards are badly suited for this application. Magnetic tape, because of its compactness, speed, fixed-sequence mode of recording, and reusability, is superior. After discussing the checking-account update problem using magnetic tape as the storage medium, we mentioned a number of other examples of computer-based master-file updating; all are batch-processing applications involving highly active files.

We used magnetic sound-recording tape to explain the reusability and the fixed-sequence nature of computer tape. Density, typically 800 or 1600 characters *per inch,* can be used to explain both the speed and compactness of tape. Data was shown to be stored as a series of magnetized spots, with a single cross section normally holding one coded character. Both seven- and nine-track tapes were discussed. The concept of parity was explained, as well as the physical nature of a tape drive.

Fields, records, and files have the same meaning on tape as they did on cards, with a few important differences. Because data is stored on tape as a pattern of electronic or magnetized spots, numeric fields can be stored without conversation. A single file might be spread over two reels (or volumes) of tape, or a single volume might contain two or more files. For this reason (plus the fact that people cannot directly read data on tape), most magnetic tape files are created with labels.

Because of the physical nature of a magnetic tape drive, individual records must be separated by an interrecord gap. To make more effective use of the tape, individual logical records are often combined into blocks called physical records. This creates problems for the programmer who must block and deblock logical records in main memory. Typically these problems are handled by an access method, a software module that is normally grafted onto the object module by a linkage editor as it creates a load module.

Magnetic tape is sometimes called secondary storage because it is fast and able to hold data in any format available to main memory. Direct access devices, the topic of Chapter 17, are another example of secondary storage.

KEYWORDS

access method	field	parity
activity	file	physical record
batch processing	file processing	read/write head
block	file ring	record
blocking	interblock gap	reel
blocking factor	interrecord gap	runbook
bootstrapping	label	secondary storage
buffer	library	sequential file processing
bulk memory or storage	linkage editor	
	load module	sorting
cassette	loadpoint marker	subprogram
character	logical record	subroutine
data cartridge	magnetic tape	volume
deblocking	master file	volume serial number
density	master-file update	

EXERCISES

1. Define once again the following terms: character, field, record, and file. Write the definitions in your own words *before* referring to the glossary.
2. In a file processing application such as updating checking accounts, why is sorting desirable?
3. Why is the computer used to maintain records?
4. Why is magnetic tape, rather than cards, used to hold the files in so many master-file update applications? What advantages does magnetic tape enjoy over cards?
5. What is meant by sequential file processing?
6. For what is the parity bit used?

7. What is the difference between a file and a volume?

8. Why is blocking desirable on magnetic tape?

9. What is an access method? What do access methods do? How is an access method added to a program?

10. What is a load module? Explain the difference between a load module, an object module, and a source module.

16

UPDATING INVENTORY ON A COMPUTER

OVERVIEW

In Chapter 4, a case study of a manual solution to an inventory data processing problem was presented. Here in Chapter 16, we'll turn our attention to computer data processing, showing how inventory might be updated by using magnetic tape as the medium for the master files.

OUR FIRM

The business concern to be analyzed in this chapter is a large department store selling thousands of dollars' worth of merchandise from each of dozens of different departments, seven days a week. Using straight dollar volume of business, the department store is bigger than the automobile dealership of Chapter 4's study. There is another factor, however, which leads to even greater complexity in tracking inventory. Where the automobile dealership dealt with relatively few units, each costing thousands of dollars, the department store must keep track of thousands of different items ranging in price from a few cents to thousands of dollars, with the average product probably running around ten dollars. In order for the department store to match the total dollar sales of the automobile dealer, many, many more pieces must be sold. This increases the magnitude of the inventory problem by increasing the volume of inventory.

It is essential that the managers of a department store know exactly what is in the inventory at any time. A department store deals in current fashions, and, as we all know, current fashions can change almost without warning. The ability to make quick decisions as to what to reorder and what to put on sale is what separates the successful department store from the business failure. Information on the current status of inventory is crucial to this decision making process.

THE BASIC SOLUTION

The basic solution to this problem is the master file update application described in the last chapter (Fig. 16.1). Products are removed from inventory in one of two ways: through sales or through returns to suppliers. When a product is sold, the sales clerk removes half of the price tag (Fig. 16.2); the holes in this tag represent a code through which the part number and other information concerning the product can be read by a machine. Products that do not sell can sometimes be returned to the supplier for credit; when this happens, a return card is prepared, identifying the product and indicating the quantity returned. As the first step in the inventory system, the sales tickets and then the return cards are read and copied to tape.

Additions to inventory can also occur in one of two ways: shipments from a supplier or returns for credit by a customer. With customer returns, if the second half of the price tag is still attached it becomes the input record to the inventory update programs. If, as is often the case, the price tag has been removed, the sales clerk fills out a number of paper forms, one of which goes to keypunch where a customer return card is prepared. Shipments from a supplier are always accompanied by shipping papers similar to those we discussed in Chapter 4; these papers are the basic source documents for preparing "addition to inventory" cards.

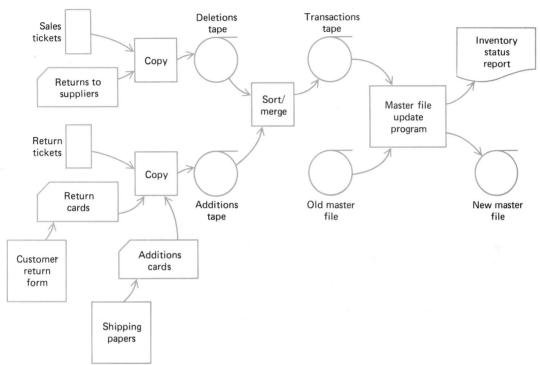

Figure 16.1
The master file update application as applied to our inventory problem.

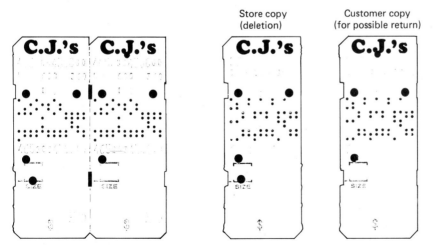

Figure 16.2
Sales tags like these are key input documents to our inventory system.

Once all the data is in machine readable form, it is sorted and then merged to a common tape (Fig. 16.1 again). Up to this point, the computer solution to this data processing problem is not essentially different from the manual solution. Now that the data has been successfully transcribed to a sorted magnetic tape, however, the similarity ends. Under control of a computer program, the records on the transaction tape are read and matched with a master file record, the correct new balance for the part number in question is computed, and a new master file is created, record by record. Once the two input tapes and one output tape have been mounted on tape drives and the proper program has been loaded into main memory and started, the process is completed automatically, needing no additional human intervention.

THE MASTER-FILE UPDATE PROGRAM

The heart of this system is the master-file update program. What exactly does this program do? The objective of the program is to read an old master-file record and then to read all the transactions against this part number, adding any additions to inventory and subtracting any deletions from inventory, so as to compute the new inventory balance. After all the transactions against this part number have been read, a new master-file record can be written to an output tape. The program then directs the CPU to proceed with the next master file record.

The key to this program is sorting. As a by-product of the sorting process, records (as you may remember) are grouped by key, meaning that all transactions against part number 1234, for example, will follow the last transaction for part number 1233, and will precede the first transaction for part number 1235. This means that, once we locate the first transaction against a given part number, all other transactions for the same part number will follow in sequence. To put it another way, as soon as we run into the first transaction for part number 1235, we *know* that there are no more to be found against 1234.

Perhaps the best way to illustrate the logic of this program is through an example. Assume that we have the data presented in Fig. 16.3; since there is

Master file		Transactions		
Part number	Quantity	Part number	Type	Quantity
0001	14	0001	A	5
0005	92	0001	D	1
0006	35	0006	D	14
0009	57	0008	A	50
0010	104	0009	D	3
		0009	D	14
		0009	A	25

Figure 16.3

Test data to support the discussion of the development of the master file update program.

only a small amount of data, we can handle this problem manually. The master file contains five records; the part number (four digits) is shown in the left column, and the quantity currently in inventory is shown in the right column. Beside the master file is a group of transactions, sorted, as is the master file, into part number order. The part number of each transaction is shown on the left again. The letter in the middle represents the transaction type: A for an addition to inventory and D for a deletion from inventory.

Let's start by looking at the first record from each file. Both have the same part number: 0001. What does this mean? Obviously, since the master file entry and the transaction both carry the same part number, they must represent a record for the same part. What should we do? Since the transaction is a type A, we add the quantity on the transaction record to the quantity on the master file record.

Are there any more transactions against this same part number? How can we find out? By reading another transaction. The next transaction is also against part number 0001; since it's a type D card, we subtract the quantity from the old inventory balance.

We've now considered what we would want to do whenever we find a transaction whose part number matches the master file record we are currently working with. The steps are summarized in the flowchart of Fig. 16.4.

Are there any more transactions against this part number? The only way in which we can find out is by reading another transaction. Since our data is sorted, if there are any other transactions against this same part they must follow in sequence; if the next transaction is for a different part number, we know that there are no more against 0001.

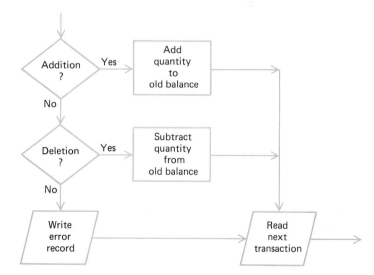

Figure 16.4
The logic steps to be followed when the part numbers of the transaction and the master file match.

Part number	Quantity
0001	18
0005	92
0006	21
0009	65
0010	104

Figure 16.5
The new master file.

ERROR ON PART NUMBER 0008; NO MASTER FILE ENTRY

Figure 16.6
The logic to be followed
when the part number of
the transaction is higher
than the part number of
the master file.

The third transaction (Fig. 16.3) is a deletion from the inventory of part number 0006, a different number. There are no more transactions against 0001; thus we know that all additions have been added to and all deletions have been subtracted from the inventory balance, meaning that we have the new inventory balance for part number 0001. A new master-file record can now be written (Fig. 16.5).

Having taken care of part number 0001, we can turn our attention to the next record in the master file, which is for part number 0005 (Fig. 16.3 again). The steps we must take whenever the part number of the transaction we are currently looking at is greater than the part number of our current old master file entry are summarized in Fig. 16.6.

We are now looking at master-file record 0005 and a transaction for part number 0006. What does this mean? Are there any transactions against 0005? If there were, they would have preceded the transaction we have in front of us now. Our conclusion: There are no more transactions against 0005. In fact, there are no transactions at all against this part number; we're looking at a product which did not sell. What should we do? Since we still have the product in inventory, we want part number 0005 to be a part of our new master file. We can achieve this by simply copying it to the new master file (Fig. 16.5 again). Will the steps described in the flowchart of Fig. 16.6 achieve this objective? Certainly they will. If we haven't added anything to or subtracted anything from the old master-file's quantity field, then we haven't changed it, and this quantity can simply be copied to the new master file.

Having written a new master-file entry for part number 0005, we turn our attention to the next master-file record; it's part number 0006 (Fig. 16.3). Once again we have a match. The transaction is a deletion of 14 units; thus we subtract 14 from the old master file balance and go on to the next transaction, an addition of 50 units of part number 0008. Since this transaction is for a higher part number than the master-file entry we are currently working with, it's time to write a new record to the new master file (Fig. 16.5) for part number 0006 and turn to the next master-file record.

The next master-file record is for part number 0009. We are working with a transaction for part number 0008. They don't match, but this situation is different from the "transaction high" situation we encountered before. In this case, the part number of the transaction is lower than the part number for the master file. Do we know that there are no more transactions against part number 0009? No, we haven't even hit the first transaction for this part number yet. When the part number of the transaction is lower than the same key in the master file, we know that there is no master-file entry for this part number. Either that, or the data is out of sequence. In either case, we have an unusual condition that cannot be handled normally.

There are many possible explanations for our current situation. Since this transaction is an *addition,* we might be looking at the first shipment of a new product. This transaction card might be a keypunch error, or an error derived from a price tag that had been "bent, folded, stapled, or mutilated." The transactions might be out of sequence.

Rather than get into the details of error handling, we'll simply consider each "transaction low" condition to be an error, print a message identifying the error, and move on to another transaction (Fig. 16.7). The next transaction is for part number 0009; since the transactions file and the master file match, we're back to normal operations again.

Now that we've seen how we handle an equal condition, a "transaction high" condition, and a "transaction low" condition, let's put these three pieces of logic together (Fig. 16.8). Our objective is to compare the part numbers of a

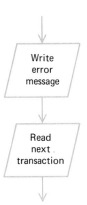

Figure 16.7
The logic to be followed in the event of a "transaction low" condition.

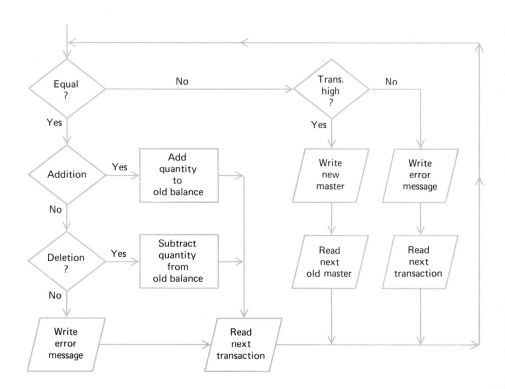

Figure 16.8
The basic logic of the inventory program.

master-file record and a transactions-file record. If they match, we take one set of actions. If the transaction part number is high, we take a second set of actions. If the transaction part number is low, we take a third set of actions, identifying this transaction as an error. Are there any conditions we may have missed? Having compared two fields and indicated what is to be done if the first is greater than, less than, or equal to the second, we haven't left much to chance. This basic logic forms the core of the master-file update program.

Getting Started

A part of each piece of logic in Fig. 16.8 involves the reading of a new record from either the master file or the transactions file; thus, after a comparison has been made and an action taken, we'll always have one new record to compare against one old record. There is only one problem: What are we comparing on the very first comparison? If we have not yet read a record from either file, we have nothing to compare.

The logic of this program relies on comparing the keys of two records. It assumes that each record is preceded by another record that can be used for comparison. The first record is different, in that there is no record preceding it. Thus it is necessary to "prime the pump," providing the initial record of both types before actual processing begins. This is illustrated in the flowchart of Fig. 16.9.

Finishing

The first record in a file is unique because there are no records preceding it. The last record in a file is unique because there are no records following it. Just as handling the first record involved special logic, handling the last record will involve special logic.

What if we were to run out of transactions while several old master-file records remained to be processed? Obviously, there are no transactions against any of the remaining master-file entries. This means no change in the inventory level of these products. Each remaining record must simply be copied to the new master file without change.

What if we were to run out of master-file records and still had several transactions to process? Obviously, there is no master-file entry for the part numbers represented by these transactions. We have already defined this condition as an error condition. Each remaining transaction must be copied to an error list.

Some Added Touches

The logic that we've covered to this point merely creates a new master file from the old master and the transactions. We want a bit more. We want a printed

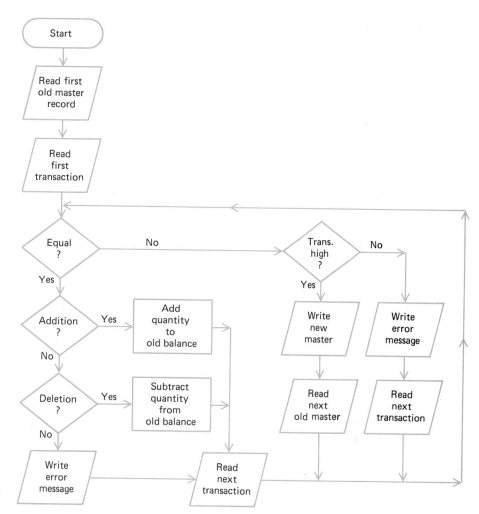

Figure 16.9
Our inventory program with start of job routines.

report that lists, for each and every part number, the old balance, the total of all additions to inventory, the total of all deletions from inventory, and the new balance. Thus, our program logic, although basically the same as what we've seen to this point, will be just a bit different. When a match is found, we'll *accumulate* deletions and additions, depending on the transaction type. When a "transaction high" condition is encountered, we'll compute the new balance by subtracting the total of all deletions from and adding the total of all additions to the old balance, we'll write the new master file, we'll write a single line of our desired report including the old balance, accumulators, and new balance, and we'll set the accumulators back to zero in preparation for the next master-file record. These steps can be seen graphically in Fig. 16.10.

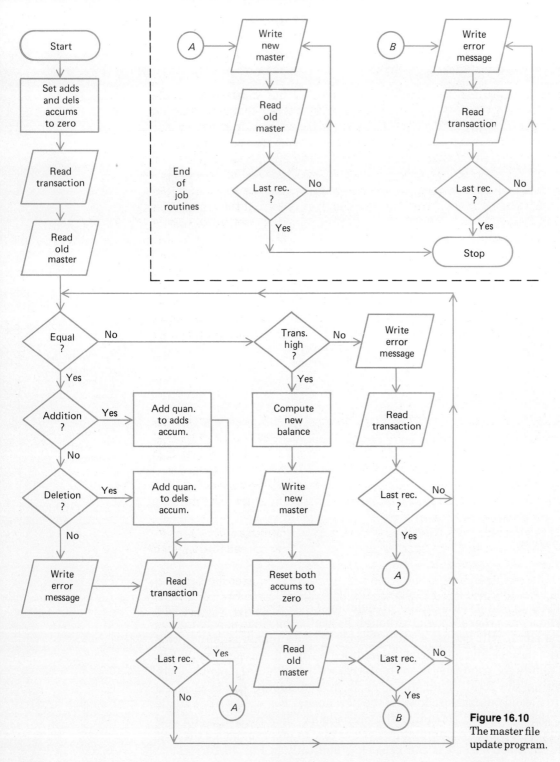

Figure 16.10
The master file update program.

Putting the Pieces Together

Having discussed all the blocks of logic required by this master-file update program, we're ready to put the pieces together and create a complete program flowchart (Fig. 16.10). Note that we begin by reading a record from each of our two files, thus "priming the pump." Once the process has started, the program logic settles down to comparing the part number of the transaction against the part number of the master-file entry currently being worked on by our program and, based on the results of this comparison, taking the appropriate action and reading a new record from the appropriate file so that the comparison step can be repeated. Additional blocks of logic have been set up to handle last-record conditions.

We've gone about the design of this program in modular fashion, developing the solution piece by piece. In its current form, the flowchart of Fig. 16.10 could be translated to some programming language such as COBOL or RPG, compiled, and implemented on a computer. The professional programmer might, however, see a number of places where parts of logic can be combined, yielding a more efficient program. It is not our intent in this chapter to take that extra step.

OUR SOLUTION IN OPERATION

After the program to support this master-file update has been written, debugged, and tested, it is released to production; i.e., it becomes a program that can be used to update a real master file. Once a program has been released, it is normally compiled and link-edited, and the load module is cataloged and stored on a library. Now, the actual program can simply be copied from the library into main memory; since it is in load module form, there is no need for additional compilation or link editing.

The process begins with the copying, sorting, and merging of the transactions to a single transactions tape. This is, to a degree, a semi-automated operation involving considerable human interaction.

Next, the operator mounts the transactions and old master-file tapes on tape drives, making sure that there are no file rings in place (we don't want this data to be destroyed by an accidental write operation). Next, a blank tape with file ring in place is mounted on a drive; this will eventually become the new master file. After checking to make sure that the printer holds enough paper for the printed report and the error listings, the operator is ready to start the program. The name of the master-file update program is typed on the operator's console, a special system program finds the desired application program on the library and loads it into main memory, the master-file update program assumes control of the computer, and the new master file is created without further human intervention.

SECURITY AND BACKUP

Mistakes happen even on the best of systems. In order to minimize the impact of errors and provide recovery capability in the event that things really do go wrong, most computer installations impose a number of security and backup procedures on the master-file update application.

We've already seen one such procedure—the requirement that the operator make sure that there is no file ring in an input tape volume. The most common backup procedure, however, involves keeping a number of history tapes.

What might happen, for example, if, two hours after the master file was updated, the new master file is accidentally destroyed? If the old master file and the transaction tape had been kept, we could simply rerun the program and recreate the tape. Normally, three sets of files are kept: the new master, the old master, and the *old* old master, which was used, one period ago, to create the old master.

Remember the relationship between the master files in a master-file update operation. The old master is used to create the new master. One period ago, the old old master was used to create what we now call the old master. It's almost like a bloodline; in fact, such interrelated master files are called a **generation data set.** In this context, the old old master file is known as the grandfather, the old master is known as the father, and the new master is known as the son. Three generations are normally kept for backup purposes.

PROGRAM MAINTENANCE

Once the program has been installed, maintenance begins. In this example, we are certainly going to want to make some changes. We have, for example, made no provision for adding or deleting a part number from the master file. (A real programmer would certainly have included these capabilities in the original program; we left them out for simplicity.) Certain conditions that we simply flagged as errors might not be errors at all, but simply unusual conditions that can be easily handled; error-handling routines that make sense will have to be added. Eventually, we might produce a program that satisfies everyone. By that time, the basic inventory system will most likely have changed anyway, meaning that it's time to write a new inventory master-file update program. Such is the life of the programmer.

SUMMARY

In this chapter, we considered the steps involved in a computer solution to the inventory problem, using a large department store as our model. By far the best summary of the material in this chapter is the flowchart of Fig. 16.10; if you can follow the logic, you know this material. The only new topic introduced in this chapter was the idea of a generation data set.

KEYWORDS

generation data set

EXERCISES

1. It has been said that a bank checking account is really nothing but an inventory of money. In a checking account, what would represent additions to and deletions from inventory for each account?

2. Updating checking accounts is another example of a master-file update application. Using either English paragraphs or a flowchart, explain the basic logic (at the level of Fig. 16.9) of this application.

3. Each term, your school updates the grade history file, adding current grades for each student and computing new grade-point averages. What are the basic transactions for adding a record to this file? Can you think of any transactions that might delete a record from the file?

4. Explain the basic logic of the program that updates a grade history file.

5. Relate the master file update application of this chapter to a library circulation system.

17

FILE PROCESSING AND DIRECT-ACCESS STORAGE DEVICES

OVERVIEW

Sequential processing is often inadequate. In this chapter, we will examine a number of applications that require quick response or access to specific records, making sequential access unsuitable. We will also examine a number of devices that support direct access, primarily disk and drum. The chapter ends with some comments on file processing economics.

SEQUENTIAL FILES AND BATCH PROCESSING

Let's review briefly the characteristics of sequential files as presented in Chapter 15. On a sequential file, the individual records follow one another in a fixed sequence: To process record number 500, it is necessary to go through the first 499 records. Typically, these records are sorted into logical order by some **key** such as a part number, social security number, name, or some other "key" field. Magnetic tape is well suited for such files because tape, by its very nature, preserves this sequence.

For a master-file update, this type of organization makes a great deal of sense. A master file and a number of transactions can be sorted by the same key and, in essence, merged together, allowing the new master file to reflect all current activity: The sequential nature of the files makes the updating process much simpler than would be possible with transactions in random order.

This application is a good example of batch processing. The transactions are collected into a batch, and the master file is updated (usually) at regular intervals. There is a very strong financial reason for collecting a substantial batch of records: If only a few of the records on a file are updated each time the program is run, the cost per change becomes prohibitive. Let's examine this statement more closely. Do you recall the discussion of the breakeven point in Chapter 3? That's really what we're dealing with here. The cost of processing a sequential file (on magnetic tape) is essentially a fixed cost (Fig. 17.1). It costs x dollars to read and to update an entire tape, and the nature of a sequential file makes it necessary to read the entire tape. If we could find a technique that would allow us to update records one at a time, this approach would be less expensive until the number of record changes reached some critical point (Fig. 17.1)—in other words, the breakeven point.

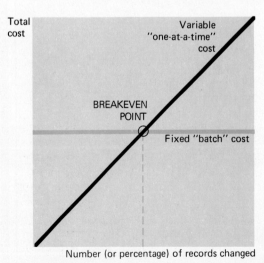

Figure 17.1
"Breakeven" on the file update application.

For example, let's say that we have a deck of punched cards in alphabetical order, each one containing an individual's name and address. What is the easiest way to change one individual's address? The answer should be obvious: Select that individual's card, change it, and replace the corrected card in the deck. This is not sequential file processing. Would anyone seriously consider reading the old master file one record at a time, merging the transactions file (a single record) with it, and creating a complete new master file? No. Why not? Because it is so much easier and less expensive to select and change the single record.

Now let's change the problem. We'll go back a few years and assume that the post office has just decided to require zip codes on all addresses. If all the individuals on our name-and-address file live in the same general area, we could write a program that would read the old master file one record at a time, check the street address and figure out the zip code, and punch a new master file. Would it be simpler to automate this process or to have a group of clerks add the zip code to one record at a time? The answer depends, of course, on the size of the file. A thousand records or so could be updated by hand, but a few hundred thousand would probably make the cost of writing a program worthwhile.

Consider a magazine with one million subscribers, several thousand of whom change addresses every month. Given the size of the master file and the volume of change (or the activity), it would be quite unusual for such an operation to be performed manually. With most magazines, address changes and other subscription modifications (new subscriptions and cancellations) are collected into a batch and processed at regular intervals (which is why it takes several weeks for an address change to become effective).

BATCH PROCESSING WON'T ALWAYS DO

Among the typical sequential file-processing applications discussed in Chapter 15 were the updating of checking and savings accounts. Checking accounts are generally quite active, but what about savings accounts? Although there are exceptions, most people do not maintain an extremely "active" savings account, making deposits and withdrawals perhaps only a few times a month. If the bank were willing to wait until the end of the month to update all savings accounts, an economically sound batch of transactions might be collected, but the bank cannot wait that long. What would happen, for example, if a customer intentionally overdrew and had a 30-day head start before the crime was even detected?

Have you ever been in a bank or a savings and loan institution that processed your deposit or withdrawal through a terminal? This is becoming a very common approach, with individual account records updated directly, one at a time. A sequential file organization just will not do for this application; the cost and time delay inherent in processing an entire file for each transaction would be prohibitive.

Why won't simple, sequential batch processing do in this case? For reasons involving such factors as risk, security, and control, the master file must be updated at least daily. There is not enough activity to economically justify a daily, sequential master-file update.

Let's look at another application in which sequential file processing just won't do, this time for quite different reasons. Our national air defense system is computer-coordinated. Information on regularly scheduled flights, nonscheduled charter or private flights, the weather, and wind conditions is kept in a massive *data base*. Radar, ground spotters, airborne units, and sea installations constantly feed current information to the system. If an unidentified aircraft is spotted, an attempt is made to identify it, starting with calculations to determine, for example, whether a known flight might have been blown off course and ending with the dispatching of interceptors and the alerting of responsible personnel.

An operation of this type cannot run in a batch mode. Imagine insisting that we wait until 5:00 P.M. to determine the identity of the aircraft because "5:00 P.M. is the scheduled time for our batch run." By 5:00 P.M., Chicago might not be there. This is a good example of an **on-line, real-time** application. It's on-line because the equipment providing or displaying the information is directly attached to the computer, with no keypunch operator or data-entry clerk involved. It is real-time because data is processed so as to influence a decision that must be made "right now" in "real time."

Air defense is an extreme example of an on-line, real-time system; let's take a look at a different one. Many airlines run an on-line, real-time reservation system. A ticket agent, using a terminal, requests a reservation for a customer. The information is sent to a central computer that checks the status of the desired flight and, in a matter of seconds, confirms or rejects the reservation. Transactions are processed one at a time. Obviously, transactions are not batched. Why? Most airlines are private organizations in business to make money. What if you, as a customer, were to approach Tree Top Airways to request a reservation on the next flight to New York and were told to wait until one half-hour before flight time (when the batch of reservation requests is run) for confirmation? While waiting, you walk across the aisle to the ticket agent for Kamikaze Airlines who gives you an immediate, firm reservation on a flight leaving only a few minutes after the Tree Top flight. Which airline are you going to choose? Ignoring any qualitative differences, you'd probably select the "sure thing" over the "come-back-later" response. Although there are other reasons for putting a reservation system on-line, such as minimizing the impact of "no-shows" and handling a last-minute rush, it is basically done for competitive reasons. This, of course, translates into money—lost customers mean lost revenue.

DIRECT ACCESS

The applications that we have just finished discussing have at least one characteristic in common: They require the processing of each transaction as it occurs, one at a time. Batch processing is not acceptable.

Sequential files leave a lot to be desired in such applications. We might get lucky and try to update the very first record on the master file, but we might get unlucky and try to update the last record. On the average, we would have to go through about half the file for each transaction. This is very time-consuming and very expensive.

What is needed is a storage medium that allows us to go directly (or almost directly) to the one record we need without going through all the intervening records. Consider a telephone book. It is organized sequentially, but we can bypass the sequence when looking for a specific phone number or address: When looking for Joe Smith's number, we do *not* start with the A's and read until we encounter the name we want. A deck of punched cards gives us this ability. We can pull, change, and replace selected cards, but cards are too slow and bulky, and provide this "direct access" capability only when processing is done manually. What we need is a device with the density and speed of magnetic tape.

What if we were to cut a volume of magnetic tape into strips (Fig. 17.2), each strip containing exactly 100 records? Assume that the file had been organized sequentially and that there are no missing records. Records 1 through 100 would be found on the first strip, records 101 through 200 would be on the second strip, and so on. Let's say that we wanted record 1132. It's a simple matter to figure out which strip holds this record; all we need do is find this strip, mount it on some magnetic I/O device, and search the selected strip for the desired record. This process is not quite direct, but we do get fairly close without going through all the intervening records.

Several early direct access devices were designed around the "strips of tape" idea. On one, loops of tape were fed continuously through a read/write

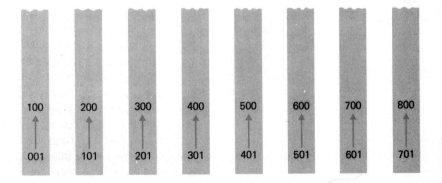

Figure 17.2
The direct access concept illustrated by a volume of magnetic tape cut into strips.

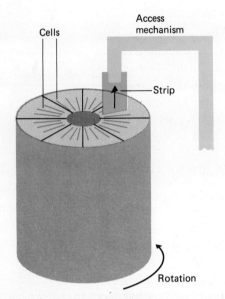

Cells

Access
mechanism

Strip

Rotation

Figure 17.3
A data cell.

mechanism (almost like in a modern 8-track stereo tape cartridge). On another, data was stored on foot-wide strips of tape that, following selection, were dropped down a chute and wrapped around a drum-like surface. Perhaps the best known of these devices was the **data cell** (Fig. 17.3). Here, the individual strips of tape were stored in a number of cells on top of the device. The programmer (through a program) simply asked for a given tape strip in a given cell. The device would then select the strip, wrap it around the outer surface of the data cell, and read or write it. At the conclusion of the I/O operation, the strip was returned to the proper location. The data cell never really became popular because of problems with reliability and access speed, but it does illustrate the basic idea of what is now called **direct access.**

MODERN MASS STORAGE SYSTEMS

Although the data cell was never a commercial success, a number of modern **mass storage systems** show greater promise. Everyone knows what a jukebox is; it's a device that plays records. After depositing some coins, you select a song by pressing some buttons. Once a song has been selected, an access arm in the jukebox moves across the stack of available recordings, pulls out the one you selected, and places it on a turntable to be played. Several newer mass storage devices work on much the same principle.

Rather than 45-RPM records, these devices use small reels of magnetic tape or small cylinders coated with magnetic material. These storage media are arranged in a matrix pattern (Fig. 17.4). If the data we want is on the data cartridge stored at location (3,5) and we know that the first number in the address indicates how far we must move to the right, while the second number indicates the number of cells we must move up, we can find the data cartridge holding our data. Once located, the tape on this cartridge can be mounted on a tape drive and processed.

Examples of mass storage systems that work pretty much as described above include IBM's 3850 Mass Storage System and Control Data Corporation's Mass Storage Facility. These systems are composed of at least three primary components: a bank of cells in which data cartridges can be stored, an **access arm** to move cartridges from the storage matrix to a read/write area, and a mechanism to read data from or write data to the cartridges. The operation of one of these devices begins with a request from the computer for a particular data cartridge. The access arm moves into position over the desired cartridge and removes it from the matrix, transferring it to the read/write mechanism. There the data can be read and transmitted into the computer. On output, information from the computer can be recorded on the magnetic surface. When

Figure 17.4
A modern mass storage device; a section of the data storage matrix.

the operation is finished, the access arm returns the data cartridge to its proper position in the storage matrix.

The process of transferring a data cartridge from the storage matrix to the read/write mechanism takes time. Control Data Corporation estimates that the average **access time** on its Mass Storage Facility is about 2.5 seconds. To a computer, this is a very long period of time; still, it's much faster than having a human operator walk into the tape room, select a tape, walk back to the computer room, and mount it on a tape drive.

The storage capacity of these devices is impressive. The CDC Mass Storage Facility can hold up to 2052 cartridges, each capable of storing as many as eight million bytes or characters of data. This means that there are close to eight billion bytes of data on-line at one time. IBM's 3850 can handle up to 472 billion bytes! The effective storage capacity of a mass storage device can be augmented by off-line storage, in that individual cartridges can be removed or inserted manually.

Data on a mass storage device such as the ones we've been discussing is accessible by the computer without human intervention. It is not necessary to begin at the data cartridge located at cell (0,0) and work through the cartridges one at a time until the needed record of data is located. It is instead possible to access directly the single data cartridge desired. In effect, we have taken the individual strips of tape discussed earlier and placed each one in its own little cell, thus allowing direct access.

MAGNETIC DRUM

The mass storage devices described above are relatively new to the marketplace. The first commercially important direct access device was the **magnetic drum.** The name is quite descriptive. Imagine a cylindrical drum-shaped device with the "strips of tape" wrapped around the outer surface. If we replace these individual strips with a continuous coating of the same material that coats magnetic tape, we have a magnetic drum (Fig. 17.5). Data is stored around the surface in a circular pattern called a **track.** Just as on tape, individual bits are represented by magnetized spots; these bits are grouped into characters which, in turn, form fields which, again in turn, form records. On tape, one cross section holds one character; on drum, although it's possible to store the bits of a given character on parallel tracks, the individual bits are normally stored in series around the track, with the first nine (eight-bit code plus parity) holding the first character, and so on.

Most drums have one read/write head for each track. This makes data access very fast. The drum normally rotates constantly at a very high rate of speed. With one read/write head per track, all that is needed to access data is to specify a track, turn on the associated read/write head, and wait for the desired data to rotate under the head.

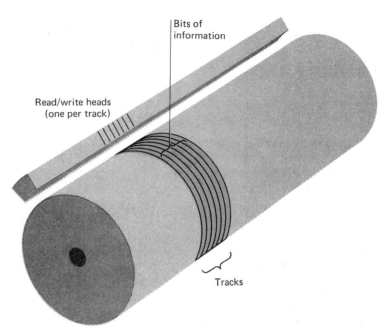

Bits of
information

Read/write heads
(one per track)

Tracks

Figure 17.5
A magnetic drum.

This does take time; even a drum is slower than the internal processing speeds of a computer. Turning on the proper head can be done electronically— it's very fast. The major delay involves waiting for the data to rotate beneath the head. We might get lucky and have the record just about to pass under the head as we turn the head on. We might get unlucky and have to wait for the record to come all the way back around. On the average, we'll wait for about one-half revolution for the data. This is called **rotational delay.**

The final component of a drum's total data access time involves the transfer of data between the device and main memory. **Data transfer time** is normally measured in microseconds.

A magnetic drum is a fixed storage medium in that the data storage cylinder cannot be removed. A typical drum can hold approximately four million bytes or characters of data.

MAGNETIC DISK

Today's most commonly used direct access device is the **magnetic disk.** In describing magnetic tape, we used the analogy of reel-to-reel sound-recording tape. A magnetic disk is analogous to a long-playing record album. It is a disk-shaped device with a magnetic coating on the flat surface (Fig. 17.6). Unlike on the long-playing record album, data on a magnetic disk is not stored in a spiral pattern, but instead is stored on a series of concentric circles called

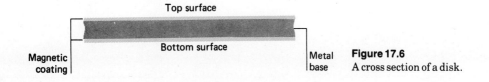

Top surface

Bottom surface

Magnetic
coating

Metal
base

Figure 17.6
A cross section of a disk.

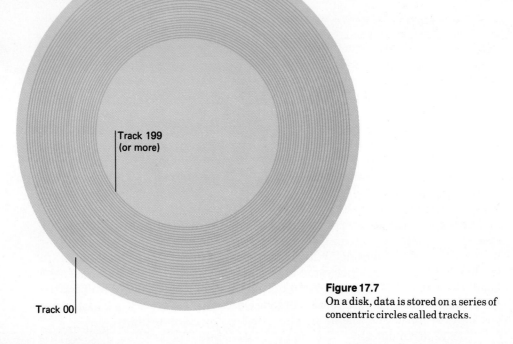

Track 199
(or more)

Track 00

Figure 17.7
On a disk, data is stored on a series of
concentric circles called tracks.

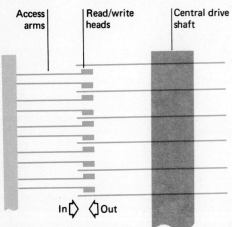

Access
arms

Read/write
heads

Central drive
shaft

In ▷ ◁ Out

Figure 17.8
A typical disk arrangement showing a stack of individual disks
and movable read/write heads.

tracks (Fig. 17.7). Individual bits are represented by magnetized spots, bits are grouped to form characters, characters are grouped to form fields, etc.

On a long-playing record, it is possible to play the fourth song on the first side by simply picking up the tone arm and placing it at the beginning of the desired song. Since we can skip the intervening three songs, we have a form of direct access. A magnetic disk is equipped with a movable read/write head that works in analogous fashion, moving over the track holding the desired data. (Fig. 17.8).

Finding a specific record on a disk is a bit more complex than on a drum. On a drum, the first step is to simply turn on the proper read/write head, but on a disk, the head must be physically moved so as to position it over the proper track. The times for rotational delay and data transfer are roughly the same, but this physical motion, called **seeking**, does make disk somewhat slower than drum. Why use disk if it's slower? Because disk has greater storage capacity than drum.

A long-playing record album has two sides. Similarly, data can be stored on both sides of a magnetic disk. In fact, a **disk pack** normally consists of a stack of individual disks (10 to 20) rotating on a single spindle and accessed by a comblike set of read/write heads (Fig. 17.8). One position of the read/write mechanism gives us access to one track on each surface. This single access-arm position is called a **cylinder.**

Accessing data on a disk involves three distinct steps:

1. Locate the read/write heads over the proper cylinder.
2. Turn on the head corresponding to the proper track and wait for the desired record to rotate beneath the head.
3. Transfer the data to (or from) the computer.

The time delay associated with the first step is called **seek time** and is measured in milliseconds. The second step involves a **rotational delay;** although still measured in milliseconds, it is not nearly as slow as seek time. Finally, there is **data transfer time,** which is measured in microseconds.

As you can see in Fig. 17.7, the "outer" tracks on a disk surface are considerably bigger than the "inner" tracks. Does this imply that we can store more data on the outer tracks? No. Every track holds the *same* amount of data. No, it isn't an optical illusion. Have you ever played "crack the whip"? In this game, often played on ice skates, a group of people join hands, and the individual on one end begins turning slowly in a circle. Proceeding outward, each individual moves around the center in circles of increasing radius. Since the people further along the chain must travel in bigger circles, they must skate faster in order to keep up. The person at the end has to skate like mad just to stay even.

The same principle applies when using a disk. The surface rotates at a constant speed. If that speed is, for example, 1000 revolutions per second, then a particle on either the inner *or* the outer track would make exactly 1000 revolutions in one second. But the particle on the outer track would have to travel further, and therefore faster, in that second.

What if we were to place 100,000 particles on the inner track and another 100,000 particles on the outer track? Those on the inner track would be fairly tightly packed, while those on the outer track would be (relatively speaking) fairly spread out. But if the disk is rotating at exactly 1000 revolutions per second, a read/write head stationed on the inner track would see 100,000 particles per millisecond. The same head moved to the outer track would also see 100,000 particles per millisecond. The read/write head is designed to read "so many" characters per second; timing, and not physical distance, is the controlling factor. Each track has the same capacity.

Typically, what is this capacity? Since there are many different types of disk packs, there are many possible answers to this question. Some packs have only two data surfaces, while others have ten; still others stack as many as twenty surfaces on a single spindle. IBM's 3330 disk system uses packs that hold 13,030 characters of data on each track. There are 404 tracks (plus seven alternate tracks) on each surface and 19 surfaces per pack, giving a total of 7676 data tracks. Given the capacity of each track, there is something in excess of 100 million characters of storage capacity (100 **megabytes**) on each pack. IBM's 3330 is also available in a dual-density version, yielding twice the capacity. Other manufacturers offer similar products.

Disk drives are often sold in clusters; Fig. 17.9, for example, shows a drive housing two packs. As with any I/O device, a disk drive is attached to a computer through a channel and a control unit. When several disk drives are housed in a single package, they usually share a control unit. Disk, being a high-speed I/O device, usually communicates through a selector channel in burst mode, meaning that only one disk can be communicating with the computer at any one time. Since only one drive can be active at a time anyway, it makes sense to share the control unit. A typical 3330 system might consist of a cluster of eight drives sharing a single control unit; this means that eight disk packs with a combined total of 800 megabytes of storage capacity are on-line with the computer.

Disk packs are normally removable; in other words, they can be taken off their drives and stored off-line (Fig. 17.10). An installation with eight disk drives might well have twelve to sixteen packs containing active data, switching packs to match the needs of the current programs. Switching disk packs does, however, take time—time during which the drive is not available for other use. As a consequence, many data processing centers frown on switching disk packs, perferring to keep the same packs spinning all day. It is possible to purchase fixed-head disks that cannot be removed.

Incidentally, an individual disk pack, like an individual reel of magnetic tape, is sometimes called a **volume.**

Photograph courtesy of IBM Corporation.

Figure 17.9
Disk drives.

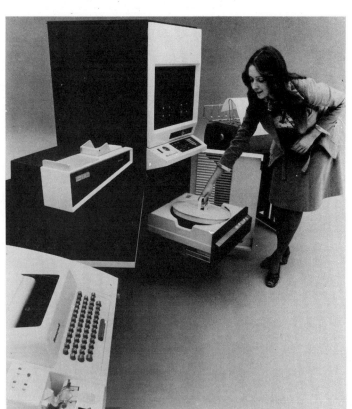

Figure 17.10
Disk packs can often be removed. Here the operator is removing a small disk pack from a mini-computer system.

Photograph courtesy of Honeywell, Inc.

Floppy Disks and Diskettes

Not all disk applications call for the massive storage capacity of a full-sized disk pack. In Chapter 7 we discussed key-to-disk data entry systems on which an operator entered data directly to disk; how many characters can the average terminal operator type in one day? This application calls for a smaller, more easily handled disk pack. A similar need can be found on smaller minicomputers, where the amount of data that must be stored is usually less than might be expected on a larger machine. In both cases, the answer is the floppy disk or the diskette.

A **floppy disk** (Fig. 17.11) usually consists of a single recording surface (sometimes two) with a capacity of roughly 250,000 bytes. On a regular disk drive, the read/write heads ride on a cushion of air, never actually touching the surface of the disk pack. On a floppy disk system, the read/write heads ride directly on the surface, which means that a certain amount of up-and-down movement that would be intolerable on a regular disk drive is acceptable. In effect, the floppy disk can "flop" around. The term **diskette** is synonymous with floppy disk.

Photograph courtesy of Maxell Corporation of America.

Figure 17.11
A floppy disk.

BUBBLE MEMORY AND OTHER NEW TECHNOLOGIES

The big problem with most direct access devices—disk, drum, and mass storage systems—is the fact that they contain moving parts. Mechanical motion is a source of wear, and it tends to limit speed. Core and semiconductor memories are far superior in terms of both speed and reliability. Unfortunately, they are too expensive to use as mass storage devices.

For years, there has been a recognized gap between the high-speed, highly reliable, but very expensive main-memory devices and the slower, less reliable, but significantly less expensive bulk memories. An ideal device would combine the speed and reliability of core with the cost of disk. A recent innovation, **magnetic bubble memory,** shows promise of filling this gap, at least for certain applications. Bubble memory is manufactured in much the same way as other solid-state electronic devices. Individual bits are represented by tiny bubbles. The fact that millions of these bubbles can be stored in a square inch of material makes bubble memory remarkably compact. Add to this compactness a very high level of reliability (bubble memory is virtually maintenance free). Bubble memory is also nonvolatile; in other words, the data remains in memory even after the power has been turned off. Compact, reliable, and nonvolatile memory is perfect for a lightweight, portable terminal or a small, occasional-use personal computer; thus it is not surprising to find bubble memory used in these two products today.

The cost of bubble memory lies between that of core and disk. Its speed is comparable to that of disk. Charged-coupled devices (CCDs), another recent innovation, are faster and just a bit more expensive, but volatile. Other new technologies are presently being tested in research labs throughout the world. The memory of the future, both main and secondary, may well be composed of 100% nonmechanical, solid-state components.

Don't bet against disk, however. Disk is quite reliable, economical, and proven—it works and it works well. Innovation is rapid, and disk systems with faster access speeds and greater data storage capacity are announced with surprising frequency. Disk should remain number one for at least the next several years.

THE ECONOMICS OF DATA STORAGE

Core memory (or its modern equivalent) is a direct access device, which allows the programmer to directly access the data stored at any memory location. In fact, main memory is the ideal direct access device. It is very fast, and using it, we can go directly to the desired data rather than just get "in the ballpark," as is the case with disk and drum. Why not just use core or integrated circuit memories exclusively? It's a question of economics: Main memory is very expensive, and disk and drum are relatively inexpensive.

Let's examine this question of economics a bit more closely. All types of data storage have their advantages and their disadvantages; some of these are summarized in Fig. 17.12. Let's begin with punched cards. Cards are very inexpensive. If the actual cost of the medium were the only consideration, most computer data would probably be stored on punched cards. But cards are also quite slow, being limited to access speeds of approximately 1000 characters per second. A slow I/O medium wastes computer time, and computer time is very expensive; this tends to wipe out the apparent cost advantage of cards.

Next, there is magnetic tape. Some tapes are as slow as 20,000 characters per second, while some are as fast as 1.2 million characters per second, but 300,000 characters per second is a reasonably typical figure. Under ideal conditions, as many as six million characters of data can be stored on a single tape volume, and, if you are willing to accept the argument that a tape file can be spread over as many volumes as necessary, it is possible to claim that the storage capacity of tape is limitless.

Tape is a bit more expensive than punched cards, but much of this added expense is offset by the fact that tape is reusable. As we discussed in Chapter 15, tape enjoys many advantages over punched cards, particularly on the master-file update application.

But tape has its problems too. It is a sequential medium, period. You can't store anything but a straight sequential file on magnetic tape. On some applications, this is fine. On others, however, this lack of flexibility is a definite handicap. The biggest problem in using tape, however, is its accessibility. Before a program can access a tape file, a human operator must first mount the volume on a tape drive. This takes time—often five minutes or more, which in the world of computers is an eternity.

To gain accessibility, we can utilize one of the newer mass storage devices. The data cartridges are on-line and can be accessed without human interven-

Storage type	Access time to locate a record	Data transfer rate in characters per second	Storage capacity in characters for a typical configuration	Cost to store 1000 characters for one year
Punched cards	Minutes	1,000	-------	Pennies
Printer paper	------	2,000	-------	-------
Magnetic tape	Minutes	300,000	------	Nickels
Mass storage	Seconds	800,000	16 billion	Dimes
Disk	Several milliseconds	1,000,000	100 million	Dimes (a few more)
Drum	A few milliseconds	1,200,000	4 million	Quarters
Core memory	Several microseconds	4,000,000	1 million	$25
Semiconductor memory	Microseconds	8,000,000	1 million	$50 (but dropping)

Figure 17.12
A comparison of the speed, storage capacity, and cost of a number of storage media.

tion in a matter of seconds. The data transfer rate of mass storage devices is higher than standard magnetic tape. They do, however, cost more.

To a human being, the ability to locate a record within a few seconds is nothing short of phenomenal, but to a computer it is slow. By using disk, the time required to find the right record can be reduced to several milliseconds. Access speed is about the same as on the mass storage system, but look at storage capacity (Fig. 17.12). We dropped from 16 billion to 100 million characters, which is, to say the least, significant. We are paying a price for the ability to locate data quickly: We cannot store as much data in one place. The actual cost of data storage is a bit higher on disk too.

When very fast data access is essential, the use of a magnetic drum is a good choice. Since a drum has one read/write head for each track, there is no seek time with which to be concerned. Thus a record of data can normally be located in the few milliseconds needed to turn the drum. Data transfer time is faster too, averaging approximately 1,200,000 characters per second. But storage capacity is way down, and storage costs are much higher.

Tape is restricted to sequential files. Direct access devices are not so restricted in that both direct and sequential files can be stored on a direct access device. With every advantage, however, comes a cost; data storage on a direct access device costs more than data storage on tape.

Stop for a minute and evaluate what you've just read. Starting with punched cards, we moved through a series of data storage devices, eventually working our way up to drum. At each step (Fig. 17.12), the new device was able to locate a record more quickly and to transfer this data into the computer at a higher speed; in every sense of the word, as we moved from cards through tape, mass storage, disk, and drum, the speed of the device increased. At the same time, storage capacity dropped off, and the cost of storing data rose. What we are looking at is a trade-off. Sure we can have faster I/O devices, but they're going to cost more and they won't allow us to store as much data. Sure we can have low-cost data processing, but our response time is going to be very slow. There's an old saying, "What you get for nothing is nothing." This is as true in data processing as in any other field.

We might consider core memory next (Fig. 17.12). As expected, it is faster than anything we have seen to this point. But it is also more expensive and, largely because of the expense, there is less of it on most systems. Semiconductor memory is even faster but, once again, it's more expensive.

WHAT'S THE BEST DATA STORAGE DEVICE?

In Chapter 12, we considered the question, "What's the best programming language?" We answered that it depends on the application. Not surprisingly, the answer to the question What's the best data storage device? is the same.

The selection of a storage device depends on a number of factors. Cards are inexpensive but slow; what is the cost, in terms of wasted computer time, of slow I/O? Semiconductor memory is very expensive but very fast; is the extra speed worth the extra cost? In general, the selection of a storage device depends on the answer to two crucial questions: How fast do we have to be and how much are we willing to spend?

A national air defense system must be fast. How much time do we have to react to a possible enemy attack in this nuclear age? Is cost a limiting factor? Yes, but it's not *very* limiting; our leaders are not willing to gamble our lives for a few hundred thousand dollars. Therefore, high-speed I/O will be used.

What about processing payroll? This job can be scheduled, so speed is not really essential. This, as we've seen, is a tape job, with tape being selected over cards for economic reasons.

The best data storage medium for a given job depends on the requirements of that job. The selection of a storage device involves a number of trade-offs, as we sacrifice speed for capacity and lower cost. There is no simple answer to the question, What's the best data storage device?

SUMMARY

This chapter began with a discussion of a number of computer applications for which the batch processing approach is less than adequate. Direct access was presented as a solution.

The concept of direct access was introduced through the imaginary exercise of cutting magnetic tape into a number of strips and then selecting and mounting the strip containing the desired record of data. An unsuccessful attempt to implement this concept, the data cell, and an apparently successful attempt, the modern mass storage device, were then presented.

Magnetic drum was the first of the commercially successful direct access devices. A drum is a cylinder coated on the outside surface with a magnetic material. Data is stored around this surface in circular patterns called tracks. Drum normally has one read/write head for each track; thus the only delay involved in locating data is a rotational delay.

Magnetic disk is today's most popular direct access medium. A disk is a plate-shaped object with a magnetic coating on both flat surfaces. Data is stored on these surfaces in a series of concentric circles called tracks. A movable read/write head allows access to any single track; the time required to move this head is called seek time. Frequently, several disks are stacked on a single spindle, with a single access mechanism simultaneously handling all surfaces. One position of this read/write mechanism defines a cylinder, which contains several tracks.

Small floppy disks or diskettes are growing increasingly popular on minicomputers and terminals. Nonmechanical memory devices such as magnetic bubble memory and charged-coupled devices may well represent the wave of the future.

The chapter ended with a discussion of the economics of storage device selection. Storage capacity and speed tends to be inversely related; as speed increases, storage capacity drops. Higher speed also costs more.

KEYWORDS

access arm	**disk pack**	**megabyte**
access time	**diskette**	**on-line**
cylinder	**drum, magnetic**	**real-time**
data cell	**floppy disk**	**rotational delay**
data transfer time	**magnetic bubble memory**	**seek time**
direct access		**track**
disk, magnetic	**mass storage device**	

EXERCISES

1. What is meant by the term batch processing?
2. What do the terms on-line and real-time mean? How does an on-line, real-time system differ from a batch processing system?
3. Why is magnetic tape less than adequate on an on-line, real-time system?
4. What is direct access?
5. Briefly explain how a modern mass storage device accesses data.
6. How does a magnetic drum work?
7. Reading data from disk (or writing data to disk) involves three distinct steps: seek time, rotational delay, and data transfer time. Explain each of these three steps.
8. Explain the difference between a track and a cylinder on disk.
9. What is a floppy disk? Why is it used?
10. Compare magnetic tape, a mass storage device, disk, and drum in terms of their speed, storage capacity, and physical limitations (direct access, sequential access, etc.).

18

DATA
MANAGEMENT

OVERVIEW

In Chapter 15 we discussed how data can be stored on magnetic tape, while in Chapter 17 we covered data storage on a direct access device. In both chapters, we concentrated on the physical nature of the I/O devices, using examples to illustrate main points. In this chapter, we turn our attention to the data that is stored on these devices, describing a number of techniques for organizing and managing files. Both sequential and direct files will be covered in some detail, and brief discussions of indexed sequential and virtual files are included. The key ideas of data base management, one of the more important trends in current information processing, will be explained. The chapter ends with a discussion of the factors to be considered in selecting a file organization.

DATA MANAGEMENT

In Chapter 15 we introduced the concept of a program library—a place in which programs are carefully cataloged and stored for future recall. A library is more than just a place where programs can be stored; careful cataloging to ensure retrievability is every bit as important as the physical fact of storage.

Data too must be retrieved. Once a file has been created, how can we be sure that we'll be able to find it when we need it again? Once a file has been located, how can we find the individual records we need? These are the kinds of questions with which **data management** deals.

The telephone book provides a number of excellent examples of what is meant by the term data management. First, how can you be sure that you have the correct phone book? (A New York City directory would not be very useful in Los Angeles.) The cover clearly identifies the city or area covered by that particular telephone book. Inside the book, data is arranged in alphabetical order; in other words, it is organized sequentially. Knowing the rules used by the telephone company in organizing the phone book, we can very quickly find the specific name and telephone number that we need.

Our first concern in the discussion of computer data management is one of locating the proper file. Once a file has been found, we must know the rules used to create that file if we want to be able to find individual records. Thus our second concern is to describe some of the more commonly used sets of rules: the access methods.

LOCATING FILES

A reel of magnetic tape is called a volume. Typically, each tape file consumes a single volume, although there are multivolume files and multifile volumes. Since people cannot read the data on tape, labels are used to identify files.

A single disk pack or a single drum is also known as a volume; the term volume is used to refer to a single physical unit of some data storage medium. The existence of multiple files on a single volume is the exception on magnetic tape; on a direct access volume, this is the rule rather than the exception. On tape, individual files are preceded by a label. Direct access files need labels too. Typically on a direct access volume, the labels of all the files on that volume are grouped at the beginning of the volume, usually on the first cylinder or two. This **volume table of contents** identifies each file and indicates where the file begins, in terms of the actual cylinder and track address.

If you refer to the chapters on software you should be able to find an OPEN instruction in the COBOL program. The function of the OPEN instruction is to get an I/O operation started. On magnetic tape, this means mounting the tape volume on a drive. On a direct access device, OPEN involves, among other things, finding the desired file in the volume's table of contents and positioning the read/write heads at the start of this file.

On most systems, however, there are many different direct access volumes; disk, for example, is typically installed in clusters, with several drives sharing a common control unit. Before finding a volume's table of contents, we must first find the correct volume. One approach is to search all the volume tables of contents until the one containing the desired file is located. This might work on a small system, but on a larger system with perhaps dozens of direct access volumes on-line, the task of searching each one in turn would be too time-consuming.

An alternative is to maintain a **catalog** or **index** listing the name and location of each file on the system. This catalog could be stored at a known location on one of the direct access volumes. When a programmer wants a particular file, this catalog can be read into main memory and searched by the computer; through this approach, the proper volume and the location of the file on that volume can be determined.

On some systems, magnetic tape files are cataloged too. Such catalog entries might tell an operator or a tape librarian exactly where a particular tape volume is located (for example, shelf 3, tape 14).

Having located our file, we are now ready to turn our attention to finding a particular record on the file. The key to understanding almost all file organization methods is the relative record address, our next topic.

THE RELATIVE RECORD ADDRESS

Imagine that you are looking for a house located at 838 Main Street. You have just passed 832 Main and are approaching 834 Main. Are you heading in the right direction? How many more buildings can you expect to pass before arriving at your destination? Assuming that standard street addresses have been assigned in this town, you are heading in the right direction, and you can reasonably assume that you are only a few buildings away from 838 Main Street.

Imagine that you are looking for the number of Robert Smith in a telephone book. At the top of a column you find the name "Smith, Jane." Do you move forward or backward to locate the entry for "Smith, Robert"? Knowing that the data in the phone book is in alphabetical order, you move forward.

In both these examples, you were dealing with the idea of relative location; in other words, how far you would need to move from your present location to get to where you wanted to be. The idea of relative location can also be applied to computer data files.

On magnetic tape, we know that records are stored in a fixed sequence. It might be reasonable to number the records, assigning the number 0 to the first record, 1 to the second, 2 to the third, 99 to the hundredth, and so on. We begin with zero because then the first record on the file is located at the start of the file plus 0 records, the second record is at the start plus 1 record, the third is at the start plus 2 records, and so on. We might refer to these numbers as **relative record numbers;** they give the position of a given record relative to the start of the file.

This relative record number, sometimes called a **relative record address,** is not particularly useful on magnetic tape, but it is tremendously useful on a direct access device. Let's assume that we are working with the drum shown in Fig. 18.1. Five of the tracks on this drum hold a file. There are exactly 100 records on each track; thus, records 0 through 99 are on the first track (*relative track* 0), records 100 through 199 are on relative track 1, records 200 through 299 are on relative track 2, and so on (Fig. 18.1).

Where would you expect to find relative record 432? It should be on relative track 4. How do we know this? Well, records 0–99 are on 0, 100–199 are on 1, 200–299 are on 2, 300–399 are on 3, and 400–499 are on 4. Since record 432 lies between records 400 and 499, it too must be on relative track 4. Also, since record 400 is the first record on track, its position relative to the start of the *track* is 0. Record 401 is relative record 1 on this track, and record 402 is relative record 2 on the track; thus record 432 must be relative record 32 on the track. By knowing a record's relative record number, we can determine its physical location.

Given that there are exactly 100 records on each track in this imaginary file (Fig. 18.1), we might go about computing the address of record number 432 in a different manner. What do we get when we divide 432 by 100? The answer is 4, with a remainder of 32. We want the 32nd record on relative track 4. We can always compute a relative track location by simply dividing a relative record number by the number of records per track. This method works for any number of records per track, not just 100. If, for example, a file were stored

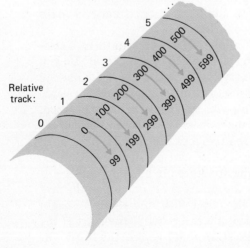

Figure 18.1
A file on magnetic drum.

with exactly 20 records per track, we would divide the relative record number by 20.

Let's refer again to the drum file shown in Fig. 18.1. We now know how to locate a record relative to the beginning of the file. How do we find the **absolute address,** in other words, the actual physical location of the record on the device?

Let's assume that our file starts on track number 50. The first track used by our file is number 50, the second track is 51, the third track is 52, and so on. (Don't forget that we start numbering relative tracks at zero.) Given this starting point, we can compile the following table.

Relative track	Absolute track
0	50
1	51
2	52
3	53
4	54
5	55
.	.
.	.
.	.

Our file starts on absolute track 50. In every case, if we add the relative track to the address of the start of our file, we arrive at the correct absolute address.

Where does our relative address come from? Knowing the relative record number and the number of records on a track, we can compute it. Where does the absolute address of the start of the file come from? From the volume table of contents. Given these two numbers, the location of the actual track holding our data can be computed, the associated read/write head can be turned on, and the data can be accessed.

In this example, we computed a relative track address because we were working with a drum. If the file had been stored on a disk, we would have computed the relative track and relative cylinder addresses, since the physical nature of a disk drive requires both a track and a cylinder location. On a mass storage device, our objective would have been to compute the relative data cartridge. Using core, we would simply multiply the relative record number by the length of the record and compute the relative memory location. Our objective is to compute an address that is compatible with the physical device being used. In every case, however, the starting point is the relative record number.

In the above discussion, the relative record number was always known. Where did it come from? Over the next several pages, we will answer this question for a number of different **file organizations.**

SEQUENTIAL FILES ON A DIRECT ACCESS DEVICE

One of the biggest problems with using magnetic tape arises from the fact that a human operator must mount tape volumes on a tape drive. This is a source of error and, although the few minutes needed to mount a tape may seem insignificant to us, tape mounting represents a substantial waste of time to a computer capable of executing a million or more instructions per second.

Because of this cost, many firms maintain key **sequential files** on disk. An on-line direct access device also makes a great deal of sense when intermediate results must be stored on a secondary medium. As a result, even though disks and drums are called direct access devices, it is not at all unusual to find sequential files stored on them.

How do we access data sequentially when it's stored on a direct access device? Simple. The first record on the file is relative record 0, next we have relative record 1, then 2, then 3, and so on. Do you see the pattern? Just add the number 1 to the preceding relative record number. The starting point, the address of the beginning of the file, is in the volume table of contents.

We have not yet mentioned how the computer "knows" when there is no more data on a file. If you again refer back to the material on software, you will notice a CLOSE instruction near the end of the COBOL program. One of the functions performed by this CLOSE macro is the writing of an end-of-file marker. Later, when it is reading the file, the computer "knows" that there is no more data when this marker is encountered.

DIRECT ACCESS

Direct access means that we can go directly (or almost directly) to the single record we want without working through all the records that precede it in the file. The way we use a telephone book is a perfect example of what is meant by the term direct access.

To get a good example of a simple direct access file, let's take a look at a small store that stocks and sells 5000 different items. Each of these items is assigned a unique part number—0001 through 5000 would make sense. A file is created to hold records for each of these part numbers (Fig. 18.2); individual records might hold the part number, description, stock on hand, selling price, cost, source, and other information.

This file would probably be created sequentially. But look at the relationship between the part number (the logical **key**) and the relative record number (Fig. 18.2). Part number 0001 is relative record 0, part number 0002 is relative record 1, part number 0003 is relative record 2, and so on. The relative record number can be computed directly from the actual key (in this case, the part number) simply by subtracting one. Once we have the relative record number, we can compute the actual location of the record and move the

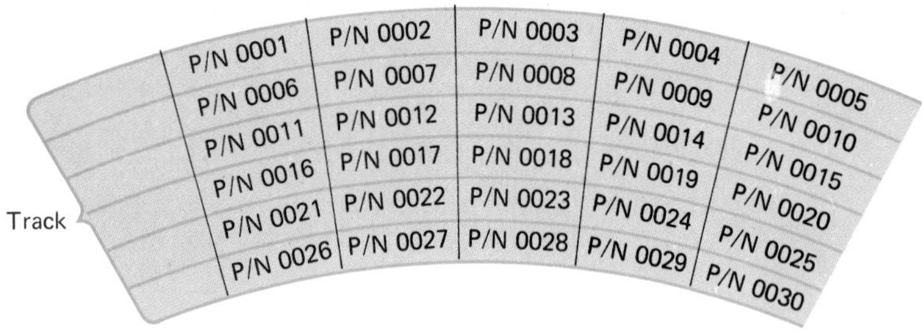

Figure 18.2
Simple direct access with the actual key being (with limited modification) the relative record address. For simplicity, the individual records are shown as they might be arranged on a single-surface disk, with exactly five records on each track. The "P/N" stands for "part number."

read/write heads directly to the desired cylinder and/or track location, by-passing the intervening records. This is the simplest form of direct access. For this technique to work, there must be one record for every possible actual key; given this restriction, the actual key becomes the relative record number (with a possible slight adjustment, such as subtracting one).

Simple direct access does not always work. What if your school were to decide to create a file of every student's academic record? If the key to the file were the student's social security number (as is often the case), how many records would the school have to allow for in order to use the simple "actual-key equals relative-record-address" approach? Since the social security number is nine digits long, space for 999,999,999 records would be needed! Even if we were to identify carefully the lowest and highest social security numbers among the students in the school, we would still need 100,000 or more records (probably more) to cover even this limited range. If you compare the number of different records needed to the number of students actually attending your school, you will see that a great many record slots would be wasted.

Try a little experiment in your own class (or even your own home). Find the lowest and highest social security numbers in the class or group. How many different numbers lie between these two extremes? How many people are in the group? To use simple "actual-key equals relative-record-number" direct access, you must assign enough direct access space to hold one actual record for each possible key. What percentage of these keys is actually utilized by your group? What percentage of the direct access space would be wasted?

A common solution to this problem is to maintain an **index** showing the relative record number of each record. As the file is created, a table is built showing the actual key and the relative record number of the associated record of data (Fig. 18.3). Normally, this index is kept in sequence by actual key. Later, when a record is to be retrieved, the actual key can be looked up in the index, the matching relative record number found, the actual physical address computed, and the data accessed.

On large files, the index can become so big as to be difficult to maintain. When this happens, a technique known as **randomizing** is sometimes used.

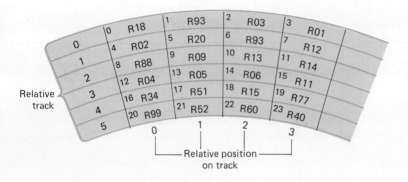

Index		Computed	
Actual key	Relative record number	Track	Record
01	3	0	3
02	4	1	0
03	2	0	1
04	12	3	0
05	13	3	1
06	14	3	2
09	9	2	1
11	15	3	3
12	7	1	3
13	10	2	2
14	11	2	3
15	18	4	2
18	0	0	0

and so on

Figure 18.3
Direct access using an index.

The basic idea of randomizing is to take the actual key and grind it through a number of mathematical computations so as to compute a relative record number.

For example, let's say that our actual key is a social security number. The social security number is nine digits long, much too long to use as a relative record number. But what if we were to create a new number by selecting only the second, fourth, sixth, and eighth digits? Social security number 123–45–6789 would, for example, become relative record number 2468. We now have a four-digit number, and there are only 9999 possible different four-digit numbers. This computed key could be used as a relative record number.

Although not too many people would be expected to have social security numbers with the same four digits in these four positions, some would. What happens when the actual keys of two different records compute to the same relative record number? Obviously, we cannot store both records at the same place on a direct access device. When two or more different actual keys produce the same relative record number, we have a **synonym.** Synonyms must be stored in an **overflow** area. Later, when the data is to be retrieved, a check of the record at the computed location might show that it is the wrong record. In such a case, the read/write heads must be moved to the overflow track or overflow area so that the proper record can be found.

The randomizing algorithm described above is a very simple one; most are far more complex, involving mathematical computations that are beyond the scope of this book. The whole purpose of randomizing is to produce relative record numbers that are evenly distributed throughout the space available to the file, with a minimum of synonyms.

INDEXED SEQUENTIAL FILES

A major problem with the index approach described above is the difficulty encountered in maintaining the index. Using an indexed sequential approach, special system software maintains the index.

To create an **indexed sequential file,** data must first be sorted into sequence by key. The individual records are then copied to successive locations on disk, with no space (except for the usual interrecord gaps) between records. As a track is filled, the key of the last record added to the track is placed on a track index. Later, when searching for data, if the actual key is found to be less than the key of the last record on this track, then we know that the record must lie on this track.

As more and more records are added to the file, more and more tracks will be filled, increasing the number of entries in the track index. Eventually all the space on an entire cylinder is filled. When this happens, the key of the last record added to the cylinder is placed in a cylinder index. A cylinder, remember, consists of several tracks.

Moving along to the next cylinder, a new track index is started, containing the key of the last record stored on each of the tracks in this second cylinder. When this cylinder is filled, another entry is made in the cylinder index, and the system moves along to the next cylinder. Note that there is one cylinder index for the entire file and one track index for each cylinder.

Once the file has been created, the records can be accessed either sequentially or directly. How sequential access is achieved should be obvious, since the file was created sequentially. To access a record directly is a three-step operation:

1. Get the cylinder index and locate the cylinder holding the desired record.

2. Get the track index associated with this cylinder and identify the track holding the desired record.

3. Move the read/write heads to the indicated cylinder, turn on the head associated with the indicated track, and search for the record with the correct key.

The ability to access data either directly or sequentially is the major advantage cited for the indexed sequential technique. This advantage, of course, also exists with the "actual-key equals relative-record-number" and the "programmer-maintained table-of-contents" approaches.

Because of the need to access both a cylinder and a track index prior to locating a record of data, direct access is relatively inefficient on an indexed sequential file. The indexes are normally stored on disk, along with the data. To find a given record means a seek and a read for the cylinder index, another seek and a read for the track index, and a final positioning of the read/write heads to get the data. Careful file design can help to minimize some of the time lost on these multiple I/O operations, but the fact remains that a process involving three I/O operations for each record is inefficient.

Since an indexed sequential file must be created in sequence, it is difficult to add and delete records using this approach. Every possible storage location is filled in creating the file; thus there are no blank spaces for new records. The need for absolute sequence creates other problems as well. Let's assume that on a particular indexed sequential file the last record stored on the first track has a key of 52. What this means is that all the other records on this track have keys of less than 52; if this were not true, the indexing method would not work. If we want to add record number 50, it must go onto this first track, but there is no room for it, making the process of adding **overflow** records to an indexed sequential file very complex. Such records complicate both direct and sequential file access, adding to the inefficiency of an indexed sequential file.

Perhaps the major disadvantage of the indexed sequential approach to file management is its "disk only" orientation. Cylinder and track indexes are maintained in support of an indexed sequential file. Cylinders and tracks exist on disk, and on no other input/output device. There are a number of new technologies which show promise of eventually supplanting disk. When these new devices become commercially available, they probably won't support indexed sequential files in quite the same way as on disk. On files using relative record numbers, a switch to one of the newer devices should be relatively transparent to the programmer. Programs accessing indexed sequential files may, however, require substantial revision.

FUTURE APPROACHES

By far the best of the available direct access devices is core memory or its modern equivalent. Since no mechanical motion is involved, it is very fast. Also, it is possible to go directly to the desired record (or even character), rather than just getting as close as the desired track. The only deterrent to using main memory for bulk data storage is its high cost.

Future memory developments will probably try to copy the best features of main memory. Specifically, future bulk memory will involve less mechanical motion and will be addressed more like main memory than are the present disk and drum.

What does this mean in terms of the file organizations we have discussed in this chapter? These trends will really not create a problem for techniques using the relative record number approach to direct access. Main memory is addressed by numbering the memory locations sequentially. When relative record numbers are used, secondary memory is "addressed" by numbering the records sequentially. Let's assume that each of the records in some future file is 100 memory locations in length. The first record, relative record 0, is zero memory locations away from the start of the file (because it *is* the start of the file). The second record, relative record 1, is exactly 100 memory locations away from the start of the file. The third record, relative record 2 is 200 memory locations away from the start, and so on. The pattern should be obvious; relative record addresses are much like main-memory addresses.

The conversion is not quite as easy with an indexed sequential file. Cylinders and tracks exist because of, *not* in spite of, the physical mechanical nature of a disk drive. When disk is eventually supplanted by faster and more cost-effective secondary-storage devices, the indexed sequential technique will also change.

Many modern computers support a new type of file organization based on a virtual storage approach. Virtual storage is a technique for expanding the capacity of a computer by putting much of what would normally be in main memory on a secondary-storage device (we will be discussing this in more detail in a later chapter). To simplify the task of the programmer, virtual memory systems include special hardware or software that assumes the responsibility for converting the secondary-storage addresses into their main-memory equivalents. In other words, the programmer can program as though everything were in main memory, and the fact that portions of the program might actually be on secondary storage is completely transparent, with any necessary address translation being handled by the system.

This is a very important concept from the standpoint of data access too. Why not simply give the "system" a relative record number and allow it to do whatever is necessary in order to figure out the actual secondary-storage location of the data? Using this approach, the actual physical input or output device used by the system would be of no concern to the programmer; data access would be device-independent. If at some time in the future the actual physical device were to change, so what? Only the special system software or hardware, and *not* all the programs, would need to be changed.

The special software or hardware needed to implement virtual storage normally assumes a rather rigid organization of data on the secondary-storage device, usually requiring a series of fixed-length blocks. Given this restriction, such virtual storage access methods are available (and widely used) today.

THE LINK TO SOFTWARE: THE ACCESS METHOD

Is it necessary that the programmer be aware of the intimate details of file access in order to write a program? No. Typically, the programmer states, in some formal way as part of the program, that either a sequential file, a direct file, an indexed sequential file, or a virtual file is to be used. The exact procedure for defining the file type varies from language to language and from manufacturer to manufacturer, but once a programmer learns the rules, it is a fairly straightforward procedure.

This definition is subsequently used by the linkage editor program in selecting an **access method.** Let's briefly review the functions performed by the linkage editor. A compiler program converts a programmer's source code to an object module (Fig. 18.4). The linkage editor adds such things as access

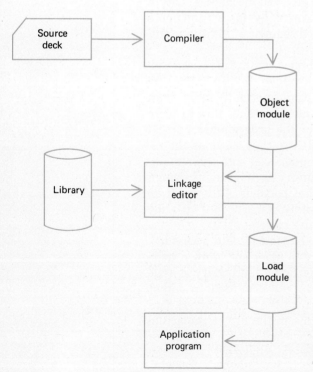

Figure 18.4
The compile, link-edit, and execute sequence.

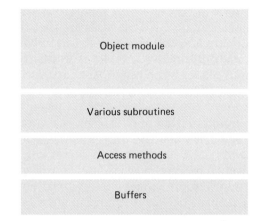

Figure 18.5
A load module.

methods and buffers to the object module to form a load module (Fig. 18.4). The resulting load module (Fig. 18.5) can then be loaded and executed.

There are many different kinds of access methods available. On an IBM machine, for example, there are two types of sequential access methods: a Queued Sequential Access Method (QSAM), which automatically performs blocking and deblocking, and a Basic Sequential Access Method (BSAM), which leaves these responsibilities to the programmer. The Indexed Sequential Access Method (ISAM) also has both Queued (QISAM) and Basic (BISAM) versions. Only a Basic version (BDAM) is provided for direct access. Virtual files are accessed through VSAM, the Virtual Storage Access Method. BTAM, QTAM, and VTAM allow the program to access files over telecommunication lines, a topic to be covered in a later chapter.

DATA BASE MANAGEMENT

The fact that a computer is an information processing machine is what makes this machine so valuable. Information is the key to decision making in an organization, and the computer is a warehouse of information. Logically, this information should be available to management, but all too often it is not.

Files have historically been designed to match a specific application. Payroll files contained all the data needed to support the payroll application. Inventory files held only those fields that were necessary to the processing of inventory. The personnel department might maintain a different set of files to keep track of employee progress. This approach is not unique to business: At a university there are files for a student's academic record, different files for financial matters, and still other files for housing and financial aid.

On the surface, it makes sense to customize a file to an application, but this does cause problems. Your name and address, for example, probably appear on several different university files. What if you move, marry, or legally change your name? The chances are that the financial files will reflect the change quickly and accurately, but what about the other files? What we have here is **redundant data,** in other words, the same data appearing in several different places. With redundant data, a simple name change must be processed several different times in order to correct every copy; unfortunately, it seems that one or two of the versions are usually incorrect. Redundant data is difficult to maintain; hence it is often inaccurate.

Why not store just a single copy of each student's name and address and allow every program to access it from this single location? In this way, data redundancy would be minimized. Data accuracy would improve because a change, once made, would immediately be available to every program. This is one of the basic ideas behind a concept known as **data base management**.

Using the data base approach, data is treated as an important organizational resource, *not* as the property of an individual programmer or department. The emphasis is on the accuracy and the accessibility of the data. Often, to improve accessibility, logically related elements of data are linked together. Perhaps the best way to illustrate these ideas is through an example.

A university maintains a number of files on every student: academic records, financial records, financial aid records, housing records, and others. Under a data base management system, each student might be assigned a master record (Fig. 18.6) containing such key data as the student's ID number, name, address, class, parents' name and address, major, and so on. Also contained in this record are a number of **pointers** to other records (Fig. 18.6), including this student's academic, financial, and housing records. These pointers might be the relative record numbers of the related records that are located in other physical files on, perhaps, physically separate pieces of equipment.

Beginning with this master record, it is possible to collect all the data the university has on any one student. The secondary files can still be processed independently (the academic history file, for example, would be updated each term), accessing the master file record through its key (the social security number in this example) when data such as the student's name and address are required. Since all requests for a name and address will access the same copy, the chances are that the data obtained will be the most accurate and up-to-date information available.

When the records in a data base are connected in this way, they are said to be **integrated**. On a well-planned **integrated data base**, all relevant data can be tracked down and found; in other words, the data is accessible. Building such a data base is not an easy task. Data base design starts with a definition of all of an organization's data resources, identifies key interrelationships between individual elements of data, and then puts the pieces together as an

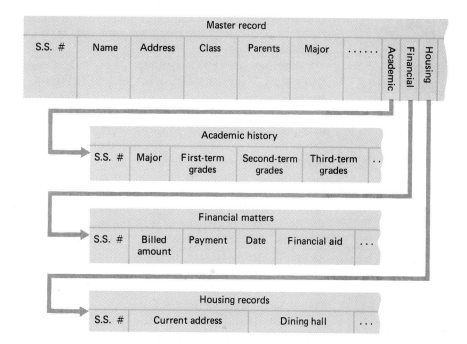

Figure 18.6
Data relationships on an integrated data base.

integrated whole rather than as a collection of separate and independent files. The whole point of a data base is to make the data resources of the organization available to whoever needs them.

Physically, the elements of a data base are the same records and files we discussed earlier; the only difference is the integration of these files. A data base management system might use sequential direct, indexed sequential, or virtual files, actually accessing the data through one of the standard access methods. The physical devices are the same too—disk, drum, tape, and mass storage. The pieces are merely put together in a different way.

WHAT'S THE BEST FILE ORGANIZATION?

The best file organization for a given application depends on a number of factors, perhaps the most obvious of which is the available hardware. An installation with no direct access devices is rather obviously restricted to sequential files. VSAM makes little sense to the manager of a computer center if the computer does not have the special hardware and software needed to support virtual memory. Although hardware limitations may keep an installation from using the "ideal" organization, the cost of obtaining the extra equipment needed to support the ideal approach may make it uneconomical (hence, not ideal).

Another important and often overlooked restriction is the format of existing files. If an installation is using ISAM, for example, its programmers are trained in ISAM. Switching to a new or different access method would create a need for additional training and might require the reorganization of several existing files; both training and reorganization can be costly. The status quo can sometimes keep a programmer or system designer from using what is obviously the best approach.

Another important consideration is **file size**. It makes little sense, for example, to use a direct or indexed sequential organization on a file that consumes only a single track of a disk pack. The best approach is to organize the file sequentially and search for the desired key since you can't get closer than the nearest track anyway. On a small file, it is easy to maintain an index; as the file grows in size, however, this becomes a real problem. A huge file—a complete metropolitan telephone book, for example—might be just too big to keep on an expensive direct access device, thus leading to the choice of a sequential organization on tape.

What about sequential files on disk? Disk storage is more expensive than tape storage, but magnetic tape must be handled by an operator. On relatively small, frequently accessed sequential files, the cost of handling the tape may offset the added cost of disk storage. Again, file size is a key.

Activity is another important consideration. By activity, we mean two things: the frequency with which the records in a file are accessed, and the distribution of this access. A payroll year-to-date file is considered to be very active because almost every record in the file is accessed each time the payroll program is run. When a significant percentage of the records in a file are accessed frequently, that file is highly active. Such files are good candidates for the sequential master-file update application described in Chapters 15 and 16.

A bank's checking-account master file is quite active, but not nearly as active as a payroll file; every employee in a company gets paid, but in any given period of time there will be many bank customers who do not write a single check. Savings-account master files are even less active. Because of this lower activity, many banks and savings and loan institutions use direct or indexed sequential organizations for these files, feeling that it is less expensive to individually look up each of the relatively few records requiring modification than it is to read the entire file in order to update a small percentage of the records. As activity declines, sequential files become less and less attractive.

An airline reservation system calls for a file to hold records for each scheduled flight. Although there may be many transactions against the file on a given day (a few hundred requests for a seat on a particular flight, for example), these requests are generally not distributed throughout the file.

Very few people really care about information on a flight scheduled to leave three months from now; the greatest emphasis is on flights leaving in the near future. This concentration of activity on a small number of records (localized activity) tends to favor a direct organization.

A file's **volatility** is a measure of the frequency of additions to and deletions from the file. It is possible for a file to be very active but not very volatile—a payroll file in a company with very little turnover is a good example. A list of the current prices of each of the firms currently being traded on the stock market would be quite active (the prices change frequently) but not very volatile (new firms and bankruptcies do not occur every day, at least not on the "big board").

The indexed sequential organization is not a good approach for highly volatile files. On a sequential file, volatility is simply handled as part of a regular master-file update. A well-designed direct access file encounters little trouble with additions or deletions.

Becoming more and more important as a file attribute is **response time**, which is a measure of the delay between making a request for information and receiving an answer. In an air defense system, quick response is essential for obvious reasons. In an airline reservation system, response time is important (though not quite as crucial) for competitive reasons. If quick response is needed, the sequential access method will not do. Direct access is probably the best alternative.

The term **integration** is used to refer to the relationship between files and between various applications. A payroll application might, for example, involve a number of related files, such as the time-cards file, the year-to-date earnings file, and a personnel file. Even though the rate of personnel turnover and other personnel changes (marriages, births, etc.) might argue for a direct access file, the fact that this file is so closely related to the payroll application (integration) might mean that sequential is the best choice.

Integration can also occur between different applications. A file of current income tax rates might be used by payroll, accounting, and financial applications. In such a situation, the file's organization might well be chosen by compromise.

More and more firms are beginning to recognize the true extent of the relationship between their various data files, and the question of file integration is thus gaining in importance. Data base management is an outgrowth of this concern.

Two other factors, **security** and file **backup,** are also growing in importance today. The computer is being used to house very sensitive and important information ranging from key operational data for a business concern to classified governmental and military secrets. The theft or loss of this information could prove to be disastrous. These factors must be taken into account when planning a file organization.

SUMMARY

In Chapters 15 and 17, we considered a number of devices used to physically store data. In this chapter, we concentrated on the data itself, discussing how data can be organized, stored, and retrieved.

The chapter began with the topic of data management. Next, techniques for locating a file were discussed, followed by a presentation of the relative record address concept, the key to understanding most file organization techniques.

A direct access device can hold both sequential and direct files; sequentially accessing records involves simply incrementing a relative record number. Several techniques for organizing a direct access file were then discussed, including the "actual-key equals relative-record-number" approach, the "programmer-maintained index" approach, and randomizing. Indexed sequential files can support both sequential and direct access.

Since main memory is the ideal direct access device, future hardware will probably be similar to main memory, with a form of straight sequential addressing. Files organized along relative record number lines will be easy to convert, but conversion to these new devices may be a problem for the indexed sequential file. The virtual-storage access methods that are currently available represent a move toward device-independent files, perhaps in anticipation of these trends.

Access methods added to a program by the linkage editor represent the link between an application program and its files.

Many organizations are moving in the direction of data base management. By treating the organization's information as the valuable resource that it is, and collecting all the information into a single integrated data base (as opposed to a series of independent files), data redundancy can be reduced, accuracy can be improved, and the data can be made more readily available to those who need it.

Several factors should be considered in selecting a file organization. The existing hardware of an installation is an obvious limiting factor. The format of existing files should also be considered. File size, activity, volatility, the need for response time, the degree of file integration, and the need for security and backup are other important factors.

KEYWORDS

absolute address	data base management	file size
access method	data management	index
activity	direct access	indexed sequential file
backup	file organization	integrated data base
catalog		

integration

key

overflow

pointer

randomize

redundant data

relative record address

relative record number

response time

security

sequential file

synonym

volatility

volume table of contents

EXERCISES _____

1. What is data management?
2. Explain how a file can be located on a direct access device.
3. Explain the concept of a relative record number.
4. How can data stored on a direct access device be retrieved sequentially?
5. Discuss several techniques for organizing a direct access file.
6. What is meant by an indexed sequential file organization?
7. Explain the concept of an access method. Why are there so many different kinds of access methods?
8. What is data base management? Discuss the advantages of this approach.
9. Why is it so difficult to select a single best access method?
10. Why are each of the following considered to be important in selecting a file organization?

     a) file size   b) activity

     c) volatility   d) integration

     e) security   f) backup

19

AN ON-LINE, REAL-TIME SYSTEM

OVERVIEW

This chapter is another case study similar to the ones presented in Chapters 4 and 16. Here, we'll be examining an on-line, real-time, airline reservation system, designed to process each transaction as it occurs, instead of collecting transactions into a batch for sequential processing. The files supporting this application are maintained on a direct access device; the basic input and output device is a keyboard terminal.

The manual and batch processing case studies were based on a variation of the inventory file maintenance problem. To an airline, a flight can be viewed as an inventory of seats, which can be filled by passengers.

THE FIRM

Tree Top Airways is one of the top ten airlines, in terms of passenger miles per year, in the country. Their business is strictly domestic, being restricted to providing connecting flights between a large number of small-to-medium cities and the major airports. In some cities, they are the only airline available; in most, however, competition with one or two other similar firms is a fact of life.

THE PROBLEM

The problem faced by Tree Top Airways is basically one of filling as many of the available seats as possible. The cost of flying from city A to city B is essentially a fixed cost, in that a full crew must be paid, a certain amount of fuel must be consumed, a certain amount of maintenance must be performed, and landing fees must be paid whether there are two or two hundred passengers on board the plane. The breakeven point is approximately 50 percent; in other words, if half the seats are filled, the costs of flying the plane are just about covered by the passengers' fares. Every passenger over the 50 percent loading factor represents pure profit.

One major problem is "no-shows," those people who make a reservation, do not cancel that reservation, and yet do not show up for the flight. Another problem is the last-minute cancellation; there may be other passengers who desire a seat on the flight, but if the airline can't get word to them in time, the seat can't be sold.

Several company policies enable us to utilize some of the unclaimed seats. Special, half-fare standby tickets can be purchased by students, servicemen, and senior citizens; if a seat is unclaimed a few minutes before the flight is scheduled to depart, persons holding standby tickets are allowed to board. From the company standpoint, this policy serves two purposes: it's good public relations, and since we can't sell the seat anyway, we might as well get half-fare for it.

Another policy relates to freight. If, a few minutes before departure time, a plane is not filled, extra freight weighing about as much as the expected weight of the passengers who might have been present (but aren't) can be added to the cargo hold. Freight shipped in this way (basically, another form of standby) is given a special, lower rate than is assigned to guaranteed-delivery freight, but, again, something is better than nothing.

If we are to be able to make these last-minute adjustments on the passenger and freight loads, we must know exactly how many passengers are on the plane. This sounds simple—just count them. But what about the regular passenger who has called ahead and indicated that he or she will be at the airport five minutes before flight time? Would we rather have this person's full fare or someone else's half-fare? And what happens when a potential customer attempts to make a last-minute reservation?

One solution might be to assign to a member of the ground crew the responsibility for keeping track of the number of people on the plane and for handling any telephone calls relating to last-minute reservations. The crucial time is the fifteen or twenty minutes right before scheduled departure. What happens if three different travel agents are attempting to contact this individual at the same time? At least one is probably not going to get through in time. As if this is not enough, consider the number of flights scheduled by Tree Top on any given day. If a potential customer wants a reservation on Flight 713, but *only if* space on a connecting flight is also available, the flight clerk would have no way of knowing this information. Manual data processing isn't adequate.

If Tree Top were the only airline around, these problems would not be significant; customers could either "take it or leave it." But, in most cities, competition is fierce, and even in those cities where Tree Top is "the only game in town," federal regulations and consumer groups prevent them from gouging the public. If a potential passenger were to request a reservation only to be told to "Come back at 5:00 P.M. when we update our batch reservation files," he or she would probably find another flight on another airline. Batch processing isn't adequate here either.

What is needed is a reservation system that provides rapid response to customer requests for reservations and that provides up-to-the-minute status information on a given flight during the last several minutes before departure. We need an on-line, real-time, air reservation system.

THE BASIC SOLUTION

The heart of our reservation system is a direct access file, stored on disk, holding information for all scheduled flights one month in advance. The key to this file is composed of the flight number and the date. Let's assume, for example, that a customer wants to make a reservation on Tree Top Flight 713 on December 22, 1988. The combination of the flight number and the date identifies a specific flight. Information on this flight is stored on the disk file and can be accessed by referring to the following key:

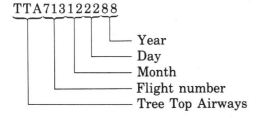

Once a reservation clerk has entered this key via a terminal, the computer converts the key to a relative record address through a simple table look-up approach. The relative record address is then converted to an absolute address, and the desired record is found and read into the computer, thus allowing new reservations to be added and cancellations to be deleted. Once the reservation clerk has completed making changes to the flight record, the record is written back into its original position on the disk, thus replacing the old version of the record. In this way, flight information reflects the status of the flight as of the most current transaction.

The master flight file is kept on a centralized computer located in St. Louis. Terminals are located in each airport serviced by Tree Top, with special private leased communication lines connecting each airport to the centralized computer. When a travel agent or a customer wants to make a reservation on a Tree Top flight, a call is made to the nearest airport, and a reservation clerk takes it from there, accessing the master file through a terminal.

What about connecting flights? The reservation clerk can access information on any Tree Top flight departing from any city through the same terminal; a series of connecting flights are simply handled as a series of separate requests.

Just before flight time, the value of the computer is really brought to bear on the problem. Given the computer's tremendous speed, last-minute reservations and cancellations represent no real problem, and concurrent requests from several different customers can easily be handled. The decision to allocate seats to standby passengers can be left to the last possible minute. Again, at the last minute, the computer can figure out the estimated weight of the passengers on board and send a message to the ground crew telling them how much additional freight can be put in the cargo hold. The net result of computerization might be the equivalent of two or three extra seats per flight being filled, but, on a basically fixed cost operation, these two or three extra seats represent almost pure profit. Multiply by the hundreds of flights per day and factor in the roughly $100.00 average cost per passenger, and you have a very significant amount of money.

DAILY OPERATION OF THE SYSTEM

On a day-by-day basis, the operation of the system begins with the reservation clerk. Let's assume that we are watching a clerk who has just received a call from a customer requesting a reservation for three on Flight 713 for December 22. As the clerk turns to the terminal, he is about to engage in a conversation with the computer; a copy of this conversation is shown in Fig. 19.1. As you read the conversation of Fig. 19.1, all comments generated by the computer are shown in simple capital letters, while the responses of the clerk are shown in lower case.

The clerk starts by pressing an ATTENTION button on the terminal; in response, within (usually) a fraction of a second, the computer causes the words ENTER FLIGHT? to be printed on the terminal (the question mark is

```
ENTER FLIGHT?tta713122288
FLIGHT: 713
DATE:   12/22/88
CAPACITY: 125
ASSIGNED: 112
AVAILABLE: 13 SEATS


DO YOU WISH TO MAKE A RESERVATION?yes
HOW MANY SEATS?3
RESERVATION CONFIRMED

PASSENGER NAMES?smith
               ?jones
               ?baxter

THANK YOU
```

Figure 19.1

A request for a reservation on an on-line, real-time reservation system.

the computer's way of asking the clerk to enter some data). The clerk types the flight number and date and hits the RETURN button on the terminal keyboard. The flight and date are then printed, under control of the computer, for visual verification by the reservation clerk, and the status of the flight—capacity, number of seats assigned, and number of seats available—is printed. This information is followed by a question, "DO YOU WISH TO MAKE A RESERVATION?", after which control returns to the clerk.

The reservation clerk responds by typing YES or NO; in this example, the response was YES, followed by the hitting of the RETURN key. The computer asks "HOW MANY SEATS?" The clerk responds with the number of seats requested, after which the computer confirms the reservation and asks for the passenger names. Once all the names have been entered, the computer thanks the clerk, and moves on to the next transaction. Total elapsed time for this transaction was in the neighborhood of 30 seconds.

What actually happened within the system? As the clerk entered the flight number, the computer converted this number into a relative record number and then into an absolute direct access address, and retrieved the record associated with the flight. Key information was extracted from this record and sent to the terminal where it was displayed for the benefit of the human clerk. Later, when the clerk indicated that a reservation was to be made, the computer responded with a question: "HOW MANY SEATS?"; in response, the clerk typed a number, and the computer added this number to the count of assigned seats and subtracted it from the count of available seats, after which the record was written back to disk. What about the request for passenger names? At this point in time, the request for names is done primarily for public relations purposes. The names are not actually entered into the flight record, but the fact that names are requested tends to make passengers feel good and helps to minimize the multiple booking problem, where one passenger books a reservation on a number of different, competitive flights. Eventually, a cross-checking

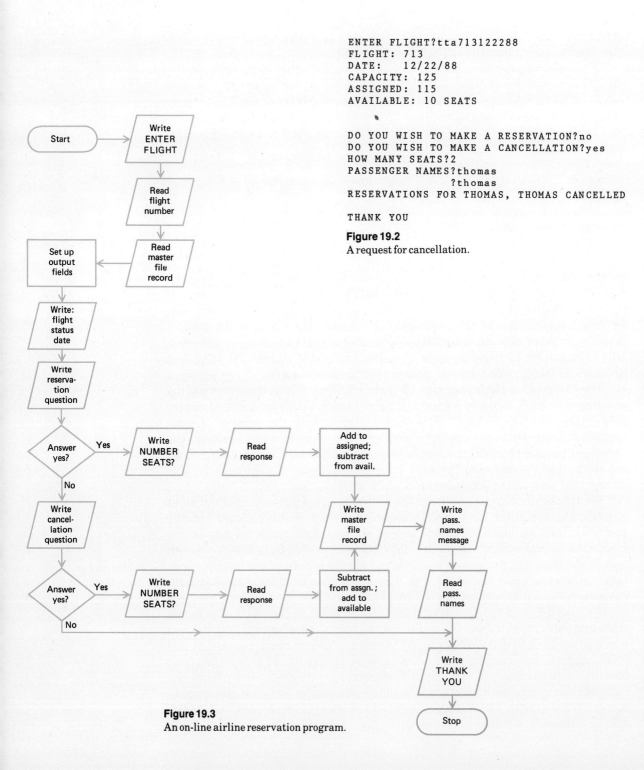

```
ENTER FLIGHT?tta713122288
FLIGHT: 713
DATE:   12/22/88
CAPACITY: 125
ASSIGNED: 115
AVAILABLE: 10 SEATS


DO YOU WISH TO MAKE A RESERVATION?no
DO YOU WISH TO MAKE A CANCELLATION?yes
HOW MANY SEATS?2
PASSENGER NAMES?thomas
              ?thomas
RESERVATIONS FOR THOMAS, THOMAS CANCELLED

THANK YOU
```

Figure 19.2
A request for cancellation.

Figure 19.3
An on-line airline reservation program.

capability based on passenger names is planned; right now, however, it is regarded as being more trouble than it's worth.

Cancellations are handled in much the same way (Fig. 19.2). Note, on Fig. 19.2, that when the response to the "reservations" question was NO, another question involving cancellations was asked. Since the response to this question was YES, the number is requested and the number of seats assigned (subtraction) and available (addition) are updated, after which the record is written back to disk.

What if the answer to the cancellations question had been NO? The computer would have assumed that this was just a request for information and gone directly to the THANK YOU message.

Basic Program Logic

The basic logic of the airline reservation program is shown in the flowchart of Fig. 19.3. See if you can follow the logic. You might find it easier if you reread the material of the last several paragraphs as you follow the flowlines.

SOME ADDITIONAL DETAILS

Why was the master-file record copied back to disk just as soon as it was updated? The answer to this question involves the possibility that several different reservation clerks need access to data on the same flight at the same time. By putting the updated version of the flight record back out to disk as quickly as possible, the computer makes this up-to-date data available to the other clerks as quickly as possible.

What might happen, however, if two or more clerks really were trying to change the record for the *same* flight at the *same* time? Consider, for example, the following sequence of events:

1. Clerk A starts a transaction for Flight 732 on December 15, 1988. The computer finds the record and displays the fact that three seats are available.

2. Clerk B begins a transaction for the same flight, again being told that three seats are available.

3. Clerk A makes a reservation for these three seats, the seat inventory is updated to reflect a new total of zero seats available, and this record is written back out to disk.

4. Clerk B, still believing that three seats are available, makes another reservation for three more seats and this copy of the flight record is updated and written back to disk, destroying the version just written at the request of clerk A.

If we were to allow this kind of thing to happen, we would have overbooked Flight 732 by 3 passengers.

How do we avoid this problem? By **locking** individual records. As soon as clerk A starts processing a transaction against Flight 732, all other clerks are barred from access to this record. Only when clerk A has completed making changes and the updated record has been written back to disk are other clerks permitted access. In this way, only the most current version of the record is shown to a clerk, and the accidental destruction of a transaction is avoided.

What happens if a clerk is involved in a long telephone conversation with a customer and ties up a record for several minutes? Other clerks might be able to sell seats on this flight if the line were available. This problem is handled by a time control; once a clerk indicates that a reservation or cancellation is pending, he or she has thirty seconds to respond with a number before the record is unlocked and released to another clerk, forcing the original clerk to start over again.

Other checks embodied in the program include tests for obviously incorrect transactions, such as a request for five seats when only two are available. For the sake of simplicity, these additional details were not incorporated into the flowchart of Fig. 19.3.

LONG-RANGE CONTROLS

Flights for today and for the next fourteen days are considered to be current; the index for accessing the records on these flights is kept in main memory at all times. Flights covering the period of 15 days through 30 days from now are kept on disk, but their index is not maintained in main memory. Requests for information on such flights are not common, so we can afford the extra time needed to read the index from disk before accessing the data.

Flights more than 30 days in advance are kept on magnetic tape. Our policy is to automatically confirm a reservation on such flights; if the demand for a given flight is unusually heavy, the fact that we have at least 30 days' advance notice gives us plenty of time to schedule a larger plane or an extra flight if it is needed.

Each evening, this tape file participates in a standard, batch master-file update. Flights that have already departed are removed from the master disk file. Flights that, because of the passage of time, have moved from being 31 days in the future to being only 30 days in the future are transferred from the tape file to the on-line disk file. At the same time, any "far future" reservations are added to the tape records as a new tape is created.

SUMMARY

In this chapter, we considered an on-line, real-time, airline reservation system in a case study form. By far the best way to review this material would be to go through the logic of the flowchart of Fig. 19.3.

KEYWORDS_____

locking (file)

EXERCISES _____

1. You may have, at some time in your life, come in contact with a hotel or motel reservation system. On such systems, the customer can get confirmation of a room reservation in a distant city. How do you suppose such a system would work?

2. How do you suppose the reservation system run by a nationwide car-rental agency might work?

3. Many savings banks have installed a computerized system for controlling access to passbook savings accounts. Under such a system, the teller inserts your passbook into a terminal and types in the amount of the deposit or withdrawal, and the computer updates your account. How do you suppose this system works?

4. A coming "thing" in supermarkets is computer-controlled checkout. Under such systems, the bar-code printed on most supermarket packages is read by a scanner device directly into a computer, which keeps track of the purchases in an order. How would you suppose this system might work?

5. Many department stores have installed special terminals that allow a clerk to insert a customer's credit card and obtain approval from a central computer before granting credit. Explain how this system might work.

V

MODERN COMPUTER-BASED INFORMATION SYSTEMS

20

OPERATING SYSTEMS AND SYSTEM SOFTWARE

OVERVIEW

In this chapter, we'll consider the way in which modern, large-scale computers actually operate. Starting with smaller computers, we'll introduce such concepts as the importance of scheduling, the use of compilers, program libraries, and access methods. Moving along to the larger machines, we'll consider the extreme disparity between the speed of the computer and its I/O devices, presenting the concepts of multiprogramming and time-sharing as solutions to this problem.

The fact that a multiprogrammed computer works on a number of different programs concurrently creates a distinct risk of interference; we'll examine how collections of system software called operating systems have been developed to deal with these problems and consider a number of different types of operating systems including those based on modern virtual memory techniques. The basic ideas of system generation and initial program loading will be explored. The chapter ends with a brief discussion of job control language, a language that allows the programmer to communicate with the operating system.

FIRST-GENERATION COMPUTERS

During the first generation, computers were brand-new and completely untried. They were very expensive and quite rare. Only a few large companies and research centers used them. These early computers were largely regarded as very powerful calculators and were used to solve scientific, mathematical, and military problems that were too lengthy or too complex for manual solution.

This early phase of computer development was a veritable "do your own thing" period. Only a few experts knew how to program the computers (in binary, initially), and only a very dedicated (or very interested) individual was willing to tolerate the difficulties inherent in the programming task. Typically, a programmer scheduled a block of time, took over the computer room, wrote a program on the machine, executed and tested the program, made necessary modifications, and kept at it until the problem was solved (or the programmer became totally frustrated).

For our purposes, perhaps the most important development of the first generation was the basic idea of an assembler or a compiler program. Assembler language and FORTRAN were in use by the end of this period—this is not surprising when you consider the fact that one of the prime purposes of a computer was to save the time of talented human beings.

THE SECOND-GENERATION AND MODERN MINICOMPUTERS

The second generation of computers began when the electronic tubes of the first generation were replaced by transistorized components. These machines were faster, more reliable, and less expensive (on a cost per transaction basis) than their predecessors. This made second-generation machines attractive to business and meant that computers began to be used to solve more general problems such as computing payrolls, keeping track of inventories, and maintaining accounting records.

Business was willing to convert to computers for these applications simply because with the declining cost and increasing speed and reliability the computer was able to perform these functions at a lower cost than human labor, a factor we considered in some detail earlier. Since computers were selected to minimize cost, it is reasonable to assume that business management would be quite concerned with controlling computer costs. For example, why spend $10,000 per month on a computer when a smaller machine, costing perhaps $7500 per month, can do the job?

A computer may save a company money, but it is still a very expensive piece of capital equipment—a fixed-cost item. If the machine costs $7500 per month it will cost that much whether it is used one hour a day or 24 hours a day. It's only natural to try to get as much work from an expensive machine as you possibly can—in other words, to try to keep the computer as busy as possible.

The term **throughput** is used as a measure of the amount of work going through a computer. Usually it is expressed in terms of time (for example, last week the computer was busy for 142 of the available 168 hours, giving 85-percent throughput). Throughput is a measure of how efficiently the computer is being used.

Suppose we are running a supermarket and decide to increase the throughput of our checkout clerks. One way of improving throughput would be to keep only a single checkout line open, forcing all our customers to wait. This tactic would, of course, keep that one checkout clerk very busy. However, it would not work for the obvious reason that too many of our customers would find another store in which to shop. Throughput is not the only measure of efficiency.

Since early second-generation computers were still quite expensive, the cost of the equipment tended to dominate the total-cost picture. The fact that programmers had to wait to have their jobs run was irrelevant, since human time was less costly than computer time. Gradually, as computers became even faster and computer costs continued to drop, this emphasis began to change. **Turnaround time**, a measure of how long an individual must wait to get the results of a computer run, and **response time**, a measure of how quickly the computer responds to a request for information or service, have become very important today. But we are digressing. Let's concentrate for the moment on throughput and consider a number of techniques that can help to increase the amount of work going through a computer.

SETUP AND THE VALUE OF SCHEDULING

Before you start to bowl, it is necessary to spot the pins. Before a play is begun, the stage must be set. Before you begin a school term, it is necessary to register for courses. These are examples of an activity known as **setup.** They describe functions that must be performed before actually beginning an activity.

Setup is present in all areas of human activity. A supermarket must stock its shelves. A bank teller's cash drawer must be prepared. Fires must be started before a steel mill can be put into operation. Apparatus must be made ready before a scientific experiment can begin. To the businessperson, setup time is nonproductive time. No steel is made when the fires are being started. No cars are made when the new tools needed to produce a new model are being installed. Since setup time is "wasted" time, it is highly desirable to minimize it.

Setup occurs on the computer too. Paper must be loaded into a printer; disk packs must be mounted; cards must be loaded. Let's take a look at one common setup activity—loading paper on a printer.

Just as a typist can make multiple copies of a letter by using carbon paper, a computer printer can produce multiple copies by using what is called multi-part paper—several sheets of paper bonded together at the edges with carbon paper between them. Imagine that you are an operator and have programs calling for the following:

Program	Paper requirements
A	four-part
B	two-part
C	four-part
D	two-part

It takes about five minutes to change the paper in a printer and, for simplicity's sake, we'll assume that each of the four programs takes exactly five minutes to run.

What would happen if we were to run the four jobs in exactly the order given? First we would set up job A, putting four-part paper into the printer (Fig. 20.1). After the program was finished, we would set up job B, and so on. During the time in which we are setting up the printer, the computer does nothing. In the 40 minutes needed to complete these four programs, the computer actually works for only 20 minutes: The throughput rate is 50 percent.

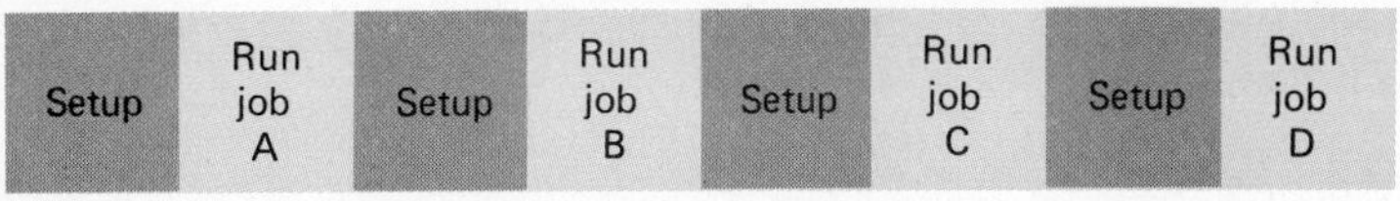

Figure 20.1
The impact of setup.

What if we were to use a little intelligence and run job A first, followed by job C, and then jobs B and D? We would only need two setup operations (Fig. 20.2). The total time needed by all three jobs would be reduced to 30 minutes; the computer would be "doing something" for 20 of these 30 minutes; and the throughput rate would rise to 66.7 percent, just from a little intelligent planning. There are other instances in which **scheduling** and planning can help. Tapes and disk packs can be mounted during the execution of programs not needing these facilities. Paper can be changed during the running of a tape-to-tape program.

Scheduling is not, however, easy or automatic. It's one thing to tell an operator to run all the four-part paper jobs together; it's quite another for the

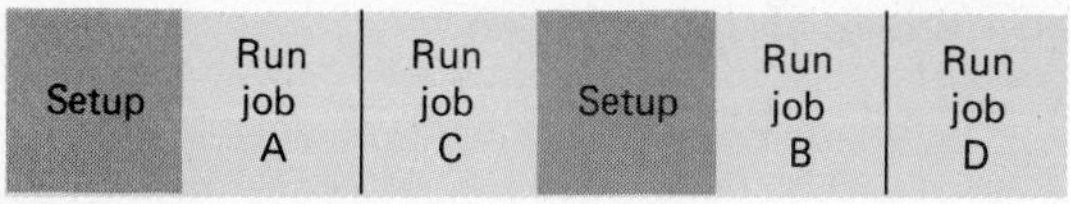

Figure 20.2
The impact of setup can be minimized by scheduling.

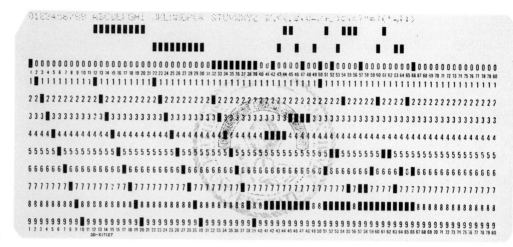

Figure 20.3
A JOB card.

operator to select all the "four-parters" from the thousands of jobs that might be in the computer room at any one time. What is needed is a system—a set of rules and procedures designed to simplify the identification of jobs by type.

In many early computer centers, the system used was a very simple one. All jobs requiring only card input and single-part paper output were thrown on table A; jobs requiring tape were thrown on table B; those requiring multipart paper went on table C, and so on. Once the jobs had been grouped according to their setup requirements, it became a simple matter for the operator to run all the similar jobs together, resulting in a minimization of the time lost to setup. Modern computers rarely use such simple scheduling systems. Rather than allowing a programmer simply to toss his or her program onto the proper table, most computer centers insist that each program be preceded by a **JOB card** (Fig. 20.3) which very clearly indicates the job's class, either through a keypunched parameter such as CLASS = A, through color coding, or through some other technique. In effect, the JOB card allows the operator or the computer itself to determine the job's setup requirements and decide where it fits in the scheduling system.

Scheduling helps to improve throughput by minimizing the time lost to setup.

COMPILATION AND THE USE OF LIBRARIES

The fact that a computer is active does not necessarily mean that it is doing useful work. Consider, for example, what happens during the compilation process. A source module is "translated" into an object module (Fig. 20.4), which usually is subsequently converted into a load module by a linkage editor. The compile and link-edit steps take time. But is any useful work

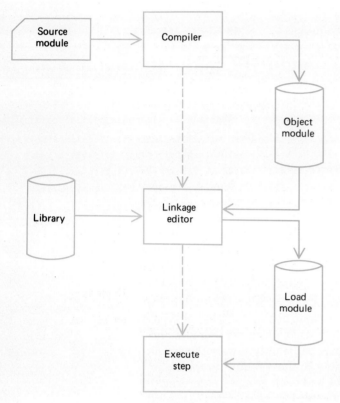

Figure 20.4
The compile, link-edit, and execute sequence.

performed during these operations? Are any checks printed? Are any inventory records updated? No. Why not make a copy of the load module? Disk, tape, or even cards could be used. Once this is done, the program can be executed by simply loading a load module, bypassing the compile and link-edit steps.

In a regular computer center, this is what is usually done. A program goes through the compile and link-edit steps until it is successfully debugged. At this point, a copy of the current load module is cataloged and placed on a library for future use. From this point on, the program can be retrieved and executed simply by copying the library entry into main memory.

A library is not created and maintained simply by discussing it. Librarian programs and storage space are needed, and both are expensive. On a program library, the storage space is usually on a direct access device, although tape and cards are sometimes used for less frequently accessed programs. The functions of a librarian are carried out by a series of service programs that control the addition of programs to and the deletion of programs from the library, maintain the catalog needed to retrieve a program, and keep track of things in general.

I/O DEVICE SPEEDS VERSUS COMPUTER PROCESSING SPEEDS

A good card reader is capable of handling 1000 cards per minute; if a card holds 80 characters, the rate is approximately 1333 characters per second. A good tape drive can transmit 100,000 characters per second. Main memory is capable of moving 4,000,000 characters per second, and modern noncore memories are capable of doing even better. The speed disparity between a computer and its I/O devices is significant.

Consider the typical data processing pattern (Fig. 20.5) in which we read one record of data, process that data, write a record of output information, and go back to the top to repeat the cycle. What does the computer do during the "read" portion of the cycle? Is it possible to process data that has not yet gone into the computer? No. During the input operation, the computer waits for the I/O device. This also happens during output.

Since cards are quite slow, relatively speaking, it makes a great deal of sense to eliminate the reading of cards as much as possible. It is better to make the computer wait for a record from tape or disk, because they are faster. Speed of data transmission was one of the primary considerations in the decision to use tape rather than cards to store a master file. The speed of the magnetic media, tape and disk, represents another advantage of the use of libraries; copying a load module from disk to main memory is much faster than reading a source deck through a card reader.

Still, some data must be read from cards. Source programs must be written. Time cards must be processed. How can the time lost in reading this data be minimized? One technique that has proved quite effective in minimizing card reading (and printing) time is called **spooling**. During the computer's second generation, spooling was often implemented off-line (Fig. 20.6). Cards were read into an inexpensive "controller" which simply copied the card images to tape. When a tape was filled, it was hand-carried over to the "real" computer and read in. Output from the computer went to tape. Full tapes were hand-carried to another off-line controller, which dumped logical records to the printer.

What advantages are to be gained from this approach? During the input stage, the data is copied from cards to magnetic tape. Since it is impossible to copy data faster than the data can be read, this process is paced by the rather slow card reader. On eventual output, information is dumped from magnetic tape to the printer where, once again, the slower device (the printer) sets the pace.

With a card reader and a printer attached directly to the computer, the speed of the computer is limited by these slow devices. With spooling, however, all data has been transferred to magnetic tape before being input to the computer and all data is transferred to magnetic tape (or a direct access device) before being dumped to the printer. Thus the computer always reads and

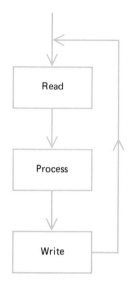

Figure 20.5
The typical data processing pattern.

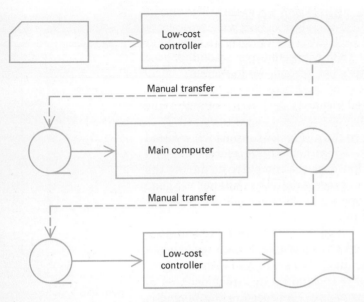

Figure 20.6
Off-line spooling.

writes high-speed magnetic tape. High-speed I/O means that the computer wastes less time waiting for its input and output devices, leaving more time for useful work.

There is, of course, an added expense: Special card-to-tape and tape-to-printer equipment must be purchased. Such devices are, however, considerably less expensive than computers are. It is better to waste the time of such inexpensive devices than to waste the time of a very costly computer.

Card readers and printers function in the range of from 1000 to 2000 characters per second; on magnetic tape, speeds in excess of 80,000 characters per second are common. It might take a minute or more to copy 1000 cards to tape; at 80,000 characters per second, these card images could all be read into a computer in about one second. At these speeds, the computer could easily keep up with several card-to-tape and several tape-to-printer devices. Imagine three or four input controllers feeding and three or four output controllers being fed by a single computer—this is the basic idea of spooling. Picture the computer as a superhighway, with the spooling devices being the on/off ramps that allow plenty of time for acceleration and deceleration.

In this example, the slow I/O operations took place off-line. Later we'll see how spooling can be performed on-line on a faster, more modern computer.

SYSTEM SOFTWARE

All this efficiency is not, of course, without cost. Scheduling requires highly trained operators and tightly controlled procedures. The use of libraries implies extra storage space and a number of librarian programs. The use of magnetic tape and disk means that data will often be blocked; we can expect to use access methods and may require the resources of a linkage editor. Spooling requires additional equipment and special access methods.

Several of these extra costs are really extra programs. Let's take a brief inventory of this special software. We already know about compilers and the linkage editor. We also considered the existence of sort routines and other "utility programs" in prior chapters; these are nothing more than programs that are used so frequently and in so many different applications that, rather than requiring the programmer to recode them each time they are needed, a single copy is made available to everyone, usually through a library. We covered access methods earlier; generally speaking, access methods are kept on a library and added to the load module by the linkage editor. Librarian programs are also needed.

What do all these programs have in common? They do not participate directly in any application. They are support programs, helping the "real" application programs to read data, to write data, to access a library, or to create a load module. They do not compute payroll, or update inventory, or figure out a grade point average. They support the programs that actually perform these primary functions.

In a business environment, these programs would be called **overhead**. In a manufacturing operation, the people who actually put products together are known collectively as direct labor. Everyone else—the people who prepare payroll, manage, keep track of inventory, run the computer, program the computer, keep the books, type letters, answer the telephone, purchase raw materials—is considered indirect labor. This is not to say that these functions are unimportant, since the president of the company is an indirect worker. It just means that they are not *directly* involved with building the product.

An application program performs a direct function, taking data and processing it into information of greater value. Compilers, the linkage editor, utility programs, librarian programs, access methods, and similar software packages are more indirect, functioning in a support role. The term **system software** is sometimes used to describe such programs and program modules; they belong to the entire system, rather than to any one application or programmer. This system software represents an early form of operating system, a topic we will consider in more detail shortly.

In the next section of this chapter, we'll be taking a look at larger, third-generation computers that require larger and more complex system software packages. Before we begin, it might be wise to mention the fact that many modern minicomputers still function in much the same way as a second-generation machine did, and even the larger machines continue to use most of these techniques.

THE THIRD GENERATION

Advances in electronics, most notably the development of the modern integrated circuit, have made possible a third generation of computers. These machines are faster, more powerful, and less expensive than their earlier counterparts. As a result, the use of computers continues to increase because as costs drop, the breakeven point also drops.

The beginning of the third generation is generally considered to be the mid-1960s when IBM announced its System/360 series of computers. Since that time, additional improvements and refinements have convinced many observers that we have moved into a fourth generation, with IBM's System/370 as the chief example. In the past, the change from one generation to another was abrupt and rather extreme, with modifications in program structure and file access creating significant problems for users. Since the mid-1960s changes in technology have been implemented much more smoothly, with most modifications being largely transparent to the user. Rather than become involved in an argument over which generation we are in, we will simply refer to these newer machines as the "current" generation.

CPU VERSUS I/O SPEED IN THE CURRENT GENERATION

Modern computers are very fast, easily handling 1,000,000 instructions per second (and more)! During the second generation, a speed disparity between the computer and its I/O devices was recognized, causing the cost-conscious manager to switch as much I/O as was possible to faster devices such as tape and disk. Although I/O devices have been improved, their essentially physical nature puts a limit on their speed. Computers—electronic devices requiring no physical motion—have advanced much further. As a result, the speed disparity is much more significant today.

An example might help to explain this point. Let us assume that we have a program that (1) reads a record, (2) executes 100 instructions in processing that record, and (3) writes a record of output before going back and repeating the process (Fig. 20.7). Let's take a look at this program with card input and printer output (Fig. 20.8). Our computer is a modern machine capable of executing 1,000,000 instructions per second.

A typical card reader can handle 600 cards per minute—a rate of 10 per second or 0.10 second per card. On a machine capable of executing 1,000,000 instructions per second, how long will it take to execute 100 instructions? Simple division tells us 0.0001 second. Printers (at least the normal line printer) normally operate in a range of from 1000 to 1500 lines per minute. If we use a speed of 1200 lines per minute (which makes our computations easy), we can calculate 20 lines per second, or 0.05 second per line. What does the computer do during the card read and print operations? Nothing. It sits and

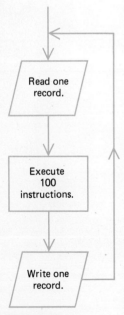

Figure 20.7
A simple program.

Read one record	0.1000 seconds
Execute 100 instructions	0.0001 seconds
Write one record	0.0500 seconds
Total cycle time	0.1501 seconds

Effective utilization $= \dfrac{0.0001}{0.1501} = 0.000666$ or 0.0667%

Figure 20.8
The program with card input and printer output.

waits. Thus the time needed to read, process, and write one record can be obtained by adding the three components of the cycle; in this case, it takes 0.1501 second.

If the computer does nothing during the card read and print operations, how much time does it spend on productive activities during each cycle? The answer is 0.0001 second. In other words, if we were to read cards and print lines for 1501 seconds (a little less than 30 minutes), we would get exactly one second of work from our computer, which is less than one minute of work in a 24-hour day! No businessperson will buy or lease a piece of capital equipment that can be used for only one minute per day.

High-speed I/O devices solved this problem back in the second generation; let's take a look at tape as the input and output medium (Fig. 20.9). Tape is much faster than cards; a typical drive can easily handle an 80-character record in 0.001 second or so. Since an output line is a bit longer than a card (120 rather than 80 characters, for example), the output operation will take a little longer—0.0015 second. Have we done anything to change the computer? No, we have just changed the input and output devices, so the time required to execute 100 instructions doesn't change. Our cycle time (Fig. 20.9) is now 0.0026 second. During each cycle, the computer is performing useful work for only 0.0001 second—slightly less than four percent of the time. This works out to roughly one hour per day, which is better than a rate of one minute per day but still not enough to excite the average controller.

Read one record	0.0010 seconds
Execute 100 instructions	0.0001 seconds
Write one record	0.0015 seconds
Total cycle time	0.0026 seconds

Effective utilization $= \dfrac{0.0001}{0.0026} = 0.03846$ or 3.846%

Figure 20.9
The program with tape input and output.

Picture yourself as a salesperson trying to sell a computer. "I have a great machine for you, Charlie. It's a thousand times as fast as your old machine, costs only ten times as much, and does almost twice the work." Unless Charlie is unbelievably naïve, he will point out that by spending only *twice* the money, he can do twice the work by purchasing another of his old machines. Extra power is useless if it·cannot be used. Why build a 200-mph train when roadbed conditions in many parts of the country restrict the engineer to 20 or 30 miles per hour? Before the current generation of computers could be effectively marketed, something had to be done to make more of the computer's power available to the user.

MULTIPROGRAMMING

The problem with which we are trying to deal arises from the extreme speed disparity between a modern computer and its I/O devices. Since a computer can't process data that it does not yet have, processing must wait for the completion of an input operation. Normally, to avoid possible errors, the computer also waits for an output operation. When computers were slow this was no problem, but today a computer might process data for a few microseconds, wait for several hundred microseconds as an input or output operation takes place, process for a few microseconds, wait for a few hundred microseconds, and so on (Fig. 20.10).

Imagine yourself running a telephone answering service. You have one customer. Over the course of your eight-hour shift, you expect, on the average, to handle three or four calls. Your job would be much like the computer's, with brief periods of activity surrounded by long periods of waiting.

What would you do with your **wait time**? Would you simply sit and wait? Probably not. You would find something else to do—read, listen to the radio, do homework, watch television, work on a hobby. If you were ambitious, you might consider taking on another client. Surely, six to eight calls a day could be handled with a minimum of interference. Why not three extra clients? Or four? Or even more? Eventually, the number of clients might climb so high that your telephone would always be busy; this inability to "get through" would tend to defeat the purpose of the answering service, so there is a limit to the number of clients you could have. But the idea of doing other work during time that would otherwise be wasted is still solid.

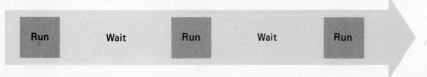

Time

Figure 20.10
During an I/O operation, the computer waits.

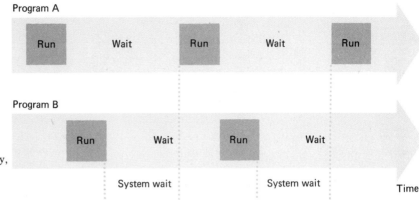

Figure 20.11
With two programs in main memory, the CPU can switch its attention to program B when program A is waiting for I/O.

Why not apply the same idea to the computer? Why not put two different programs in the computer's memory? Then, when program A is waiting for the completion of an input or output operation (Fig. 20.11), the computer can work on program B. And why stop at two programs? With three, even more of the otherwise wasted time can be utilized (Fig. 20.12).

This technique is known as **multiprogramming**. Basically, a number of programs (10, 15, 20, and even more on some modern computers) are placed in memory (Fig. 20.13) and the central processing unit switches its attention

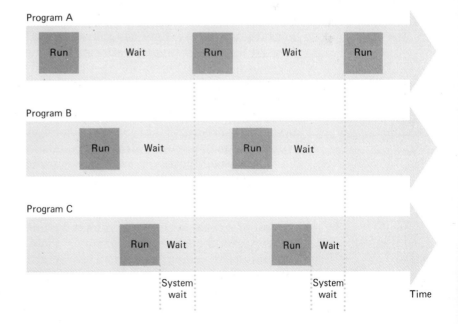

Figure 20.12
More programs in main memory means that even more "wait" time can be utilized.

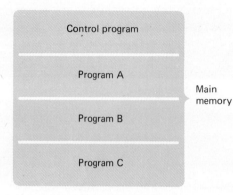

Figure 20.13
Under multiprogramming, main memory contains several different programs, with the CPU switching its attention from one, to another, to another, and back again, in turn.

from one program to another to another, taking advantage of time that would otherwise be spent waiting for I/O.

Have you ever seen (or heard about) a chess master taking on 25 concurrent opponents? The master starts with the first board, quickly sizes up the situation, and makes a move. Then he or she moves on to the second board where the pattern is repeated, and so on. Eventually, the chess master comes back to the first board to begin a second cycle. If the expert is good (and those who participate in such exercises usually are), opponent number one has had just about enough time to analyze the board situation, decide on a move, and make it. The chess master has probably forgotten about the first move made on this first board, but has the skill and experience to recognize the board situation quickly and to make an intelligent decision.

The central processing unit on a multiprogrammed computer works in much the same way. Let's say that we have three programs in main memory (Fig. 20.13). The CPU begins working on program A. A few microseconds later, A requests the start of an I/O operation and drops into what is called a **wait state**. Since nothing can be done in support of program A for the time being, the CPU can turn its attention to program B. A few microseconds later, B needs some input data and drops into a wait state. Thus the CPU turns its attention to program C. Eventually the I/O operation requested by program A will be completed, and control can be returned to this program.

Take careful note of a few very important points. The CPU works on only *one program at a time*. We may have a number of programs in memory at the same time, but the CPU can work on only one at a time.

Thus it is not correct to say that multiprogramming means executing several programs at the same time or simultaneously. Like the chess master playing several opponents, a computer (more specifically, the central processing unit of a computer) implements multiprogramming by switching its attention from one program to another, in turn. The word **concurrent** is sometimes used to describe activities of this type. Although the words *simultaneous* and *concurrent* are very close to being synonymous, there is a very subtle difference in meaning, at least so far as computer-related usage is concerned. Simultaneous means "at the same instant of time." A central processing unit cannot execute two or more programs simultaneously. Concurrent means "over the same period of time." A central processing unit can certainly execute two or more programs concurrently.

OPERATING SYSTEMS

The advantages of multiprogramming are obvious; more programs can be run in the same amount of time and, since the cost of a computer is fixed, this means that we can do more work for the same amount of money. But where do we pay for this gain?

Multiprogramming causes a number of problems that did not arise in the old one-program-at-a-time serial batch days. These problems occur because of the conflicts that are inevitable whenever we try to do too many things at the same time.

What happens, for example, when two or more programs are ready to be executed at the same instant? Who goes first? We could print a message on the operator's console asking for a human decision, but by the time the human operator got around to making the right decision, the computer could have taken all the conflicting programs to their next break point. Computers are so fast that human beings cannot possibly react quickly enough to control them at this level.

Memory management represents another area where conflicts can occur. What happens if two different programs both decide to use the same main memory location? And what happens if program A were to decide to use space allocated to program B to store its input data? Can a human operator possibly stop one program from accidentally or intentionally destroying another? Consider the fact that the problem might occur during any given microsecond, and it's easy to see that this task is beyond the capacity of a human being (one blink would be more than enough time to wipe out the entire system).

What about **I/O device allocation**? What would happen if two programs were allowed to take turns writing data to the same printer? Or what would happen if program A was reading data from a tape at the same time that program B was writing new data to that same tape? Chaos! This cannot be allowed to happen. Again, can a human operator be expected to control the allocation of dozens of I/O devices among dozens of different programs? No!

An **operating system** is a collection of support programs. Most experts consider the old, second-generation system software (compilers, linkage editors, access methods, utilities, librarian programs) to be part of the operating system; these software packages are still in common use. In addition to these system programs, multiprogramming creates a need for software to perform such functions as making the "who goes first" decision, managing main memory, protecting programs from each other, allocating I/O devices, scheduling jobs, queueing jobs, spooling, and handling interrupts. Many of these functions must be performed on-line by software modules that are resident in the computer's main memory—that is the only way these functions can be handled in a reasonable (computer) time frame. The resident portion of the operating system goes by such names as the **supervisor**, the **monitor**, the resident **operating system**, and the nucleus; each computer manufacturer seems to use a different set of words. The various functions performed by an operating system are summarized in Fig. 20.14.

An operating system is a collection of system software programs and program modules. These programs are written in the same languages (usually assembler) and use the same instructions as any application program. The only characteristic that sets operating system modules apart is the fact that they perform a support rather than a direct function. The basic idea of an operating system is crucial to understanding how a modern, large computer works. The environment is considerably more dynamic than was the case in the old, one-program-at-a-time days.

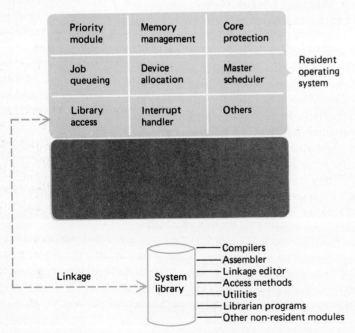

Figure 20.14
The functions of an operating system.

TIME-SHARING

Many of you have undoubtedly seen a computer terminal that is connected to a computer via telephone; perhaps your school has such terminals. Typically the person working at a terminal can write programs in languages such as BASIC, FORTRAN, or PL/1, or execute previously written programs. How can we possibly limit a high-speed computer to the typing speed of a human being? A card reader is considered too slow, although it can handle 600 cards per minute, or 10 cards per second, or 800 characters per second! How fast can you type?

A person sitting at a terminal can economically be given access to a computer only if there are many such terminals (and persons) attached to the same machine. That way, while one terminal user is thinking, the computer can turn its attention to another. Thus a number of terminals might be attached to a single computer, some via telephone lines and some locally over regular wires (Fig. 20.15). The term used to describe such arrangements is **time-sharing**. Since time-sharing involves a number of users (programs) sharing the time of a single central processing unit, it is, at least from the computer's point of view, much like multiprogramming.

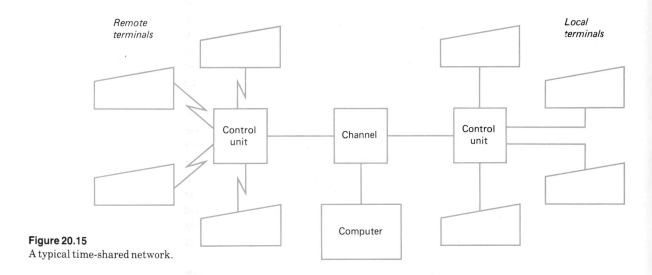

Figure 20.15
A typical time-shared network.

TYPES OF OPERATING SYSTEMS

Not all operating systems are the same; there are many different varieties. Some divide the available main memory into a number of fixed-length **partitions**; these are called **fixed-partition memory management** systems (Fig. 20.16). In a typical configuration, one partition is assigned to the resident

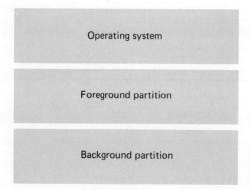

Figure 20.16
Fixed-partition memory management.

operating system, a second is assigned to a **foreground** program, and a third is assigned to a **background** partition; in the event of conflicts, the program in the foreground has higher priority. IBM's Disk Operating System (DOS) is a good example; it can handle as many as six concurrent partitions. Other fixed partition systems can handle even more.

How might a fixed-partition system work? First, visualize a number of programs queued on disk waiting to be loaded and executed. As the program in the foreground partition of main memory is completed, this partition becomes available. The operating system thus searches the queue (or waiting line) of high-priority programs, selects the next one to be run, and loads the complete program into the foreground partition. Once the program is in, the CPU can begin to work on it. When another partition becomes free, another program can be loaded, and so on.

A fixed-partition memory management system can waste memory space. Under another technique known as **dynamic memory management**, space is allocated as needed rather than ahead of time (Fig. 20.17). By allocating only

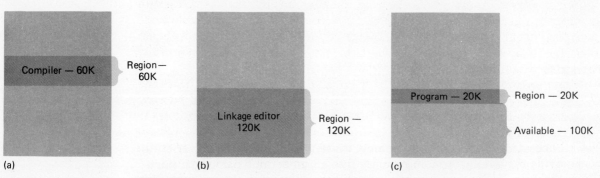

Figure 20.17
Under dynamic memory management, main memory is allocated as needed.

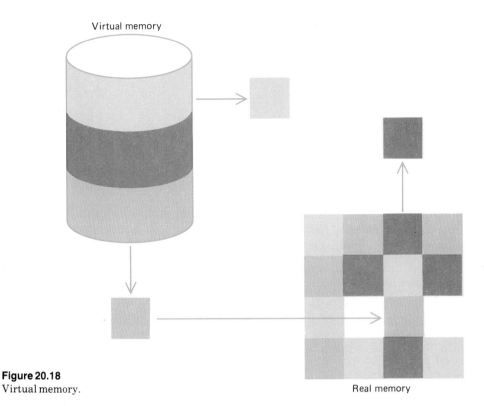

Virtual memory

Real memory

Figure 20.18
Virtual memory.

as much space as is actually needed, such systems use main memory more efficiently. The problem of variable space allocation is, however, much more complex than simple fixed-partition memory management, so the dynamic systems tend to be bigger and more costly.

Even better main memory utilization can be achieved under a technique known as **virtual memory** management. Under virtual memory, an entire program is stored on a secondary device such as disk or drum. The program is divided into a number of pieces called **pages** or **segments**. A few of these pages or segments are moved into main memory (Fig. 20.18), with the bulk of the program remaining on the secondary storage device.

The computer's main memory is referred to as **real memory**. Since the secondary device that holds the major part of the program isn't "real" memory (at least not in this context), we need another name for it. The term used to describe this bulk memory is virtual memory. The word virtual means, according to Webster, "being in essence but not in fact." Virtual memory is "in essence" just like real memory, but "in fact" it is not real memory.

How does a virtual memory system work? Consider, for example, the system sketched in Fig. 20.19(a). Real memory is large enough to hold exactly

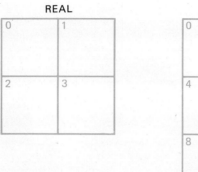

Figure 20.19
A virtual memory system (a) as we begin our example; (b) as real memory is filled.

four pages. On the virtual memory, however, we have loaded three complete programs, each containing four pages. Thus, virtual memory (a direct access device) contains a total of twelve pages of program instructions and data; three times the available main memory space.

The CPU can execute only instructions that are in main memory; thus, it is necessary to transfer pages from virtual to real memory. The CPU can execute only one instruction at a time. Thus it is *not* essential that the *entire* program be in real (or main) memory; all we need is the page containing the current instruction.

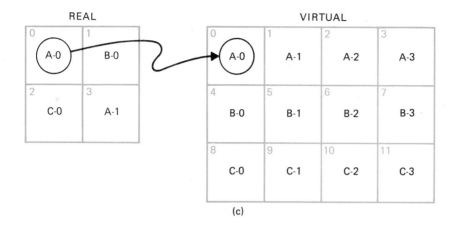

(c)

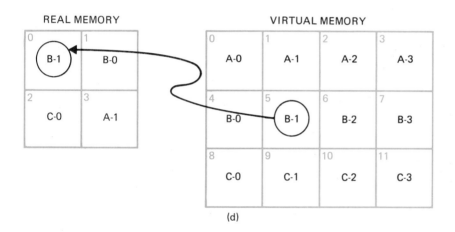

(d)

Figure 20.19 (cont.)
A virtual memory system (c) as an unneeded page is copied back to virtual memory; (d) as a new page is copied from virtual to real memory.

Imagine that real memory contains the pages shown in Fig. 20.19(b). Assume that page B-0 is in control, and that it refers to an instruction located on page B-1. The referenced page is out on virtual memory and must be brought into real memory, but real memory is full. What happens next? We'll assume that program A is finished with the instructions on page A-0, having moved along to page A-1; thus page A-0 can be copied back to virtual memory (Fig. 20.19c), freeing a real memory page. Now, the needed page, B-1, can be copied into real memory (Fig. 20.19d). In this way, by swapping pages back and forth between virtual and real memory, many different programs can be concurrently executed in a limited amount of main memory space. More programs means more efficient utilization of the CPU.

Virtual memory does, of course, use secondary memory, but space on disk or drum is perhaps one hundred times less expensive than an equivalent amount of main memory. It simply makes good economic sense to keep inactive portions of a computer program on an inexpensive storage medium. Most modern large computer systems use the virtual memory technique to implement multiprogramming.

SYSTEM GENERATION AND INITIAL PROGRAM LOAD

Where does the operating system come from? Generally, such system software is developed by the supplier of a computer and sold or leased along with the mainframe. How does the operating system get onto a customer's computer?

The first step in this process is called system generation, better known as SYSGEN. During SYSGEN, a representative of the customer gets together with the supplier of the computer and makes a copy of the operating system or selected portions of the system from the manufacturer's master copy, onto magnetic tape or disk. This customer master is then taken back to the customer's computer where it can be mounted on a tape drive or a disk drive and made available to the computer.

An operating system on a secondary device is not of much use; it must be copied into main memory. This is done during a process known as **initial program load** (or IPL). At the start of each day's work and following any shutdowns due to system problems, the operator "IPL's the system," entering commands through the system card reader, the console, and, perhaps, through switches on the control panel to cause the resident portion of the operating system to be read from its disk or tape into main memory. IPL is done once or twice a day; SYSGEN is (barring accident) done once in the life of a system.

COMMUNICATING WITH THE OPERATING SYSTEM

A modern operating system performs many of the functions previously handled by a human operator. Because the operating system is doing so many things for the programmer, it is sometimes necessary for the programmer to communicate directly with this software module. The mechanism for this communication is **job control language.**

Through job control language (or JCL), the programmer can tell the operating system such things as what programs are to be loaded and executed and what input and output devices are to be used by a program. Different computer manufacturers have taken different approaches to job control language, and we will not attempt to catalog all the types here; in all cases, however, the objective of JCL is to provide a mechanism to allow the programmer to communicate with the operating system.

OTHER SYSTEM SOFTWARE

One of the topics we covered in Chapter 18 was the basic idea of data base management. Software to implement data base management is commercially available. Since these programs are intended for the use of all programmers rather than just one or two, data base management software is another example of system software.

Time-sharing, given the fact that it typically involves a number of different terminals sharing a CPU, represents unique problems, which must be managed. Data communication packages and partition management systems can be purchased to help manage the multiple-terminal problems.

In discussing the second-generation advances earlier in this chapter, the concept of off-line spooling was introduced. With multiprogramming, on-line spooling is possible, with the spooling system reading a record from card or writing a record to disk when the computer has nothing else to do anyway. A number of commercial spooling packages are available today.

In fact, the development and sale of commercial software is one of the fastest growing submarkets of the computer field. Not all system software is supplied by the computer manufacturer.

SUMMARY

We began this chapter with a brief discussion of the computer's first generation, a period of expensive machines used primarily for mathematical and scientific problem solving. Second-generation computers were faster, more reliable, and, in terms of what they could do, less expensive. These improvements made the machines attractive to business, and with business use came a concern for cost. Throughput, a measure of the amount of work going through a computer, became the accepted standard of computer efficiency.

We explored a number of techniques for improving throughput including scheduling, the use of libraries, and spooling. The system software needed to support these activities represents the beginnings of modern operating systems.

The computers of the current generation are even faster than their second-generation counterparts; the tremendous disparity between the speed of these machines and their I/O devices led to a need for solutions such as multiprogramming and time-sharing, techniques that allow the computer to work concurrently on a number of different programs. To handle the inevitable interference, resident operating systems were developed. Among the problems handled or resolved by the resident operating system are the determination of internal priority, memory management, memory protection, I/O device allocation, scheduling, queueing, spooling, and interrupt processing.

The term operating system is sometimes used in a broader sense to refer to the collection of *all* the system software. In addition to the resident portion (called the supervisor, monitor, or nucleus), this broader concept of an operating system includes such system software as compilers, the linkage editor, access methods, librarian programs, and utilities.

We next turned our attention to a number of different memory management techniques, mentioning fixed-partition memory management, dynamic memory management, and virtual memory. The chapter ended with some brief comments on SYSGEN and IPL, job control language, and other types of system software.

KEYWORDS

background	monitor	setup
concurrent	multiprogramming	spooling
dynamic memory management	nucleus	supervisor
fixed partition memory management	operating system	SYSGEN
	overhead	system software
foreground	page	throughput
IPL (initial program load)	partition	time-sharing
	real memory	turnaround
I/O device allocation	response time	virtual memory
JOB card	scheduling	wait state
job control language	segment	wait time
memory management		

EXERCISES

1. Define throughput and turnaround time.
2. How can scheduling help to reduce the time lost to setup?
3. From the standpoint of throughput, why is magnetic tape so much better than punched cards?
4. What do we mean when we refer to system software?
5. What is multiprogramming?
6. Why is a technique such as multiprogramming necessary on a fast, modern computer?

7. What is an operating system?

8. Discuss some of the functions performed by an operating system.

9. What is meant by fixed-partition memory management?

10. How does dynamic memory management differ from fixed-partition memory management? Which technique would you expect to require the bigger, more complex operating system? Why?

11. Explain how virtual memory works.

21

DISTRIBUTED INFORMATION PROCESSING AND TELECOMMUNICATIONS

OVERVIEW

In this chapter, we'll consider the phenomenon of distributed information processing—the trend toward moving computer access away from the exclusive control of those who run the main computer, and out into the "real" world. This trend involves terminals, minicomputers, microprocessors, and communication facilities.

The chapter begins with a discussion of data communications, concentrating on communication lines and services, data sets or modems, and the need for buffering. Next we'll move on to remote job entry terminals, gradually building up to the idea of an intelligent terminal. A number of special-function terminals designed to support such activities as data entry, supermarket checkout, and banking will be illustrated. The trend toward declining hardware costs will be shown as a key factor behind these trends.

TERMINAL NETWORKS

In discussing time-sharing in Chapter 20, we mentioned the idea of a time-shared network (see Fig. 20.15). The network consisted of a number of terminals, some "remote" and some "local"; the **remote** terminals were attached to the computer via telephone lines, while the **local** terminals were attached directly to a control unit. These terminals were used to support a number of activities, such as data entry, scientific or engineering problem solving, and managerial information retrieval.

A local terminal, though it's quite slow, is much like any other input or output device. It can be connected directly to a control unit that is connected directly to a channel that, in turn, is connected to the computer (Fig. 21.1). A remote terminal is different in that a telephone line or other communication link is involved. What is it about data communications that makes a remote terminal different?

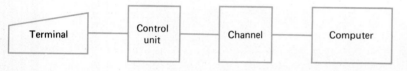

Figure 21.1
The hardware involved in connecting a local terminal to a computer.

DATA COMMUNICATION: MODULATION

Within a computer, data can be represented as individual pulses of electricity; a pulse of current is a 1-bit and "no" pulse is a 0-bit. Since the individual components of a computer system are generally pretty close to one another, this does not present a problem. When we attempt to send information over a long distance, however, several things happen. First, the signal tends to drop in intensity, to "die down," due to the resistance of the wire, much as a bicycle coasts to a stop on a level surface. The second problem is that the signal tends to pick up interference. If you've ever tried to listen to a distant radio station, or if you've ever heard other voices in the background on a long-distance telephone call, then you have experienced this interference, called **noise.**

An electronic signal traveling along a wire or a radio signal traveling through the air will lose strength and pick up noise. As it gets further and further away from the source, the signal gets weaker and weaker, and the noise becomes more intense until eventually the noise overwhelms the signal and the signal is lost. When this happens, no information can be transmitted.

But, you say, our telephone system allows us to talk from coast to coast and even halfway around the world, and we see television programs from virtually every spot on earth (not to mention the moon and Mars). If signal loss and noise create problems for long-distance data communications, how can we explain these obvious discrepancies? Data *can* be transmitted over long dis-

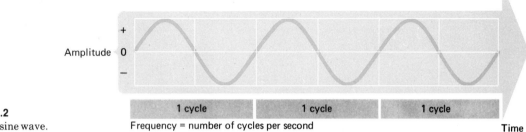

Figure 21.2
A typical sine wave.

Amplitude

+
0
−

1 cycle   1 cycle   1 cycle

Frequency = number of cycles per second

Time

tances. In order to transmit information over long distances, however, it is necessary to boost the signal occasionally. It's a bit like swinging on a swing; in order to keep going high, we must pump every so often.

Boosting an electronic signal is, however, not quite that simple. Some signals are easier to boost than others. As it turns out, the easiest signal to boost is in the form of a sine wave (Fig. 21.2). The "electronic pulse" approach within the computer is one of the most difficult patterns to boost. Thus, in transmitting computer data over any communication facility, it's highly important that the data first be converted from the computer's internal "pulse of current" form to a wave pattern. The process of converting a binary pattern to a wave pattern is called **modulation.**

Data Sets or Modems

Let's stop for a minute and think about what happens when a computer communicates with a remote terminal. First, the data is in the computer in "pulse" form. Next it enters the communication system—telephone or radio—where it must be modulated or converted to a "wave" form. Finally, it arrives at the terminal where, since most terminals are designed to be used locally as well as remotely, it must be converted back to a "pulse" form.

The device that performs the conversion from pulse to wave and back to pulse form is called a **data set** or **modem** (Fig. 21.3); the word modem is an acronym that stands for *mo*dulator/*dem*odulator, a name that accurately describes the functions performed by this device. Normally, there is a data set or modem on each end of the communication line (Fig. 21.4). These devices must be present because of the electronic incompatibility between a computer and the common communication facilities.

Perhaps the most recognizable type of data set is the one pictured in Fig. 21.3. Near the top, you can plainly see what looks like a set of earphones; this part of the data set is called an **acoustical coupler** and is used to hold the telephone receiver. Inside the device are a number of electronic circuits that perform the modulation and **demodulation** functions; this is the modem.

Photograph courtesy of Anderson Jacobson, Inc.

Figure 21.3
A typical data set or modem.

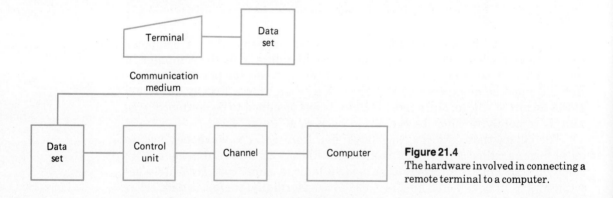

Figure 21.4
The hardware involved in connecting a remote terminal to a computer.

COMMON COMMUNICATION FACILITIES

Now that we have identified the various parts of a remote terminal network (terminal, data set, communication medium, data set, computer system) let's turn our attention to the communication facilities. We'll start with the telephone system. Our national **telephone network** connects just about every point in the world, and it's extremely reliable and dependable.

The type of telephone **line** that we all use for voice communication is called a **voice-grade line.** It can also be used for data communication. A voice-grade line normally transmits between 2000 and 2400 bits of data per second. A man named Emile Baudot was an early pioneer in the data communication field; in his honor, the basic unit of *data transmission* speed, one bit per second, is called a **baud,** making a voice-grade line a 2400-baud line.

If 2400 baud isn't enough, it's possible to transmit the data at a higher frequency. To preserve compatibility with the switching equipment of the telephone company, even multiples of 2400 (such as 4800, 7200, and 9600) are commonly used. Special modems are needed to transmit at these higher rates. If 9600 baud is not enough, **wide band channels** with data transfer rates ranging from 19,200 to one million baud can be leased. If 2400 baud is more than is needed, telegraph channels supporting from 75 to 300 baud are available. There really is a broad range of alternatives.

In many cases, the need for data communications is not continuous; short occasional bursts of **connect time** are all that is needed. In such cases, the user will typically take advantage of the regular public telephone system, dialing the computer, making a connection, and hanging up the phone when the work is finished. This approach is called **dial-up.**

Dial-up can get expensive if the call is long distance. Even if the call is local, many data communication users are not willing to accept the noise, interference, occasional busy signal, and other problems that are inherent in the dial-up approach. As an alternative, it's possible to lease a **private line.** This is a very common solution when line speeds in excess of 2400 baud are involved.

Digital Communications

When you say "hello" into a telephone receiver, it is not your actual sound waves that are transmitted over the line. Instead, the sound waves are converted into an electronic wave form that "represents" the actual data being transmitted. In other words, the telephone line transmits an **analog** signal rather than a true signal.

We use analogs every day. The height of a column of mercury in a thermometer really isn't the temperature, it just represents the temperature. The needle on your automobile's control panel really isn't the speed, it just represents the speed. The signal passing over a telephone wire isn't a sound wave—it is merely analogous to a sound wave.

Most of our telephone equipment is "analog" in nature. Most computers are digital in nature, representing data as patterns of binary digits. This is the basic incompatibility that makes equipment like modems necessary.

Actually, it is possible to transmit **digital** data. A 1-bit might be sent as a normal sine wave; a 0-bit would then be the absence of a normal sine wave. To boost an analog signal, it is necessary to amplify the signal; the result is to amplify the noise as well as the data. Rather than amplifying a digital signal, it is possible to simply retransmit it, sending out strong sine waves for each 1-bit, and no wave for each 0-bit; the result is that noise is filtered out from the signal. With voice communication, you, the human being, tend to filter out noise; thus, analog communication is fine. Computers are not as smart as you and are more easily confused by noise; thus there is a real advantage to digital communication.

Given today's electronic technology, digital data transmission is actually superior to analog data transmission. Why then hasn't the telephone company switched to digital? Simply because they have such a tremendous investment in existing analog equipment—equipment that, incidentally, works quite well. As new facilities are added, however, most are digital.

Microwave Communications

There are alternatives to the telephone system. Data can be transmitted between two points via radio waves, and many organizations doing a significant amount of data communication have installed private **microwave** relays. When microwave is used, transmission is restricted to a "line of sight"; in other words, if any large solid object gets in the way, microwave transmission will not work. The earth, as we all know, is round; it curves. The curvature of the earth limits the maximum distance of data transmission, making expensive relay stations necessary (Fig. 21.5). In an attempt to circumvent this problem, data communication satellites have been placed in orbit, thus allowing installations located anywhere in the United States to send data, via microwave, to any other spot (Fig. 21.6). Eventually, this satellite network will be worldwide.

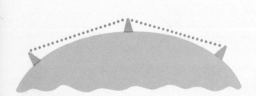

Figure 21.5
Since microwave data transmission is limited to a "line of sight," relay stations must be used to compensate for the curvature of the earth.

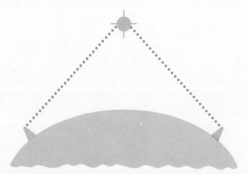

Figure 21.6
Satellites can also be used for microwave data communication.

A considerable amount of data is transmitted via satellite even today; the future promises only growth. In fact, one new company, Satellite Business Systems (SBS), was established by IBM, Comsat, and Aetna for the express purpose of developing and operating a private, leased satellite service.

Data Communication Service Bureaus

SBS is a good example of a rapidly growing type of business organization, the data communication **service bureau.** A typical communication service bureau leases a network of wide-band channels connecting a number of major cities (Fig. 21.7). Customers sublease portions of these communication channels. A typical customer might utilize regular telephone lines to get from a local office to the communication center in city A, have the message transmitted to city B over the wide-band facilities of the service bureau, and return to regular telephone lines to get the message from the communication center in city B to the local city B office. Getting to and from a communication center involves regular lines and regular rates; the city-to-city leg involves private wide-band lines and a lower-than-normal cost.

A key problem in operating such data communication service bureaus is keeping track of the source and destination of each of the messages passing through the system. Consider a simplified **network** linking two cities as an example. In city A, perhaps 100 or more different customers use the facilities of the service bureau. At any given instant in time, messages from dozens of these customers may be descending on the communication center. The service bureau is responsible for accepting all these messages and funneling them through a single wide-band line toward city B. The communication center in city B must, in turn, accept a continuous stream of data from the wide-band channel, separate this data into individual messages, and route each message to its proper destination along regular telephone lines. It's a very complex operation even on a two-city network; imagine how complex this **message switching** task becomes on a network connecting 20 or 30 cities.

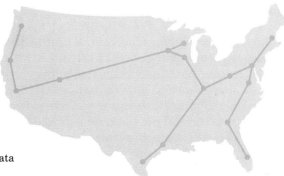

Figure 21.7
The leased-line network of a typical data
communication service bureau.

Message switching, at least at this level, is so complex and requires such speed of response that unaided human beings cannot do it. Thus a communication service bureau typically has a computer located in each city served by the network; the sole purpose of this computer is to keep track of the source and destination of each message going over the line. The telephone company uses similar computers to handle regular telephone communications; that's why a direct-dial call is less expensive than an operator-assisted call.

THE SPEED DISPARITY PROBLEM

Let's return to a typical keyboard terminal/data set/voice-grade line/data set/ computer system network. At the computer's end, data can be manipulated at speeds of four million characters per second and more. A voice-grade line is rated at 2400 baud; if we assume an eight-bit code, we get 300 characters per second, which is significantly less than four million. What about the terminal? Typical terminals are rated in the range of from 20 to 30 characters per second and, given the typing speed of most people, the rated speed is probably an exaggeration.

We have a 20-characters-per-second device attached to a 300-characters-per-second line which, in turn, is attached to a four million-characters-per-second computer. That's quite a range!

How can we possibly deal with this speed incompatibility? We can use buffers and we can handle a number of terminals at the same time. Let's deal with the first part of the solution first.

Most terminals contain a buffer (Fig. 21.8). Typically, a terminal's buffer is just big enough to hold one line of data. As the user types at a certain rate of speed, the individual characters go into the buffer. The RETURN key usually signals the end of a line, be it a partial or a full line. When the RETURN key is depressed, all of the data is in the buffer in an electronic form. This means that it can be transmitted at electronic speeds—300 characters per second is easy. Output data can be written into the buffer at a rate of 300 characters per second and transferred to the printed page at a rate of 20 or 30 characters per second. With a buffer in the middle, both the terminal and the telephone line can work at peak speed.

What happens at the other end of the line? Once the data has passed through a modem, it enters a control unit to begin its trip into the computer. A modern **transmission control unit,** often called a **front-end device,** is made up of a series of **ports** and associated buffers (Fig. 21.8). A port is nothing more than a connection point for a communication line, and we already know what a buffer is. Data enters the control unit at a rate of 300 characters per second and is moved into the buffer associated with the "port of entry." Once all the data is in the buffer, the transmission control unit can signal the channel which, in turn, can signal the computer (an interrupt, remember?) that data is available

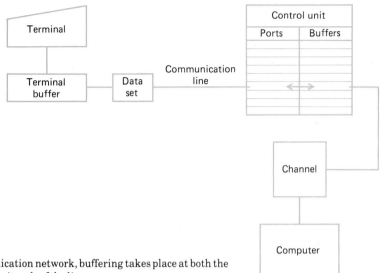

Figure 21.8
On a typical data communication network, buffering takes place at both the
terminal and the control unit ends of the line.

for transfer into the computer. As soon as the computer is ready, the data
transfer can be achieved at close to the computer's internal speed. Going back
out, data can be dropped in one of the transmission control unit's buffers at
four million characters per second, parceled out to the communication line at
300 characters per second, dumped into the terminal's buffer at this rate, and
printed at a rate of 20 characters per second.

But this is only half the story. If the computer supplies data to the
transmission control unit at a rate of four million characters per second and
the communication lines at the other end of the control unit can accept only
300 characters per second each, how many lines can the front-end transmission
control unit handle? At 4,000,000 per second in and 300 per second per line out,
the transmission control unit could, in theory, take care of a full 13,333 lines at
the same time (or at least concurrently)! Most front-end machines do not
operate nearly this high—25 to 100 lines is a more reasonable range. But the
idea that a single control unit can easily keep pace with a number of lines
should be obvious to you. Buffering makes it possible.

Getting back to the terminal end of the line, we might note that attaching
a single 20- or 30-character-per-second terminal to a 300-character-per-second
line represents a bit of a speed mismatch, too. It's possible to put a **multiplexer**
or concentrator at the terminal end (Fig. 21.9) and assign to this piece of
hardware the responsibility for controlling several terminals or several local
or low-speed lines. By so concentrating the data transmission requirements of
several devices, we can get closer to full utilization of the communication line.

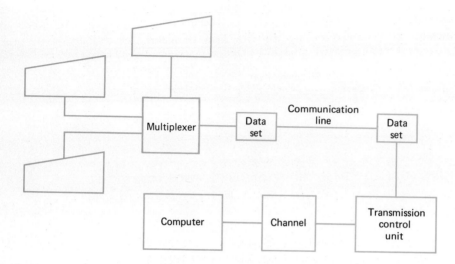

Figure 21.9
It is possible to improve the utilization of a communication line by placing a multiplexer or concentrator at the remote end of the line.

HANDSHAKING AND POLLING

One of the basic skills of a computer is, as you may recall, the ability to request the start of an I/O operation. Many computers, strangely enough, are not particularly good at dealing with I/O operations that they did *not* request. On a terminal network, it's very difficult to predict exactly when any given user will complete a line of input data and hit the RETURN button, and a totally unexpected I/O operation can "drive a computer bananas."

Even though the data really originates "out there somewhere," the computer must be led to believe that *it* really started things. This is done through a process known as **polling,** which works as follows.

1. The computer, being ready to accept some data, asks the channel if it has any.

2. The channel, being little more than a data path anyway, asks the transmission control unit.

3. The transmission control unit asks the first terminal on the network if it is ready to transmit data.

4. If the terminal is ready (in other words, if there is data in the buffer and the user has already hit the RETURN key), the terminal sends a message (essentially, yes) back to the control unit, and

    a) the control unit tells the terminal to send it;
    b) the terminal sends it;
    c) the control unit tells the channel it has data;
    d) the channel tells the computer it has data;
    e) the computer tells the channel to send it;

f) the channel tells the control unit to send it;

g) the control unit sends the data through the channel;

h) the channel signals the computer when it has finished;

i) the process starts all over again.

5. If the terminal is *not* ready (i.e., the user is still typing), no message is returned to the control unit, which (apparently feeling ignored) goes on to the next terminal.

6. If *no* terminals are ready, the process starts all over again.

That was not a comedy routine; polling really works that way. The signals that pass back and forth between the various machines are, as you probably assumed, in binary. The term given to this exchange of signals is, believe it or not, **handshaking.**

Many modern transmission control units have been designed to simplify this task a bit. Rather than wait for the computer to start things, they continuously poll their terminals, transferring data into the control unit's buffers as soon as a terminal makes it available. Later, when the computer asks for data, it's already in the control unit and can be quickly transferred. A front-end control unit with this kind of logical capability is a very complex piece of electronics in its own right, approaching minicomputer status. Such front-end controllers are quite expensive.

While we're on the subject of transferring data, it might be wise to mention a few points that students sometimes find confusing. In our discussion of terminals and communications, we have consistently pictured a terminal as working from a buffer—data is typed, character by character, into a buffer and then transferred over the communication line. However, not all terminals work this way. Some transmit each character as it is typed. When buffers are used, we have what is called **synchronous** data communication. When individual characters are transferred one at a time, we have **asynchronous** data communication.

Let's start at the terminal and try to visualize what happens during data transmission. First the modem at our end takes the binary code of a character and modulates it into a sine-wave pattern. At the other end of the line, another modem must demodulate the sine wave back into a binary form. But how does that modem know exactly when to expect that data? Is it possible to predict the precise instant at which a user will depress a key? No.

Since predicting the exact time of arrival of data is impossible, the modem must be given some warning. This warning is provided by placing special **message characters** in front of and behind the data (Fig. 21.10). Now, just

Figure 21.10

When transmitting data, message characters are normally placed in front of and behind the data.

before the data hits the modem, the modem gets a message that says, in effect, "Here comes the data." This gives the modem time to react and get itself aligned and "in synch" with the incoming signal. The data can then be demodulated, with the end-of-message characters marking, as you may have guessed, the end of the message.

Under asynchronous communication, message characters surround each character of data. This means that more total bits must be transferred than would be necessary under the synchronous mode, where a single set of start- and end-message characters might do for 80 or more characters of data. Since the speed of a line is limited to so many bits per second, asynchronous communication, with its need for more bits per character, will be able to transfer fewer characters per second. On the other hand, the modem that handles synchronous communications, since it must stay "in phase" with the incoming signal for a longer period of time, will be more complex and more expensive than the asynchronous modem—another trade-off.

PROTOCOLS

Handshaking involves an exchange of prearranged signals. Message characters follow a prearranged pattern. Together, the signals associated with handshaking and the pattern of message characters define a very specific set of rules for exchanging information over a communication line. Many different sets of rules are used, with the "correct" rules being dependent on the computer manufacturer, the front-end device, the modem, the telephone company, and every other device or organization involved in the data transmission. In connecting a specific terminal to a specific computer (or front-end device) over a specific communication medium, however, a specific set of rules must be used. This specific set of rules governing handshaking and message characters is called a line **protocol.**

REMOTE JOB ENTRY TERMINALS

The only real difference between a remote terminal and a local terminal is the fact that there is a communication line and associated hardware involved with the remote terminal. Otherwise the link to the computer is identical—device, control unit, channel, and computer.

Keyboard terminals are not the only devices that can be located away from the mainframe. What's wrong with taking a card reader or a printer, breaking the line connecting the device to its control unit, inserting a telephone line and a pair of data sets, and teleprocessing card data? Nothing.

In fact, the use of remote card readers and printers is very common today. Typically, rather than simply dropping the device out there on its own (which would involve some major modifications to the equipment), a small control unit accompanies the card reader and printer (Fig. 21.11). The resulting collection

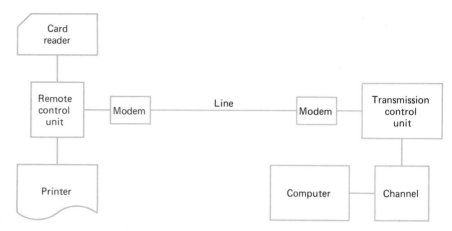

Figure 21.11
A remote job entry configuration.

of hardware is called a **remote job entry** terminal (Fig. 21.12). With such a terminal, cards can be entered from a remote site and placed on one of the computer's regular batch job queues. When the job's turn comes, the printed output can be routed directly back to the remote site. In effect, the remote location gets many of the advantages of a computer at the cost of a terminal. Jobs that are much too big or too complex for a keyboard terminal can be run without the long delays that a courier system might entail.

Photograph courtesy of Data 100 Corporation.

gure 21.12
remote job entry terminal.

Typically, the control unit associated with a remote job entry terminal performs blocking and buffering functions. A number of cards are read into the controller's buffer and then transmitted in a block to the transmission control unit at the computer end of the line. While this buffer is being emptied, data that is in the printer buffer can be printing, in parallel. Later, while the card-read buffer is once again being filled by the card reader, the terminal's controller can be accepting another buffer full of output data from the computer. By overlapping input and output in this way, the line is kept as busy as possible.

HALF DUPLEX AND FULL DUPLEX

Some terminals are capable of transmitting data in both directions at the same time, accepting output data from the computer at the same time that input card data is being sent to the computer. When data transmission takes place in both directions at the same time, we call it the **full duplex** mode. **Half duplex** means that data is transferred in only one direction at a time.

LINE SPEED AS A BOTTLENECK

A card reader can handle 600 cards per minute, which is 10 per second. At 80 columns per card, this reader handles 800 characters per second.

A 2400-baud line can transmit only 300 characters per second. If we were to attach a 600-card-per-minute card reader to a 2400-baud line, the card reader would spend a considerable amount of its time waiting for the transmission line. On a remote job entry terminal, the transmission line often becomes the limiting factor on speed.

It is essential that the input and output devices attached to a remote job entry terminal be carefully matched with the line speed. At 2400 baud, with an eight-bit code for each character, a total of 300 characters per second can be transmitted. A card reader or a printer capable of going faster than 300 characters per second represents wasted, unusable power. For a card reader, a reasonable upper limit is about 225 cards per minute; for a printer, 150 lines per minute. These speeds can be doubled for a 4800-baud line, tripled for 7200 baud, and so on. Wasted capacity is worthless.

TERMINAL INTELLIGENCE

There are things that can be done to improve the performance of a remote system. One such technique is called **data compression.** The typical card contains quite a few blank columns. The typical output line contains even more, since spacing for readability is considered important. Why transmit these blanks? With data compression, the terminal controller strips blanks from the input cards, replacing them with a control field telling the transmission control unit at the other end how many blanks to put back in. Coming the other way, the transmission control unit strips the blanks from a line of output, and the terminal's controller puts them back in.

What's the advantage of this? Fewer characters must be transmitted over the line. At 120 characters per print-line, a 2400-baud line can drive a printer at 150 lines per minute. If, through data compression, we could reduce the average print-line as actually transmitted to 100 characters, we could drive the printer at 180 lines per minute.

Data compression is a logical function. It requires some intelligence. A terminal that can support data compression will be somewhat more complex and a bit more expensive than a terminal that doesn't have this feature.

Some terminals are even more "intelligent," being locally programmable. It's possible on terminals of this type to write a program to "edit" input cards for accuracy, eliminating obvious errors before they are transmitted. After all, why send bad data to the computer? An important part of most printed output is information that serves only to identify the data, such as page headings and column headings. On a programmable terminal, only the "raw" data need be transmitted; the column headings, page headings, and spacing can be added locally. By eliminating the transmission of unneeded information, it's possible to get more performance from the terminal.

As we begin to add more and more logical functions to the terminal, it begins to look less like a terminal and more like a small computer in its own right. These devices are called **intelligent terminals.** The dividing line between an intelligent terminal and a minicomputer is nebulous at best. Many terminals contain features like cassette tape storage and floppy-disk drives.

For many years, the high cost of the central processing unit and other mainframe components forced firms into centralization, concentrating all information processing in one or two large, expensive machines. Today, however, the declining cost of minicomputers and intelligent terminals is forcing these same organizations to take another look at this decision. What seems to be developing is a trend toward what is now known as **distributed data processing.**

At its core, distributed data processing doesn't seem to be too different from the centralized approach of the recent past—we still have a large, central computer (Fig. 21.13). Typically, this computer houses the organization's data base and handles key corporate-wide functions. The difference lies in all the intelligent terminals spread throughout the organization. Given this widely distributed intelligence, the individual functional groups of the organization can do most of their information processing locally, dialing the central computer at the beginning of the day (to get current information), at the end of the day (to report activity to the central data base), and only as required at other times. The local groups enjoy the flexibility of having their own computer at a

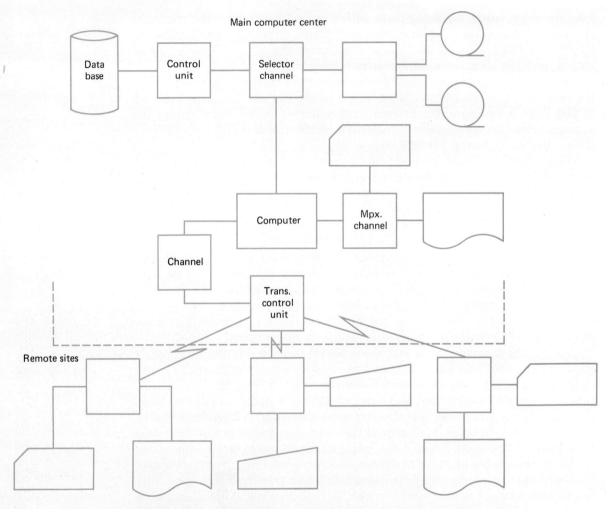

Figure 21.13
Distributed data processing.

very reasonable cost, with the central machine being available to handle an occasional large job. The organization still enjoys the advantages of a centralized data base.

The term distributed data processing is not restricted to systems with a large centralized computer. A network of interconnected minicomputers might be considered a distributed system too.

SPECIAL SINGLE-FUNCTION TERMINALS

The use of single-function terminals is another interesting trend. One variety, mentioned in Chapter 7, is an on-line data collection terminal used to collect data from manufacturing employees. These terminals typically contain a card reader, a badge reader, and a very limited manual entry keyboard. To report on progress, the employee might enter his or her own badge, a card that identifies the activity just completed, and, via the keyboard, the number of units of work completed; the resulting record goes directly into the computer. The terminal is designed to perform one and only one function—in this case, data collection.

Many banks have installed automatic teller terminals (Fig. 21.14) that allow the customer to handle everyday banking transactions at any time of day without human intervention. Supermarkets are experimenting with automatic computer-controlled checkout systems capable of reading a bar-code printed on the side of a package. Many department stores have installed special terminals to check on a customer's credit rating. Though single-function in

Figure 21.14
An automatic bank-teller
terminal.

Photograph courtesy of NCR Corporation.

nature, these terminals can be quite sophisticated, approaching the status of minicomputers.

The fact that minicomputers are continuing to drop in cost will tend to lead to more and more such examples. Do you remember our discussion of a breakeven point? As the cost of the computer drops, what happens to the breakeven point? It becomes possible to economically justify automation for applications with fewer and fewer repetitions. As recently as the early 1970s no one really believed that the job of the bank teller would begin to fall to computerized automation. It has, because computer costs are dropping while labor costs are rising.

Of particular importance in the world of single-function terminals is the rapid development of **microcomputers. A microprocessor,** as the name implies, is an extremely tiny processor, usually consisting of a single integrated-circuit chip. Microprocessors are found in pocket calculators and digital watches, to cite two of their more common applications. They can also perform more complex functions, and they are inexpensive—*very* inexpensive. Look at the current cost of pocket calculators and digital watches.

In addition to being inexpensive, microprocessors are very flexible. A chip can be designed to perform a myriad of functions, and the individual design can be mass-produced. Even more important, these microprocessors can be combined to perform even more complex functions. In the future, look for such things as a full-function computer in a briefcase weighing perhaps 20 pounds, microprocessor control of pacemakers and other medical equipment, an inexpensive box that will convert your television set into an electronic gameboard—an almost endless list can be compiled.

SUMMARY

The chapter began with a discussion of a terminal network. The unique problems of transmitting data over any distance were pointed out, and the need for converting the electronic pulses of the computer into a wave for data transmission was established. We also discussed the concept of modulation and demodulation and the need for a modem or data set to bridge the electronic incompatibility.

We then moved into a discussion of data communication facilities, starting with the standard voice-grade telephone line. Combinations of two, three, and four voice-grade lines can be used. Higher transmission speeds can be obtained from wide-band channels. A major alternative to the telephone is microwave; special satellites are planned. Service bureaus are common and growing.

Keyboard terminals are very slow, creating a serious speed disparity problem. The line transmission speed is also quite slow when compared to the computer's internal processing speed. Buffering and the assignment of multiple terminals to a single control unit are two techniques that help to minimize the impact of this speed disparity.

Because of the fact that most computers are not very good at handling unexpected I/O operations, terminals are coordinated through a process known as polling. The exchange of electronic signals that usually accompanies polling is called handshaking. A specific set of rules for handshaking and message characters is called a protocol.

Keyboard terminals are not the only devices that can work over data communication lines; a remote job entry terminal is often used to control a card reader and a printer. If data transmission takes place in only one direction at a time, it is known as half duplex; a full duplex system allows for transmission in both directions at the same time.

The speed of the transmission line is frequently a bottleneck, limiting the speed of the attached devices. Data compression and intelligent terminals can allow the user to get more performance from the system. Special-function terminals with intelligence limited to a single area of application are also growing in popularity. There is a very strong trend toward the use of intelligent terminals, both single-purpose and general-purpose; this trend toward distributing computing power throughout the organization is known as distributed data processing.

KEYWORDS

acoustical coupler	handshaking	polling
analog	intelligent terminal	port
baud	line	private (leased) line
connect time	local	protocol
data compression	message characters	remote
data set	message switching	remote job entry
demodulation	microcomputer	service bureau
dial-up	microwave	synchronous
digital	modem	telephone network
distributed data processing	modulation	transmission control unit
front-end device	multiplexer	voice-grade line
full duplex	network	wide-band channel
half duplex	noise	

EXERCISES

1. What is a communication line? What is a communication network?

2. What is meant by modulation and demodulation?

3. What is a data set or modem? Why is it necessary?

4. What is a voice-grade line? What does the term baud mean?

5. What is the difference between microwave data transmission and telephone data transmission? Why is microwave transmission limited as to distance?

6. Why is buffering so important in communicating between a computer and a terminal?

7. What is handshaking? What is polling? What is a line protocol?

8. Often a transmission control unit or a front-end device is used at the computer's end of a communication line. What functions are performed by this device?

9. Contrast synchronous and asynchronous data communication.

10. Contrast half duplex and full duplex.

11. What is remote job entry? What is an intelligent terminal?

12. What does the term distributed data processing mean?

22

A DISTRIBUTED SYSTEM

OVERVIEW

Our final case study will describe a distributed information processing system. The firm is a large chain of supermarkets. Certain information processing functions must be performed at the store level; thus local computer equipment is needed. Other functions must be centralized; thus the system includes a large central computer. The local and central machines are connected by communication lines; the central machine incorporates several system software functions such as data communication management and data base management.

We'll analyze the operation of this system first at the local level, considering how a new, computer-controlled supermarket checkout system might function. We will then move back to the central computer and investigate the supermarket chain's inventory and distribution systems. Finally, the use of the computer data base to support an on-line management information system will be discussed.

THE FIRM

TLD Superstores is a major, midwestern chain of supermarkets. Roughly 100 stores are spread over a four-state area. Headquarters are located in a large city near the geographic center of the service area; the individual stores are supplied from a large warehouse near the headquarters.

Competition is intense, with several local supermarkets vying with TLD Superstores and some of the better-known national chains. Profit margins are tight; last year, TLD made only about 2¢ on each dollar of sales. Cost control is essential to the continued health of the business. A second key, of course, is volume. Last year TLD controlled about 20% of the local supermarket trade. Management wants more.

THE PROBLEM

Perhaps the biggest problem facing TLD Superstores in these inflationary times is cost control. With such a small profit margin, a few cents per dollar of sales, there is little margin for error. Given the competitive nature of the marketplace, cost increases cannot all be passed on to the customer. Increases in the basic cost of the product impact every retailer, of course, and can be passed on, but internal costs of distribution and sales are subject to control. The lower they are, the greater the profit margin.

Of particular concern to management are labor costs. The union just won a substantial pay increase; and checkout clerks, stock people, meat cutters, and other personnel will be earning between ten and twelve percent more than last year. These labor costs alone could wipe out as much as 25% of the profit margin. Future union agreements are certain to have a similar impact. Clearly, something must be done to bring labor costs under control.

Another major controllable cost item is inventory. Before a supermarket can place stock on its shelves, it must purchase that stock. Customers will (hopefully) eventually buy the products, but some time will elapse between the purchase and the sale of the products. TLD Superstores borrows the money to buy stock, repaying the loans from sales. The cost of borrowing varies with the prime interest rate, but it's usually about 1% per month. Other costs of carrying inventory include building and space costs, insurance costs, the risk of spoilage or theft, materials handling costs, and many others. Inventory is expensive.

Inventory is also essential. Customers simply will not continue to shop at a store where desired products are not available. The secret is to have "enough" inventory, but not "too much." Tighter control over inventory, both in the central warehouse and in the stores, is highly desirable.

Distribution costs represent another sizable and controllable component of the supermarket's business expense. Typically, TLD Superstores buys in large quantity and sells individual items; the difference between the bulk cost and the selling price represents the profit potential. A boxcar full of canned beans

COMPUTER CONTROL IN THE SUPERMARKET

1. Over the past few years, the modern supermarket has undergone significant change.

2. The key to this change is the universal product code, or UPC, a computer-readable bar code that is printed on most prepackaged supermarket products.

3. Because of the UPC, it is no longer necessary to stamp the price on each package. Instead, the customer will find price tags, often including unit price information, on the shelves near a product display.

4. With non-prepackaged products, such as fresh produce, clerks can add a UPC sticker in the store.

5. At the checkout counter, the bar code is read into a computer by a scanner, and the computer simply looks up the price. Here, you see the computer cabinet opened; inside you can see the electronic components of the machine.

7. As in any supermarket, the customer pushes a cart through the store and selects products for purchase, eventually placing the packages on the checkout counter. Here, however, the similarity ends.

5

6

7

6. The manager of the store can access the computer through a terminal and change a price or enter a store special.

8. Directly in front of the checkout clerk is a scanning device; you can see it in the foreground of this picture.

8

9. Selecting a package, the clerk locates the UPC and simply passes it over the scanner.

9

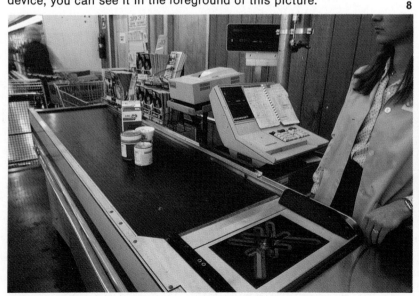

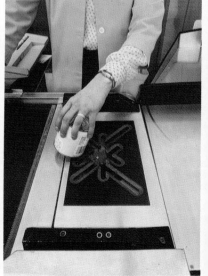

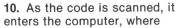

11

10. As the code is scanned, it enters the computer, where

    a) the UPC is used to search a table of product information;

    b) the price, a product description, sales tax, and any deposit due on this product are located;

    c) the value 1 is subtracted from the inventory of this product; and

    d) the cost is added to the customer's bill.

The price, sales tax, deposit, and product description are printed on a sales receipt back at the checkout station. Note that all this happens in less than the time it takes for the clerk to place the package in a bag.

11. Located near the computer is a telephone and other equipment needed to transmit the data over telephone lines.

12. At the end of each business day, current inventory information on each item in the store is sent to the supermarket chain's centralized computer.

12

13

14

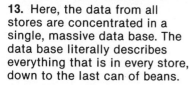

13. Here, the data from all stores are concentrated in a single, massive data base. The data base literally describes everything that is in every store, down to the last can of beans.

14. The supermarket gains its competitive advantage by purchasing large quantities, storing this inventory in a centralized warehouse, and then distribut-

ing to individual stores from the warehouse. The accurate information found in the central data base is invaluable in managing this hugh inventory.

15. Product distribution is another massive problem. Sales data coming in from the store clearly define the products that are selling and thus must be replenished in the store. By

analyzing the needs of all the stores as defined in the central data base, the large computer can generate efficient shipping routes.

15

16

The photographs in this "tour" were taken at the facilities of Heartland Food Warehouse, Malden, and Purity Supreme, North Billerica, Massachusetts. We gratefully acknowledge the help and cooperation of all personnel involved.

16. Finally, the information on the data base is an invaluable aid to management decision-making. Using a management information system that rests on this data base, management can evaluate the likely results of a possible strategy or course of action *before* making an irreversible decision.

might be stored in the central warehouse, but before the beans can be sold, they must be distributed to the stores. The more efficiently products can be distributed, the less the cost of distribution. The lower the distribution cost, the greater the profit margin. Better control of these costs represents another key management objective.

Finally, the management of TLD Superstores is concerned with increasing its market share; in other words, in gaining new customers. A 2% profit margin on sales of $100 million is $2 million. If sales could be increased to $125 million, that same profit margin would yield a profit of $2.5 million, a significant improvement. The official target for this year is a 10% increase in total sales; the 5-year target is for a 25% increase. Management has a number of ideas, but needs significant computer support to investigate the potential impact of these ideas.

THE BASIC SOLUTION

In our earlier case studies, the computer was asked to help solve one well-defined problem. This time, several rather complex problems have been cited. Is this unusual? Not at all. The efficient management of a large, modern corporation requires such a broad, multiapplication point of view. The modern computer makes such a viewpoint practical. A computer professional working today probably finds such large projects much more common than batch applications such as payroll.

Let's assume that, after careful analysis of the problem, the systems analysis staff of TLD Superstores has recommended the installation of a computer-controlled checkout system. Electronic checkout stations controlled by an in-store minicomputer, will be placed in each store. The minis will, in turn, be connected by communication lines to the central computer system. At the store level, computer-controlled checkout is expected to reduce labor costs and will significantly improve the quality of inventory data. This improved data can be sent to the central data base. A better data base means better inventory control and more efficient product distribution. Finally, the more accurate data can be used to support a management information system, with corporate officers accessing the data base via desk-top CRT terminals to request the generation of special reports or to ask the computer to answer important "what if" questions. It is a most ambitious project.

Systems analysis has developed a presentation in which they will attempt to "sell" management on this system. Let's see how they might describe each phase of this system.

THE "IN-STORE" SYSTEM

The key to the proposed computer controlled supermarket checkout system is the Universal Product Code (UPC) printed on most supermarket packages. The code uniquely identifies the product. The Universal Product Code is a bar

Figure 22.1
A computer-controlled checkout
station.

code—black bands on a light background. It can be read electronically by taking advantage of the reflectivity of light. Thus, it is possible to identify the product in a form acceptable to a computer.

The system begins with a checkout station (Fig. 22.1). Attached to the station is a bar-code scanner built into the checkout counter. As the customer unloads his or her purchases, the clerk picks up the product, locates the UPC, and passes it over the scanner (Fig. 22.2). An audible beep from the checkout controller tells the clerk that the code has been successfully scanned; other tones are used to signify a need for rescanning. The clerk then bags the purchase and repeats the process for the next item in the order. When all items have been scanned, the clerk presses a button on the controller (which, incidentally, is designed to look much like a traditional cash register; see Fig. 22.1), and the total amount of the customer's bill is printed and displayed. Accepting payment, the clerk enters the amount of payment, the system computes the change due, and the clerk gives the customer the change and a printed receipt (Fig. 22.3).

Neither the customer nor the clerk need be aware of the fact that the checkout counter is controlled by an in-store minicomputer (Fig. 22.4). As the product code is scanned, it is fed as input data to the mini. Here, a program accepts the code, checks it for accuracy and completeness, and then uses the code to access a direct access file on disk. On this file, keyed by UPC, such

Photograph courtesy of IBM Corporation.

Figure 22.2
The bar-code scanner.

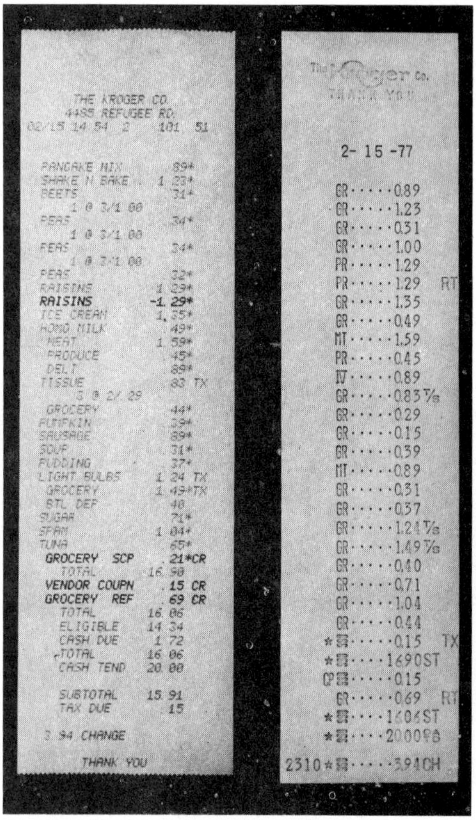

Figure 22.3
A sample of the printed receipt generated by a computer-controlled
checkout station is shown on the left. For comparison, a receipt, for the
same purchases, produced by an old, noncomputerized cash register is
shown on the right.

Photograph courtesy of the Kroger Company.

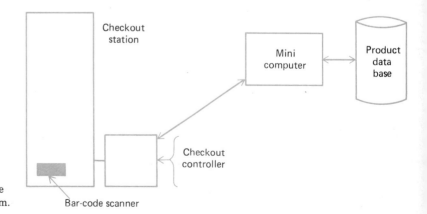

Figure 22.4
A schematic drawing of the in-store
computer-controlled checkout system.

information as the current selling price, any required sales tax, a description of the product, and the current inventory level is found for each product. Retrieving the appropriate record from the file, the computer

1. adds the price to the customer's bill;
2. adds any tax to the customer's bill;
3. prepares a message consisting of the product description, selling price, and tax;
4. sends this message back to the checkout counter, where it is printed and displayed;
5. subtracts 1 from the current inventory balance of the product (one unit is about to leave the store).

All this happens while the clerk is bagging the item. In fact, this same minicomputer can concurrently keep pace with all the checkout stations in the store (Fig. 22.5).

Advantages

Some of the advantages of this system will accrue to the customer. Checkout will be faster, as the clerk no longer must enter the price of each item digit by digit. The annoyance of waiting for a stock clerk to run back and check on the price of an unmarked item will be eliminated. Overcharging due to clerical error will no longer be a problem; the correct price of the "sale item" will be known to the system. Finally, the customer will receive a printed inventory of all items purchased, including both a product description and a price.

Other advantages accrue to the store. Labor costs will be cut. Faster checkout means that, under ordinary conditions, fewer checkout counters need be open. The simplicity of operation of this system means that checkout clerks will need less training. The big labor saving, however, arises from the fact that it will no longer be necessary to stamp the price on each item. The current price is in the computer. The UPC is already on the package. The computer-controlled checkout system uses the UPC to "look up" the correct price. We simply will not need an army of clerks stamping prices at several dollars per hour. (The customer will, of course, find the price of each product clearly displayed on the shelf.)

The potential for labor cost reduction may, however, be dwarfed by the anticipated improvement in our inventory control. At present, the only way to get an "accurate" count of the stock on hand of a given item is to assign a stock clerk the job of "counting cans." This process is expensive (labor costs, again), prone to error, and can be used on only a few specific products at a time. With the computer-controlled system, however, all that will change. As stock is received by the store, the manager simply enters the number of items received

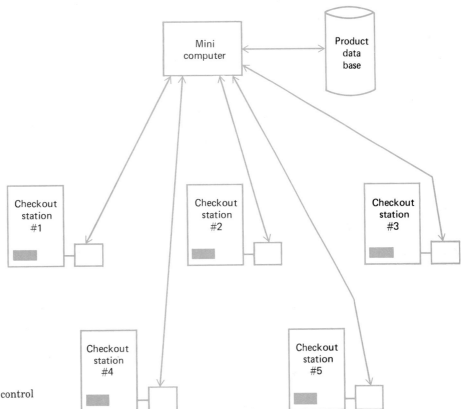

Figure 22.5
A single minicomputer can control
several checkout stations.

into the computer. Only shipping cartons need be counted, since the number of packages or cans per carton is known. (Often, the quantities can be transmitted from the central computer, thus saving the manager's time.) As units are sold, the computer automatically subtracts 1 from the inventory level; thus, the direct access product file reflects, with as much accuracy as possible, the actual stock on hand of *every* item in the store. Such accurate and complete information is simply impossible to obtain with existing methods. Later, we'll see just how valuable this information really is.

   Other, secondary advantages should be recognized as well. The process of entering an order and making change will be more accurate. By comparing the computer's inventory levels with the results of selected physical inventories, the extent of the pilferage problem can be identified. Finally, once this system is installed, the company might be able to connect this system with a bank system, allowing for direct funds transfers and taking us out of the check-cashing business.

THE NETWORK

The system does not, of course, stop at the level of the store. Our stores are part of the TLD Superstore chain, and it is this multistore relationship that gives us our competitive clout. Thus, the minicomputer in each store will be tied to a central computer at corporate headquarters by telephone lines (Fig. 22.6).

The basic operation of the system begins at corporate headquarters. Here, the current selling price for each product will be determined and entered onto the central data base. At the start of each business day, this information will be communicated to the individual stores; thus each store will start the day with the same prices. The store manager will have the authority to change the price of several items as store specials, but essentially the entire chain will be consistent.

Once the price information has been communicated to the stores, control can be given to the individual store computers, and the communication link can be broken. At the end of the day, communication will be reestablished, and

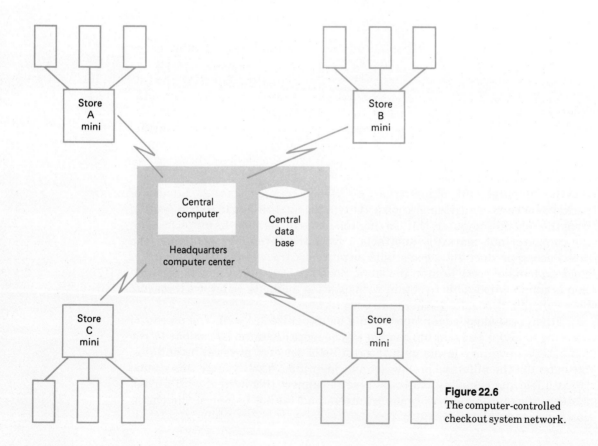

Figure 22.6
The computer-controlled
checkout system network.

current, end-of-day inventory balances for each product in the store will be sent back to the central computer. The difference between the start-of-day and end-of-day balances is the amount sold. This number, and the amount of new stock on hand, can be used to update the data base. Such accurate numbers will prove invaluable in the inventory system, the distribution system, and the proposed management information system.

Clearly, the need for centralized control means that we cannot do the whole job on the local minicomputers. Why not do the entire job on the central machine? While it is technically feasible to control all our checkout stations from a single, centralized, large computer system, such an approach would expose the supermarket chain to great risk. Downtime on a store mini inconveniences that store and only that store. Downtime on a centrally controlled system would impact every store in the chain. Given the relatively low cost of the minis, that risk is simply unacceptable. (In fact, the minis are so inexpensive that most stores use two: an on-line unit and a completely redundant "back-up" unit just in case the primary computer fails.)

THE INVENTORY CONTROL SYSTEM

Inventory is expensive. It is also essential. The important thing is that we have the correct amount of inventory on hand. What exactly is meant by "correct"?

There are two costs associated with inventory. One is the cost of placing an order. Purchasing agents must contact suppliers, papers must be filled out, shipping costs must be paid, the fact that a new order has arrived must be reported to the computer. Many of these costs are fixed; in other words, the cost of placing an order remains about the same whether one or one million units are purchased. Given the fixed nature of these costs, the obvious conclusion is to order as much as possible each time an order is placed. This would result in a large inventory.

The other major cost associated with inventory is the carrying cost. Money must be borrowed to purchase the inventory, and interest must be paid on this money. Warehouse space must be constructed, purchased, or rented. Insurance must be carried. Products can spoil, become obsolete, or be stolen. These costs tend to increase as the size of the inventory increases. Considering only these costs would tend to argue for a small inventory. In other words, the two major cost factors tend to pull us in opposite directions.

There are mathematical techniques that allow us to balance these costs and compute, for each product, an **optimum** inventory level that results in the minimization of the *total* expected cost. The algorithm generates an ideal reorder point for each item in stock; when the stock on hand drops below this critical point, it is time to place another order. The accurate stock-on-hand data that the computer-controlled checkout system will generate will allow us to implement an inventory control system based on this algorithm. One set of reorder points can be used to trigger the transfer of central stock to the individual store. Another set can be used to reorder product for the central warehouse. The potential cost savings are simply enormous.

THE DISTRIBUTION SYSTEM

A supermarket gains its competitive advantage over smaller stores by buying in large quantities. Generally, the price per unit for products purchased in carload lots is significantly lower than the cost per unit of materials purchased one can or one box at a time. A small store doesn't have this purchasing power and thus must pay more for its stock. The result is either higher retail prices or a lower profit margin.

Bulk purchases imply a need for a central warehouse. Basically, as large lots are bought, they are stored in a warehouse. As needed, the central stock is distributed to the individual stores for retail sale. Obviously, it is to the advantage of TLD Superstores to distribute the products as efficiently as possible.

Consider the distribution problem. Each store has certain requirements that must be filled; these are the reorders generated by the inventory control system described earlier. There are also a number of constraints or limitations on our distribution system. There are only so many delivery trucks, and they are available only so many hours per week. Each store has only so much space for storing products. The requirements and constraints tend to limit the distribution system, but there are probably dozens (perhaps even hundreds or thousands) of alternative strategies that fall within these limits. What is the best strategy?

Earlier, we discussed the *optimum* reorder point in our inventory system; it was simply the reorder point that tended to yield the minimum total expected inventory cost. By using mathematical techniques, it was possible to generate this optimum point for each product in inventory. Our objective in the distribution system is to minimize distribution costs. We might state our problem thus: Find the distribution strategy that minimizes total distribution costs subject to the requirements and constraints described above. A mathematical technique known as *linear programming* can be used to solve such problems.

How do we define the cost of distribution? It may not be easy to measure distribution costs directly. Labor is certainly a factor. Miles driven must be considered. Maintenance costs on the trucks are important. Product must be loaded and unloaded, and each stop is expensive. While a complete cost analysis might prove unworkable, it is possible to measure such factors as total trucking time or total miles driven, and total distribution cost is certainly going to vary with these criteria. Thus, we might design our system to generate distribution strategies that minimize total trucking time, subject to the requirements and constraints.

Common sense might suggest a few rules. It is absurd, for example, to have two delivery trucks pass each other moving in opposite directions. One truck should ideally handle all deliveries to the east side of town, while another covers the west side. With 100 stores, dozens of trucks, and thousands of individual product requirements, however, common sense solutions simply cannot handle the problem. The computer is essential. Without accurate input data, the value of even a computer-generated solution would be at best questionable. An essential part of the distribution system, therefore, is the highly accurate inventory data collected by the computer-controlled checkout system.

Inventory data can be compared with the critical reorder points of the inventory system to generate the individual stores' requirements. Store capacity and truck capacity are known. A weekly analysis by the distribution linear programming model can be used to generate a weekly shipping schedule. If necessary, daily runs can be used to "fine tune" this schedule. Once again, the potential cost savings are enormous.

THE MANAGEMENT INFORMATION SYSTEM

It is relatively easy to define areas of potential cost saving. It is much more difficult to define new sources of revenue. Clearly, population growth is one factor. Increasing our share of the available market is another. Still a third possible source of new revenue lies in the introduction of new departments—a delicatessen counter, for example.

How can TLD Superstores capture a large share of the "new customer" market? How can TLD Superstores increase its market share? What new products should be introduced? These are not easy questions, and there are no easy answers. Management must carefully consider its alternatives and select the best marketing strategies; no simple algorithm can be substituted for informed managerial decision making.

Perhaps the key word in that last sentence was "informed." If management is to make good decisions, they must be able to anticipate the consequences of those decisions. Suppose that management is considering using milk as a "loss leader," selling it below cost in hopes of generating more business. How much would the company stand to lose on milk sales? Can increased sales of other products reasonably be expected to generate enough new revenue to offset that loss? Unless such questions can be answered, management is merely guessing.

The inventory data base might be tapped to help answer such questions. It is easy to extract such information as the average daily sales of milk. Multiplying by the anticipated loss per gallon generates the total expected loss. Management might then increase this figure by a percentage to allow for expected increases in sales. Additional computations might involve finding the average daily sales volume of other selected products, factoring in the projected increase in sales, figuring the increase in profit resulting from these new sales, and then comparing the result with the cost. In this way, the projected impact on total profits of a decision to use milk as a loss leader can be estimated. By changing the selling price of the milk, or the projected increase in sales, or both, a number of alternative strategies can be tested. While no one can predict the future with certainty, the manager armed with such information can make more informed (and hence better) decisions.

Several other examples might be cited. Consider a basic marketing question: Is it better to place the dairy products near the front of the store (for "quick purchase" convenience), or is it better to place the dairy products near the rear of the store and have the customer pass by a number of "impulse" products in order to get that quart of milk? Several stores might be set up with the dairy case in front; an equal number of stores might have the dairy case placed in the rear. A careful analysis of several weeks of actual sales data should reveal which strategy (if either) is better. Once again, the data needed to support such a study would be found on the inventory data base; the ultimate source of this information would be the computer-controlled checkout stations.

If management is to use the data base, management must have access to the data base. Since the data base is on the computer, management must have access to the computer. Although some decisions can be postponed, many must be made quickly; thus the traditional, data-processing approach of waiting until a professional programmer is available to do the job is simply not acceptable.

We need a **management information system.** The hardware needed to support such a system (Fig. 22.7) would consist of a control unit and a local network of desk-top CRT terminals. On the computer itself, we would need both a data base manager and a data communication manager. A manager enters the system via a CRT terminal. The transaction is accepted and the individual's identification verified by the data communications manager, a software package occupying a foreground partition. Part of the data communication manager will be a **query system** designed to allow the manager to ask questions of the computer system (to query the system) in an English-like language.

A typical query session might begin with a request for the average daily sales of milk. Subsequent requests might produce the current selling price and current cost of milk. All these data elements, of course, would be extracted from the data base by the data base manager. Now, the manager can "play with" the data. "What if" the price of milk were reduced to a few cents below cost? How much would we stand to lose? What if the lower cost generated an increase of 20% in the amount of milk sold? How much would we lose now? Given this number, the manager can now make a value judgment: "We can (or cannot) reasonably expect to make up this loss in the increased profits generated by the increased customer traffic taking advantage of our lower milk prices."

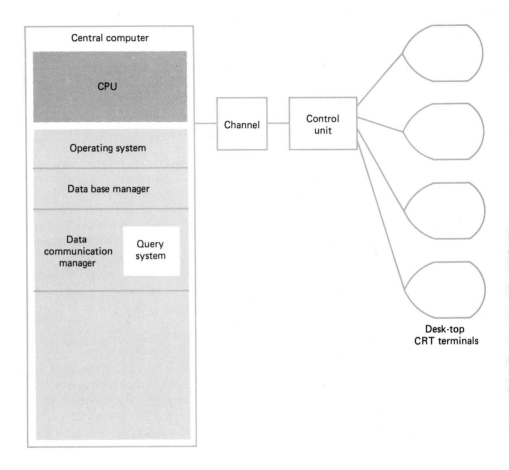

Figure 22.7
The hardware and soft-
ware components of a
typical MIS system.

Some queries might be handled in real-time, with the manager essentially using the computer as a high-speed calculator and data base. Other queries might call for significant amounts of output. These can be handled in a background mode, with a printed report being generated within an hour or two of the request for data. Still other queries might produce such valuable information that management wants it on a continuing basis. Such reports can be assigned to the regular programming staff, with the query serving as a clear and unambiguous statement of management needs.

The starting point for any management information system is accurate data. The computer-controlled checkout system assures that accuracy. The use of a data base (rather than independent files) assures that this data will be accessible. Finally, the local terminal network provides a physical mechanism for accessing the data, and the data communication manager makes such access by nontechnical people logically possible.

The potential cost savings listed above are more than adequate to pay for this system. Given the data collection system and the data base, a management information system can be installed for a relatively small additional cost; in effect, the management information system is a by-product. While it is difficult to estimate the precise benefits of the MIS, the competitive advantage it gives our management team may well prove to be the most valuable contribution of the entire system.

A SYSTEM OVERVIEW

Note how all these components are interrelated. The computer-controlled checkout system, in addition to supporting significant cost savings, serves as an outstanding source-data collection system. The highly accurate data it collects allows us to create a complete, centralized inventory data base. This data base, in turn, is the key to our inventory control system, our product distribution system, and our management information system. Yes, it is more complex than a simple payroll or sequential master-file update application, but with the added complexity comes added power. The potential for a system like this is almost unbelievable!

A CAUTIONARY NOTE

A systems analyst is a technical person. Once a good analyst has designed a well-conceived system, however, he or she tends to assume a different role— that of salesperson. You will note that, in the presentation of this chapter, very little was said that was negative. Ideally, the analyst should point out both the good and the bad, but it is simply unrealistic to assume that the designer, in effect the creator of a complex system, will be able to function as an unbiased critic. That is management's role.

In fact there are numerous problems associated with computer-controlled supermarkets. Customers often object to the lack of price information on individual packages. Boycotts (both organized and individual) and even lawsuits have been threatened. Any significant loss of business could easily offset the potential gains.

Human labor may be expensive and inefficient, but at least it is flexible. In the event of unforeseen problems, the work force in a given supermarket always seems to find a way to "muddle through." Computer control of the store introduces a note of rigidity. What happens when the computer fails? There are no prices on the packages. There is no master file on which prices can be found, and even if a printed list can be found, it could take hours to search the list for the items in even a handful of orders. Coupled with the reduction in the number of workers, computer downtime could mean that the store must close. A duplicate computer system designed to provide backup could be installed in each store, but that would tend to almost double the system cost.

The reduction in labor presents several problems. The union won't like it; a strike is certainly possible. Looking beyond the dollar and cent considerations, is it morally right to replace people with a computer? Of particular concern is the fact that the jobs being eliminated are the traditional entry-level positions, those slots where young people find their first jobs. That is troubling.

The high degree of accuracy claimed for the system is also suspect. What happens if the store manager forgets to report incoming products to the computer? How do we handle customer returns? What happens to that jar of jelly that some customer is always dropping on the floor and breaking? How can we factor in the impact of theft and shoplifting except by physically counting the stock on hand (which negates some of the claimed cost savings)? How much work are we creating for the store manager just to keep the inventory up to date? Certainly the new system will be more accurate than the old system. But can we call it "highly" accurate?

What about the inventory system? The algorithms used to compute optimum reorder points are derived from a field of applied mathematics known as *inventory theory*. The model makes a number of assumptions, some of which are of questionable validity in our environment. The model is also very sensitive to relatively minor changes in the estimated inventory carrying cost; a change in inventory accounting methods can, for example, radically change the computed optimum reorder points. Still, a consistently applied rule is probably better than no rule at all. But the claim of "enormous" savings may have to be cut a bit.

The distribution system comes next. The problem of distributing all those products to all those stores *is* beyond the limits of human control; computer support is essential. Linear programming is probably the best available technique, and the more accurate inventory data will certainly help. Still, the data will not be quite as accurate as the system designers would have us believe. Once again, the potential for cost savings may be overstated.

The usefulness of a management information system is also subject to question. Clearly, direct access to the computer's data base as an aid to the decision-making process would be invaluable to management. But only if the individual managers take advantage of it. Is it reasonable to expect a manager who cannot type to willingly embrace a keyboard-oriented MIS? Is it reasonable to expect a manager who has been a successful decision-maker for years to suddenly change his or her work habits? If MIS is to work, high-level management had better be behind it and had better be willing to spend money on training its executives in the use of such a system. And the system had better work, almost from day number one. A few major errors in the beginning, and management simply won't trust the system. If they don't trust it, they won't use it.

In other words, management must consider the risks, and not all the risks can be reduced to simple dollars and cents. If the benefits outweigh the risks, the system should be installed. If not, the system should be scrapped. It's not an easy decision, but management is paid to make such decisions.

SUMMARY

In this chapter, we investigated a distributed system. We started in the supermarket, where a computer-controlled checkout system was to be installed. The checkout counters were controlled by an in-store minicomputer. A bar-code scanner was used to read the Universal Product Code from a package and into the mini, where a direct access table was searched for a product description and selling price. Inventory levels were updated on the mini. Major reductions in labor cost and significant improvements in inventory status data were claimed.

The store minis were to be connected to a large centralized computer by communication lines. The organization's data base was maintained on the central computer. Using this data base, it was possible to implement sophisticated inventory control and product distribution systems, yielding additional potential cost savings. Allowing managers to tap this data base through a management information system promised to significantly improve the decision-making process. The proposed system was highly complex but had great promise.

The chapter ended with a discussion of some of the hidden costs of such a system. Management must consider these costs.

KEYWORDS

management   optimum   query system
information system

EXERCISES

1. Would a system such as the proposed computer-controlled supermarket checkout system have been possible without the Universal Product Code presently found on most packages? Why or why not?

2. Do a little research into the UPC and see if you can determine what the codes mean.

3. Visit a store that has installed a computer-controlled checkout system. If possible, ask the store manager about the problems as well as the benefits.

4. Do some research into consumer publications to determine how consumers react to some of the procedures of the computerized supermarket.

5. The various systems described in this chapter were all interrelated. Discuss these interrelationships.

6. Do you suppose that such interrelated systems are common or uncommon in modern business? Why?

7. Briefly, what is a management information system?

8. Why do you suppose that it might be difficult to convince management to use a management information system such as the one described in this chapter?

23

TRENDS, OPPORTUNITIES, AND CONCERNS

OVERVIEW

In this, the final chapter, we'll begin by pointing out a number of trends in the information processing field and then try to translate these trends into possible future employment opportunities.

Not all of you will become computer professionals following graduation. Some will choose management and become regular users of computer-generated information. Others will choose a different path, perhaps interacting with the computer only indirectly, as a consumer. No matter what path you choose, however, the computer will have an impact on your life, and not all aspects of computerization are positive. The chapter ends with a brief discussion of some of these concerns.

TRENDS IN HARDWARE

Computers and computer-related equipment are electronic in nature. Modern integrated electronic devices have been declining in cost for some time now; pocket calculators and digital watches are two good commercial examples. This trend toward declining cost continues unabated. Computer hardware, being electronic, benefits from this trend. The declining cost of information processing equipment will be a very important factor in the future, allowing this equipment to economically compete for more and more new applications.

Along with cost, the size and weight of this equipment is also dropping. At the same time, speed, reliability, and computing power are increasing. Except for the computer, very few products offered by our modern industrialized society have shown such marked improvement as their cost declined.

Another important improvement in modern electronic computers is the lifting of *environmental constraints*. Until recently, a computer, to ensure reliable performance, had to be kept in a climate-controlled room, maintaining constant temperature (72°F ±2°) and relative humidity (50% ±5%). Newer computers, especially minicomputers, are designed to work almost anywhere. This represents another cost reduction, saving the customer the expense of special climate-control equipment.

The claim that the cost of computers is dropping may seem a bit strange to the manager contemplating the purchase or lease of a large machine; they always seem to cost more than the big machines of the prior generation. What changes is the capacity of the newer machine: A System/370 computer might cost 1½ times as much as a System/360 computer at the same relative spot in the product line but might be capable of doing three or four times the work. The customer contemplating the addition of another early-third-generation machine may well find that a newer model, more expensive than one but cheaper than two earlier models, provides more than enough extra power.

The cost decline is most obvious in the minicomputer market. Machines every bit as powerful as a second-generation computer can be *purchased* today for what would have been a few months' *rental* cost for the old machine. We even have personal computers today—about as big as a suitcase, powered by electrical current from a standard wall outlet, fully programmable in languages like APL and BASIC, and costing less than $1000. This may seem like a great deal of money, but consider the fact that the UNIVAC I, a considerably less powerful machine, sold for over two million dollars as recently as the early 1950s. Eventually, if current trends continue (and there is no reason to believe that they won't), look for very powerful personal computers in about the same price range as a typical household appliance.

Microprocessors—very small, often single-function computers—represent another remarkable growth market. Using microprocessors, special-function computers can be designed to perform almost any imaginable task. The manufacturing process used in making these devices is highly automated; the big cost factor is concentrated in designing, building, and testing the first unit, with subsequent copies being produced at a nominal cost. This is why, as the demand continued to grow and more and more units were produced, the cost of pocket calculators and digital watches has shown such a marked decline. Pocket calculators and digital watches are controlled by special microprocessors.

What happens as a particular special-function computer begins to decline in cost? More and more are demanded; this is the basic law of supply and demand. As more and more are demanded, even more are built, and the cost per unit drops even further, fueling even greater demand. This is a tremendous potential growth area. Many experts foresee the day when even the small grocery store on the corner has a small, inexpensive computer dedicated to the tasks of billing, maintaining tax records, paying bills, and tracking inventory.

Microprocessors are beginning to significantly impact the design of larger computers as well. Consider, for example, the problem of introducing a new program into a large, multiprogrammed computer system. Generally, a queueing module in the operating system is given control, and it locates and loads the next program. In effect, while this queueing module is in control, the CPU (since it can execute only one instruction at a time) is giving its complete attention to the overhead function of loading a program; it is doing nothing in support of its primary responsibility, the application programs. Why not assign this task to a small microcomputer? The logic of the queueing module (software on the old system) can be burned into a ROM (read-only memory) chip, thus providing a control program for the microprocessor. Now when a new program must be loaded, the micro can assume full responsibility, leaving the main CPU free to work, in parallel, on the application programs. In effect, a computer with two processing units can literally do two things at once.

The term **multiprocessing** is used to refer to computer systems in which two or more processors share a common memory. I/O processors, communication processors, data base processors, and array processors are available today on many large computer systems. Essentially, such multiprocessing configurations tend to be quite efficient, as the secondary processors free the CPU from the burden of numerous overhead functions, thus leaving more time for the primary application functions. The declining cost of micros makes multiprocessing economically viable.

Another area where the potential for technological change is tremendous is in memories. Current bulk memories (disk, drum, and tape) move; this movement limits the speed and storage capacity of these devices and makes them susceptible to wear and eventual failure. It's only a matter of time before economically competitive static memories are developed. Numerous technological approaches, none of which we'll discuss in any detail, are under active study today.

These newer memories will probably be addressed much like main memory by simply counting memory locations in sequence. No longer will the programmer be forced to consider tracks, cylinders, and other factors that relate to physical efficiency. This will have a significant impact on the use of traditional access methods, causing a probable decline in the indexed sequential approach and tending to favor sequential access and techniques that are based on the relative record number concept.

The programmer will also be significantly affected. Today one of the most valuable individuals in any computer center is the programmer who fully understands the intricacies of physical I/O and can advise the other programmers as to the most efficient approach. With bulk memory addressed much like main memory, the complexity disappears, and with it the need for this individual. In effect, those who are today considered to be at the very top of their profession will be among the "first to go."

Probably the biggest potential growth area in the entire information processing field is in terminals of all types—keyboard typewriters, CRTs, remote job entry, intelligent terminals, and special-function terminals. More and more banks will begin to use the automatic teller terminal. Supermarkets will tend to increase the pace of checkout automation. Retail stores will place the credit-checking function on-line more and more. Schools will use terminals for instruction and administrative problem solving. Even personal terminals, roughly analogous to a pocket calculator but making a powerful computer as close as the nearest telephone, will come into general use. (Already it's possible to purchase a terminal, complete with communications equipment, for less than $1000.) The growth potential here is just tremendous!

TRENDS IN FIRMWARE

Traditionally the designer of a computer system was forced to choose between hardware and software for performing key logical functions. Hardware is highly reliable and very fast, software is slower and more prone to error, but it's also much more flexible and less expensive. Until recently, economics has tended to dictate a software solution for most logical functions.

Modern trends in electronics have tended to change this picture. It's possible, for example, to design a single circuit chip to find a square root. Traditionally, square roots have always been estimated by using a software algorithm. It was not implemented through hardware because the cost was too high. Today, however, with the tremendous growth of calculators with a square root function built in, the development cost of this piece of hardware has been spread over so many copies that the cost per unit has declined, making the hardware solution both faster *and* less costly than the software solution. Look for built-in square root functions (and other common mathematical functions) on many future computers.

Typically these electronic circuits are assembled on a single card or two and can be installed or removed from a computer almost at will. Where do they fit? They are obviously not software, but from the standpoints of cost and flexibility, they are different from traditional hardware too. The term **firmware** has been coined to describe these electronic circuits, which fall somewhere between traditional hardware and software.

Almost any function can be implemented through firmware. The big cost is in developing and building the first copy; subsequent copies are relatively inexpensive. What this means in practical economic terms is that a firmware solution to an information processing problem is only viable when a significant number of copies can be sold.

On a large computer, expect to see many of the system software functions (operating systems, I/O control, data base management, data communications management, utility programs and sorting) implemented through firmware. The control logic of the secondary processors (described above as part of a multiprocessing system) will almost certainly be implemented through firmware, as will certain commonly used "application" programs. The line separating hardware from software will become increasingly blurred.

At the other extreme, the small, single-function minicomputer (the device used to control checkout at each of hundreds of supermarkets, for example) will be totally controlled by firmware programs. Supermarket employees will probably view the minicomputer in their store as a "magic sealed black box," never to be tinkered with or modified. Along the same lines, a small business can even today purchase or lease a minicomputer with "built-in" firmware programs to perform such typical business functions as payroll, accounts receivable, accounts payable, and inventory analysis. These computers look much like a normal piece of office furniture and require no professional operators and no programming staff.

TRENDS IN SOFTWARE

The trend in software is toward simplicity. Although some experts believe that a new, human-like language is about to take over, this does not seem to be the case. Instead, a few languages—COBOL, FORTRAN, BASIC, PL/I, APL, RPG, and, at least in Europe, ALGOL—seem to be gaining stature as "de facto" standards. Although the "perfect" language, perhaps even spoken language, is not beyond the realm of possibility, the trend toward simplicity will probably be seen in other ways first.

The first and perhaps most obvious trend is away from assembler-level languages and toward the higher-level compiler languages, at least for application programming. The major advantages of assembler language are related to computer efficiency; an assembler program usually runs faster and needs less main memory than an equivalent program written in a compiler language. New technology won't change this basic fact. Why then is the use of assembler-level languages expected to decline?

As the computer becomes faster and less expensive, the value of efficiency on the computer begins to decline. In the middle 1950s, eliminating 1000 instructions from a program might have amounted to a savings of a second or two each time that the program was run. On a modern high-speed computer, the same saving might yield a few microseconds at best and, given the fact that we might only be using 35 percent of the available time, who cares?

Even more important is the growing awareness of the true cost of writing a program. Debug, documentation, and maintenance are key components of this total cost, and programs written in a compiler language are much easier and much less expensive to debug, document, and maintain than are programs written in assembler. With declining "on-the-computer" costs, a program must be used with great frequency before the "on-the-computer" economies catch up with the much higher debug, documentation, and program maintenance costs arising from the use of assembler language.

One approach that should tend to simplify programming is the trend toward structured programming. Structured programming is implemented through a series of rules, restrictions, and guidelines for writing programs in a simple, straightforward, easy-to-read, and easy-to-maintain manner. Tricky programming is out. The simplified approach is in.

Purchased software also has an impact. Once a programmer becomes used to the syntax of a data base management package, the writing of application programs is greatly simplified because the programmer can forget about the details of input and output and concentrate on the logic of the program. With purchased, vendor-supplied system software, the modern programmer need do little more than sequence a series of add, subtract, multiply, divide, compare, move, read, and write statements, paying absolutely no attention to such details as physical I/O or converting coded data to numeric form. He or she can concentrate on solving a problem rather than fitting the solution to a particular computer.

Not only system software but also application software can be purchased today. Look for an acceleration of this trend as more and more managements begin to realize that what they do really isn't that much different from what many others do and decide to stop "reinventing the wheel."

DATA COMMUNICATIONS

Data communications is a major bottleneck today. The cost is very high, tending to limit the use of terminals and intelligent terminals. Line speeds limit the speed of the entire remote system.

Although the American telephone system is without a doubt the best in the world, it was not designed with data communications in mind. The telephone company is, of course, aware of the present limitations and is taking steps to deal with them; recent advertising tends to stress new technology. Look for major changes in the area of digital data transmission, with laser technologies, glass fibers, and other new approaches carrying messages.

Other changes will come in the area of rate structures. Look for new data transmission rates, and don't be surprised if the new structures make over-night, "off-prime-time" data transmission very attractive. Many major firms manage to save a great deal on their long-distance communications by leasing special WATS lines, which allow any number of long-distance calls for a fixed fee; the future will bring similar arrangements on data communications.

The trend toward the use of intelligent terminals or minicomputers feed-ing a large centralized computer is partially due to existing telephone rate structures. It's much cheaper to allow a remote computer to handle its own load, dialing up the central computer only when necessary, than to attach a less expensive but less intelligent terminal directly to the main machine. The cost of telephone time is a function of connect time.

There are, of course, competitors. Microwave radio can be used for data transmission, and there are plans to launch a private communications satellite to support a national microwave network. Such a system would probably be designed to transmit data from city to city, with local telephone lines being used from the transmission station to the customer's installation. Given the fact that the demand for data communications is almost certain to continue to grow, new technologies are equally certain to be developed.

A growing submarket of the data communications field is the private leased network. Such networks are set up by private companies that lease wide-band facilities (similar to the cables that carry television programs from the network to its stations) connecting major cities, and then sublease the use of these lines to a number of customers. Generally, these communication service operations use special-purpose computers at the terminal points of the line; these computers control the transmission of data, making certain that messages get to the proper party.

COMPUTER NETWORKS

Distributed data processing implies a number of different computers intercon-nected by communication lines. Such configurations are often called computer networks. Some networks are composed of a number of minicomputers. Others are centered around a large "maxi" computer that houses the organizational data base and performs organizational data processing activities. Terminals of all kinds are attached to this central computer, including keyboard terminals, simple remote job entry terminals, intelligent terminals, and single-function terminals. The communication facilities, including perhaps special computers whose sole responsibility is message concentration or message switching, are also considered to be part of the computer network. Planning and balancing such networks has become a discipline of its own.

NEW MARKETS

Traditionally, a relatively small number of mainframe manufacturers supplied their customers with both hardware and software support. Independent software and "foreign" hardware did, of course, exist but was relatively rare.

Today one of the major markets within the information processing field is supplying **peripheral hardware,** primarily input/output devices, memory, control units, and terminals. Such devices are said to be **plug-to-plug compatible** with the mainframe of a given supplier; this term means that the equipment can simply be plugged into the mainframe. Plug-to-plug peripherals succeed mainly because they are quite cost-competitive, often selling or leasing for considerably less than equivalent peripheral equipment supplied by the mainframe manufacturer.

Believe it or not, there are even **plug compatible mainframes** (PCM). A computer that plugs into another computer? Not really. The PCM market has developed in response to a recognized fact of computer life: IBM is the dominant force in the computer marketplace. It is much easier to find an already-written program or an experienced programmer for an IBM machine than for the computer of any other manufacturer. Why not design a new, competitive computer that runs IBM software? That is the essential idea behind a plug compatible mainframe. The hardware may be quite different, but the software looks just like IBM's.

Probably the biggest growth potential, at least in the hardware area, can be found in the manufacture and sale of terminals, all types of terminals. Closely associated with terminals is the equipment needed to support data communications—data sets, modems, acoustical couplers, data communications control units, and teleprocessing line controllers. This is another potential growth market. Remember, however, that communication facilities are controlled by a relative handful of high-technology companies. A major technological breakthrough or a significant new approach to marketing data communications by one of these giants could significantly alter this picture.

With the advent of small, inexpensive, special-purpose minicomputers, many small firms that have never even considered the possibility of computer use before will "take the plunge." These firms will need help getting started. There is a growing market for people who are able to provide this service. The market is presently served by a number of independent consultants who purchase equipment from the various manufacturers and assemble a number of what are called **turnkey systems;** ideally, the customer should merely have to "turn the key" to make the system work. These consultants install the systems at customer locations, get things started, and provide follow-up support when necessary. The first-time user needs this kind of service. With the declining cost of minicomputers, there will be more and more first-time users entering the market, and that translates again into growth potential.

Closely related to the development of small, inexpensive computers, particularly microcomputers, has been the emergence of the computer hobbyist and the whole new field of **personal computing.** "Build-your-own-computer" kits are available at prices ranging from a few hundred to several thousand dollars. Computer hobby clubs are springing up all over the nation. There is even a possibility of nationally franchised personal computing centers along the lines of the more popular electronics and hardware chains.

Not only computers but terminals are beginning to have an impact on the hobby market. By constructing or purchasing a small, low-cost keyboard, it's possible to convert a regular black-and-white television set into a CRT terminal, which can in turn be connected to a computer via telephone lines. We already have firms that, for a fee, will allow the terminal owner to access a computer and play computer games such as Star Trek, chess, electronic football, and countless others until his or her interest (or money) runs out.

System software has been supplied by private concerns for quite some time now, and this will continue. By using standard operating systems and vendor-supplied data base management, data communication, and spooling packages, many companies have, in effect, given full responsibility for maintaining all system software to outsiders. In fact, there are **independent software vendors** who will gladly accept full responsibility for a fee. Given this approach, programmers at the customer's location write only application programs. As more and more system functions are taken over by hardware or firmware, this trend will become more and more pronounced. If you want to be a **system programmer** working on operating systems and data base managers, you should plan to work for one of the mainframe manufacturers or for a large software vendor.

Many companies have "gotten out" entirely, assigning full responsibility for all systems and application programs and even the operation of the computer center to an outside vendor. In other cases, a firm will decide not to even own or lease a computer, sending all work to an **information processing utility.** There is a growing demand for services of this type.

Systems analysis and design is another growing field. Organizations are just now beginning to become aware of the value of a total-system approach to system planning. A particularly strong subfield within this general market involves the planning and implementation of data communications networks.

EMPLOYMENT OPPORTUNITIES

As the computer field goes through what seems to be an almost continual period of change, employment opportunities are certain to shift too. Let's take a look at some of the traditional jobs within this field and comment on the probable future of these jobs; then we'll consider some of the newer employment opportunities. The comments that follow are based to a large degree on the opinions of the author.

One traditional data processing job is that of keypunch operator. Don't look for any significant growth here. The newer data entry terminals and the trend toward on-line data collection via special terminals will, if anything, decrease opportunities in this area. Punched cards will not disappear, of course, and many former keypunch operators will find work operating one of the newer keyboard data entry devices. But this is *not* a growth field.

The traditional job of computer operator is another that will probably tend to stabilize or even decline in the future. The trend toward distributed data processing should reduce the emphasis on the large machines while increasing the use of minicomputers; a minicomputer does not require as many operators as a big machine does. Continued growth in the computer field will probably create enough new jobs to offset the expected job loss and thus maintain some stability, but operations is not a real growth field.

The demand for programmers will grow, but there will be changes in this job category. The trend toward implementing many system functions in firmware, coupled with changes in the way in which bulk memory is addressed and the switch to purchased software, will tend to cut the demand for the systems programmer, the person who traditionally has been at the top of the programmer "pecking order." The mainframe manufacturers and the independent software houses will still need good system programmers, of course; stability or a mild improvement in the employment opportunities for these individuals can be expected.

Application programming should grow simply because more and more organizations will be using the computer. Here again, however, there will be changes. As programming is simplified, the emphasis will shift from clever coding to problem solving. Perhaps we will someday be able to say that an accountant with a reasonable amount of computer training can be expected to write better *accounting* programs than a programmer with no accounting experience. Programming skill will become a valuable "companion skill" to go along with solid preparation in almost any major field. This may become the entry-level skill needed for that first post-college or post-technical school job.

Systems analysis will be a real growth area. Individuals who can attack problems from a broad total-system point of view will always be in demand. The increasingly technical world of the future will only increase this demand.

The trend in hardware design—electronics, specifically—is a bit more difficult to pin down. While it is true that more and more computers and related electronic devices will be manufactured and sold, it's also true that the economics of modern integrated circuitry insist that a great many copies of a circuit be manufactured in order to recover the development costs. In the past, the designer could always concentrate on redesigning a circuit to make it better. To justify the redesign and replacement of a modern integrated circuit demands a potential for a really significant improvement before it becomes economically viable. This factor might tend to limit employment opportunities for newly minted computer designers. Look to the mainframe manufacturers and the major electronics firms for possible positions.

Sales and service will be affected too. As the sale of computer equipment increases, the impact on these two groups should be obvious. The fact that modern electronic devices are significantly more reliable than their predecessors could tend to dampen the growth in service a bit. And the fact that these modern machines are electronically very complex will certainly increase the amount of training required of these people.

Where there are employees, there are managers. As the number of computer installations increase, so will the demand for installation managers.

Current trends are creating a number of new positions, too. As more and more small computers and intelligent terminals are installed, there will be an increasing demand for professional *programmer/operators*. As the name of the position implies, these individuals will be responsible for both operating and programming a machine. Typically, the demands placed on the operator of a minicomputer or intelligent terminal amount to something less than a full-time job. By effectively "wearing two hats," the programmer/operator becomes a very valuable employee. Current and potential operators should strongly consider learning a programming language or two—RPG and BASIC are good ones—to improve their own marketability.

Data communications is potentially a very strong growth market. The data communications consultant will find increasing demands for his or her services in the future.

One of the relatively unseen new markets is related to the anticipated growth in first-time computer users, the small "mom-and-pop-type" business establishment which, due to the rapidly declining cost of minicomputers, has decided to move into computer-controlled record keeping, accounts receivable, accounts payable, payroll, and inventory control. Such organizations rarely have any technical expertise and don't really want any. What the small, first-time user needs is a pure turnkey system. Someone must design and install these systems. The demand for people capable of doing this kind of work is bounded only by the number of small businesses in this country. If you want to succeed in this market though, solid training and experience are essential.

One traditional occupation that is bound to undergo some change as a result of all these trends is the position of the office secretary. Typing and shorthand skills used to be enough, but the secretary of the future may also have to know how to use a word processing terminal and how to operate an intelligent terminal. In the office of the future, the person who can handle more than one job will be more than welcome.

The growth of personal computing spells opportunity too. Personal computing franchises and personal computing services are certain to grow in the near future. This could well be another of those "ground-floor" opportunities.

Finally, with more and more people being exposed to the computer, the demand for computer-related training is certain to grow. In spite of the fact that the computer can, in some cases, be used to teach, the expected increase in the demand for such training is welcome to those who teach (and write books) in the field.

To summarize this author's view of the employment potential for those who have trained themselves for computer-related jobs, the prospects look solid.

THE COMPUTER: A MIXED BLESSING

Not all who take an "introduction-to-computers" course plan to become computer professionals, however. For the business student a common goal is management. Others will enter politics, become engineers, train for a profession, or simply become "consumers." It really doesn't matter; computers have come to so permeate our society that you simply cannot escape their influence. Like the automobile and television, the computer is here to stay.

We hear that the automobile is largely responsible for the air pollution and congestion of our major cities. And television has been accused of literally "rotting our minds." Technology is usually a bit of a mixed blessing, and the computer is no exception. In the next several pages, we'll examine some of the problems caused by or associated with the computer.

Computers and Unemployment

The image of a human being replaced by a computer is a common one. We see an automated bank-teller terminal and know that somewhere a human teller is out of work. Computerized supermarket checkout certainly has an impact on the jobs of supermarket clerks. In fact, one of the major reasons for using the computer is that it can do a job at a lower cost than its human competition can, but what happens to that human competition? There is little question that the use of computers does in fact displace some human workers.

How many? What is the real impact of this problem? The answer depends a great deal on the attitude of the respondent. Trade unions consider worker displacement to be a very serious problem, part of what they see as a general trend toward automation in this country. The union leader might look at a decision to computerize payroll and point out the five or ten people who would be replaced immediately. Should the company double in size as projected, the number of clerks who might have been employed would be twice the number being displaced today.

Management and the computer industry tend to look at the problem differently. From their point of view, the use of computers creates new jobs— keypunch operators, computer operators, programmers, systems analysts, and a new management group. Not only that, but without the computer the increase in paperwork would tend to swamp the growing concern, thus slowing growth; the use of computers, according to this group, creates jobs simply by allowing growth to proceed at a more rapid rate.

Just as there is little question regarding the fact that the computer does displace some people, there is little question that the computer creates new jobs. In a recent survey of the top 100 companies in the data processing industry (*Datamation,* July 1980), the number of people employed by these companies is estimated to be in excess of 2,250,000. These are people who build, sell, and service computers; without the computer, these jobs would not exist. This survey certainly does *not* count the people who program, operate, or manage computer operations for almost every medium-sized to large-sized organization in the country.

Dire prophecies of the impact on employment have accompanied the arrival of almost every technological advance in history—none have come true. Major technological breakthroughs tend to create growth, leading to additional jobs in the long run. The computer, at least in the opinion of the author, is no exception.

There is, however, one potentially very serious problem with the computer. The jobs that can be automated are highly repetitive and require little or no advanced training; the jobs that are created tend to be more sophisticated, requiring training, experience, or special skills. Given this shift toward skilled jobs and away from the low-skilled, entry-level positions, we can see a very real potential shift in the job mix. Without special technical training, the young person just entering the job market will have a difficult time "cracking" the computer field. Some form of training will be necessary.

This creates a companion problem in retraining those people who are displaced by the computer. Given the fact that the computer can best be applied to relatively simple, repetitive tasks, the army of the displaced will tend to include a disproportionate number of the unskilled and low-skilled. Is it reasonable to assume that an individual who has been working on an assembly line for 20 years and who has not attended any school during that time can be retrained as a computer programmer? The problem is that the very people who are displaced tend to be the most difficult to retrain. There is no easy answer to this problem.

Computers and Privacy

In his classic novel *1984,* George Orwell envisioned a future society in which the lives of human beings were tightly controlled and structured by an absolute dictatorship personified by "Big Brother." These controls were implemented by a fantastic array of electronic surveillance devices. Today, many fear that the combination of modern electronic "bugs" and the computer provides all the technology needed to make Orwell's nightmare come true.

Consider the data that is today held in computer data banks. Let's start with the federal government, where many agencies and bureaus maintain files containing personal information (Fig. 23.1). Add to this the files maintained by local and state governments and by private concerns, and you have an imposing array of personal information in the hands of others. Have you ever done anything wrong? Have you ever made a mistake that you would rather forget? The chances are that it's on a computer file somewhere, and the computer never forgets. The potential for blackmail, particularly political blackmail, is enormous.

Fortunately these files are not interrelated, belonging to a number of independent and often hostile groups. The possibility of combination does, however, exist, probably with the social security number as a key. This was suggested several years ago, and the idea of a **national data bank** was widely

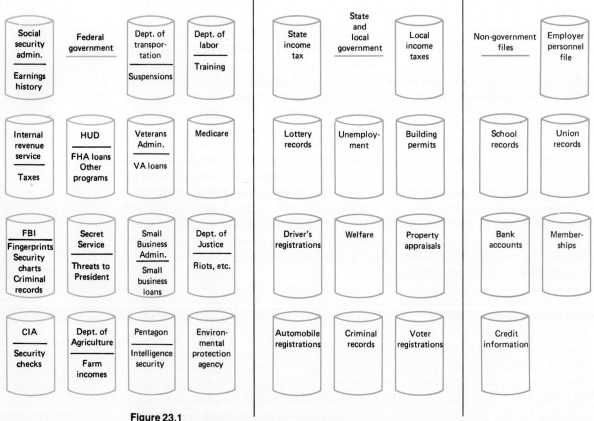

Figure 23.1
Personal data is maintained by many groups.

discussed. Among the strongest opponents were the members of the data processing profession. The potential for a misuse of power and the invasion of personal privacy was just too great. In effect, the slow wheels of bureaucracy serve to protect us from excessive misuse of existing files.

People are (rightfully) concerned about this. As business becomes more and more computerized, more and more personal data finds its way onto business computer systems. Is it secure? Is it protected? Business has a responsibility—both moral and legal—to ensure that the answer to both questions is yes.

Computer Crime

There once was a programmer who was assigned the task of writing a program to compute the interest due on savings accounts. Very early in his work, he recognized the fact that interest did not always compute exactly to the penny; frequently, fractions of a cent were involved. "What," he asked, "is the rule I should use for rounding?" "You don't round," he was told, "you truncate. We (the bank) keep those fractions of a cent."

Being well-versed in mathematics, it didn't take our programmer very long to realize that this "unpaid" interest amounted to an average of one-half penny per account. On 100,000 accounts, that's $500.00! "Why," he reasoned, "should the bank get all that money? I want some for myself."

So he wrote the program to add these fractions of a penny to his own account. It worked, for several years, but eventually he was caught and convicted of theft—one of the very first computer crimes.

Computer crime is an increasing problem. Recently a large insurance company was found guilty of creating and selling (to other insurers) bogus insurance policies. The key to making this scheme work was the computer; the fraudulent policies were simply added to the list of good policies on the company's data base. The crime was so well implemented that a well-known national auditing firm verified the accuracy of the insurance company's financial records, detecting nothing wrong. It took the testimony of a disgruntled employee to expose the scandal.

Numerous other cases could be cited. A young man in California used the computer to bilk the telephone company out of millions of dollars' worth of communications equipment. A bank employee used his knowledge of a computer system to "borrow" the funds needed to support his gambling habit. An unknown bank customer used a knowledge of the national banking system to postpone discovery of a number of bogus checks until it was simply too late to trace him (or her). Programmers have been known to intentionally sabotage an employer's computer system in retaliation for a real or an imagined slight. College students often consider the theft of computer time (using an unauthorized access number, for example) as little more than harmless fun.

Computer Security

If it were possible to guarantee that only authorized persons could gain access to a computer data bank, much of the concern for potential invasions of privacy would disappear. Likewise, if computer access could be limited to only authorized persons, much of the opportunity for computer crime would similarly disappear. The problem in both cases is one of **security.**

A common image of "security" is the bank vault. We tend to believe that anything stored behind those massive steel doors is secure, protected from theft, fire, or natural disaster. What does the safe manufacturer say? Most safes or vault doors are rated on a time scale. A "four-hour" safe is designed in such a way that a professional thief, given the proper tools, will need about four hours to break through. An "eight-hour" safe will probably take twice as long. Very simply, the risk of getting caught increases with the quality of the safe. Note, however, that *no* safe claims to be absolutely secure. Given enough time, a determined crook *will* break in.

Actually, that massive bank vault is more for show than for protection. Most of the bank's resources do not reside in the vault anyway. Instead, these resources are represented as patterns of bits on a magnetic surface, usually tape or disk. How secure is this computer data?

Unfortunately, in most cases, the answer is "not very." To the average person, who knows very little about computers, anything stored on an electronic medium is bound to be safe. To the computer professional, however, breaking the secuity codes of a computer-based system is often little more than a mental exercise. Given enough time, almost any modern computer security system can be broken. Financial data, personal data, military data, and corporate trade secrets are all stored on computers, and all are subject to the risk of unauthorized access.

How can security be implemented on a computer? First, you must realize that there are several different types of security risks. At one extreme is the "crime of opportunity," where an untrained individual accidently or maliciously begins "pushing buttons." On a poorly designed system, such activities can raise havoc, but a reasonable amount of planning can eliminate or at least minimize such risks. At the other extreme is the determined professional. Like the professional bank robber, when this individual (or group) decides to breech a computer's security system, it is only a matter of time. The key to security is to make such access as risky and as expensive as possible.

Often the first line of defense is a sign-on procedure that requires the user of a computer to supply a valid accounting number or **password** before access is authorized. The weakness of most password systems is that they really don't identify the individual; they merely determine that the person attempting to gain access (whoever he or she may be) has a valid password. Perhaps someday, an individual's fingerprints, hand print, facial features, signature, or voice print will become the basis for true personal identification; such techniques are already in use in several research labs and in a few highly sensitive computer centers. For the moment, however, the sophisticated equipment needed to implement these tests remains too expensive for common use.

Within the computer system, second- and third-level passwords are used to restrict access to selected parts of a data base, preventing an employee from reading the boss's salary, for example. Another common internal security function involves **logging** all transactions against the data base. The idea here is that unauthorized access will be discouraged by the simple fact that "somebody" (the computer) is watching.

Highly confidential or sensitive data is sometimes protected by techniques borrowed from the field of **cryptography;** in essence, it is translated into a "secret" code that can be understood only by a certain program. The data thief, of course, might use a computer to break the code, but the cost would be very high. If the cost is high enough, "crime doesn't pay."

As computers have developed, security has tended to lag behind. It is only fairly recently that the industry, prompted by a number of new federal and state laws, began to take the problem seriously. The past few years have seen significant improvement, but much remains to be done.

THE COMPUTER IMPACT: A FINAL COMMENT

No major technological advance has ever been without its social cost. Mass production is probably responsible for bringing us up to our present high standard of living, but mass production brings drudgery into the lives of the assembly-line workers. The automobile provides us with unparalleled mobility, but automobiles pollute and take up precious space for parking and roads. Television provides entertainment, putting us in touch with the entire world, but television has been accused of creating a generation of passive followers.

We must deal with these problems. Solutions must be found. But in solving the problems arising from technological achievement, we must be careful not to destroy the advantages we derive from technology. Technology is not always right, nor is it always wrong.

SUMMARY

In this chapter we summarized a number of trends in the computer field. Hardware costs are dropping, particularly in the minicomputer area. Size and weight are also dropping, while speed, reliability, and computing power are increasing. These trends are opening the possibility of computer use to a number of brand-new markets. Memory is also changing, with the trend growing away from "moving" memory and toward electronic memories that are addressed much like main memory. Perhaps the biggest area of potential hardware growth is in terminals.

Firmware is a name given to certain modern integrated circuits that can be manufactured at a very low cost and used within a computer in a very flexible manner. These circuits combine the speed of hardware with the relatively low cost and flexibility of software. Firmware is being used to perform many system functions on larger computers, and this use should grow. These circuits are also used for controlling applications on smaller, special-purpose computers.

Software is becoming easier to use. More and more of the computer's details are being hidden in system software and in hardware, allowing the programmer to concentrate on the application.

Data communications is a major bottleneck; improvements are almost certain to occur. Information processing networks, with a number of computers interconnected by communication lines, are becoming common. Some networks are composed of a number of minicomputers; on others, various types of terminals and minicomputers are connected to a centralized "maxi" computer.

These trends are creating a number of new markets. The sale and support of traditional mainframes continues to be strong. Plug-to-plug compatible equipment and terminals are examples of new and growing segments of the computer hardware market. The growth of minicomputers creates a demand for people who can plan and install turnkey systems for the first-time or unsophisticated user. The demand for personal computers is growing too; a brand-new hobby is beginning to develop.

Independent software vendors are very important in the modern computer marketplace. These organizations sell both system and application software. Systems analysis, systems consulting, and communications consulting are other examples of new and growing market activities.

The chapter presented an analysis of the potential for job opportunities in computer-related fields. Generally speaking, the outlook is optimistic.

The chapter ended with a brief discussion of some of the problems caused by computerization. Computers do, in some cases, replace people, and this can lead to unemployment. On the other hand, the computer has created a number of new jobs. An unfortunate problem is that those who are replaced by a computer usually hold low-skilled jobs, while the work created by these machines calls for a very high level of training. As a result, those who lose their jobs are among the most difficult to retrain.

The privacy and confidentiality of data stored on a computer is a growing concern, as is computer crime. Both are (at least partially) related to the problem of security. The security procedures on a modern computer are far from ideal; improvements are, however, being made.

KEYWORDS _____

computer crime

cryptography

firmware

independent
software vendor

information
processing utility

logging

multiprocessing

password

peripheral hardware

personal computing

plug compatible
mainframe

plug-to-plug
compatible

purchased software

security

turnkey system

EXERCISES _____

1. Why will the declining cost of hardware have an impact on software?

2. Why will the declining cost of firmware have an impact on software?

3. Why does the high cost of data communications tend to push users in the direction of distributed data processing?

4. What is a turnkey system?

5. Do some research on your own and write a paper on the future job opportunities in the data processing field.

6. Select a possible area of future employment (for yourself) and do some reading to determine the impact of the computer on this field.

7. Do computers lead to unemployment? What do you think?

8. It has been said that the victim of a computer crime often does not even realize that a crime has been committed. Why do you suppose that this might be so?

9. Investigate the password or identification number system used to control access to your school's computer. How does it work? Based on your own experience, how effective is it?

APPENDIX:
THE IBM 029
KEYPUNCH

BASIC IDEAS

The whole point of keypunching is to convert the characters printed on a source document into a pattern of punched holes on a card. Each column of a card holds one character of data; the hole pattern within the column determines which character it is. The keypunch is designed to be used much like a typewriter, with the operator depressing keys on a keyboard; the only difference is that the characters are punched into a card rather than printed on a sheet of paper.

The keyboard (Fig. A.1) is similar to a typewriter keyboard. There are, however, a few differences. To the experienced typist, the most obvious difference is the position of the digits 0 through 9; rather than being located across the top of the keyboard, they are gathered into an adding machine-like group just beneath where your right hand would normally be positioned. This is intentional; the experienced operator soon learns to enter numeric data with one hand, using the other to depress the numeric shift key or to track the data on the source document. Another difference between a typewriter and a keypunch is that there are no lowercase letters on a keypunch; every letter is a capital letter.

Photograph courtesy of IBM Corporation.

Figure A.1
The keyboard of an IBM 029 keypunch.

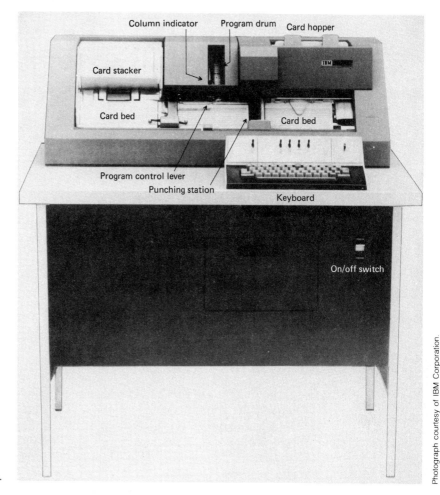

Column indicator   Program drum   Card hopper

Card stacker

Card bed

Card bed

Program control lever

Punching station

Keyboard

On/off switch

Figure A.2
An IBM 029 keypunch.

Above the keyboard shown in Fig. A.1, you should be able to see a series of switches. These are called the control switches or the selector switches; they are used to control the operation of the keypunch. More about these switches later.

Let's step back a bit and take a look at the whole keypunch (Fig. A.2). The on/off switch is located near the bottom right, underneath the keypunch proper. The keyboard sits atop a table-like ledge. Behind the keyboard are the card-feed and punching mechanisms. A card moves from the card hopper (at the right), down into the card bed, through the punching station where it is punched and, continuing its movement to the left, into the card stacker; look for each of these basic positions in the diagram of Fig. A.2.

Normally, the contents of each card column are printed at the top of the card. This is for the convenience of the keypunch operator or other individual who wishes to visually verify the cards; the computer needs only the holes.

LOADING CARDS

Before using a keypunch, it is necessary to have a supply of blank cards in the card hopper. To place cards in the hopper,

1. push the pressure plate at the rear of the card hopper back until it catches;
2. grab a stack of cards;
3. fan through the cards to loosen any that might be stuck together;
4. use the edge of the keyboard to straighten and align the cards in the deck;
5. look at the edges of the cards and remove any that look nicked or warped (they can jam the machine);
6. place the cards in the hopper 9-edge (bottom) down and with the printing facing you;
7. release the pressure plate.

You are now ready to begin punching.

BASIC KEYPUNCH OPERATION

Most beginners are concerned with punching a series of cards; thus our basic operating steps are designed around a "multiple card" assumption. The on/off switch is located at the bottom right of the machine, underneath the ledge; turn the machine on. As you begin, all the control switches at the top of the keyboard should be flipped up. One, the CLEAR switch, won't stay up; don't worry about it.

The first step in the keypunching operation is to move a card from the card hopper to the punching station. The following two steps achieve this objective.

1. Depress the FEED key (it's a blue key, near the right edge of the keypunch in the second row down from the top).
2. Depress the FEED key again.

The first feed operation feeds one card from the card hopper down to the card bed. The second feed operation moves the first card into the punching station and feeds a second card.

You are ready to begin punching data into a card. Each keystroke causes one character to be punched, with the character being printed at the top of the column; after being punched, the card automatically advances to the next column, where another character can be punched. Alphabetic characters and any symbols located on the lower half of a key can simply be punched; numeric characters and symbols on the upper half of the key must be punched while the NUMERIC key (bottom left of keyboard) is being held down.

An extremely useful aid to the keypunch operator is the column indicator, a small red indicator, which can be viewed through the window near the center of the keypunch (see Fig. A.2). This marker indicates the card column that is about to be punched.

After completing the punching of a single card, hit the REL key; it's in the top row, near the right edge. The REL key causes the card that has just been punched to be released from the punching station, the second card to be moved to the punching station, and a third card to be fed from the card hopper to the card bed. The "just punched" card now rests near the center of the card bed, where it can be visually checked (if desired) by the keypunch operator.

A second card can now be punched. When all the data has been keyed, the card is released; at this time, the first card moves to the card stacker, the second card (the one just punched) moves from the punching station, the third card moves to the punching station, and a fourth card is fed. This process is continued until all the cards have been punched. By flipping up the CLEAR switch at the top right of the keyboard (Fig. A.1), you can move all cards on the card bed to the card stacker, and the job is finished.

Basic Operations: A Summary

1. Load cards.
2. Turn keypunch on.
3. Flip all control switches up.
4. Feed first card.
5. Feed a second card.
6. Punch the card.
   a) For numbers, hold down NUMERIC button.
   b) For alphabetic characters, just keypunch.
   c) Check column indicator for position.
7. When finished with card, depress REL key.
8. Visually check card.
9. Go back to step 6 and punch another card.
10. When finished, flip up CLEAR switch.

DUPLICATING A CARD

Programmers and keypunch operators often find it desirable to duplicate all or part of a card. Assume that you have just finished keypunching a card. Hit the REL key, moving this card to the middle position on the card bed and moving a second card to the punching station. Now, hold down the DUP key (top row, just to the right of center). You will get a column-by-column copy of the first card.

If only a portion of a card is to be duplicated, the DUP key can be "tapped," causing one column at a time to be copied; the column indicator can be used to determine which column will be punched next. If several consecutive columns, 1–25, for example, are to be duplicated, the DUP key can be held down until the column indicator shows that you are "getting close," at which time you can shift to a one-column-at-a-time mode of duplication.

PUNCHING A SINGLE CARD

To punch a single card, the AUTO FEED switch should be flipped down. This turns off the automatic card feed feature, meaning that no additional cards will be fed when the REL key is depressed.

Hit the FEED key, feeding one card to the card bed. Now hit the REG key (it's just below and slightly to the right of the FEED key); this moves the card to the punching position. Now you can punch this card. When you are finished, flip the CLEAR switch and retrieve the card from the stacker.

CORRECTING AN ERROR

Every keypunch operator makes errors. It's very frustrating to have to re-punch an entire card just because one character is incorrect, especially when you know that the process of rekeying the card may well produce additional errors. Don't. Take advantage of the DUP feature.

Start by turning the automatic feed feature off (flip the AUTO FEED switch down). Feed one card. Now, take the card containing the error and slip it into the center position of the card bed; if you look closely (Fig. A.2), you'll see a set of small openings at the top and bottom of the plastic card guides that provide an ideal path for slipping the card in. Once the card containing the error has been successfully inserted into the center position, hit the REG key; both cards should move into place. Carefully check and note the number of the card column containing the error. Using the column indicator as a guide, duplicate (DUP key) over as far as the column containing the error. Type the correct character or characters in the column(s) to be corrected and then duplicate the remainder of the card. Use the CLEAR switch to move both cards to the output stacker, visually check the new card for accuracy, and throw the error card away.

Correcting an Error: A Summary

1. Turn AUTO FEED off.
2. Feed one card.
3. Slip the error card into the center position.

4. Hit the REG key.

5. Make sure you know which column contains the error.

6. Duplicate over to the error column.

7. Punch the correct character or characters.

8. Duplicate the remainder of the card.

9. Flip the CLEAR lever.

ADDING A CHARACTER OR CHARACTERS TO A CARD

Beginners, be they programmers or keypunch operators, often make the error of simply forgetting to punch one or more characters; this often happens with the period at the end of a COBOL sentence or the semicolon at the end of a PL/I statement. Assuming that sufficient blank columns exist on the card, characters can be added without duplicating the whole thing.

Start by slipping the card to which characters are to be added into the rightmost position of the card bed; again, a convenient set of guides is provided for this purpose. Make sure the card lies flat on the card bed, and then hit the REG key. Now, simply space over to the desired column (using the column indicator as a guide), type the desired character or characters, and flip the CLEAR switch.

PROGRAM CARDS

The work done by a keypunch operator is often very repetitive, involving the punching of thousands of cards all having the same format. By using a program card, the operator can

1. automatically cause the keypunch to shift into a numeric mode, thus eliminating the need to depress the NUMERIC key while entering digits;

2. automatically duplicate selected fields;

3. automatically skip several columns, thus eliminating the need to skip one column at a time using the space bar.

The use of a program card saves keystrokes.

Program cards are prepared on a keypunch, using the following codes:

Code	Meaning
blank	Designates start of a manual numeric field; i.e., starts automatic numeric shift
0	Start of automatic duplication
1	Start of a manual alphabetic field
11	Start of an automatic skip field
12	Used to define the length of a numeric field
A	Used to define the length of an alphabetic field

To cite an example, let's say that you've been assigned the task of punching several thousand cards all having the following format:

Columns	Contents
1–9	Social Security number
10–20	Blank, unused
21–35	Customer name
36–50	Name of our firm; constant for all cards

We have a numeric field, a string of 11 consecutive unused columns, an alphabetic field, and a constant field that can be duplicated. A control card for this job (Fig. A.3) would contain the following:

1. A blank in column 1 marking the beginning of a numeric field.

2. Ampersands (&) in columns 2–9, indicating the length of this field. The ampersand (&), an uppercase P, is represented as a 12-punch.

3. An 11-punch (a minus sign) in column 10, marking the beginning of an automatic skip field.

4. The letter A in columns 11–20, marking the length of this skip field.

5. A 1 in column 21, marking the beginning of the customer name field (it's alphabetic).

6. The letter A in columns 22–35, indicating the length of this field.

7. A 0 in column 36, marking the beginning of an automatic duplication field.

8. The letter A in columns 37–50, indicating the length of this field.

9. An 11-punch in column 51 (the rest of the card is to be automatically skipped).

10. The letter A in columns 52–80, taking us to the end of the card.

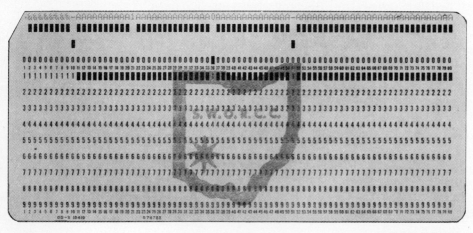

Figure A.3
A sample program card.

Program cards should be prepared one at a time. Switches are to be set as follows:

1. AUTO SKIP off (down).
2. AUTO FEED off.
3. PRINT off.
4. L Z PRINT off.
5. PROGRAM switch to ONE.

USING A PROGRAM CARD

In order to use a program card, the card must first be mounted on the program drum, which can be found behind the little window near the top center of the keypunch. Refer to Fig. A.2; the program drum is right above the column indicator. If you have access to a keypunch, lift the cover to get a better look.

At the left of the program drum is a set of starwheels that read the hole pattern on the program card. A switch, the program control lever, can be found just beneath the program drum area. This switch controls the starwheels. In the off position, the starwheels are up; in the on position, the wheels are down, contacting the program drum.

To insert a program card, turn the starwheels off and pull the program drum cylinder straight up; it should slide off the spindle with very little effort. Inside the drum is a lever called the clamping strip handle; turn it away from you (counterclockwise) to open the clamping strip. Slide the 80-edge of the card in under the clamping strip, making sure that the program card is straight; then turn the clamping strip handle back toward you, locking the card into place. Roll the card around the drum, making sure that it is straight and smooth; if you are inserting the card correctly, you should be able to read the printing on the card. Insert the 1-edge of the program card under the clamping strip, and turn the clamping strip handle toward you as far as it will go, thus locking the card into place. Replace the program drum on the spindle, engage the starwheels, and you are ready to go.

TWO PROGRAMS ON THE SAME CARD

Another problem sometimes faced by the keypunch operator is the job for which cards must be punched to one of two different formats. Rather than having the operator change control cards each time the format changes, two different programs can be punched into the same card, one in the top six rows and the other in the bottom six rows. The program select switch (PROG SEL) allows the operator to indicate which of these two programs should be in control; ONE is for the top program and TWO is for the bottom program.

OTHER FEATURES

One switch we have not yet mentioned is the one labeled PRINT. This switch turns the printer on or off. Certain applications call for the punching of confidential information (a wage rate, for example); such information might well be punched with the printer off.

Another feature sometimes used by professional keypunch operators is left zero punching. Let's say that we have a numeric field five columns long. What if the number 8 is to be punched? Using all five columns, the operator would punch 00008.

Using the left zero feature, the operator would simply punch the digit 8 and hit the LEFT ZERO key. The data, rather than being punched directly into the card, is placed in a buffer; when the LEFT ZERO key is depressed, nonsignificant zeros are added to the left and the card field is punched automatically. The left zero feature requires the use of a program card. The L Z PRINT switch is used to control printing when this feature is used.

THE AUTO SKIP DUP switch controls another special feature. This one allows the operator to automatically duplicate a card up to the column containing an error. A keypunch operator, like a typist, often senses that an error has occurred as soon as the wrong key is depressed. The automatic skip duplication feature allows the operator to automatically duplicate the card over to this point, correct the error, and continue punching.

GLOSSARY

Sources

1. *American National Standard Vocabulary for Information Processing.* American National Standards Institute (1970), Publication number ANSI X3.12-1970.

2. *A Data Processing Glossary.* IBM Publication C20-1699.

3. *Webster's New World Dictionary of the American Language,* College Edition. Cleveland, Ohio: World Publishing.

4. Weik, Martin H., *Standard Dictionary of Computers and Information Processing,* Revised Second Edition, Rochelle Park, New Jersey: Hayden Book Company, Inc., 1977.

The sources are listed in order of preference: A definition was first sought in the ANSI standard, with the other sources being consulted only when no definition was present in this primary source. The source of each definition is indicated as follows: (ANSI), (IBM), (Webster), or (Weik). If no source is indicated, the definition is the author's.

Abacus An early computing device on which numbers are represented by the pattern of a series of beads on a number of strings. Still in common use in many parts of the world.

Absolute address (ANSI) (1) An address that is permanently assigned by the machine designer to a storage location. (2) A pattern of characters that identifies a unique storage location without further modification. (3) Synonymous with machine address, specific address.

Access arm (ANSI) A part of a disk storage unit that is used to hold one or more reading and writing heads.

Access method (IBM) Any of the data management techniques available to the user for transferring data between main storage and an input/output device.

Access time (ANSI) (1) The time interval between the instant at which data are called for from a storage device and the instant delivery begins. (2) The time interval between the instant at which data are requested to be stored and the instant at which storage is started.

Accounts payable A file of bills representing payments owed to others. The data processing operation of handling the accounts payable, including the paying of bills and the recording, tabulating, and summarizing of these payments.

Accounts receivable A file of payments due a firm. The data processing operation of handling accounts payable, including preparing bills, distributing bills to customers, recording payments and amounts due, and tabulating and summarizing this data.

Acoustical coupler A device that converts digital signals into acoustic signals suitable for transmission over telephone lines.

Acronym (IBM) A word formed from the first letter or letters of the words in a name, term, or phrase; e.g., SAGE from semi-automatic ground

environnent and ALGOL from algorithmic language.

Activity (IBM) A term used to indicate that a record in a master file is used, altered, or referred to.

Address (ANSI) (1) An identification, as represented by a name, label, or number, for a register, location in storage, or any other data source or destination such as the location of a station in a communication network. (2) Loosely, any part of an instruction that specifies the location of an operand for the instruction.

Aiken, Howard Developer of the MARK I, the first modern computer.

Algorithm (ANSI) A prescribed set of well-defined rules or processes for the solution of a problem in a finite number of steps, e.g., a full statement of an arithmetic procedure for evaluating $\sin x$ to a stated precision.

Alphabetic data Data that is composed exclusively of letters of the alphabet and the blank character. Occasionally, the period and the comma are also used.

Analog (Weik) (1) Pertaining to a device that represents numerical quantities by means of physical variables. (2) Pertaining to representation of information by means of physical quantities that are continuously variable.

Analysis (ANSI) The methodical investigation of a problem and the separation of the problem into smaller related units for further detailed study.

Analytical engine A hypothetical mechanical computer developed by Charles Babbage in the mid-1800s.

Application program A program that performs a user function. Contrast with system program. For example, the program that actually computes and prints paychecks would be an application program, while the program that compiles the payroll program from COBOL to machine level would be a system program.

Arabic numerals Common, base 10 numbers.

Arithmetic and logical unit The portion of a central processing unit in which arithmetic and logical operations are performed.

ASCII (American National Standard Code for Information Interchange) (ANSI) The standard code, using a coded character set consisting of 7-bit coded characters (8 bits including the parity check), used for information interchange among data processing systems, communication systems, and associated equipment.

Assemble (ANSI) To prepare a machine language program from a symbolic language program by substituting absolute operation codes for symbolic operation codes and absolute or relocatable addresses for symbolic addresses.

Assembler (ANSI) A computer program that assembles.

Assembler language The source language for an assembler.

Assignment statement A statement, written in the FORTRAN language, to indicate a computational step in a program.

Asynchronous (IBM) Without regular time relationship.

Atanasoff, Dr. John Vincent Inventor of an early digital computer (1939); regarded by many as the inventor of the first true digital computer.

Auxiliary storage (ANSI) A storage that supplements other storage. Contrast with main storage.

Babbage, Charles A computer pioneer who developed the difference engine and who visualized an analytical engine in the mid-1800s. Both machines were commercial failures.

Background (Author's definition, based on ANSI) The partition or region of a multiprogramming system holding lower priority programs, which are executed only when higher priority programs are not using the system.

Backup A procedure, technique, or hardware intended to be used in an emergency to help recover lost or destroyed data or to keep a system running.

Bar-code scanner A device used to read a bar-code by means of reflected light, such as the scanners that read the Universal Product Code on supermarket products.

Base (ANSI) (1) A reference value. (2) A number that is multiplied by itself as many times as indicated by an exponent. (3) Same as radix.

BASIC Acronym for Beginners All-purpose Symbolic Instruction Code; a programming language.

Batch processing (ANSI) (1) Pertaining to the technique of executing a set of computer programs such that each is completed before the next program of the set is started. (2) Pertaining to the sequential input of computer programs or data. (3) Loosely, the execution of computer programs serially.

Batch processing (IBM) A systems approach to processing where a number of similar input items are grouped for processing during the same machine run.

Baud (ANSI) A unit of signaling speed equal to the number of discrete conditions or signal events per second. For example, one baud equals one-half dot cycle per second in Morse code, one bit per second in a train of binary signals, and one 3-bit value per second in a train of signals each of which can assume one of eight different states.

BCD (ANSI) Binary-coded decimal notation.

Billing The data processing operation involving the tabulation, preparation, and distribution of bills for services rendered or products delivered.

Binary (ANSI) (1) Pertaining to a characteristic or property involving a selection, choice, or condition in which there are two possibilities. (2) Pertaining to the number representation system with a radix of two.

Binary coded decimal (ANSI) Positional notation in which the individual decimal digits expressing a number in decimal notation are each represented by a binary numeral, e.g., the number twenty-three is represented by 0010 0011 in the 8-4-2-1 type of binary-coded decimal notation and by 10111 in binary notation.

Binary number system (ANSI) Fixed radix notation in which the radix is two.

Bit (ANSI) A binary digit.

Block (ANSI) (1) A set of things such as words, characters, or digits, handled as a unit. (2) A collection of contiguous records recorded as a unit. Blocks are separated by block gaps and each block may contain one or more records. (3) A group of bits or *n*-ary digits, transmitted as a unit. An encoding procedure is generally applied to the group of bits or *n*-ary digits for error-control purposes. (4) A group of contiguous characters recorded as a unit.

Block gap See Interblock gap.

Block multiplexer A type of data channel that multiplexes or overlaps the operation of a number of high-speed I/O devices.

Blocking (IBM) Combining two or more records into one block.

Blocking factor The number of logical records in a single physical record or block.

Boole, George Developer of the system of logic that has come to be known as Boolean algebra.

Bootstrap (ANSI) A technique or device designed to bring itself into a desired state by means of its own action, e.g., a machine routine whose first few instructions are sufficient to bring the rest of itself into the computer from an input device.

Branch (ANSI) (1) A set of instructions that are executed between two successive decision instructions. (2) To select a branch as in (1). (3) A direct path joining two nodes of a network or graph. (4) Loosely, a conditional jump.

Break point (IBM) A place in a routine specified by an instruction, instruction digit, or other condition, where the routine may be interrupted by external intervention or by a monitor routine.

Breakeven point The point at which the total cost of a fixed-cost alternative and the total cost of a variable-cost alternative are equal.

Budget An estimate, target, or limit placed on expenditures.

Buffer (ANSI) A routine or storage used to compensate for a difference in rate of flow of data, or time of occurrence of events, when transmitting data from one device to another.

Buffered keypunch A keypunch containing a buffer. In typical operation, data is keyed as rapidly as the operator can type into the buffer, and punched into the card from the buffer, thus allowing the operator to work at a pace somewhat faster than that imposed by the punch mechanism. On some buffered keypunches, the operator can check data for accuracy before punching a card.

Bug (ANSI) A mistake or malfunction.

Bulk memory See Auxiliary storage.

Bulk storage See Auxiliary storage.

Burst mode Transferring data between a single high-speed I/O device and main memory via a selector channel.

Bus line (Weik) One or more conductors used for transmitting signals or power from one or more sources to one or more destinations. (Author) The cables used to connect the internal components of a computer.

Byte (ANSI) A sequence of adjacent binary digits operated upon as a unit and usually shorter than a computer word.

Calculating Performing arithmetic operations.

Calculation specifications In an RPG program, the source statements that specify the calculations to be performed by a program.

Calculator (ANSI) (1) A data processor especially suitable for performing arithmetic operations that require frequent intervention by a human operator. (2) A device capable of performing arithmetic. (3) A calculator, as in (2), that requires frequent manual intervention. (4) Generally and historically, a device for carrying out logic and arithmetic digital operations of any kind.

CALL A statement or macro instruction, available in most compiler and assembler languages, that performs the function of linking between a main program and a subroutine.

Card column (ANSI) A single line of punch positions parallel to the short edge of a 3¼-by-7⅜-inch punched card.

Card punch (IBM) A device to record information in cards by punching holes in the cards to represent letters, digits, and special characters.

Card reader (IBM) A device that senses and translates into internal form the holes in punched cards.

Card row (ANSI) A single line of punch positions parallel to the long edge of a 3¼-by-7⅜-inch punched card.

Cassette A small, self-contained volume of magnetic tape used for data storage. Similar to a sound-recording cassette.

Catalog (ANSI) An ordered compilation of item descriptions and sufficient information to afford access to the items.

Cathode ray tube terminal (IBM) A device that presents data in visual form by means of controlled electron beams.

Central processing unit (ANSI) A unit of a computer that includes the circuits controlling the interpretation and execution of instructions. Synonymous with mainframe.

Chain printer (ANSI) A printer in which the type slugs are carried by the links of a revolving chain.

Channel (ANSI) (1) A path along which signals can be sent, e.g., data channel, output channel. (2) The portion of a storage medium that is accessible to a given reading or writing station, e.g., track, band. (3) In communication, a means of one-way transmission.

Character (ANSI) A letter, digit, or other symbol that is used as part of the organization, control, or representation of data.

Character printer (ANSI) A device that prints a single character at a time. Contrast with line printer.

Checkpoint (ANSI) A place in a routine where a check, or a recording of data for restart purposes, is performed.

CLOSE An instruction or macroinstruction, common to many languages, whose function is to perform end-of-program activities on a given file and to return the physical device to the use of the system.

COBOL (ANSI) (COmmon Business Oriented Language) A business data processing language.

Code (ANSI) (1) A set of unambiguous rules specifying the way in which data may be represented, e.g., the set of correspondences in the standard code for information interchange. Synonymous with coding scheme. (2) In telecommunications, a system of rules and conventions according to which the signals for representing data can be formed, transmitted, received, and processed. (3) In data processing, to represent data or a computer program in a symbolic form that can be accepted by a data processor. (4) To write a routine.

Coding The act of actually writing program statements in a source language.

Collator (IBM) A device to collate sets of punched cards or other documents into a sequence.

Comments Verbal explanations added to a program for purposes of documentation.

Communication link (ANSI) The physical means of connecting one location to another for the purpose of transmitting and receiving data.

Communication medium See Communication link.

Compile (ANSI) To prepare a machine language program from a computer program written in another programming language by making use of the overall logic structure of the program, or generating more than one machine instruction for each symbolic statement, or both, as well as performing the function of an assembler.

Compiler (ANSI) A program that compiles.

Compute-bound A program or a computer system that is restricted or limited by the speed of the CPU.

Computer (ANSI) A data processor that can perform substantial computation, including numerous arithmetic or logic operations, without intervention by a human operator during the run.

Computer crime Any criminal activity in which the computer is the victim or an accomplice.

Computer data processing Automated data processing performed with the aid of a computer.

Computer network (ANSI) A complex consisting of two or more interconnected computers.

Computer operator An individual who operates a computer.

Computer output microfilm (1) An output device that records character or graphic data on microfilm. (2) The medium used on such a system.

Computer program (ANSI) A series of instructions or statements, in a form acceptable to a computer, prepared in order to achieve a certain result.

Computer system The hardware, software, and procedural components that must function together in order that a computer might actually process data into information.

Concurrent (ANSI) Pertaining to the occurrence of two or more events or activities within the same specified interval of time.

Connect time The time interval from the initial connection to the final breaking of a communication.

Constant (IBM) A fixed or invariable value or data item.

Control card The first card in an RPG source deck. Defines a number of compiler options.

Control unit An electronic device, intermediate between a computer and an I/O device, that performs such functions as buffering and standard interface.

Control unit portion of CPU (ANSI: instruction control unit) In a digital computer, those parts that effect the retrieval of instructions in proper sequence, the interpretation of each instruction, and the application of the proper signals to the arithmetic unit and other parts in accordance with this interpretation.

Core memory (IBM) A form of high-speed storage using magnetic cores. See also Magnetic core.

Core storage See Core memory.

CPU (ANSI) Central processing unit.

CRT See Cathode ray tube terminal.

Cryptography (Webster) (1) The art of writing in or deciphering secret writing or code. (2) A system of secret writing.

Cycle stealing Taking an occasional machine cycle from a CPU's regular activities in order to control things such as input or output operations. Commonly used on minicomputers.

Cylinder One position of a disk access arm, allowing access to a number of tracks.

Data (ANSI) (1) A representation of facts, concepts, or instructions in a formalized manner suitable for communication, interpretation, or processing by humans or automatic means. (2) Any representations such as characters or analog quantities to which meaning is or might be assigned.

Data base (ANSI: data bank) A comprehensive collection of libraries of data.

Data base management Software, hardware, and organizational techniques designed to manage a data base.

Data cartridge A small, self-contained reel of magnetic tape used to store data.

Data cell A mass storage device that utilizes strips of magnetic tape housed in a rotating cylinder.

Data collection (IBM) The act of bringing data from one or more points to a central point.

Data communication (IBM) The transmission of data from one point to another.

Data communication consultant An expert in the design, planning, and implementation of a data communication system.

Data compression A technique for minimizing the amount of data actually transmitted over a communication line by removing blanks at the sending end of the line and replacing blanks at the receiving end.

DATA DIVISION The section of a COBOL program that includes detailed specifications for allocating main memory to the program, describing the detailed format of each data record and all work areas.

Data entry Introducing data into a data processing or information processing system.

Data entry terminal A terminal for entering data.

Data format A position-by-position description of each of the data fields in a record.

Data management (IBM) A general term that collectively describes those functions of the control program that provide access to data sets, enforce data storage conventions, and regulate the use of input/output devices.

Data manipulation Data processing, particularly the calculation steps.

Data processing (ANSI) The execution of a systematic sequence of operations performed upon data. Synonymous with information processing.

Data processing card See punched card.

Data processing system (IBM) A network of machine components capable of accepting information, processing it according to a plan, and producing the desired results.

Data set (IBM) A device that performs the modulation/demodulation and control functions necessary to provide compatibility between business machines and communications facilities.

Data set A general term for a data file or program library.

Data transfer time The time required to transfer data from point A to point B.

Data transmission (IBM) The sending of data from one part of a system to another part.

Deblocking Separating blocked data into individual logical records.

Debug (ANSI) To detect, locate, and remove mistakes from a routine or malfunctions from a computer.

Decimal number system (ANSI) A fixed radix notation where the radix is ten.

Decision table (ANSI) A table of all contingencies that are to be considered in a description of a problem, together with the actions to be taken.

Demodulation (IBM) The process of retrieving intelligence (data) from a modulated carrier wave; the reverse of modulation.

Density (ANSI: recording density) The number of bits in a single linear track measured per unit of length of the recording medium.

Detail line On a data processing report, one line of output that contains information from exactly one record of input. Contrast with summary line.

Detailed planning In the program development or systems analysis process, the step dealing with the planning and definition of a specific, detailed solution to a problem.

Dial-up (IBM) The use of a dial or pushbutton telephone to initiate a station-to-station telephone call.

Difference engine A mechanical calculating device developed by Charles Babbage.

Digit (ANSI) A symbol that represents one of the non-negative integers smaller than the radix.

Digit-times-place-value rule A rule for determining the value of a number written in any number system by summing the products of each digit and its place value.

Digital (Weik) Pertaining to data in the form of digits.

Digital computer (ANSI) (1) A computer in which discrete representation of data is mainly used. (2) A computer that operates on discrete data by performing arithmetic and logic processes on these data.

Digitizer A device for converting graphical data into digital form.

Direct access (ANSI) (1) Pertaining to the process of obtaining data from, or placing data into, storage where the time required for such access is independent of the location of the data most recently obtained or placed in storage. (2) Pertaining to a storage device in which the access time is effectively independent of the location of the data. (3) Synonymous with random access.

Disk, magnetic (ANSI: magnetic disk) A flat circular plate with a magnetic surface on which data can be stored by selective magnetization of portions of the flat surface.

Disk pack A stack of magnetic disks.

Diskette A small disk pack.

Distributed data processing Decentralized data processing.

Documentation (ANSI) (1) The creating, collecting, organizing, storing, citing, and disseminating of documents or the information recorded in documents. (2) A collection of documents or information on a given subject.

Drum, magnetic (ANSI: magnetic drum) A right circular cylinder with a magnetic surface on which data can be stored by selective magnetization of portions of the curved surface.

Dynamic memory management See Dynamic storage allocation.

Dynamic storage allocation (ANSI) A storage allocation technique in which the location of computer programs and data is determined by criteria applied at the moment of need.

EBCDIC (Extended Binary Coded Decimal Interchange Code) An eight-bit code for representing characters.

Eckert, J. Presper Along with John W. Mauchly, the developer of the ENIAC, the first electronic computer. Later worked on developing the EDVAC and the UNIVAC computers.

EDVAC One of the first stored-program computers.

END statement In many computer programming languages, a statement to indicate the physical and/or logical end of a program.

ENIAC The Electronic Numerical Integrator and Calculator; the first electronic computer.

ENVIRONMENT DIVISION In a COBOL program, the section of the program where linkages to input and output devices are coded.

Environmental constraints Temperature and humidity limits that must be maintained for the proper operation of a computer.

Execution The act of carrying out an instruction or performing a routine.

Execution time (E-time) The portion of a CPU's cycle during which an instruction is executed.

Expression (IBM) A source-language combination of one or more operators.

Feasibility study An early step in the system development process aimed at determining if a proposed project is possible and practical.

Field (ANSI) In a record, a specified area used for a particular category of data, e.g., a group of card columns used to represent a wage rate, a set of bit locations in a computer word used to express the address of the operand.

File (ANSI) A collection of related records treated as a unit.

File description specifications That portion of an RPG program where the linkage to physical files is coded.

File maintenance (ANSI) The activity of keeping a file up to date by adding, changing, or deleting data.

Filename The logical name assigned, within a compiler- or assembler-level program, to a file.

File organization (1) The physical arrangement of records on a data storage device. (2) The logical set of rules used to physically arrange data. (3) Loosely, the access method used to read or write a file.

File processing Creating, utilizing, or maintaining files.

File ring A small plastic ring that may be inserted into the back of a magnetic tape volume. With the ring in place, the volume can be used for output; without the ring, the tape is limited to input operations only.

File size The number of records in a file.

Firmware Electronic circuits, typically arranged in the form of a card or a board, that can easily be added to or deleted from a computer's electronics. Firmware is often used to house the computer's instruction set.

First generation (IBM) A computer utilizing vacuum tube components.

Fixed cost A cost that remains the same for all levels of activity.

Fixed logic In an RPG program, certain logical functions such as basic input and output and checking for break points that are performed without a need for actual coding by the programmer.

Fixed-partition memory management A memory management technique in which main memory is subdivided into a number of fixed-length partitions.

Floppy disk A small disk of relatively limited storage capacity often used on a minicomputer or an intelligent terminal. See also Diskette.

Flowchart (ANSI) A graphical representation for the definition, analysis, or solution of a problem, in which symbols are used to represent operations, data flow, equipment, etc.

Foreground The partition in a multi-programming system containing the high-priority application program.

FORMAT statement In FORTRAN, a statement used to describe the precise format of an input or output record.

FORTRAN (ANSI) (FORmula TRANslating system) A language primarily used to express computer programs by arithmetic formulas.

Front-end device A transmission control unit capable of controlling polling and buffering independent of the CPU.

Full duplex (ANSI: duplex) In communications, pertaining to a simultaneous two way independent transmission in both directions. Contrast with half duplex.

General-purpose computer (ANSI) A computer that is designed to handle a wide variety of problems.

Generation data set (IBM: generation data group) A collection of successive, historically related data sets.

GO TO statement In many compiler languages, an unconditional branch.

Half duplex (ANSI) In communications, pertaining to an alternate, one way at a time, independent transmission. Contrast with duplex.

Handshaking (IBM) Exchange of predetermined signals when a connection is established between two data sets.

Hardware (ANSI) Physical equipment, as opposed to the computer program or method of use, e.g., mechanical, magnetic, electrical, or electronic devices. Contrast with software.

Hexadecimal number system (ANSI: sexadecimal) Pertaining to the numeration system with a radix of sixteen.

Hierarchy chart A diagram showing the relationship among modules in a large program.

HIPO Hierarchy and Input/Processing/Output. The use of hierarchy charts in combination with input/processing/output charts for planning and/or documentation.

Hollerith, Herman Developer of the first commercially successful punched card data processing systems in the late 1800s.

Hopper, Grace One of the first of the software pioneers, she was instrumental in the development of the COBOL programming language.

IDENTIFICATION DIVISION In COBOL, a section of the program set aside for key documentation such as the program name, program purpose, programmer name, and so on.

IF statement In most compiler languages, a statement for performing logical comparisons and making decisions based on the results of these comparisons.

IF . . . THEN . . . ELSE logic A form of logical test supported in many languages and consisting of three parts: a condition, a first conditional statement or series of statements usually preceded by the word THEN, and a second conditional statement or series of statements usually preceded by the word ELSE. If the condition is true, then the first conditional statement or group of statements is executed; if the condition is false, then the second statement or set of statements is executed.

Impact printer A printer that forms characters by physically striking a ribbon and paper.

Implementation The act of finishing or installing a program or a system.

Independent software vendor A business concern, other than a hardware vendor, that offers computer programs for sale or lease.

Index (ANSI) (1) An ordered reference list of the contents of a file or document together with keys or reference notations for identification or location of those contents. (2) To prepare a list as in (1).

Indexed sequential A file organization technique in which data are placed on a file in sequence and an index is maintained, thus allowing both sequential and direct access. This technique is designed to be used on magnetic disk exclusively.

Indicator In RPG, a program-controlled switch used to indicate conditions or states of a program.

Information (ANSI) The meaning that a human assigns to data by means of the known conventions used in their representation.

Information processing (ANSI) See Data processing.

Information processing utility A business concern that offers numerous computing facilities including programming, software, systems analysis, computer time, etc., for sale or lease.

Initial program load (ANSI: initial program loader) The procedure that causes the initial part of an operating system or other program to be loaded such that the system can then proceed under its own control.

Input (ANSI) Pertaining to a device, process, or channel involved in the insertion of data or states, or to the data or states involved.

Input device (ANSI) The device or collective set of devices used for conveying data into another device.

Input specifications In RPG, that portion of a program concerned with describing the contents of the input records.

INPUT statement In BASIC, a program statement for reading data from the input terminal or a card reader.

Input/output (ANSI) Pertaining to either input or output, or both.

Instruction (ANSI) A statement that specifies an operation and the values or locations of its operands.

Instruction control unit See Control unit portion of CPU.

Instruction set (ANSI: instruction repertoire) The set of operations that can be represented in a given operation code.

Instruction time (I-time) The portion of a CPU cycle during which an instruction is fetched and decoded.

Integer number In FORTRAN and other computational languages, a whole number with no fractional part. Internally, integer numbers are usually stored as pure binary numbers.

Integrated adapter A hardware device, built into the CPU, that performs the functions of a channel by stealing cycles.

Integrated data base A data base whose parts are linked or otherwise integrated.

Integration In file processing, the degree of relationship between files.

Intelligent terminal A terminal with some logical capability.

Interblock gap (ANSI: block gap) An area on a data medium used to indicate the end of a block or record.

Interface (ANSI) A shared boundary.

Interpreter (ANSI) (1) A computer program that translates and executes each source language statement before translating and executing the next one. (2) A device that prints on a punched card the data already punched in the card.

Interrecord gap (ANSI: record gap) An area on a data medium used to indicate the end of a block or record.

Interrupt (ANSI) To stop a process in such a way that it can be resumed.

Inventory control A data processing operation concerned with keeping track of inventory.

I/O (ANSI) An abbreviation for input/output.

I/O-bound A program or computer system that is restricted or limited in processing speed by its I/O devices.

I/O device An input or output device.

I/O device allocation Controlling the allocation of I/O devices among the several programs in a multiprogramming system.

IPL See initial program load.

IPO chart Input/Processing/Output chart. A chart listing, for a single program module, the inputs, necessary processing steps, and outputs. Often used with a hierarchy chart for planning and/or documentation.

Jacquard, Joseph Marie Inventor of an automatic weaving machine or loom controlled by punched cards (1804).

Job (ANSI) A specified group of tasks prescribed as a unit of work for a computer. By extension, a job usually includes all necessary computer programs, linkages, files, and instructions to the operating system.

JOB card or **JOB statement** (IBM) The control statement in the input job stream that identifies the beginning of a series of job control statements for a single job.

Job control language A set of programmer generated commands supporting communication with the operating system.

Job control statement (ANSI) A statement in a job that is used in identifying the job or describing its requirements to the operating system.

K (ANSI) (1) An abbreviation for the prefix kilo; i.e., 1000 in decimal notation. (2) Loosely, when referring to storage capacity, two to the tenth power, 1024 in decimal notation.

Key (ANSI) One or more characters within an item of data that are used to identify it or control its use.

Key field A field that serves as a key.

Key-to-disk Hardware designed to transfer data entered via a keyboard to magnetic disk or diskette. Also, the process of transferring data from a keyboard to magnetic disk.

Key-to-tape Hardware designed to transfer data entered via a keyboard to magnetic tape. Also, the process of transferring data from a keyboard to magnetic tape.

Keyboard terminal A terminal through which data can be entered to a data processing system by means of a typewriterlike keyboard.

Keypunch (ANSI) A keyboard-actuated device that punches holes in a card to represent data.

Label (ANSI) One or more characters used to identify a statement or an item of data in a computer program.

Label A header or leader on a volume of magnetic tape or on a direct access device containing information identifying the file, files, or records stored thereon.

Ledger Accounting books and records; often, a firm's master accounting record.

Leibniz, Gottfried Wilhelm Inventor of the first mechanical calculator capable of multiplication (1673).

LET statement In BASIC, a program statement that defines one or more operations which are to be performed on data.

Library (ANSI) (1) A collection of organized information used for study and reference. (2) A collection of related files.

Line A communication medium connecting two or more points.

Line printer (ANSI) A device that prints all the characters of a line as a unit. Contrast with character printer.

Link (Webster) To join together . . .

Linkage editor (IBM) A program that produces a load module by transforming object modules into a format that is acceptable to fetch, combining separately produced object modules and previously processed load modules into a single load module, resolving symbolic cross references among them, replacing, deleting, and adding control sections automatically on request and providing overlay facilities for modules requesting them.

Load module (IBM) (1) The output of the linkage editor. (2) A program in a format suitable for loading into main storage for execution.

Loadpoint marker On magnetic tape, a reflective strip, visible to the operator, marking the beginning of the area of the tape actually used to store data.

Local Connected to a computer by regular electric wires. In close proximity to the computer. Contrast with Remote.

Locking (file) Preventing access to a file or a record.

Logical record (ANSI) A collection of items independent of their physical environment. Portions of the same logical record may be located in different physical records.

Logging Maintaining records of computer use.

Long-range planning Business planning for the future, usually involving a period of time 1 to 5 years in the future.

Loop (ANSI) A sequence of instructions that is executed repeatedly until a terminal condition prevails.

LSI Acronym for Large Scale Integration; a technique for manufacturing electronic devices that integrates many circuit elements on a single chip at very high density.

Machine cycle The basic operating cycle of a CPU during which a single instruction is fetched, decoded, and executed.

Machine-level program A computer program in binary form capable of being executed on a computer.

Magnetic bubble memory A type of storage in which data are stored as a series of bubbles in a thin substrate.

Magnetic core (ANSI) A configuration of magnetic material that is, or is intended to be, placed in a spatial relationship to current-carrying conductors and whose magnetic properties are essential to its use. It may be used to concentrate an induced magnetic field as in a transformer induction coil or armature, to retain a magnetic polarization for the purpose of storing data, or for its nonlinear properties as in a logic element. It may be made of such material as iron, iron oxide, or ferrite and in such shapes as wire, tapes, toroids, rods, or thin films.

Magnetic strip card A card, usually a plastic card of wallet size, with a strip of magnetic tape on one surface. A good example is a bank credit card.

Magnetic tape (ANSI) (1) A tape with a magnetic surface on which data can be stored by selective polarization of portions of the surface. (2) A tape of magnetic materials used as the constituent in some forms of magnetic cores.

Mainframe (ANSI) Same as Central processing unit.

Main memory See Main storage.

Main storage (ANSI) The general-purpose storage of a computer. Usually, main storage can be accessed directly by the operating registers. Contrast with Auxiliary storage.

Mainline The primary route of logical flow through a program.

Maintenance (ANSI) Any activity intended to eliminate faults or to keep hardware or programs in satisfactory working condition, including tests, measurements, replacements, adjustments, and repairs.

Management information system (ANSI) (1) Management performed with the aid of automatic data processing. Abbreviated MIS. (2) An information system designed to aid in the performance of management functions.

Manual data processing Data processing by manual means.

MARK I The first modern computer; developed by Aiken.

Mark sense (ANSI: mark sensing) The electrical sensing of manually recorded conductive marks on a nonconductive surface.

Mass storage See Auxiliary storage and Bulk memory.

Mass storage device A hardware device on which amounts of data are stored on individually addressable data cartridges or cells.

Master file (ANSI) A file that is either relatively permanent or that is treated as an authority in a particular job.

Master file update The process of maintaining a master file.

Matrix printer A printer that forms characters by printing a pattern of dots.

Mauchly, John W. With Eckert, developer of the ENIAC, the first electronic digital computer.

Megabyte One million bytes; more accurately, 1000K bytes.

Memory See Storage.

Memory management The allocation of main memory space on a multiprogramming system.

Merge (IBM) To combine two or more sets of items into one, usually in a specified sequence.

Message characters Characters that precede and follow a message transmitted over a communication line.

Message switching The process of transferring messages between various communication media so as to ensure accurate transmission from the correct source to the correct destination.

MICR (ANSI) Magnetic Ink Character Recognition.

Microcomputer (Weik) A complete general- or special-purpose electronic digital computer, with central processing unit, storage, and I/O bus, usually constructed of one LSI chip, with up to 16,000 32-bit words of high-speed internal (main) storage. (Author) The typical micro has an 8-bit word.

Microprocessor (Weik) (1) The arithmetic, logic, or control unit of a minicomputer, usually constructed of a single LSI chip. (2) A processor that executes the microinstructions of a microprogram.

Microprogramming (IBM) Programming with microinstructions.

Microsecond One millionth of one second.

Microwave (IBM) Any electromagnetic wave in the radio frequency spectrum above 890 megacycles.

Millisecond One thousandth of one second.

Minicomputer A small, digital computer.

Mnemonic code (ANSI: mnemonic symbol) A symbol chosen to assist the human memory, e.g., an abbreviation such as "MPY" for "multiply."

Modem (ANSI) (MOdulator-DEModulator) A device that modulates and demodulates signals transmitted over communication facilities.

Modular programming Writing a program as a series of separate but linked blocks of logic.

Modulation (IBM) The process by which some characteristic of one wave is varied in accordance with another wave or signal. This technique is used in data sets and modems to make business machine signals compatible with communications facilities.

Monitor (ANSI) Software or hardware that observes, supervises, controls, or verifies the operations of a system.

Multiplex (ANSI) To interleave or simultaneously transmit two or more messages on a single channel.

Multiplexer channel A data channel which multiplexes or overlaps the operation of two or more low-speed I/O devices.

Multiprogramming (ANSI) Pertaining to the concurrent execution of two or more programs by a computer.

Nanosecond One billionth of one second.

Napier, John Published the first table of logarithms in 1614.

Napier's bones A primitive slide rule developed by Napier.

Network (ANSI: computer network) A complex consisting of two or more interconnected computers.

Network (IBM) (1) A series of points interconnected by communications channels. (A private line network is a network confined to the use of one customer, while a switched telephone network is a network of telephone lines normally used for dialed telephone calls.) (2) The interconnection of electrical components.

Noise (ANSI) (1) Random variations of one or more characteristics of any entity such as voltage, current, or data. (2) A random signal of known statistical properties of amplitude, distribution, and spectral density. (3) Loosely, any disturbance tending to interfere with the normal operation of a device or system.

Nonimpact printer A printer that forms images through electrostatic or other nonimpact means.

Nucleus (IBM) That portion of the control program that must always be present in main storage. Also, the main storage area used by the nucleus and other transient control program routines.

Number system (ANSI) Loosely, a number representation system.

Numeric data Data consisting exclusively of digits; occasionally, in some languages, a decimal point is also permitted. Data whose individual digits are written in the positional notation of some number system.

Numeric punch A punch in any one of the rows 0 through 9 on a punched card.

Object code (ANSI) Output from a compiler or assembler that is itself executable machine code or is suitable for processing to produce executable machine code.

Object deck An object module in punched card form.

Object module (ANSI) A module that is the output of an assembler or compiler and is input to a linkage editor.

OCR (ANSI) Optical Character Recognition.

Octal number system (ANSI: octal) Pertaining to the number representation system with a radix of eight.

Off-line (ANSI) Pertaining to equipment or devices not under control of the central processing unit.

On-line (ANSI) (1) Pertaining to equipment or devices under control of the central processing unit. (2) Pertaining to a user's ability to interact with a computer.

OPEN An instruction or macroinstruction common to many languages whose function is to prepare a specific physical device and/or file for I/O.

Operand (ANSI) That which is operated upon. An operand is usually identified by an address part of an instruction.

Operating system (ANSI) Software that controls the execution of computer programs and that may provide scheduling, debugging, input/output control, accounting, compilation, storage assignment, data management, and related services.

Operation code (or op code) (ANSI) A code that represents specific operations.

Operator In a compiler language, a symbol that represents an operation to be performed, such as + for addition or * for multiplication.

Operator, computer The person who operates a computer.

Optical character recognition (ANSI) The machine identification of printed characters through the use of light-sensitive devices.

Optimum (Webster) The most favorable degree, condition, amount, etc.

Output (ANSI) Pertaining to a device, process, or channel involved in an output process, or to the data or states involved.

Output device (ANSI) The device or collective set of devices used for conveying data out of another device.

Output specifications In RPG, that part of a program concerned with describing the output records.

Overflow (ANSI) That portion of the result of an operation that exceeds the capacity of the intended unit of storage.

Overhead Support, as opposed to direct, functions.

Page A fixed-length portion of a program or data that can be transferred between main memory and a secondary storage device on a virtual memory system. Also, a fixed-length portion of a program that can be loaded into main memory and addressed independently of the rest of the program.

Page printer (Weik) A printer in which an entire page of characters is composed and determined within the printer prior to printing and the entire page is printed during a single cycle of operation, such as in a xerographic printer or in a cathode ray tube, camera, and film printer.

Paper tape An input/output medium, similar to magnetic tape, on which data can be recorded as a pattern of punched holes.

Paragraph name In COBOL, a logical name or label assigned to a block of logic in the PROCEDURE DIVISION.

Parallel run (Weik) Operating a newly developed system concurrently with the system that it is to replace, until there is sufficient confidence in the new system's performance to justify discontinuing the old system.

Parity bit (ANSI) A check bit appended to an array of binary digits to make the sum of all the binary digits, including the check bit, always odd or always even.

Partition A portion of a computer's main memory set aside to hold a single program on a fixed-partition memory management system.

Pascal, Blaise Inventor of the first mechanical adding machine.

Password (Webster) A secret word or phrase used by the members of a military unit, etc., to identify themselves, as in passing a guard. (Author) A secret word or phrase used to identify a user to a computer system.

Payroll A data processing operation concerned with computing and distributing paychecks and tabulating and recording the information contained in the paychecks.

PERFORM statement In COBOL, a statement that links with an internal subroutine.

Peripheral equipment (ANSI) In a data processing system, any unit of equipment, distinct from the central processing unit, that may provide the system with outside communication.

Personal computing A hobby concerned with the building and use of small, personal computers.

Physical record A single block of data as transferred between an I/O device and main memory; may contain several logical records.

Picosecond One millionth of one millionth of a second.

PICTURE clause In COBOL and several other compiler languages, a clause or portion of an instruction concerned with describing, character by character, a given field.

Planning In the program development or systems analysis process, the act of determining the outline of a single, optimum solution to a problem.

Plotter A device that generates output from a computer in graphic form.

Plug-compatible mainframe or PCM. A computer that is capable of running operating systems and application software written for a computer manufactured by another company.

Plug-to-plug compatible A peripheral device that can function with the mainframe of another manufacturer without modification.

Pointer A link.

Polling (IBM) A technique by which each of the terminals sharing a communications line is periodically interrogated to determine whether it requires servicing. The multiplexer or control station sends a poll that, in effect, asks the terminal selected, "Do you have anything to transmit?"

Port A connection point for a communication line on a front-end device or a transmission control unit.

Port-o-punch A type of punched card in which the holes are prescored and are punched out manually with a stylus.

Positional notation (ANSI) A numeration system in which a number is represented by means of an ordered set of digits, such that the value contributed by each digit depends upon its position as well as upon its value.

Powers, James The successor to Hollerith at the Census Bureau, and the inventor of a number of improved punched card data processing machines.

PRINT statement In BASIC, a statement to cause results to be displayed on a printer or terminal.

Printer (IBM) A device that expresses coded characters as hard copy.

Private (leased) line A communication line intended for the use of a single customer.

Problem definition The first step in the program development or systems analysis process, concerned with determining, in general terms, what must be done.

PROCEDURE DIVISION In COBOL, that portion of the program where the actual logical operations are coded.

Process (ANSI) A systematic sequence of operations to produce a specified result.

Process-bound See Compute-bound.

Processing (1) Executing instructions. (2) Converting data into information.

Production control A data processing function concerned with keeping track of the status of a production operation.

Program (ANSI) (1) A series of actions proposed in order to achieve a certain result. (2) Loosely, a routine. (3) To design, write, and test a program as in (1). (4) Loosely, to write a routine.

Program See Computer program.

Program card On a keypunch, a control card used to allow portions of the card to be punched or skipped automatically.

Program implementation See Implementation.

Program planning See Planning.

Program testing See Testing.

Programmer (ANSI) A person mainly involved in designing, writing, and testing computer programs.

Programmer, application A person who writes or maintains application programs.

Programmer, system A person who writes or maintains system programs such as operating systems or data base managers.

Programmer/operator A person who both programs and operates a computer.

Protocol In data communications, a specific set of rules defining handshaking and message characters.

Punched card (ANSI) (1) A card punched with a pattern of holes to represent data. (2) A card is in (1) before being punched.

Purchased software Programs that are purchased or leased from outside rather than being written within an organization.

Query A request for specific data, usually made through a terminal and to a data communication monitor.

Quota A target or standard, such as an expected sales total or an expected number of pieces manufactured.

Radix (ANSI) In positional representation, that integer, if it exists, by which the significance of the digit place must be multiplied to give the significance of the next higher digit place. For example, in decimal notation, the radix of each place is ten; in biquinary code, the radix of the five places is two. Synonymous with base (3).

RAM Random access memory.

Random access See Direct access.

Random access memory Any memory that supports direct or random access, such as main memory, core, disk, or drum. The term is generally used when referring to the programmer-addressable main memory of a microcomputer.

Randomize To compute relative record numbers from actual keys through any of a number of mathematical techniques.

Read-only memory Memory that the programmer can access but cannot change.

READ statement In many compiler languages, an input statement.

Read/write head The mechanism that writes data to or reads data from a magnetic recording medium.

Real memory A computer's actual main memory that is directly addressable by the CPU. Contrast with virtual memory.

Real number In FORTRAN, a number with a fractional or decimal part. A floating point number.

Real time (ANSI) (1) Pertaining to the actual time during which a physical process transpires. (2) Pertaining to the performance of a computation during the actual time that the related physical process transpires, in order that the results of the computation can be used in guiding the physical process.

Record (ANSI) A collection of related items of data, treated as a unit; e.g., one line of an invoice may form a record; a complete set of such records may form a file.

Recording The act of making a permanent record of data or information.

Redundancy The repetition of data in two or more places.

Redundant data Data that is repeated, in whole or in part, in two or more places.

Reel A single volume of magnetic tape.

Register (ANSI) A device capable of storing a specified amount of data such as one word.

Relative address (ANSI) The number that specifies the difference between the absolute address and the base address.

Relative record address The position of a record relative to the beginning of the file.

Relative record number See Relative record address.

REM statement In BASIC, a statement that allows the programmer to insert comments.

Remote (1) At a distance. (2) Connected to a main frame via communication lines.

Remote access (ANSI) Pertaining to communication with a data processing facility by one or more stations that are distant from that facility.

Remote job entry Entering jobs into the regular batch processing job stream from a remote facility.

Response time (IBM) The elapsed time between the generation of a message at a terminal and the receipt of a reply in the case of an inquiry or receipt of message by addressee.

RJE See Remote job entry.

Rotational delay The time required for the desired record to rotate under the read/write heads once they have been positioned over the proper track on a disk or drum.

RPG (Report Program Generator) A business-oriented programming language designed to support the generation of reports.

RPG II The current version of the RPG language.

ROM Read-only memory.

Runbook A documentation manual designed to explain the details of operating a computer during the execution of a particular program.

Sales analysis A data processing operation during which the actual results of a sales group are collected, tabulated, and summarized.

Scheduling Determining the sequence in which programs will be loaded and/or executed.

Scientific notation A system for representing numbers as a decimal fraction multiplied by a power of ten.

Second generation (IBM) A computer utilizing solid-state components.

Secondary storage See Auxiliary storage.

Security (Webster) Something that gives or assures safety; safeguard.

Seek time The time required to move the read/write head mechanism of a direct access device to a desired position.

Segment (ANSI) (1) To divide a computer program into parts such that the program can be executed without the entire program being in internal storage at any one time. (2) A part of a computer program as in (1).

Selector channel A data channel designed to connect high-speed I/O devices to a computer, and operating in a burst mode without multiplexing.

Semiautomated data processing Data processing performed by a mixture of manual and mechanical means.

Semiconductor memory Memory composed of semiconductor components or integrated circuits.

Sequential file A file of records organized in a fixed sequence; e.g., a file of punched cards or a file on tape.

Sequential file processing Processing the records in a file in fixed sequence.

Service bureau A firm offering data processing or data communication services for sale or lease. Usually applied to a firm not associated with one of the main frame manufacturers or one of the communication common carriers such as Bell Telephone, or to a separate subsidiary of one of these major firms.

Setup (ANSI) (1) In a computer that consists of an assembly of individual computing units, the arrangement of interconnections between the units and the adjustments needed for the computer to solve a particular problem. (2) An arrangement of data or devices to solve a particular problem.

Short-range planning Planning for the near future. Often involves setting up the specific budgets and quotas needed to implement a long-range plan.

Software (ANSI) A set of computer programs, procedures, and possibly associated documentation concerned with the operation of a data processing system, e.g., compilers, library routines, manuals, circuit diagrams. Contrast with hardware.

Sort (ANSI) To segregate items into groups according to some definite rules.

Sorting The act of putting items into order or segregating items into groups.

Source code Program statements written in a source language.

Source data Data in the form in which it is originally recorded.

Source data automation The use of special equipment to collect data at its source.

Source deck A source module in punched card form.

Source document A document containing source data.

Source module (ANSI: source program) A computer program written in a source language. Contrast with object program.

Special-purpose computer (ANSI) A computer that is designed to handle a restricted class of problems.

Spooling Moving data from a slow I/O device to a high-speed I/O device prior to moving it into main memory so as to help minimize the speed disparity between the computer and I/O. On output, the order of data movement is reversed.

Standard interface Converting data to (or from) a common code.

Statement (ANSI) In computer programming, a meaningful expression or generalized instruction in a source language.

Statement number In many compiler languages, a number assigned to a statement for identification purposes.

STOP statement In many compiler languages, the statement marking the logical end of a program.

Storage (ANSI) (1) Pertaining to a device into which data can be entered, in which they can be held, and from which they can be retrieved at a later time. (2) Loosely, any device that can store data. (3) Synonymous with memory.

Storage allocation (ANSI) The assignment of blocks of data to specified blocks of storage.

Stored program A series of instructions placed in a computer's main memory to control that computer.

Storing Recording data for future reference, often in an electronic form.

Strategic planning See long-range planning.

Structured programming Planning and implementing a program as a series of linked logical modules, paying special attention to documentation, testability, and program clarity so as to simplify program debug and maintenance.

Subprogram See Subroutine.

Subroutine (ANSI) A routine that can be part of another routine.

Summarizing Accumulating totals from a number of input records for later output.

Summary line An output line in a report holding summary rather than detail data.

Supervisor (IBM) A routine or routines executed in response to a requirement for altering or interrupting the flow of operation through the central processing unit, or for performance of input/output operations, and, therefore, the medium through which the use of resources is coordinated and the flow of operations through the central processing unit is maintained. Hence, a control routine that is executed in the supervisor state.

Synchronous (IBM) Occurring concurrently, and with a regular or predictable time relationship.

Synonym A record whose computed or randomized relative record number is identical to that of a different record.

SYSGEN Acronym for SYStem GENeration.

System (ANSI) (1) An assembly of methods, procedures, or techniques united by regulated interaction to form an organized whole. (2) An organized collection of men, machines, and methods required to accomplish a set of specific functions.

System design The phase of the system development process in which the actual system is designed.

System generation The act of making a copy of selected portions of a vendor's master copy of an operating system for transfer to a customer's computer.

System software Programs or routines that belong to the entire system rather than to any single programmer and that (usually) perform a support function. Contrast with application program.

Systems analysis (IBM) The analysis of an activity to determine precisely what must be accomplished and how to accomplish it.

Systems analyst A person who practices systems analysis. A professional who analyzes systems from management's broad total-system point of view but who does not share in management's responsibility or authority.

Tape drive (ANSI) A device that moves tape past a head.

Telecommunications (ANSI) Pertaining to the transmission of signals over long distances, such as by telegraph, radio, or television.

Telephone network A network of telephone lines; the Bell system is a good example.

Terminal (ANSI) A point in a system or communication network at which data can enter or leave.

Terminal A piece of hardware designed to be placed at the terminal of a communication network for the purpose of entering or obtaining data.

Testing The process of assuring that an implemented program or system actually solves the problem that it is intended to solve.

Third generation (IBM) A computer utilizing SLT components.

Throughput (IBM) A measure of system efficiency; the rate at which work can be handled by a system.

Time-sharing (ANSI) Pertaining to the interleaved use of the time of a device.

Top-down approach Solving problems by starting with a broad total-system point of view and gradually introducing details, layer by layer, until a solution is obtained.

Top-down design Designing a system by starting with a broad, total-system viewpoint, defining what must be done, and then adding details (how to do it) gradually, layer by layer, until the system is fully designed.

Track (ANSI) The portion of a moving storage medium, such as a drum, tape, or disk, that is accessible to a given reading head position.

Transaction A single input record or a single query. Usually associated with a time-shared or real-time system rather than with a traditional batch processing system.

Transmission (ANSI) (1) The sending of data from one location and the receiving of data in another location, usually leaving the source data unchanged. (2) The sending of data. (3) In ASCII and communications, a series of characters including headings and texts.

Transmission control unit A control unit that interfaces data transmissions.

Turnaround (IBM) The elapsed time between submission of a job to a computing center and the return of the results.

Turnkey system A computer system that can be used by an untrained or unsophisticated operator.

Unit record (IBM) Historically, a card containing one complete record. Currently, the punched card.

UNIVAC I The first commercially available digital electronic computer.

Universal Product Code A bar-code printed on a retail package that uniquely identifies the product.

UPC Acronym for Universal Product Code.

Utility program (ANSI: service routine) A routine in general support of a computer, e.g., an input/output diagnostic, tracing, or monitoring routine.

Variable (ANSI) A quantity that can assume any of a given set of values.

Variable cost A cost that varies with activity. Contrast with fixed cost.

Verification The act of verifying. See Verify (2).

Verifier A machine similar to a keypunch used to verify.

Verify (ANSI) (1) To determine whether a transcription of data or other operation has been accomplished accurately. (2) To check the results of keypunching.

Virtual memory Memory space on a secondary storage device that is used to hold programs and data on a virtual memory system. Instructions and data must be transferred from this virtual memory into real memory prior to execution or processing.

Virtual storage See Virtual memory.

Virtual storage access method An access method or file organization in which data is stored on a secondary device in fixed-length segments or pages and transferred into real memory much as program pages or segments on a virtual memory system.

Voice-grade line (IBM: voice-grade channel) A channel suitable for transmission of speech, digital or analog data, or facsimile, generally with a frequency range of about 300 to 3000 cycles per second.

Voice recognition Direct conversion of spoken data into an electronic form suitable for entry to a computer.

Voice response Computer output in spoken form.

Volatility On data files, a measure of the frequency of additions to or deletions from the file.

Volume (IBM) That portion of a single unit of storage media that is accessible to a single read/write mechanism.

Volume serial number A serial number assigned to a disk or tape volume for identification purposes.

Volume table of contents A list of the contents of a volume, including the physical location of key fields or files.

Wait state (IBM: wait condition) As applied to tasks, the condition of a task such that it is dependent on an event or events in order to enter the ready condition.

Wait time The time during which a program or a computer waits for the completion of other activities.

Wide-band channel A communication channel capable of carrying data at a rate higher than a voice-grade channel.

Word (ANSI) A character string or bit string considered as an entity.

WRITE statement An output statement in many compiler languages.

X-punch In punched card data processing, an 11-punch.

Zone punch A 12-, 11-, or 0-punch on a punched card.

INDEX